Professional Examinations

Managerial Level

Paper P5

Integrated Management

CIMA Study Text

KAPLAN PUBLISHING
FOULKS LYNCH

British Library Cataloguing-in-Publication Data

A catalogue record for this book is available from the British Library.

Kaplan Publishing Foulks Lynch
Unit 2 The Business Centre
Molly Millars Lane
Wokingham
Berkshire
RG41 2QZ

ISBN 1-84390-909-X

978-184390-909-5

Printed and bound in Great Britain.

Acknowledgements

We are grateful to the Chartered Institute of Management Accountants, the Association of Chartered Certified Accountants and the Institute of Chartered Accountants in England and Wales for permission to reproduce past examination questions. The answers have been prepared by Kaplan Publishing Foulks Lynch.

INTRODUCTION

This is the third edition of this Study Text, under the new CIMA syllabus.

Our aim was to produce an even better, more syllabus-tailored, exam-focused and student-friendly range of publications. To achieve this we have worked closely with numerous CIMA tutors and experts, and we are confident that this Study Text forms the best resource for your exam preparation.

It covers all syllabus topics to the required depth, and contains a wealth of exam-style and practice questions. Throughout the text you will find plenty of relevant examples, activities, diagrams and charts. These will put the subject matter in context and help you absorb the material easily.

The following points explain some of the concepts we had in mind when developing the layout of this book.

DEFINITION

KEY POINT

- **Definitions**. The text defines key words and concepts, placing them in the margin with a clear heading, as on the left. The purpose of including these definitions is to focus your attention on the point being covered.
- **Key points**. Also in the margin, you will see key points at regular intervals. The purpose of these is to summarise concisely the key material being covered.
- **Activities**. The text involves you in the learning process with a series of activities designed to catch your attention and make you concentrate and respond. The feedback to activities is at the end of each chapter.
- **Self-test questions**. At the end of each chapter there is a series of self-test questions. The purpose of these is to help you revise some of the key elements of the chapter. All the answers to these questions can be found in the text.
- **End of chapter questions**. At the end of each chapter we include examination-type questions. These will give you a very good idea of the sort of thing the examiner will ask and will test your understanding of what has been covered.

Good luck with your studies!

CONTENTS

		Page
Syllabus and learning outcomes		vii
Helping you with your studies		xi
The examination		xiii
The basis of strategic management		
Chapter 1	The process of strategy formulation	1
Chapter 2	Approaches to strategy formulation	27
Chapter 3	Strategy and structure	59
Chapter 4	Concepts in strategic management	85
Chapter 5	Culture and corporate governance	107
Project management		
Chapter 6	Basics of project management	123
Chapter 7	Tools for project managers	141
Chapter 8	Project methodologies and planning	161
Chapter 9	Managing the project team	183
Chapter 10	Project control	197
The management of relationships		
Chapter 11	Management and leadership	217
Chapter 12	Control, communication and negotiation	249
Chapter 13	Managing groups	281
Chapter 14	Legal and ethical issues	303
Chapter 15	Answers to multiple-choice and exam-type questions	319
Index		363

SYLLABUS AND LEARNING OUTCOMES

Syllabus outline

The syllabus comprises:

Topic and study weighting

A	The Basis of Strategic Management	30%
B	Project Management	40%
C	The Management of Relationships	50%

Learning aims

Students should be able to:

- identify and apply management techniques necessary for decision-making that cuts across functional areas.
- analyse data in support of strategic decision making.
- contribute to decision making in these areas by advising management.

Below we reproduce the learning outcomes and syllabus content. **The numbers in brackets denote the chapters in which each topic is covered.**

Learning outcomes and syllabus content

A – The Basis of Strategic Management – 30%

Learning outcomes

On completion of their studies students should be able to:

(i) explain the process of strategy formulation. (1, 2)

(ii) evaluate different organisational structures. (3)

(iii) discuss concepts in contemporary thinking on strategic management. (4)

(iv) apply tools for strategic analysis appropriately. (2)

(v) explain the purpose and principles of good corporate governance. (5)

(vi) evaluate competitive situations and apply this knowledge to the organisation. (2)

Syllabus content

- The process of strategy formulation. (1), (2)
- The relationship between strategy and organisational structure. (3)
- The reasons for conflict between the objectives of an organisation, or between the objectives of an organisation and its stakeholders, and the ways to manage this conflict. (1)
- Strategic decision-making processes. (1)
- Approaches to strategy (e.g. rational, adaptive, emergent, evolutionary or system-based views based on Porter, Mintzberg, Bartlett and Ghoshal). (2)
- Transaction cost view of the firm (e.g. Coase, Williamson) and its implications for organisational structure. (3)
- Resource-based views of the firm and implications for strategy development. (2)
- Ecological perspective on the firm. (3)
- The determinants, importance and role of organisational cultures and ways to improve the effectiveness of an organisation. (5)
- Introduction to corporate governance, including stakeholders and the role of government. (5)
- Translating strategy into business (e.g. formation of strategic business units, encouragement of entrepreneurship inside organisations). (4)
- Contemporary issues in business management (e.g. alliances, demergers, virtual organisations, corporate social responsibility and business ethics). (4)

B – Project Management – 40%

Learning outcomes

On completion of their studies students should be able to:

(i) identify a project and its attributes. (6)

(ii) apply suitable structures and frameworks to projects to identify common management issues. (6)

(iii) produce a basic outline of the process of project management. (6)

(iv) identify the characteristics of each phase in the project process. (6)

(v) demonstrate the role of key stakeholders in the project. (6)

(vi) distinguish the key tools and techniques that would need to be applied in the project process, including the evaluation of proposals. (7)

(vii) identify methodologies and systems used by professional project managers. (8)

(viii) identify the strategy and scope for a project. (8)

(ix) identify stakeholder groups and recommend basic strategies for the management of their perceptions and expectations. (6)

(x) produce a basic project plan, recognising the effects of uncertainty and recommending strategies for dealing with this uncertainty, in the context of a simple project. (8)

(xi) identify structural and leadership issues that will be faced in managing a project team. (9)

(xii) recommend appropriate project control systems. (10)

(xiii) evaluate, through selected review and audit, the learning outcomes from a project. (10)

(xiv) apply a process of continuous improvement to projects. (10)

Syllabus content

- The definition of a project, project management, and the contrast with repetitive operations and line management. (6)
- 4-D and 7-S models to provide an overview of the project process, and the nine key process areas (PMI) to show what happens during each part of the process. (6)
- Stakeholders (both process and outcome) and their needs. (6)
- Roles of project sponsors, boards, champions, managers and clients. (6)
- Key tools for project managers (e.g. Work Breakdown Structure, network diagrams (Critical Path Analysis), Gantt charts, resource histograms, establishment of gates and milestones). (7)
- Evaluation of plans for projects. (8)
- The key processes of PRINCE2 and their implications for project staff. (8)
- The role of determining trade-offs between key project objectives of time, cost and quality. (8)
- Managing scope at the outset of a project and providing systems for configuration management/change control. (8)
- The production of basic plans for time, cost and quality. (8)
- Scenario planning and buffering to make provision for uncertainty in projects, and the interface with the risk management process. (8)
- Organisational structures, including the role of the project and matrix organisations, and their impact on project achievement. (9)
- Teamwork, including recognising the life-cycle of teams, team/group behaviour and selection. (9)
- Control of time, cost and quality through performance and conformance management systems. (10)
- Project completion, documentation, stakeholder marketing, completion reports and system close-down. (10)
- The use of post-completion audit and review activities and the justification of their costs. (10)

C – Management of Relationships – 30%

Learning outcomes

On completion of their studies students should be able to:

(i) explain the concepts of power, bureaucracy, authority, responsibility, leadership and delegation. (11)

(ii) analyse the relationship between managers and their subordinates. (11)

(iii) discuss the roles of negotiation and communication in the management process, both within an organisation and with external bodies. (12)

(iv) explain how groups form within organisations and how this affects performance. (13)

(v) demonstrate personal time management skills. (12)

(vi) construct a set of tools for managing individuals, teams and networks, and for managing group conflict. (13)

(vii) recommend ways to deal effectively with discipline problems. (13)

(viii) explain the process of mentoring junior colleagues. (12)

(ix) discuss the importance of national cultures to management style. (11)

(x) explain the importance of business ethics and corporate governance to the organisation and its stakeholders. (14)

(xi) identify methods of conducting research and gathering data as part of the managerial process. (12)

Syllabus content

- The concepts of power, authority, bureaucracy, leadership, responsibility and delegation and their application to relationships within an organisation and outside it. (11)
- The characteristics of leaders, managers and entrepreneurs. (11)
- Management-style theories (e.g. Likert, Tannenbaum and Schmidt, Blake and Mouton). (11)
- The use of systems of control within the organisation (e.g. employment contracts, performance appraisal, reporting structures). (12)
- Theories of control within firms and types of organisational structure (e.g. matrix, divisional, network). (12)

- The advantages and disadvantages of different styles of management. (11)
- Managing in different countries and cultures. (11)
- Contingency approaches to management style (e.g. Adair, Fiedler). (11)
- Theories of group development, behaviour and roles (e.g. Tuckman, Belbin). (13)
- Disciplinary procedures and their operation, including the form and process of formal disciplinary action and dismissal (e.g. industrial tribunals, arbitration and conciliation). (13)
- Personal time management. (12)
- The nature and effect of legal issues affecting work and employment, including the application of relevant employment law (i.e. relating to health, safety, discrimination, fair treatment, childcare, contracts of employment and working time). (14)
- The sources of conflict in organisations and the ways in which conflict can be managed to ensure that working relationships are productive and effective. (13)
- Communication skills (i.e. types of communication tools and their use, as well as the utility and conduct of meetings) and ways of managing communication problems. (12)
- Negotiation skills. (12)
- Creativity and idea generation. (12)
- Information gathering techniques (e.g. interviews, questionnaires). (12)
- Introduction to corporate governance, including business ethics and the role, obligations and expectations of a manager. (14)

HELPING YOU WITH YOUR STUDIES

Take control

Create favourable conditions and a positive attitude

- Plan to study at specific times each week. Devise a schedule and set goals.
- Choose a location where you can concentrate.
- Ask questions to be an active learner and to generate interest.
- Continually challenge yourself.

Study

Develop good learning techniques

- Use the **SQR3** method – it works with reading accountancy and management subjects. **Survey** (get an overall picture before studying in detail), **Question** (important things to learn are usually answers to questions), **Read** actively (to answer your questions), **Recite** (recall what you have read and connect topics) and **Review** (what you have covered and accomplished).
- Use the **MURDER** method – **Mood** (set the right mood), **Understand** (issues covered and make note of any uncertain bits), **Recall** (stop and put what you have learned into your own words), **Digest** (go back and reconsider the information), **Expand** (read relevant articles and newspapers), **Review** (go over the material you covered to consolidate the knowledge).
- Create **associations** and analogies to relate new ideas to what you already know and to improve understanding.

Practise

Practise under exam conditions

- **Practise** as much as possible – go through exam-style and standard questions under exam conditions.

Prepare for the exam

Develop exam technique

- Be familiar with the structure of your exam and know how to approach and answer the questions.

THE EXAMINATION

Format of the examination:

There will be a written examination paper of three hours, with the following sections.

	Marks
Section A: a variety of compulsory objective test questions, each worth between 2 and 4 marks. Mini-scenarios may be given, to which a group of questions relate.	20
Section B: three compulsory medium answer questions, each worth 10 marks. Short scenarios may be given, to which some or all questions relate.	30
Section C: two questions, from a choice of three, each worth 25 marks. Short scenarios may be given, to which questions relate.	50
TOTAL	100

Note: The first 20 minutes of your exam is reading time. During reading time you can read, annotate and highlight the question paper, but you are not allowed to open the answer book, write in the answer book, add any loose sheets/supplements to your answer book or use a calculator. This change to the duration of the exams has been introduced by CIMA after we published our Exam Kits. Therefore you will notice that the exam length stated in this section will differ from the one stated in the Exam Kit. The length of the exam stated here is the correct one.

Before sitting the exam make sure that you are familiar with CIMA's *Exam Rules & Regulations*. You can find this document on the CIMA website (www.cimaglobal.com).

Examination tips

- Spend the first few minutes of the examination **reading the paper** and where you have a **choice of questions**, decide which ones you will do.
- **Divide the time** you spend on questions in proportion to the marks on offer. One suggestion is to allocate 1½ minutes to each mark available, so a 10-mark question should be completed in 15 minutes.
- Unless you know exactly how to answer the question, spend some time **planning** your answer. Stick to the question and **tailor your answer** to what you are asked.
- **Fully explain** all your points but be **concise**. Set out all workings **clearly and neatly**, and state briefly what you are doing. Don't write out the question.
- If you do not understand what a question is asking, **state your assumptions**.
- If you **get completely stuck** with a question, leave space in your answer book and **return to it later.**
- Towards the end of the examination spend the last **five minutes** reading through your answers and **making any additions or corrections**.

Answering the questions

- **Multiple-choice questions**: Read the questions carefully and work through any calculations required. If you don't know the answer, eliminate those options you know are incorrect and see if the answer becomes more obvious. Remember that only one answer to a multiple-choice question can be right!

- **Objective test questions**: These might ask for numerical answers, but could also involve paragraphs of text which require you to fill in a number of missing blanks, or for you to write a definition of a word or phrase, or to enter a formula. Others may give a definition followed by a list of possible key words relating to that description.

- **Essay questions**: Make a quick plan in your answer book and under each main point list all the relevant facts you can think of. Then write out your answer developing each point fully. Your essay should have a clear structure; it should contain a brief introduction, a main section and a conclusion. Be concise. It is better to write a little about a lot of different points than a great deal about one or two points.

- **Computations**: It is essential to include all your workings in your answers. Many computational questions require the use of a standard format: company profit and loss account, balance sheet and cash flow statement for example. Be sure you know these formats thoroughly before the examination and use the layouts that you see in the answers given in this book. If you are asked to comment or make recommendations on a computation, you must do so. There are important marks to be gained here. Even if your computation contains mistakes, you may still gain marks if your reasoning is correct.

- **Reports, memos and other documents**: Some questions ask you to present your answer in the form of a report or a memo or other document. Use the correct format – there could be easy marks to gain here.

Chapter 1

THE PROCESS OF STRATEGY FORMULATION

Syllabus content

- The process of strategy formulation.
- The reasons for conflict between the objectives of an organisation, or between the objectives of an organisation and its stakeholders, and the ways to manage this conflict.
- Strategic decision-making processes.

Contents

1 Strategy formulation

2 Managing the process

3 Strategic decision-making

4 Mission, goals and objectives

5 Stakeholders and objectives

6 Conflicting objectives

1 Strategy formulation

1.1 What is strategy?

There are many different definitions of 'strategy' depending on the context being discussed and the viewpoint of the writer concerned.

DEFINITION

A **strategy** is a course of action, including the specification of resources required, to achieve a specific objective.

The definition used in CIMA's official terminology is that a strategy is course of action, including the specification of resources required, to achieve a specific objective.

Formulating strategy will thus involve three stages:

1 Where are we now?

2 Where do we want to be?

3 How are we to get there?

For the purposes of formulating **business** strategy, a more comprehensive definition comes from Johnson and Scholes, who define strategy as follows:

DEFINITION

'**Strategy** is the direction and scope of an organisation over the long-term: which achieves advantage for the organisation through its configuration of resources within a challenging environment, to meet the needs of markets and to fulfil stakeholder expectations.'

'Strategy is the direction and scope of an organisation over the long-term: which achieves advantage for the organisation through its configuration of resources within a challenging environment, to meet the needs of markets and to fulfil stakeholder expectations.'

In other words, strategy is about:

- Where is the business trying to get to in the long-term (direction)?
- Which markets should a business compete in and what kinds of activities are involved in such markets (markets, scope)?
- How can the business perform better than the competition in those markets (advantage)?
- What resources (skills, assets, finance, relationships, technical competence, facilities) are required in order to be able to compete (resources)?
- What external, environmental factors affect the business's ability to compete (environment)?
- What are the values and expectations of those who have power in and around the business (stakeholders)?

1.2 The five Ps

KEY POINT

Mintzberg suggests various definitions of strategy covering the five Ps: plan, pattern, ploy, position and perspective.

Henry Mintzberg suggests various definitions of strategy covering the five Ps.

- Strategy as a **plan** – a direction, a guide or course of action into the future, a path to get from here to there.
- Strategy as a **pattern** of consistent behaviour over time, giving the impression of a logically thought out strategy. A company that perpetually markets the most expensive products in its industry pursues what is commonly called a high-end strategy, just as a person who always accepts the most challenging of jobs may be described as pursuing a high-risk strategy.
- Strategy as a **ploy**, which can be seen as a manoeuvre in a competitive business game. For example a firm might add unnecessary plant capacity. The intention is not to produce the goods but to discourage a competitor from entering the market. The strategy is not the activity but the deterrence.
- Strategy as a **position** is a means of identifying where an organisation places itself in an environment or market.
- Strategy as a **perspective** consists not just of a chosen position but also of a unique way of perceiving the world, of interpreting information from it and judging its opportunities and choices. As such, it can refer to organisation culture. Different organisations with different strategic perspectives might respond to the same environmental stimulus in different ways. In this respect Mintzberg is suggesting that the organisation's strategy is similar to the individual's personality.

These five ways of discussing strategy are not mutually exclusive. Arguably they complement each other. In the right circumstances, any of the definitions will be the most apt. Nor is there a necessary hierarchy in which one comes before the other. Mintzberg contrasts strategy as a plan (looking ahead), with strategy as a pattern (looking at past behaviour). However, both definitions appear to be valid. Organisations develop plans for their future and they also evolve patterns out of their past. One is an 'intended' strategy and the other is 'realised'.

Activity 1

Which of Mintzberg's categories (plan, position, ploy, pattern, perspective) do the following two strategies fit into?

(a) The management team at the local hospital prepare a strategy to minimise the time doctors spend walking from place to place. The hospital has been rearranged into services that are clustered around patients. The resources are available so that this change can be phased in over three years – oncology first, then paediatrics and so on.

(b) Two market traders sell fruit and vegetables. One of them decides to specialise in Chinese vegetables as he feels there are enough interested people in his area to make it worth his while.

Feedback to this activity is at the end of the chapter.

1.3 Strategy at different levels of an organisation

KEY POINT

Johnson and Scholes identify three levels of strategy: corporate, business and functional.

Strategies exist at several levels in any organisation – ranging from the overall business (or group of businesses) through to individuals working in it.

Johnson and Scholes identify three levels of strategic activity – corporate, business and functional (operational) demonstrating a hierarchy or cascade of plans and decisions whereby activities at the lower levels are guided and constrained by policy made at higher levels.

Corporate strategy

KEY POINT

Corporate strategy is concerned with the scope of activities and matching them to the organisation's environment, its resource capabilities and the values and expectations of its various stakeholders.

Johnson and Scholes claim that corporate strategy is concerned with the scope of an organisation's activities and the matching of these to the organisation's environment, its resource capabilities and the values and expectations of its various stakeholders. This is a crucial level since it is heavily influenced by investors in the business and acts to guide strategic decision-making throughout the business. Corporate strategy is often stated explicitly in a 'mission statement'. It covers a longer time period and has a wider scope than the other levels of corporate planning and is primarily concerned with the determination of ends e.g. what business or businesses the firm is in or should be in and how integrated these businesses should be with one another.

Corporate strategy involves issues such as:

- investing in existing units or buying a new business;
- diversifying or limiting the activities of the organisation;
- surviving.

Business strategy

KEY POINT

Business strategy is concerned with how each strategic business unit (SBU) attempts to achieve its mission within its chosen area of activity.

Business strategy or competitive strategy is concerned with how each strategic business unit (SBU) attempts to achieve its mission within its chosen area of activity. It relates to strategic decisions about choice of products, meeting needs of customers, gaining advantage over competitors, exploiting or creating new opportunities, etc.

An SBU is a term often used in relation to business strategy. It is a unit within the overall corporate entity, which should have an identifiable and definable product or service range, market segment and competitor set.

Functional strategy

KEY POINT

Functional strategy ensures that the different functions of the business support the corporate and business strategies.

Functional or operational strategies are concerned with how the various functions of the organisation (marketing, production, finance, etc) contribute to the achievement of the corporate and competitive strategies, e.g. revising delivery schedules and drivers' hours to improve customer service or recruiting a German-speaking sales person to assist a UK company's sales drive in Europe. They focus on issues of resources, processes, people etc.

Examples of operational and functional strategies:

(a) *Marketing strategies* involve devising products and services, pricing, promoting and distributing them, to satisfy customer needs at a profit. Marketing and corporate strategies are interrelated.

(b) *Production strategy* involves issues such as factory location, manufacturing techniques and subcontracting.

(c) *Finance strategy* ensures that the firm has the financial resources to fund its other strategies. Pricing decisions are both marketing and finance issues.

(d) *Human resources strategy* aims to secure personnel in the right quantity, and to ensure that they have the right skills and values to promote the organisation's overall goals.

(e) *Information systems strategy* includes administrative support as well as being a tool for competitive strength. Not all IT applications are strategic, and the strategic value will vary from case to case.

(f) *Change strategies* incorporate many of the above, including changes to *organisation structure,* an important aspect of strategy.

For all levels of strategy, the common purpose is to guide the use of the company resources in achieving the organisation's objectives.

Activity 2

A traditional manufacturer of diaries opened a textbook publishing subsidiary. While the core business, diaries, declined, the publishing business was astonishingly successful. Classify the following strategic issues according to their level of strategy:

(a) Should the profits from the publishing company be used to rescue diaries, or grow the publishing company more quickly?

(b) Should the diaries move up market?

(c) How can the costs of the diaries be reduced, to improve the margin?

(d) Should the publishing company move into publishing novels?

(e) Should the diary business be sold to a rival, so that resources can be focused on the publishing company?

Feedback to this activity is at the end of the chapter.

2 Managing the process

2.1 What is strategic management?

There are many questions that you could ask about the organisations that surround us. How did they reach the situation they are in today? Why are they producing particular products or services? How did they come to be located where they are? Why are they serving a certain part of the marketplace? How did they end up with their particular set of senior managers? Why are they organised in different ways?

KEY POINT

Decisions about products, locations, structure, personnel and other resources are all major or strategic decisions.

DEFINITION

Strategic management is the decision process that aligns the organisation's internal capability with the opportunities and threats it faces in the environment.

All of these questions address different but interrelated aspects of organisations and all these aspects come together to influence how effective the organisation will be in achieving its objectives. How these major – or strategic – decisions about products, locations, structure, personnel and other resources are made and how they are implemented is the process of strategic management. There are several definitions of strategic management:

- Wright et al see it as 'top management's plans to attain outcomes consistent with the organisation's missions and goals'.
- Rowe et al describe it as ' the decision process that aligns the organisation's internal capability with the opportunities and threats it faces in the environment'.

Essentially, strategic management is going to be something to do with deriving and describing the strategy. This is something that is applicable to all organisations whether large or small, public or private, profit or non-profit making.

It covers the entire cycle of planning and control at a strategic level.

2.2 Strategic planning

Strategic planning can be defined as 'a continuous process of making entrepreneurial decisions systematically and with the best possible knowledge of their futurity, organising systematically the effort needed to carry out these decisions and measuring the results against expectations through organised systematic feedback'.

DEFINITION

Strategic planning is the establishment of an organisation's objectives in a clearly defined manner as a basis for management decision-making.

This definition sees the establishment of an organisation's objectives in a clearly defined manner as a basis for management decision-making. The sequence of planning could then be shown as:

- establish organisation's objectives;
- analyse internal and external data;
- analyse future trends;
- devise a range of alternative strategies;
- select the most appropriate strategy or mix of strategies;
- translate selected strategies into action by establishing management objectives;
- monitor performance;
- correct variations in performance and restate objectives if future trends, as they evolve, change management's perceptions.

Planning is seen as a dynamic, continuous operation rather than a once-a-year exercise. Also, it is seen as a systematic discipline, carried out by managers, not unstructured ideas proposed by a team of advisors or experts.

It starts with a detailed, continuous analysis of future markets, trade conditions, competitors and customer needs. For this analysis, opportunities are defined which are realistic in terms of expected future trends. Management then designs actions to exploit these opportunities (or combat expected threats). This change in emphasis makes planning more realistic.

3 Strategic decision-making

3.1 Characteristics

DEFINITION

Decision-making can be defined as 'making choices between future, uncertain alternatives to resolve a problem'.

Decision-making can be defined as 'making choices between future, uncertain alternatives to resolve a problem'. There are five steps in decision making:

1. Identifying the problem
2. Generating alternative courses of action
3. Evaluating the alternatives
4. Selecting the best alternative
5. Implementing the decision

Decision-making takes place at every level of management. At the strategic level, decision-making is much more dependent upon human factors and judgment. Such decision-making is often based on guided trial and error and because of uncertainty and ambiguities, all possibilities cannot be explored. This type of decision-making is known as heuristic and is based on rules of thumb rather than explicit decision rules and formulae.

Johnson and Scholes (*Exploring Corporate Strategy*) have summarised the various aspects of strategic decisions.

- Determination of the scope of the organisation's activities.
- Relating the organisation's activities to the environment in which it operates.
- Matching the organisation's activities to its resource capability.
- The allocation or re-allocation of resources.
- Constraining and providing a framework for lower level operational decisions.
- Reflecting the values and expectations of the people in power within the organisation.
- Determining the long-term direction that the organisation takes.
- Often implying change in the organisation – transformational as well as incremental change.

A strategy is a set of policies adopted by senior management that guides the scope and direction of the entity. It takes into account the environment in which the company operates. 'Scope' used in this context relates to size and range; it concerns the way in which those responsible for managing the organisation conceive its boundaries. For example, does it concentrate on one area of activity or many?

The 'direction' describes product/market positioning. Strategic decisions affect the long-term direction of the organisation. Once the wheels are set in motion it is often impossible to turn back. Large organisations are often faced with decisions related to acquisitions, mergers, takeovers, vertical or horizontal integration, internationalisation and the rationalisation of core activities to get back to the markets and customers they know best. The alternative strategies that they could pursue include market strategies (such as market penetration, market development), innovation strategies, people strategies, organisation design strategies such as joint venture, retrenchment, divestiture, and liquidation and growth strategies.

Each alternative strategy has countless variations. For example, market penetration can include adding salespersons, increasing advertising expenditures, giving away coupons, and using similar actions to increase market share in a given geographic area.

Like any other major decision, it affects and is affected by many other areas. For example strategy must be able to match the activities of the organisation to the environment in which it operates, to take advantage of environmental opportunities and cope with organisational threats. However, there would be little point in trying to take advantage of some new opportunity if the resources needed were not available or could not be made available. Strategic decisions, therefore, have major resource implications for an organisation and strategies need to be considered, not only in terms of the extent to which the existing resource capability of the organisation is suited to the environmental opportunities, but also in terms of the extent to which resources can be obtained and controlled, to develop a strategy for the future. The decision is also likely to affect the operational decisions and set off waves of lesser decisions.

The values and expectations of those that have power in and around the organisation will also affect the strategy. In some respects, strategy can be thought of as a reflection of the attitudes and beliefs of those who have most influence on the organisation.

Strategic decisions are often complex in nature. The complexity arises for at least three reasons:

- **High degree of uncertainty** – because they involve taking decisions on the basis of views about the future, which it is impossible for managers to be sure about.
- **Integrated approach** – unlike functional problems, there is no one area of expertise or one perspective that can define or resolve the problems. Managers have to cross functional and operational boundaries to deal with strategic problems.
- **Major change might be involved** – making it problematic to decide upon and implement those changes.

3.2 The link between planning and decision-making

KEY POINT

The existence of a plan is the result of certain decisions having been taken, and at the same time the plan provides a framework for other decisions.

Planning and decision-making are closely linked. The existence of a plan is the result of certain decisions having been taken, and at the same time the plan provides a framework for other decisions.

If there is an effective plan, each executive knows what is expected and why. If on the other hand an executive does not know what targets have been allocated there will be no criteria against which alternative courses of action can be evaluated. Without planning there is a danger that the various units in the organisation will be run without adequate co-ordination, and may be under-performing, pursuing different objectives, or optimising their own performance at the expense of the organisation as a whole.

Too often, management consists of managing short-term problems, of trying to find ways out of immediate difficulties, of muddling through from one crisis to the next. Planning forces attention on the longer term, gives the company a direction, and should help to avoid some of the difficulties. It should at least help to predict future difficulties before they reach crisis proportions, so that there is more time to consider possible solutions.

To take a very simple analogy, managing a business is like a planned car journey. Before setting out you decide where you are going and what route you will take. You may hear on your car radio about difficulties ahead and change your route to avoid encountering a traffic jam. However, eventually you will probably resume your normal course in order to reach your specified destination, although naturally you are quite free to change your mind halfway there. However, rational decision-making is only one way that researchers have thought about management decision-making.

The planning process by which an organisation can move from mission to strategies and actions can be expressed in the diagram below.

From mission to action

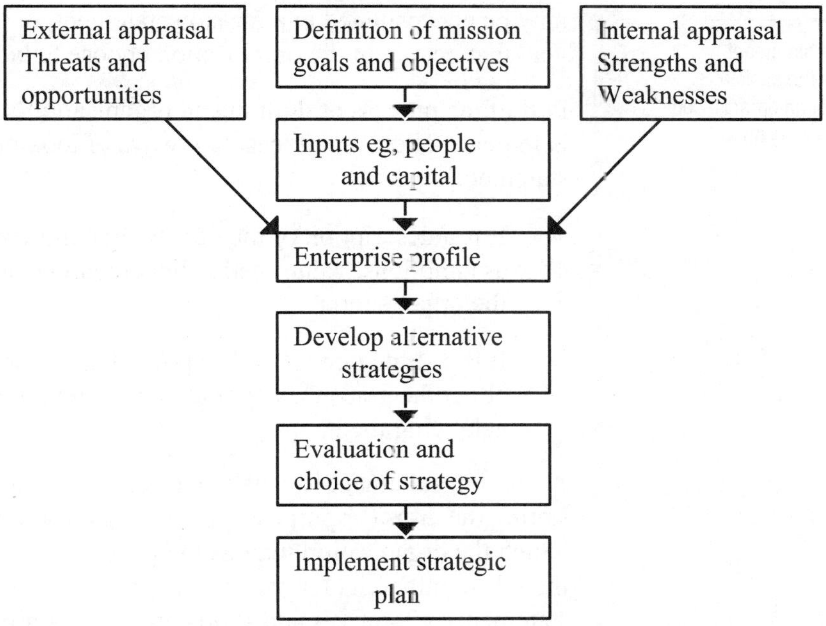

This diagram represents an approach where objectives are defined ahead of, and independently of, the strategies to be pursued. There is a logical sequence of activities. However, it is important to stress that the model is only a device for thinking through complex strategic problems. Although the steps taken in the formulation of strategy vary, the process can be identified by the key elements.

4 Mission, goals and objectives

4.1 Hierarchy of objectives

Most writers agree with the idea that there is a hierarchy of objectives, just as there is a hierarchy of managers. At each higher level in the hierarchy, the objectives are more relevant to a greater proportion of the organisation's activities so that the objectives at the top of the hierarchy are relevant to every aspect of the organisation. The following diagram illustrates the hierarchical relationship of mission, goals, objectives, strategy, tactics and operational plans.

The hierarchy of objectives

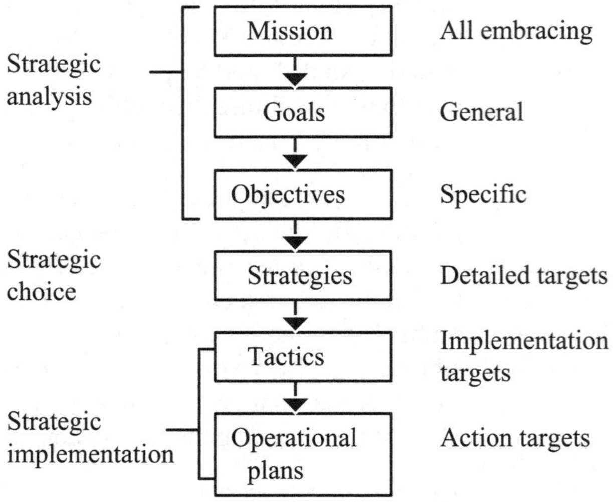

4.2 Mission

DEFINITION

A mission statement describes the basic purpose of an organisation i.e. what it is trying to accomplish.

The mission expresses the overall sense of purpose that the organisation has. It may be encapsulated in a mission statement, or it may be revealed simply by the way that people in the organisation choose to behave.

Part of the process of defining an organisation's mission is to decide what role it is to play. There are at least two ways of looking at the role of a mission statement.

- It is a description of the pervading culture of an organisation. It defines the assumptions, values and beliefs regarded as important by those managing the organisation.
- It is a strategic tool, a discipline that forces managers to think carefully about the goals they should be pursuing. It helps them to formulate plans for achieving them.

A mission statement is usually a brief statement of no more than a page in length stating the aims (or purposes) of the organisation and the business areas in which the organisation intends to operate. It is not time-assigned nor does it include commercial terms, such as profit. Because it is used to formulate goal statements, objectives and short-term targets it guides the direction of the entity's strategy and as such is part of management information.

A mission's goals do not have to be 'internal'. Some of the most effective are directed outside the company, on customers, or competitors. Federal Express Corporation's U.S. operation has a short but powerful mission statement: 'Absolutely, Positively Overnight!' Everyone in the company knows what that statement means. Almost nothing more has to be said to ensure that every action of every person is aimed at total customer satisfaction. Another short credo that says it all belongs to PepsiCo. PepsiCo's mission has long been simply to 'Beat Coke', a mission it has yet to achieve. A longer mission statement on a plaque at Lever House places the emphasis on serving the customer:

The mission of our company, as William Hesketh Lever saw it, is to make cleanliness commonplace, to lessen work for women, to foster health and to contribute to personal attractiveness so that life may be more enjoyable for the people who use our products.

4.3 Goals

KEY POINT

An organisation's goals are the intentions behind its decisions or actions.

Goals are more specific about the way the company will develop, but are not specific enough to be acted upon directly. They are mainly narrative statements derived from the mission and are set in advance of the objectives. An organisation's goals are the intentions behind its decisions or actions.

The distinction between goals, objectives and targets is a common cause of confusion. Some writers assign different meanings to the same terms, others use them interchangeably and almost all disagree about their relative values and significance.

However, in this text we adhere to the view that goals will be a narrative transformation of the mission statement (or mission), and typically a goal will be transformed into one or more specific objectives.

4.4 Objectives

KEY POINT

Objectives are time-assigned targets derived from the goals, and are set in advance of strategy.

Objectives are time-assigned targets derived from the goals, and are set in advance of strategy. They are intended to be realised in a reasonable timeframe, and should be quantifiable to allow unambiguous monitoring and control. They are used to provide direction and purpose; they allow synergy and aid in evaluations; they help to establish priorities, reduce uncertainty, minimise conflicts and stimulate exertion. They are also used to allocate resources, design jobs and motivate managers and employees.

The categories that could be involved as overall objectives have been listed by Drucker as: profitability; innovation; market standing; productivity; financial and physical resources; managerial performance and development; worker performance and attitude; and public responsibility.

Financial objectives

The financial objectives for an organisation may be very simple. The Mars Group of Companies runs its business with two main objectives – return on investment and sales growth. To meet these objectives management needs to achieve profitable growth, to manage fixed assets and working capital well and to invest wisely. Other companies use key ratios as financial objectives for example, profit to sales or profit to capital.

By accepting the notion that firms exist to make money, then managing becomes a much clearer task. The basic need to make a profit can underpin the entire management process. Other ideas can be evaluated against the profit objective and performance can be measured and compared with that of other firms.

Social and ethical objectives

Not all organisations would put profits and growth at the top of their corporate objectives ranking list nowadays because there are so many other issues to be taken into account. Not only are there doubts as to whether profits and growth are desirable ends in themselves, there are also doubts about their practicality. Other new factors are measures such as pollution control, conservation of natural resources and avoidance of environmental disfigurement by companies. Companies are now developing a social conscience, even at the cost of lower profits.

It is management's job to convert the demands placed on an organisation by public opinion and attitudes, and legal and political pressures, into opportunities for future growth and innovation. Under this heading there may well be objectives relating to preservation and improvement of the environment, consumer protection, and the avoidance of socially undesirable activities and ensuring that plans for expansion, rationalisation or other major changes are carried out without adverse effects on employees or on the community.

Measuring objectives

For a local authority, for instance, to state a goal as 'to improve the welfare of old age pensioners in the borough' is not precise enough. The goal needs to be translated into objectives, which state how it is going to measure the achievement. For example:

- the number of places made available in old people's homes by a certain date;
- the number of meals-on-wheels served in a certain period;
- the number of patients treated in geriatric wards.

As shown in this example, several targets may make up its overall objective. For objectives to be of use in practice, they must have three components:

- attribute chosen to be measured, e.g. profit, return on capital, output;
- scale by which it is to be measured, e.g. £, %, tonnes;
- target, i.e. the level on the scale which it is hoped to achieve, e.g. £1m, 12%, 350,000 tonnes.

As well as being explicit, objectives should be realistic and attainable. Ideally, existing performance statistics should be used to measure objectives; if a new system of data collection or processing has to be instituted in order to measure progress towards objectives, extra cost will be incurred.

Drucker maintains that there are several factors that should be considered when formulating objectives:

- Objectives are commitments to action through which the mission of the business is to be carried out, and provide the standards against which performance is to be measured.
- Objectives must be operational, i.e. capable of being converted into specific targets and implying certain courses of action.
- Objectives should be of a fundamental nature to ensure the concentration of resources, i.e. they must be selective.
- A number of objectives are required to manage a business adequately.
- Objectives are needed in all areas upon which the survival of the organisation depends.

Drucker is an advocate of the hierarchy approach to corporate objective setting whereby the primary objectives are defined before the lower level objectives. In this way, the overall objective specifies the lower or sub-objectives.

Primary and secondary objectives

KEY POINT

In the hierarchy of objectives, there could be a *primary corporate objective* and other *secondary objectives* whose attainment should ensure the achievement of the primary corporate objective.

Some objectives may be more important than others. In the hierarchy of objectives, there could be a *primary corporate objective* and other *secondary objectives* whose attainment should ensure the achievement of the primary corporate objective.

For example, if a company sets itself an objective of growth in profits as its *primary objective* it will then have to develop strategies by which this primary objective can be achieved. An objective must then be set for each individual strategy; many secondary objectives may simply be targets by which the success of a strategy can be measured.

Secondary objectives might be concerned with sales growth, technological innovation, customer service, product quality, efficient resource management (e.g. labour productivity) or reducing the company's reliance on debt capital. Sometimes, objectives have to be ranked in order of priority.

Unless they are discussing a not-for-profit organisation, some writers assume that an enterprise's primary objective is to make a profit and that all other objectives, e.g. sales growth, market share and social responsibility, are secondary and take a lower priority. That is not to say that the secondary objectives are not important or relevant to many firms, merely that, without the profits, firms do not survive. They view some of the secondary objectives more as ways of making a profit than as objectives in their own right, so that objectives to increase market share, extend geographical coverage or develop new products are linked to profitability. Some of the social objectives are promoted by managers for public relations reasons, with the hope of increased business and therefore increased profits.

In some enterprises, other objectives not directly related to profits can predominate. For example survival might be of paramount importance to the firm in dire straits, but this must be a temporary objective. In other circumstances, especially where the shareholders are not in a position to influence the management directly, managerial objectives, such as empire building, may come to the fore. These managerial objectives may persist, although there may be occasions when the profits fall so low that shareholders eventually reassert their power.

Objectives may also be long-term and short-term. For example, a company that is suffering from a recession and making losses in the short term might continue to have a primary long-term objective of achieving a steady growth in profits, but in the short term, its primary objective might change to survival.

Secondary objectives will also range from short-term to long-term. Planners will formulate secondary objectives within the guidelines set by the primary objective, after selecting strategies for achieving the primary objective. For example, a company's primary objective might be to increase its earnings per share from 30p to 50p in the next five years. Strategies for achieving the objective might include the following:

- increasing profitability in the next 12 months by cutting expenditure;
- increasing export sales over the next three years;
- developing a successful new product for the domestic market within five years.

Secondary objectives might then be re-assessed to include the following:

- the objective of improving manpower productivity by 10% within 12 months;
- improving customer service in export markets with the objective of doubling the number of overseas sales outlets in selected countries within the next three years;
- investing more in product-market research and development, with the objective of bringing at least three new products to the market within five years.

Trade-off between objectives

When there are several key objectives, some might be achieved only at the expense of others. For example, a company's objective of achieving good profits and profit growth might have adverse consequences for the cash flow of the business, or the quality of the firm's product. Attempts to achieve a good cash flow or good product quality, or to improve market share, might call for some sacrifice of profits.

There are different ways of dealing with goal conflict.

- **Bargaining** – managers with different goals will compete and will form alliances with other managers to achieve their goals.
- **Satisficing** – organisations do not aim to maximise performance in one area if this leads to poor performance elsewhere. Rather they will accept satisfactory, if not excellent, performance in a number of areas.
- **Sequential attention** – goals are dealt with one by one, as it were, in a sequence.
- **Priority setting** – certain goals get priority over others. This is determined by senior managers, but there are quite complicated systems to link goals and strategies according to chosen criteria.

Activity 3

Consider how goals and objectives could be important in the following situations:

(a) where the parent company has completed the takeover of a smaller competitor;

(b) where a company is considering whether to buy-in partly finished goods from countries in Eastern Europe and complete the manufacture in UK.

Feedback to this activity is at the end of the chapter.

4.5 Strategy, tactics and operational plans

Strategy is the means by which these objectives will be attained. For example, a firm might have a strategy of cost leadership, or differentiation through marketing.

Tactics are the means by which the strategy will be carried out, and would include such things as marketing mix adjustments and developments.

Operational plans are the sequence of activities that must be performed to carry out the tactics. This would involve arrangements with distributors, discussions with advertising agencies and so on, to make the adjustments to the marketing mix, set against deadlines and budgets.

5 Stakeholders and objectives

5.1 Stakeholder groups

DEFINITION

Stakeholders are individuals, groups, or other organisations that have an interest in a particular organisation and can influence it.

Stakeholders are individuals, groups, or other organisations that have an interest in a particular organisation and can influence it. They have a 'stake' in what the organisation does.

An important part of the strategic manager's job is to understand the contribution that relationships with stakeholders can make to the well-being of the organisation. Assessing the expectations of stakeholders enables an organisation to gauge whether its objectives will provide the means to satisfy the demands of its various stakeholders.

Stakeholders may include any or all of the following groups:

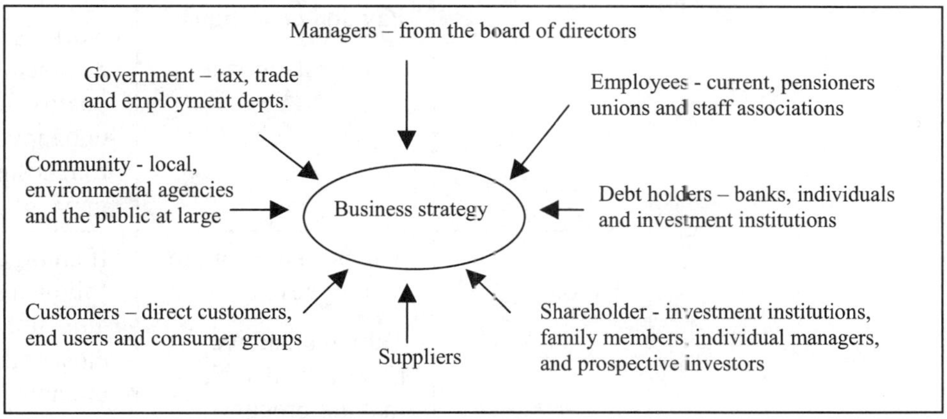

KEY POINT

Stakeholders can be broadly categorised into internal, connected and external stakeholders.

Stakeholders can be broadly categorised into:

Internal stakeholders – employees, management, etc. Because this group is intimately connected with the organisation, their objectives are likely to have a strong and immediate influence on how it is run.

Connected stakeholders – include shareholders, customers, suppliers, investors, distributors and competitors. The objective of satisfying shareholders is taken as the prime objective which the organisation's management seeks to fulfil. The customers' objectives in most companies must also be fulfilled if the company is to be successful. But clearly financiers such as banks have objectives that must be met – usually loan interest payments are contractual obligations whilst payment of dividends is not.

External stakeholders – government, local authority, pressure groups, the community, professional bodies etc. This group is likely to have quite diverse objectives and have varying ability to ensure that the organisation meets them.

5.2 Stakeholder analysis

The following table takes each stakeholder group in turn, identifies what each may generally be concerned with and gives an example for each.

Stakeholder group	Objectives	Example
Shareholders	A steady flow of income (dividends) Possible capital growth Continuation of business	If an organisation wishes to follow a strategy that will involve a large capital injection, the shareholders will be unhappy if the injection has an adverse effect on their income stream.
Managers	Pay and status Job security Individual performance measures	If an organisation wishes to follow a strategy that results in a particular department being reduced in size or abolished, the manager of that department is likely to be hostile to the plans.
Employees	Job security Pay and conditions Job satisfaction	If an organisation wishes to follow a strategy that results in workers being given more responsibility for monitoring quality, the employees may be unhappy unless this increased role is supported by an increase in wages.
Trade Unions	The problems of the employees Taking an active part in the decision-making process	If an organisation wishes to follow a strategy that results in a manufacturing plant being closed, the union will be unhappy if it has not been consulted and if there is no scheme for helping the employees find alternative employment.
Customers	Receiving goods and services of a reasonable quality Paying a reasonable price for those goods and services	If an organisation wishes to follow a strategy that increases the quality of a product at the same time as increasing the price, existing customers may not be willing to pay more for the product, while new customers are not attracted to a product that they will view as being of low quality.
Suppliers	Being paid promptly for goods and services delivered Receiving regular repayments of any capital provided (e.g., banks)	If an organisation wishes to follow a strategy that improves the working capital management by paying suppliers late, existing suppliers may decide to stop supplying the organisation leading to the increased cost of finding new suppliers.

Government and the general public	The organisation is meeting relevant legal requirements The organisation does not harm the outside environment	If an organisation wishes to follow a strategy that relies on increased use of shops based in out-of-town retail centres, this will be affected by government attitudes towards increased road building and society's attitude towards this method of shopping.

6 Conflicting objectives

6.1 Stakeholder expectations

Individual companies have their own unique permutation of corporate objectives, but there are certain common strands and themes. The basic motivators include survival, customer satisfaction and shareholder's wealth.

- Survival is an implicit, overriding objective in every organisation. Economic recessions and the activities of competitors will threaten an established company, and may cause it to re-examine its capacity for long-term survival.
- Customer satisfaction – Drucker suggests that a company exists to 'create a customer', or, as others have put it, 'to satisfy a customer need'. The view is that unless companies achieve a satisfactory level of customer satisfaction they would soon close down.
- Pursuit of profit – is a company's main objective. Shareholders are obviously a major group to be taken into account when setting objectives. If we ask 'why does the company want to survive or what about the objective of customer satisfaction?' the answer must be that the company wants survival and satisfied customers to make a profit or to maximise the wealth of investors in the company, i.e. the shareholders.

However, a company should think of profit **optimisation**, i.e. maximisation subject to constraints, rather than of profit **maximisation**. An acceptable statement of the primary objective of the private-sector company is:

'the achievement over a defined period of time of the maximum profitability consistent with keeping risk to an acceptable level and with any social responsibilities and constraints, internal or external, within which the company has to operate'

Each stakeholder to some degree has a link of dependency to the organisation. Each will make demands on, and have expectations of, the organisation. These expectations may clash and conflict with the interest of other stakeholder groups. For instance, the rate of growth expectations of the managers of a family owned company may conflict with those of the family shareholders whose main interest may be in maintaining family control.

KEY POINT

There will be occasions where the objective specified by the organisation is a formal statement of stakeholder expectations.

There will be occasions where the objective specified by the organisation is a formal statement of stakeholder expectations, for example:

- return on capital employed expressing shareholders' expectations;
- pledges on non-pollution of environment expressing society's expectations.

Clearly, some stakeholder groups wield greater power than others. The government's legislative power is comprehensive, and rulings of the Competition Commission have a direct effect upon the objectives and strategies of companies affected. Examples are:

- breweries, where Bass was required to sell off a major part of its tied public houses;
- newspaper publishing, where Rupert Murdoch was blocked from taking over other newspapers on the grounds of safeguarding freedom of opinion across a range of views.

Since stakeholder expectations are expressed through objectives and such expectations will vary over time; so we must expect objectives to change in response. Indeed, if we ask the question of any organisation, 'Why are you in this position today?', the answer will be the objectives that it has pursued in the past and the future environment as it is perceived.

6.2 Managing the conflict – the stakeholder approach

KEY POINT

The stakeholder approach suggests that an organisation's objectives should balance the conflicting claims of its stakeholders.

The 'stakeholder' approach suggests that the objectives of an organisation should be derived by balancing the often conflicting claims of the various stakeholders (or coalitions) in the organisation.

Once stakeholders are identified they can be mapped in relation to:

- the likelihood of each stakeholder group attempting to impress their expectations on others;
- the power and means available for them to do so;
- the impact of stakeholder expectations on the strategy.

Mapping out the various expectations within an organisation and where they conflict contributes significantly to an understanding of the core beliefs in the organisation and its strategic position. Together with an assessment of power structure, management can assess future strategies in relation to their cultural fit and how easy or difficult change is likely to be.

Two matrices can be developed from this analysis that aid the manager in understanding the threat and management approach to key stakeholders (following Mendelow, 1991). These are shown below. The first one maps stakeholder power against predictability and shows where political efforts are best channelled during the strategy development. The latter maps stakeholder power against interest in the strategy to understand the best way to manage expectations.

Power \ Predictability	High	Low
Low	Few problems	Unpredictable but manageable
High	Powerful but predictable	Greatest danger **or** opportunity

(a) Power/Dynamism matrix

Power \ Level of interest	Low	High
Low	Minimal effort	Keep informed
High	Keep satisfied	Key players

(b) Power/interest matrix

Power/dynamism matrix – this is a useful way of assessing where the political efforts should be channelled during the development of new strategies. The most difficult group to manage are those with high power and low predictability since they are in a position to block or support new strategies but it is difficult to predict where they stand. New strategies must be tested on these stakeholders before an irrevocable position has been established. In contrast, the powerful but predictable stakeholders are likely to influence strategy through the process of managers anticipating their stand and building strategies that will address their expectations. Stakeholders in the other two segments cannot be ignored because their active support may, in itself, have an influence on the attitude of the more powerful stakeholders.

Power/interest matrix – this classifies stakeholders in relation to the power they hold and the extent to which they are likely to show an interest in the organisation's strategies. The key players must be considered during the formulation and evaluation of new strategies. Although the other stakeholders might be relatively passive, managers must be aware that stakeholder groups tend to emerge and influence strategy as a result of specific events. It is very important that the likely reaction of stakeholders towards future strategies is given full consideration. A disastrous situation could occur if their level of interest is underrated and they suddenly become key players and frustrate the adoption of an intended strategy. Where stakeholders have low power and interest, they need to be kept informed because they can be important allies in influencing the attitudes of more powerful stakeholders.

6.3 Strategies and mapping

KEY POINT

Using the power/interest matrix, Scholes suggests four strategies:

- Direction
- Education/ Communication
- Intervention
- Participation.

Using the power/interest matrix, Scholes suggests the following strategies to deal with the four quadrants:

- Low interest/low stakeholder power – **Direction**. Their lack of interest and power makes them malleable. They are most likely to accept what they are told and follow instructions.
- High interest/low stakeholder power – **Education/Communication**. This stakeholder group may lobby others to support the strategy. If the strategy is presented in a logical way and shown to be rational, this may stop them joining forces with more powerful dissenters.
- Low interest/high stakeholder power – **Intervention**. The key is to keep these stakeholders satisfied to avoid them gaining interest. Reassuring them of the likely outcomes of the strategy well in advance usually does this.

- High interest/high stakeholder power – **Participation**. These stakeholders can be major drivers of change and also major opponents of the strategy. Initially there should be communication to assure them that the change is necessary followed by discussions on the implementation of the strategy and how it affects them.

For example, consider three different types of organisation that are investigating the same strategy of bringing down costs by reducing wages and making employees work more flexible shifts.

- **Contract cleaning company** – the main employees affected will be the cleaners themselves. Since unskilled workers are relatively easy to replace, they have high interest in this decision but low power. The organisation will therefore keep the cleaners informed of the decision but will probably impose the decision on the workforce. This imposition is likely to be enacted quickly, i.e. the strategy will take place almost immediately.
- **Accountancy training company** – the main employees affected will be the lecturers. Since these lecturers are very difficult to replace, they have high interest in the decision and high power. The organisation will need to bear in mind the feelings of the lecturers and may decide that this strategy will not succeed.
- **Local public library service** – the main employees affected will be the library staff. Although these employees may be easy to replace, they are likely to be heavily unionised. The power of the union will affect the decision-making process. The organisation may decide to consult with the union before any final decisions are made. Owing to the lengthy procedures that often exist within the public sector, it is likely that any change in working conditions will be subject to a number of reviews, and implementation will not be rapid.

In the private sector the shareholders are usually the key stakeholders. In the public sector the different groups of stakeholders should be mapped to identify who are likely to be the key stakeholders and what outcomes they want from any particular strategy. Any strategy chosen will need to be accepted by these key stakeholder groups.

Abrams emphasises the importance to an organisation of maintaining 'an equitable and working balance among the claims of the various directly interested groups'. Senior management may seek to achieve a balance. However, a dominant stakeholder group can impose its demands at the expense of others. A typical example would occur when an organisation over-expands and its gearing ratio dictates that capital restructuring is necessary for survival. In these circumstances, the company's bankers will assume a dominant role and dictate the terms of the company's future with token regard to the interest of shareholders and employees.

6.4 Stakeholder power

Power is the mechanism by which stakeholders' expectations are able to influence the organisation's strategies. In most organisations, power will be unequally shared between the various stakeholders. Stakeholder power is more elusive than stakeholder interest because it is exercised in subtle, invisible ways.

Power within organisations can be derived in a variety of ways (as we will see in Chapter 11). Sources of stakeholder power include the following:

- **Hierarchy** – provides people or groups with formal power over others and is one method by which senior managers influence strategy. Statutory authority is enjoyed by central and local government agencies and regulators.

- **Influence** – may arise from personal qualities (leadership) or because a high level of consensus exists within the organisation i.e. people are willing to support the prevailing viewpoint. An important task of management is to shape the culture of the organisation to suit its strategy because those individuals most closely associated with the core beliefs are likely to accrue power e.g. doctors in the health service have considerable power through their influence on others.

- **Control of strategic resources** – the relative importance of different resources will change over time e.g. the power of organised labour is most potent when demand for output is high and labour supply short. R&D departments may be powerful in organisations developing new products or processes and the marketing department may dominate an organisation, which is primarily concerned with developing new markets. Stakeholders that can withdraw their resources have an advantage e.g. suppliers, financiers and bankers.

- **Knowledge and skills** – is an extension of the previous point. Certain people may be viewed as irreplaceable by the organisation and some will jealously guard this privilege by creating a mystique around their positions.

- **Control of the environment** – knowledge, contact and influence where the environment is concerned can be a source of power for some groups since they are able to reduce the uncertainty experienced by others. It is probably for this reason that financial and marketing managers have traditionally been seen as dominant in strategy determination.

- **Ability to exercise discretion** – many people in an organisation will need to interpret and execute particular parts of the strategy and in doing so will use their own personal discretion in the successful adoption and implementation of the strategy.

6.5 Assessing power

There are four indicators that can be used when analysing and assessing the power of *internal* stakeholders:

- **Status** – the position in the hierarchy, the individual's job grade or salary or the reputation that a group or individual holds with others will be relevant in the assessment.

- **The claim on resources** – can be measured by the size of the department's budget or the number of people involved in that group. Assessments can be made with comparable groups in similar organisations.

- **Representation in powerful positions** – in hierarchical organisations representation on the board of directors can indicate the relative importance e.g. the weakness of the production function may result from the lack of representation either at board level or in important committees.
- **Symbols of power** – may be indicated by the size and location of people's offices and whether they have newspapers delivered daily. In more bureaucratic organisations the existence of distribution lists for internal memos and other information may also provide pointers as to who is viewed as important within the organisation.

Similar indicators can be used when analysing the power of *external* stakeholders:

- **Status** – the power of an external stakeholder such as a supplier can be indicated by the way they are discussed among employees and whether members of the organisation respond quickly to the supplier's demands
- **Resource dependence** – can be measured directly e.g. by the proportion of an organisation's business tied up with any one customer or supplier. A key indicator is the ease with which the supplier, customer or financier could be switched at short notice.
- **Negotiating arrangements** – are another indicator e.g. whether external parties are kept at arm's length or are actively involved in negotiations with the company. A customer that is invited to negotiate over the price of a contract is in a more powerful position than one that is given a fixed price on a take it or leave it basis.
- **Symbols** – may be indicated by the actions of the management team in wining and dining some customers or suppliers and not others. The care and attention paid to correspondence with outsiders will tend to differ from one party to another depending on the power held.

No single measure will give a full understanding but a combined analysis will be useful to identify who has power and to what extent.

Summary

- To formulate strategy we ask: Where are we now? Where do we want to be? How do we get there?
- Mintzberg's five Ps: strategy as plan, pattern, ploy, position, perspective.
- Johnson and Scholes distinguish between corporate, business and functional strategies.
- Mission, goals and objectives are linked in a top-down hierarchy.
- Analysis of stakeholders provides a means of dealing with conflicts in objectives.

Having completed your study of this chapter you should have achieved the following learning outcome.

- Explain the process of strategy formulation.

Self-test questions

1 Give a simple definition of strategy. (1.1)

2 What are the five Ps of strategy according to Mintzberg? (1.2)

3 List the three different levels of strategy. (1.3)

4 Describe the sequence of strategic planning. (2.2)

5 Why are strategic decisions often complex in nature? (3.1)

6 Sketch the hierarchy of objectives. (4.1)

7 What is a mission statement? (4.2)

8 What is an organisational goal? (4.3)

9 For objectives to be useful, they must have three components. What are they? (4.4)

10 Give two examples of connected stakeholders. (5.1)

11 How does the power/interest matrix classify stakeholders? (6.2)

Multiple-choice questions

Question 1

Federal Express has a short mission statement – 'absolutely, positively overnight'. Other organisations have broader definitions that can include many elements. Which of the following is unlikely to be included?

A Strategy – the commercial logic for the company; it defines the nature of the firm's business.

B Profits – return on investment.

C Values – a description of the pervading culture and the assumptions and beliefs regarded as important by those managing the organisation.

D Policies and standards of behaviour.

Question 2

In an article on stakeholders, Mirjana is surprised at how many stakeholders there are and the 'stake' they have in the organisation. She is finding it difficult to distinguish between the various groups. Indicate which of the following would not be described as a connected stakeholder?

A Customers – want products and services.

B Suppliers – will expect to be paid and will be interested in the future.

C Employees – want security of income and interesting work.

D Shareholders – want a return on their investment.

For the answers to these questions, see the 'Answers' section at the end of the book.

Exam-type questions

Question 1: Stakeholder groups

R is a large high-class hotel situated in a thriving city. It is part of a worldwide hotel group owned by a large number of shareholders. Individuals hold the majority of the shares, each holding a small number, and financial institutions own the rest. The hotel provides full amenities, including a heated swimming pool, as well as the normal facilities of bars, restaurants and good-quality accommodation. There are many other hotels in the city which all compete with R. The city in which R is situated is old and attracts many foreign visitors, particularly in its summer season.

Required:

State the main stakeholders with whom relationships need to be established and maintained by the management of R.

Explain why it is important that relationships are developed and maintained with each of these stakeholders. **(10 marks)**

Question 2: Synfib and Thetfib

C is a company which is engaged in synthetic fibre production. It is situated in Home country where it operates two production plants. C pipes raw material from an oil refinery (which it does not own) to its own production plant where it manufactures a single product, which is a special grade of polymer. The polymer is then transferred to a second production site, which produces two products, 'Synfib' and 'Thetfib'. As the polymer is of a special grade and manufactured specifically for the production of Synfib and Thetfib, there is no intermediate market for it. The transfer price for the polymer has been set at $40 per litre.

Mission and objectives

C's Chairman has declared that the firm's mission is to 'provide its customers with the highest quality product at a reasonable price'. The organisational objectives are to satisfy the demands of the shareholders, reduce pollution to a minimum, maintain secure employment and to sell a product of high quality, which satisfies customer requirements. The objectives also make reference to maximisation of shareholder wealth while at the same time keeping the shareholders' exposure to financial risk to a minimum. Approximately 75% of the shares are held by large financial institutions. The remainder are held by individual investors including employees and the Directors.

The final products

While Synfib and Thetfib are both produced at the second production site in Home, they are produced in different processes. There is strong demand for both of these specialist products worldwide and C is the only producer. However, substitute products are available and may be used in place of them.

The divisional manager (M) of the second production site has autonomy to choose the level of output, and always selects that level of output which maximises divisional contribution.

As a result of its production processes, Thetfib emits waste products, which pollute the atmosphere. The government of Home has introduced strict regulations in recent years to control waste emissions and C estimates that the firm incurs a fixed monthly cost of $2,000 million in order to comply with these regulations.

Transfer of production of Thetfib to another plant in Foreign country

The Directors of C are considering transferring production of Thetfib to another plant, which the firm owns in Foreign. The plant is already established in Foreign and could produce Thetfib in the quantities required without any other costs being incurred except for those shown in the following table. Foreign is a developing country, which encouraged the Directors of C to build a plant there by offering grants and loans at a very attractive interest rate. Foreign's government also takes a more relaxed view of pollution and, while it does have regulations in place, these are less strict than those which apply in Home. The Directors of C estimate that compliance with the regulations applying in Foreign would cost the company $600 million per month.

Required:

Produce a critical appraisal of the content of the mission statement and objectives of C as they are presented to you in the scenario.

Recommend what changes should be made to their content. **(10 marks)**

For the answers to these questions, see the 'Answers' section at the end of the book.

Feedback to activities

Activity 1

(a) This is probably strategy as plan. A document is being prepared by senior management.

(b) This is strategy as position. The market trader specialising in Chinese vegetables is trying to carve himself a niche.

Activity 2

Most of the issues require some contribution from all levels. However, the principal decision-making levels are as follows.

(a) **Corporate level**. Movement of resources between businesses can only be decided at the highest level.

(b) **Business level**. Only managers who understand the particular markets concerned can really work out the most effective strategy (technically called positioning). Senior managers will be interested in associated costs and benefits, while functions will need to know how they can produce a superior product that appeals to the new target market if this option is selected.

(c) **Functional level**. Good functional managers, in operations and cost accounting in particular, should be able to produce a range of alternative projects to reduce costs. Business level strategy will be concerned with the effect the changes may have on other functions, for example it is possible to reduce costs by lowering quality, but this may make the product harder to sell at the same price. Thus the functions would have achieved their cost reduction targets, but the strategic objective of improving the margin may fail if this quality-based option is selected.

(d) **Business level**. The publishers are best placed to know whether they have, or could gain, the skills necessary to diversify in this way. Naturally, the senior corporate levels will be concerned about costs and benefits of this move, compared with other possible projects.

(e) **Corporate level**. Acquisitions and disposals to strengthen the group of businesses can only be made at the highest level.

Activity 3

(a) Where a parent company has taken over a smaller competitor then the setting of specific goals and objectives could achieve the following benefits:

- a means of checking the operating data and results that the parent company believed existed at the time of the takeover;
- to identify areas of performance that are inferior to group standards;
- the identification of effective managers;
- to evaluate the contribution of particular processes or products;
- checking customer reactions to the takeover.

(b) Where a company is considering whether to buy in partly finished goods from Eastern Europe, then goals and objectives would be important in:

- defining the standards required in areas of quality, delivery promise, design, etc;
- setting improvement targets;
- providing a basis of comparison with other suppliers.

Chapter 2

APPROACHES TO STRATEGY FORMULATION

Syllabus content

- The process of strategy formulation.
- Approaches to strategy (e.g. rational, adaptive, emergent, evolutionary or systems-based views based on Porter, Mintzberg, Bartlett and Ghoshal).
- Resource-based views of the firm and implications for strategy development.

Contents

1 The rational process of strategy formulation

2 Alternative approaches to strategy formulation

3 Tools for strategic analysis

1 The rational process of strategy formulation

1.1 The rational model

A rational process is considered to be one 'based on reasoning', one that is not subjective but objective, and one that is logical and sensible. Using rational behaviour, policy is formed by firstly defining the goal and then selecting the means to achieve the goal by rational analysis.

In many problem-solving situations an assumption is made that the goals or objectives can be measured or assessed in quantitative terms. Rationality in this sense is based on the choice the decision-maker makes with reference to clear-cut alternatives. The following areas are present:

- complete knowledge of environmental factors;
- ability to choose the alternative that returns the best outcome;
- ability to order the preferences using some yardstick of utility, mainly with money as the common denominator.

In process terms, rationality assumes that decision-takers confront issues with known objectives. They then gather appropriate information, develop a set of options and select the optimum one. Suppose a company requires more production capacity. There may be several options available:

- buy or lease more machines;
- sub-contract;
- build or lease a new factory.

If the decision-maker's preference was to spend as little as possible (a preference for cheapness), then the rational approach would be to choose the option that cost the least.

KEY POINT

The rational approach to strategy formation assumes that the organisation takes a systematic and structured approach to its development.

The implication of the rational approach to strategy formulation is that the organisation takes a systematic and structured approach to its development. Internal and external information is collected, and decisions are integrated into a comprehensive strategy. Managers ascertain, review and evaluate every option available, and they are then able to choose what appears to be the best option in the light of rational criteria.

The rational approach to strategy involves:

- strategic plans;
- long-term objectives;
- key strategies;
- funds requirements;
- analysis of strategic options:
  - is it feasible given resources?
  - is it suitable to the firm's existing position?
  - is it acceptable to stakeholders?

This approach to strategy evolves from top down. First we have the corporate strategy. With this we can then discuss the business unit strategy which will then allow us to develop the organisational and functional strategy, (marketing, finance, HRM, etc.). Actual performance is compared with plans and assessed in the review and control process.

1.2 Johnson and Scholes rational model

This strategic planning (rational) model involves the careful and deliberate formulation, evaluation and selection of strategies for the purpose of preparing a cohesive long-term course of action to attain objectives. There are three main stages – these are strategic analysis, strategic choice and strategic implementation, which are described in the following sections.

To make it easier to remember, the process can be imagined as undertaking a journey.

- **Strategic analysis** – Where are we now (current location)? Where do we want to go (desired location)?
- **Strategic choice** – Develop a range of methods to travel from current location to desired location. Choose which method of travel to undertake.
- **Strategic implementation** – Travel to desired location.

The rational model

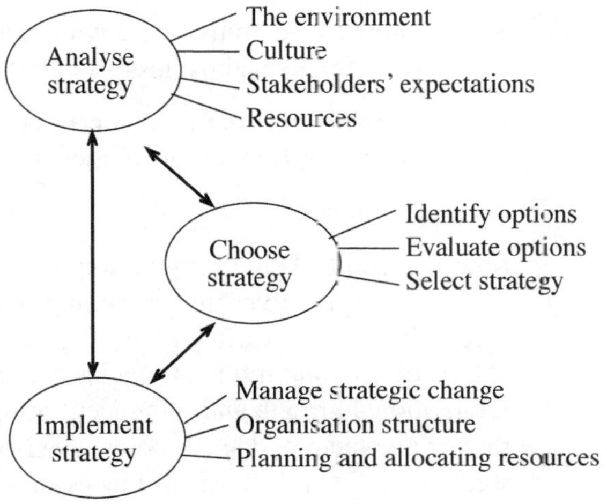

Note that once the strategy is implemented, the new position of the organisation should be analysed; in other words, we return to the strategic analysis stage and the process is continuous. It is quite likely that the elements are interlinked. For example one way of evaluating a strategy might be to begin to implement it and because strategic analysis will be an on-going activity, it will overlap with the implementation of strategy.

This process is not intended as a prescription of what strategic management should be, but as a framework that can be used to structure strategic problems.

Strategic analysis

KEY POINT

The aim of strategic analysis is to form a view of the main influences on the present and future well being of the organisation.

Strategic analysis helps gain an understanding of the strategic position of the organisation relative to its competitors. It deals with the environmental (political, economic, social and technological) and competitive factors that offer both opportunities and threats to the organisation. It also covers the strengths and weaknesses of the resources of the organisation and its mission and objectives. The aim of strategic analysis is to form a view of the main influences on the present and future well being of the organisation. This will obviously affect the strategy choice.

The process of strategic analysis can be assisted by a number of tools (discussed in more detail in section 3 of this chapter), including:

- **SWOT analysis** – a useful technique for summarising the key issues arising from an assessment of a business's 'internal' position and 'external' environmental influences.
- **PESTLE/SLEPT/PEST analysis** – a technique for understanding the external environment in which a business operates
- **Scenario planning** – a technique that builds various plausible views of possible futures for a business
- **Five forces analysis** – a technique for identifying the forces which affect the level of competition in an industry
- **Market segmentation** – a technique which seeks to identify similarities and differences between groups of customers or users
- **Directional policy matrix** – a technique which summarises the competitive strength of a business's operations in specific markets
- **Competitor analysis** – a wide range of techniques and analysis that seeks to summarise a business's overall competitive position
- **Critical success factor analysis** – a technique to identify those areas in which a business must outperform the competition in order to succeed.

Strategic choice

KEY POINT

Strategic choice is the formulation of possible courses of action and their evaluation.

Strategic choice is the formulation of possible courses of action and their evaluation. It involves understanding the nature of stakeholder expectations (the 'ground rules'). A variety of strategic options can be considered to establish a choice of possible future strategies e.g. increased market share, acquisition, international growth and/or concentration on core competencies. Each option is then evaluated e.g. does it increase existing strengths or strengthen existing weaknesses? On the basis of this evaluation, a strategy is chosen.

There are three main areas to consider.

- **Porter** describes certain strategies which an organisation may pursue for competitive advantage. They determine how you compete.
- **Ansoff** describes product-market strategies (which markets you should enter or leave). They determine where you compete and the direction of growth.
- **Institutional strategies** (i.e. relationships with other organisations) determine the method of growth – acquisition versus organic.

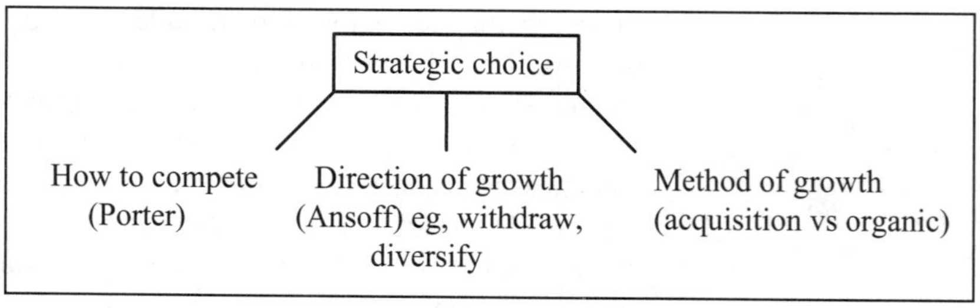

According to Hofer and Schendel, strategic choice follows logically out of the process of strategic analysis, but there are other considerations:

- A strategy might be acceptable or feasible in principle, but this does not necessarily mean it is the right one to choose.

- The choice of strategy should follow a strategic logic i.e. it should be consistently related to the objectives of the organisation and match the organisation's capability (including its structure, control systems and culture) to its environment.

The idea is that all the pieces of the strategic puzzle should fit together in a predetermined manner. For Hofer and Schendel, a strategy is the mediating force or 'match' between the organisation and the environment.

Harrison also supports the proposition that strategy is the achieving of a match between the organisation and its environment. Strategic choice involves viewing the internal capabilities of the organisation and, in the light of these, identifying the opportunities or threats that exist externally.

Strategic implementation

Strategy is translated into action via processes that become successively more specific as they move down the organisational hierarchy towards the point of implementation. It involves resource planning e.g. the changes that need to be made in the resource mix of the organisation. It also includes implementation of any changes in organisational structure or adaptation of any systems used to manage the organisation.

The implementation of strategy also requires the management of change. This may be achieved directly (by altering the attitudes, beliefs and values of individuals) or indirectly (by changing the structure, goals or technology of the organisation).

1.3 Limited or 'bounded' rationality

Most versions of the rational model, which have been advocated and tried in practice, have placed considerable emphasis on the determination of objectives, or ends. Once the ends are determined, all possible means of securing them are explored, and their consequences analysed. The course of action with the greatest net benefit is then chosen.

KEY POINT

In practice, complete rationality is seldom realised. Managers must settle for limited or 'bounded' rationality.

In practice, people seldom achieve complete rationality, especially in managing. In the first place, decisions must operate in the future and this almost certainly involves uncertainties. Secondly, it is difficult to recognise all the alternatives that might be followed to reach a goal. This is particularly true when decision-making involves opportunities to do something that has not been done before. Also, in most instances, it is difficult to analyse all the alternatives, even with the newest analytical techniques and computers.

Simon was aware that this ideal model could not readily be realised. He argued that when people face decisions they operate within the bounds or capacities of the human mind. They are limited by imperfect perceptions, wandering attention, faulty memories, and fluctuating information-processing abilities. People don't optimise, but instead resort to simplifying rules of thumb in order to proceed with their decision-making. These limitations have been investigated for decades with the repeated finding that limitations in working memory restrict the ability to make rational decisions.

A **limiting factor** is something that stands in the way of accomplishing a desired objective. Recognising the limiting factors in a given situation makes it possible to narrow the search for alternatives to those that will overcome them.

A manager must settle for limited or 'bounded' rationality. Limitations of information, time and certainty reduce rationality even though a manager tries to be completely rational. Because managers find it difficult to be completely rational in practice, they sometimes allow their dislike of risk to interfere with their desire to reach the best solution under the circumstances.

Simon evolved a 'best practicable model', which would fit the problems of real life. In this model the manager does not optimise (i.e. get the best possible solution). Instead the manager satisfices. In other words, the manager carries on searching until he or she finds an option, which appears tolerably satisfactory, and adopts it, even though it may be less than perfect. This approach Simon characterised as **bounded rationality.**

Activity 1

What is bounded rationality?

Feedback to this activity is at the end of the chapter.

1.4 Systematic planning process

At this stage, it is appropriate to examine why a systematic approach to strategy formulation and implementation is desirable. The alternative is to have no system except the approach of looking for profitable activities. In other words a firm evaluates each new opportunity on the merits of its individual profitability or as part of its portfolio of investments. It does not bother to define objectives, undertake a detailed analysis of the organisation and its environment, or evaluate existing or possible strategies.

Ansoff has examined the pros and cons of this alternative to a systematic planning process. In favour of **no planning**, he makes the following points:

- The firm would save the time, money and executive talent which are required for a thorough strategic analysis.
- The field of potential opportunities will be in no way restricted. Objectives and strategy limit the field of its search.
- The firm reaps the full advantage of the delay principle. By delaying commitment until an opportunity is in hand, it is able to act on the basis of the best possible information.

Against these advantages, Ansoff lists several significant **disadvantages**:

- Without strategy, there are no rules to guide the search for new opportunities. The firm passively waits for opportunities, or pursues a buckshot search technique.
- Project decisions are of poorer quality, not least because the firm will lack the specialist knowledge needed for competent analysis of opportunities in particular areas.
- There will be no criteria for identifying excellent opportunities or the likelihood of better opportunities occurring subsequently. As a result a firm may over-commit resources prematurely or fail fully to utilise available resources.
- The firm will be unable to anticipate change.

These disadvantages are quite severe in comparison with the advantages of an unplanned corporate development. In short it would seem highly desirable that an organisation has some form of strategic, or corporate, plan.

1.5 Top-down planning

Many organisations combine a rational strategic planning methodology with a top-down approach. The benefits and drawbacks of a top-down approach to strategy formulation are explained below:

Benefits

A top-down approach should facilitate better control by senior management. Targets can be set, for example, that are key to the whole organisation, not just one part of it.

Senior management can ensure that the objectives of each business unit are congruent with the overall mission and objectives of the firm.

Senior management are in a better position to see the whole business and can thus develop a strategy that coordinates all the different activities in a consistent manner.

Senior managers are likely to be more experienced and will thus make better decisions.

Changes in direction can be made more quickly without the need to consult throughout the organisation.

Drawbacks

Senior management are often disconnected from the real business of the firm. They may not have the understanding of market forces that local managers have, for example.

Senior managers are often older and may fail to understand the significance and essential features of modern technologies.

If the planning process is done by essentially the same group every year, then there will be little scope for radical changes in strategy in favour of preserving the status quo. This gives rise to the risk of failing to anticipate and respond to market changes in what is often a dynamic environment.

Note: To deal with these criticisms, **Hamel** and **Prahalad** advocate getting increased participation from three groups:

(1) young people;

(2) those at the geographic periphery of the organisation; and

(3) those in your company who bring experience from outside the industry.

Each of those groups adds a perspective that is unlikely to be well understood by those at the corporate centre.

Top-down approaches often become very formal, rational planning exercises with little room for emergent strategies (see below).

Top-down planning can become a once-a-year exercise rather than an ongoing process. Mintzberg argued that strategy development is as much (if not more) art than science. Strategy is crafted, not engineered, and the crafting process is as far away from routine as you can get.

Increased participation from junior and middle managers will result in better motivation and training. This is lost in a top-down approach.

2 Alternative approaches to strategy formulation

2.1 How strategies are developed

Strategy formulation is a continuous process of refinement based on past trends, current conditions and estimates of the future, resulting in a clear expression of strategic direction, the implementation of which is also planned in terms of resource allocation and structure. The strategy then comes about or is realised in actuality. The figure below shows that the actual outcome, the organisation's realised strategy, can come about through a planned, deliberate formulation and implementation.

How strategies are developed

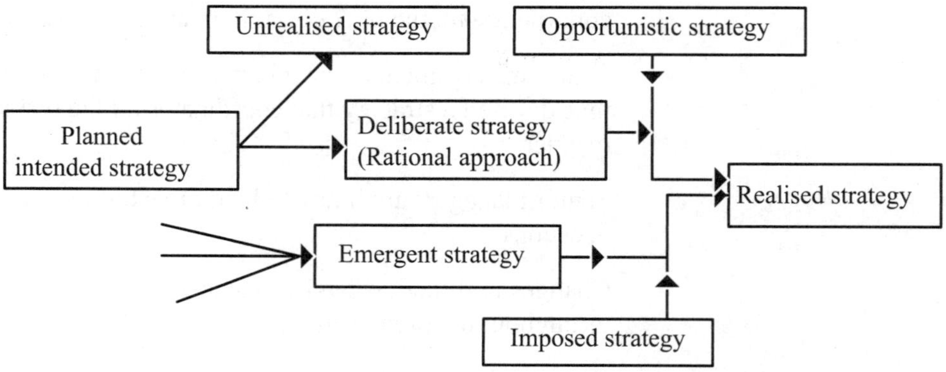

The obvious reason that an intended strategy is not implemented is because its underlying assumptions turn out to be invalid or because the pace of developments overtakes it. Factors affecting the strategy realisation will include changes in the organisation's external environment e.g. changes in the market for the goods and services that the firm produces and in the nature of the competition facing the company, and also its internal environment.

2.2 Emergent strategy – Mintzberg

The term 'emergent strategy' was developed by Mintzberg based on the idea that most of what organisations intend to happen, does not happen and is eventually rejected along the way. He argues that strategies can emerge, perhaps as a result of the processes of **negotiation, bargaining and compromise**, rather than be due to a deliberate planning process.

Emergent strategies result from a number of **ad hoc choices** that may have been made lower down in the hierarchy. They develop from patterns of behaviour; one idea leads to another, until a new pattern is formed and a new strategy has emerged. For example a salesman visits a customer out in the field. The product isn't right, and together they work out some modifications. The salesman returns to the company and puts the changes through; after two or three more rounds, they finally get it right. A new product emerges, which eventually opens up a new market. The company has changed strategic course.

KEY POINT

Emergent strategies are reactive, evolving and unpredictable, capitalising on luck/ unintended results.

Emergent strategies develop progressively over time. They are reactive, evolving, unpredictable and they capitalise on luck/unintended results

Mintzberg further maintains that the strategy development process is not so much about thinking and reasoning, as involvement, a feeling of intimacy and harmony with the materials at hand, developed through long experience and commitment. In this way, strategies 'can form as well as be formulated'.

2.3 Entrepreneurial and imposed strategies

Strategies may come about in **opportunistic** or **entrepreneurial** ways. An organisation may take advantage of changes in the environment or recognise new skills in an opportunistic manner. Alternatively, a firm may be set up by an entrepreneur because of an opportunity in the market place. This mode requires the strategy-making authority to rest with one powerful individual. Strategy is developed by significant bold decisions being made. Growth is the dominant goal of the organisation, and in uncertain conditions, this type of mode can result in the organisation making significant gains. These conditions are most typical of organisations that are small and/or young.

There are also situations where a strategy may be imposed on the organisation. Recession and threat of a takeover may force a strategy of cost cutting and retrenchment, with divestments. Technological developments may cause an organisation to develop new products to replace the ones that have become obsolescent. Government action/policies may have a direct impact on organisational strategy; for example, in the public sector; or by privatisation of public utilities or state-owned enterprises, as has happened most dramatically in recent years in eastern Europe. Again such pressure may be dealt with through planning mechanisms within the organisation; or it may be handled through some other mechanism, such as individual decision making by senior executives. In any event, such imposed strategy development can result in significant long-term changes for an organisation.

Activity 2

Differentiate between the rational model of strategy making and the concept of emergent strategies.

Feedback to this activity is at the end of the chapter.

2.4 Logical incrementalism

KEY POINT

Instead of being a comprehensive, planned, and rational process, strategy making can sometimes be disjointed and incremental.

Within the organisation, a host of behavioural, social, and political factors influence the strategy making process. Instead of being a comprehensive, planned, and rational process, strategy making can sometimes be disjointed and incremental. Quinn (1980) used the term logical incrementalism (sometimes called 'adaptive' by other writers) to describe such processes. Logical incrementalism acknowledges that organisational goals are complex, changing, and unclear. It involves artfully blending formal analysis, behavioural techniques, and power politics to move organisations toward broadly conceived goals. In this process, strategy formulation and implementation are not separate; rather, they are integrated into a single-decision making process.

Indeed, this view of strategy making is consistent with reality in many organisations where the flow of decision activities often tends to be non-sequential, fragmented, and somewhat haphazard. By acting logically and incrementally, managers can improve the quality of information used in critical decisions, overcome personal and political pressures resisting strategic changes, and deal with varying lead times and sequencing problems. They also can help build consensus and support for key decisions and create enthusiasm and psychological commitment to chosen strategies.

The outcome of this approach is a deliberate policy of **small strategic changes** within the framework provided by a general sense of strategic direction. While managers are continually learning from each other, this results in continual testing and gradual strategy implementation, which provide improved quality of information to help decision-making. Because of this continual readjustment, the organisation should be in line with the environmental demands being placed on it. Quinn advocates the cautious use of logical incrementalism over the comprehensive rational planning suggested in most strategy textbooks. He believes that it is more realistic and that it allows firms to be flexible and opportunistic. It keeps sensitive strategic information within control of key decision-makers and allows managers to seek new environmental information continually and incorporate it into strategic decisions.

2.5 The adaptive approach

KEY POINT

An adaptive approach allows for the introduction of new strategic ideas as new opportunities are spotted.

The adaptive approach to strategy formulation is the introduction of new strategic ideas as new opportunities are spotted. **Learning** is at the heart of this mode. Managers must know of opportunities and threats facing them; the organisation must be able to synthesise all the changes into a meaningful pattern, and spread learning and best practice. They should also learn from the successes and mistakes of other managers and be willing to take measured risks. For this to happen, understandable mistakes and errors of judgement should not be sanctioned harshly.

Change is gradual and comes from experimentation; new strategies involve an element of trial and error. The success of this mode is very dependent upon communications.

It is called the adaptive mode because it fits the description that managers give of how strategies come about in their organisations. They see their role as strategists as being involved in a continual proactive pursuit of a strategic goal, countering competitive moves and adapting to their environment whilst not rocking the boat too much.

This type of strategy formulation is commonly found in the public sector, non-profit making organisations and in organisations that face relatively stable environments. Strategies are developed as a result of the interaction and bargaining among various power/interest groups. As there is no one source of power or influence, strategies are not always automatically clear.

Four major characteristics distinguish the adaptive mode of strategy-making:

- Clear goals do not exist in the adaptive organisation; strategy-making reflects a division of power among members of a complex coalition. The adaptive organisation is caught in a web of political forces – unions, managers, owners, lobby groups, government agencies, and so on.
- There is no one central source of power, no one simple goal. The organisation cannot make decisions to 'maximise' any one goal such as profit or growth; rather it must seek solutions to its problems that satisfy the constraints.
- The strategy-making process is characterised by a 'reactive' solution to the existing problems rather than a 'proactive' search for new opportunities. Adaptive organisations seek conditions of certainty wherever possible. Failing that, they seek to reduce existing uncertainties by for example negotiating long-term purchasing arrangements to stabilise sources of supply, etc.
- Organisations make decisions in incremental, serial steps. Because its environment is complex, the adaptive organisation finds that feedback is a crucial ingredient in strategy-making. Strategy-making focuses on what is familiar, considering the convenient alternatives and the ones that differ only slightly from the status quo.

Disjointed decisions are characteristic of the adaptive organisation. The demands on the organisation are diverse, and cannot be reconciled easily, therefore decisions are made in a piecemeal manner.

2.6 Evolutionary theory

Evolutionary theory is one of Whittington's four generic approaches to strategy formulation shown in the matrix below:

Whittington's strategy perspectives matrix

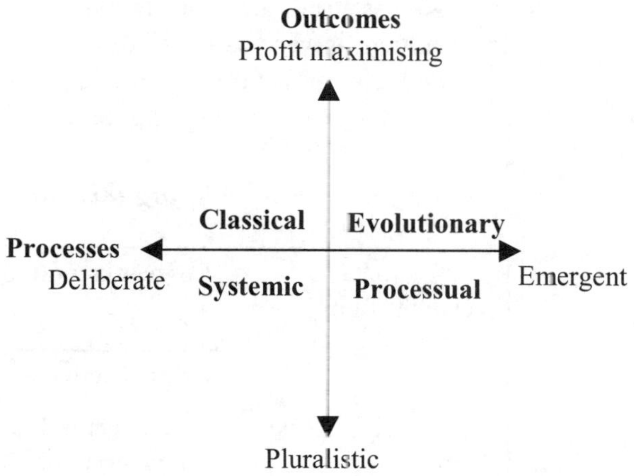

The horizontal axis characterises the process by which strategy is arrived at as *deliberate* – planned or designed, or *emergent* – arrived at by 'accident, muddle or inertia'. The vertical axis reflects the *outcomes* (perhaps better thought of as goals) of strategy – these may be entirely profit related, or may include multiple or non-profit related ends.

The *classical* perspective (deliberate processes, profit-maximising outcomes) offers a 'rational process of deliberate calculation and analysis, designed to maximise long-term financial advantage'.

KEY POINT

The evolutionary view argues that only firms that adapt constantly to their environments will survive.

Whittington's *evolutionary* perspective has the following characteristics:

- Survival of the fittest and the law of the market – those who are well-adapted to the prevailing conditions will survive, the others will go to the wall.
- The environment is too unpredictable to anticipate effectively, therefore the classical type of rational planning is often irrelevant.
- Only firms that hit upon profit maximising strategies survive in competitive, dynamic, hostile markets.
- It is the market (not managers) that makes the important choices therefore managers must fit as best they can with environmental demands. Markets are dynamic and volatile; all managers can do is to scrutinise the environment.

Evolutionists believe that environmental changes are too fast to be predicted in advance: thus rational long-term planning for an unknown future becomes a futile exercise.

Processualists (in Whittington's view) are primarily concerned with the management processes which underpin strategic change and innovation. They focus on the processes whereby strategies emerge from the imperfect decision-making and learning abilities of individuals and groups in organisations. 'Strategy emerges more from a pragmatic process of bodging, learning and compromise than from a rational series of grand leaps.'

The *systemic* perspective suggests that 'strategy reflects the particular social systems in which the strategists participate, defining for them the interests in which they act and the rules by which they survive – class and country make a difference'. This perspective stresses the social 'embeddedness' of economic activity.

2.7 The systems model

KEY POINT

Organisations can be viewed as open systems, which take inputs from the environment and through a series of activities convert or transform these inputs into outputs to achieve some objective.

Organisations can be viewed as **open systems**, which take in resources such as people, finance, raw materials and information from the environment and through a series of activities transform or convert these and return them to the environment in various forms of outputs such as goods produced, services provided, completed processes and procedures in order to achieve certain goals such as profit, market standing, level of sales or consumer satisfaction.

The organisation as an open system

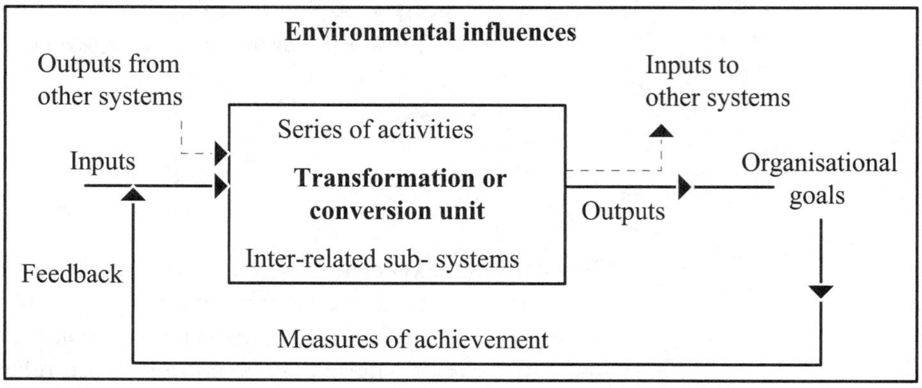

The systems model portrays decision making as primarily a function of a set of inputs, both organisational and external in origin, which, when processed by the organisation, lead to a particular set of outputs. It addresses the organisational context of decisions and can be used to analyse them by comparing inputs and outputs across organisations. Outputs (selected strategy, for example) can be analysed as a function of organisational inputs. For example, a systems-oriented strategist might look at past environmental scenarios and company circumstances and identify ones similar to the present. Then, the strategy that worked best during past situations that are similar to the present would be selected for implementation. As such, the systems model pays little attention to the internal machinations of the decision process itself, focusing instead on the relationships between inputs and outputs. Some of the benefits of the systems model for strategy selection lie in the questions that it raises:

- What are the important elements of the environment that place demands on the organisation?
- What characteristics of the organisation allow it to transform demands into strategy?
- How do environmental inputs affect the content of strategy?
- How does selected strategy affect key actors in the environment through feedback?

The major benefit of this approach is that historical analyses of relationships between inputs of the organisation or to the decision-making process and the characteristics of strategies associated with those inputs can be used to spot patterns with normative implications.

Activity 3

Look at the five different descriptions of strategy given by Mintzberg, and identify which ones imply deliberate managerial actions, and which ones imply a more emergent approach. To help, Mintzberg's five Ps are:

- Plan
- Ploy
- Pattern
- Position
- Perspective.

Feedback to this activity is at the end of the chapter.

2.8 Michael Porter – competitive advantage

Michael Porter argues that strategy is about gaining a competitive advantage. He states that competition in an industry depends upon five basic forces which help to assess the long-term attractiveness of that industry. A corporate strategist must find a position within the industry where the company can best defend itself against these forces and then choose one of three strategic directions.

The five forces are as follows:

- **The intensity of competitive rivalry** which measures the level of product differentiation, switching costs and concentration of the forces.
- **The threat of new entrants** which determines the possible barriers to entry, the role of government policy and any expected retaliation from competitors.
- **The threat of substitutes** which examines price positioning, the likelihood that buyers will provide substitute products and the changes in technology.
- **The bargaining power of suppliers** which analyses the presence of substitute inputs, the concentration in the supplier's industry and the impact of the inputs on the total cost of the product.
- **The bargaining power of buyers** considers the concentration of firms in the buyer's industry, the buyer's volume, the availability of substitutes and the incentives that the buyer may have to purchase from one firm or another.

We will re-visit Porter's Five Forces Model in Section 3 of this chapter, as a key tool of strategic analysis.

Porter explains that there are only two routes to superior performance. You either become the lowest-cost producer in your industry or you differentiate your product/service in ways that are valued by the buyer to the extent that he or she will pay a premium price to get those benefits. By applying these strengths in either a broad or narrow scope, three generic strategies result:

- **Cost leadership** – a strategy aimed at producing standardised products at low per-unit cost for consumers who are price-sensitive. The firm sells its products either at average industry prices to earn a profit higher than that of rivals, or below the average industry prices to gain market share.

- **Differentiation** – a strategy aimed at producing products and services considered unique industrywide and directed at consumers who are relatively price-insensitive. Differentiation means a company can successfully distinguish itself from other products or services on the market, thereby charging a premium.

- **Focus** – this strategy concentrates on a narrow segment (a particular buyer group, market segment, geographical region, service need, product feature or section of the product range) and within that segment attempts to achieve either a cost advantage or differentiation.

These strategies are applied at the business unit level. They are called generic strategies because they are not firm or industry dependent. The following table illustrates Porter's generic strategies.

KEY POINT

Porter's generic strategies are:

- cost leadership;
- differentiation;
- focus.

Porter's generic strategies

Competitive scope \ Competitive advantage	Lower cost	Differentiation
Broad target (industry wide)	Cost leadership	Differentiation
Narrow target (market segment)	Cost focus	Differentiation focus

2.9 Bartlett and Ghoshal

In most of the literature top managers are associated with three clearly defined jobs: to determine a firm's *strategy*, to design its *structure*, and to select its information and control *systems*. People, however, are left out of the design criterion. Christopher Bartlett of Harvard Business School and Sumantra Ghoshal of London Business School have noted the role shift of top management from being the company's chief strategist, its structural architect, and the developer of its information and control systems to being the developer of people. The first shift they document is from a top-down functional structure (vertical structure) to cross-functional business processes. This is a leap from corporate control systems to letting people make operating decisions. It is the movement towards the people side of work that encourages a diversity of views and stimulates employees to develop their own ideas. It is a shift from strategy to building corporate purpose, from framing structure to developing organisational processes, and from systems designed to control human nature to ones that create environments that enable people to take initiative, to co-operate, and to learn.

Ghoshal and Bartlett argue that managers should move beyond thinking in terms of strategy, structure and systems, and view their organisations instead in terms of purpose, process and people. They call upon managers to focus on developing their individuals' unique talents and skills. To do this requires management to:

- build a rich engaging purpose;
- focus on effective management techniques;
- develop (not control) employees.

This involves the chief executive officer recognising the need to:

- capture employees' attention and interest;
- get the organisation involved;
- build on core values.

Bartlett and Ghoshal give the example of Andersen Consulting as specifying in its recruitment literature that new employees will be trained to work for anyone.

2.10 Internationalisation strategies – Bartlett and Ghoshal

KEY POINT

Increasing internationalisation is evidenced by the integration of operations between subsidiaries in different countries, the growth and power of multinationals and the inter-dependence of the world economy.

Another contribution to strategic formulation by Bartlett and Ghoshal is their research on increasing internationalisation. International trade has always existed; what is new is its scale and penetration. This is evidenced by a number of factors:

- the standardisation and integration of operations between subsidiaries in different countries e.g. car manufacturing;
- the growth and power of multinationals, so that today they form some of the largest economic units in the world;
- the interdependence of the world economy.

In order to exploit the opportunities presented by globalisation while avoiding the pitfalls, organisations need to develop a sophisticated understanding of what globalisation really means in the context of their particular businesses. A good framework for starting this investigation was put forward by Chris Bartlett and Sumantra Ghoshal in their work on the transnational organisation. Their research showed that different organisations adopted different positionings with regard to seeking global integration across their businesses or encouraging local responsiveness to individual market needs. Global companies tend to have a single, integrated way of doing things, which is rolled out across the world. Multinationals, in contrast, have a collection of businesses that are heavily tailored to local needs

The intensification of economic competition together with the development of information technology are driving the search for new business strategies and organisational forms. Two key responses can be identified:

- uncertainty in markets has been coped with by the creation of **flexibility** in production, operations and marketing; and
- management changes have been introduced aimed at creating **lean production**, and producing higher quality with less inputs.

Many companies are changing their **models of organisation** to partly reflect these trends of market volatility, uncertainty and rapid technological change. As we see in Chapter 3, models of organisation structure have moved from vertical bureaucracies to flat collections of teams characterised by: a process focus; low hierarchy; team co-ordination; sharp focus on customer satisfaction; the close management of suppliers; attention to information sharing; and intensive employee training at all levels. To be able to internalise the benefits of network flexibility the company has had to become an **internal network** itself and energise each element in its organisational structure. An element of internal competition is often required within the organisation that is striving to meet a common objective.

Strategy formulation also has to be different: the notion of cross border strategies is being urged upon the company. Companies that operated in a variety of domestic markets are advised to use this information between markets in their business strategies and trade across market borders. The term the 'Individualised Corporation' has recently been coined by Ghoshal and Bartlett to describe this new approach, where the actual operating units of the organisation become the focus of strategy formation, and are then combined into an inter-company network.

Most of the new thinking in strategic management is concentrated upon the challenge of combining organisational flexibility and co-ordination capabilities to ensure both innovation and continuity in a fast changing market place. These new models of business organisation are all variations on utilising networking concepts.

3 Tools for strategic analysis

3.1 Strategic analysis

Strategic analysis is concerned with understanding the strategic position of the organisation and the changes going on in the environment. It also aims to identify the resource strength of the organisation in the context of these changes.

An analysis of the environment increases the quality of strategic decision-making by considering a range of the relevant features well before the need to make an irrevocable decision. The organisation identifies the threats and opportunities facing it and those factors that might assist in achieving objectives and those that might act as a barrier. It also considers its strengths and weaknesses – what it is good or not so good at doing or where it is at a competitive advantage or disadvantage.

KEY POINT

Strategic analysis is concerned with matching the activities of the organisation to its environment, taking advantage of opportunities and coping with organisational threats.

For a change of strategy to work there must be alignment between internal capability and external opportunity. This is described as 'strategic fit'. Strategic analysis is concerned with matching the activities of the organisation to the environment in which it operates, to take advantage of environmental opportunities and cope with organisational threats. To identify these, management use information provided by such activities as forecasts of general economic conditions, industry projections, market research, and technological reviews. Also factors such as competitor activities, changes in consumer preferences, and trends in government regulations have to be taken into account. The information gained from these various sources will determine the strategy that the organisation follows.

The environmental forces that affect organisations are numerous and the impact they will have over time will vary. For example during periods of high inflation the economic environment will be important in determining an organisation's strategy. The type of organisation will also determine the relative importance of each environmental factor. A computer manufacturer will be concerned with the technological environment. Each national market requires a certain degree of special treatment – global companies are faced with cultural and economic diversity. Conditions in one market are not replicated in others; the UK market for new cars might be growing when markets in Europe are contracting.

3.2 Environmental analysis tools

The environment can be divided into the internal and the external environments. An analysis of the external environment will identify **opportunities** and **threats**; the internal analysis will identify **strengths** and **weaknesses**. Conducting both forms of analysis provides a **SWOT analysis** of the organisation. (We will return to SWOT analysis in other contexts.)

The external environment consists of forces that originate outside an organisation and generally cannot be altered by its actions – an enterprise may be influenced by changes but cannot itself influence the environment. Essentially the external environment is made up of six main groups of factors – Political, Economic, Social, Technological, Legal and Ecological. This can be remembered easily by the acronym PESTLE (discussed below).

An analysis of the **internal environment** of an organisation will be concerned to identify the resources internal to the business. This involves an understanding of its major strengths and distinctive competencies, its significant organisational shortcomings and its internal performance.

It is easy enough to suggest an analysis of the environment. But how do we conduct such an analysis?

Below we briefly mention a few of the techniques available. We then go on to discuss the main techniques of internal and external environmental analysis.

Forecasting – obviously this is a technique employed in most organisations. Its scope can vary widely – from detailed forecasts of cash movements or production volumes over the next few weeks, to more complex predictions of environmental changes such as we are concerned with in this chapter. The difficulty, of course, is that most forecasts start from the basis of what has happened in the past, and this is at best an inadequate guide to the future.

The Delphi model – is based on canvassing the views of relevant experts and then applying weightings to the outcomes they predict. At worst, this gives a well-informed guess at future developments. But the technique can be refined to improve on this, for example by feeding back to individual experts the views expressed by their colleagues. Where these differ, the process of rationalisation can lead to further and more accurate analysis.

Scenario building – is the process of constructing alternative 'visions' of the future, based on differing assumptions about changes in the environment. Forecasting has a role in strategic management, but for anything other than the near future, scenarios are needed to provide appropriate views.

Scenario building is used in strategic planning to allow a number of deductions to be made about future developments of markets, products and technology. The aim is to draw up a limited number of logically consistent, but different scenarios so that managers can examine strategic options against the scenarios and ask such questions as 'what should we do if?', or 'what would be the effect of?'

Examples of scenarios that are drawn up so that the strategies can be tested against a range include:

- an optimistic scenario, where everything turns out favourably in the future;
- a pessimistic scenario, which describes the worst possible scenario;
- a 'most likely' scenario, which is likely to be between the other two.

Strategies will need to be developed which help the organisation either to gain a competitive advantage or to minimise the potential damage deriving from the environment.

3.3 PESTLE analysis

KEY POINT

The most popular way of assessing the external environment is to use PESTLE analysis.

The most popular way of assessing the external environment is to use PESTLE analysis, which divides the business environment into six related but separate systems – Political, Economic, Social, Technological, Legal and Ecological.

KEY POINT

PESTLE analysis includes:

- Political factors
- Economic factors
- Social factors
- Technological factors
- Legal factors
- Ecological factors.

Political factors – the organisation must react to the attitude of the political party that is in power at the time. The government is the nation's largest supplier, employer, customer and investor and any change in government spending priorities can have a significant impact on a business. Political influence will include legislation on trading, pricing, dividends, tax, employment, as well as health and safety.

Economic factors – the current state of the economy can affect how a company performs (e.g. entering a recession or emerging from a recession). The rate of growth in the economy is a measure of the overall change in demand for goods and services. Other economic influences include taxation levels, inflation rate, the level of unemployment, interest rates and availability of credit and Government subsidies. International economic issues include comparative rates of growth, exchange rates, wages and taxation, the freedom of capital movement and economic agreements. Even companies not marketing internationally need to appraise the international economic environment. A company is essentially a resource-conversion engine that consumes material, labour, machines and funds. The necessary resources are often obtained from overseas sources, even if indirectly. How well the company buys depends on how well it grasps the workings of the international commodity and currency-exchange markets.

Social/cultural factors – the organisation is influenced by changes in the mix in the ethnic and religious background of the population, the values, tastes and lifestyles, in patterns of work and leisure, in demographic changes and in changes in the habits and attitudes of society. For example in Western Europe people are living longer and in most countries the birth rate is falling, leading to an ageing population. This has obvious implications for the types of products and services which businesses and other organisations may plan to offer. Typical questions that need to be answered include:

- What are the current and emerging trends in lifestyles and fashion?
- What demographic trends will affect the size of the market or its sub-markets?
- Does the trend represent opportunities or threats?

Technological factors – this is an area in which change takes place very rapidly and the organisation needs to be constantly aware of what is going on. Appraisal may reveal changes in:

- retailing methods (such as direct selling via the Internet);
- production methods (greater use of automation) and the type of products that are made and sold;
- how services are provided and how we identify markets;
- integration between buyers and suppliers via computer link-ups.

The managers would need to know to what extent the existing technologies are maturing and what technological developments or trends are affecting or could affect the industry.

Legal factors – an organisation is affected by the law of contract, law on unfair selling practices, health and safety legislation, employment laws, legislation on competitive behaviour and the environment as well as how it gives information about its performance. The addition or removal of legislative or regulatory constraints can pose major strategic threats and opportunities. The organisation needs to know:

- What changes in regulations are possible and what will their impact be?

- What tax or other incentives are being developed that might affect strategy?

Ecological (physical environment) factors – issues relating to the effect of an organisation's activities on the physical environment have come to the fore in recent years. This is a cultural shift with significant political consequences.

It is possible to identify many ways in which issues of ecology will affect an organisation's strategy:

- Consumer demand for products which appear to be ecologically friendly. Companies such as Body Shop have cleverly exploited ecological friendliness as a marketing tool. Supermarkets now stock bleaches or cleansing products that are supposed to be environmentally sound.
- Demand for less pollution from industry.
- Demand that businesses be charged with the external cost of their activities.
- Possible requirements to conduct ecology audits.
- Opportunities to develop products and technologies that are ecologically friendly. Perhaps companies have more to fear from the impact of bad publicity (relating to their environmental practices) than they have to benefit from positive ecological messages as such.
- Greater regulation by government and the EU. Companies might have to face a variety of measures designed to deal with the problem of pollution, such as taxes, regulations and permits.
- Pressure to relocate to a country where ecological standards are less strict, or have a lower priority in relation to other economic and social objectives, such as economic growth.

Activity 4

Fun 'n' Sun is a UK company selling packaged holidays. Founded in the 1960s, it offered a standard 'cheap and cheerful' package to resorts in Spain and, more recently, to some of the Greek islands. It was particularly successful at providing holidays for the 18–30 age group.

What do you think the implications are for Fun 'n' Sun of the following developments?

(a) A fall in the number of school leavers.

(b) The fact that young people are more likely now than in the 1960s to go into higher education.

(c) Holiday programmes on TV that feature a much greater variety of locations.

(d) Greater disposable income among the 18–30 age group.

Feedback to this activity is at the end of the chapter.

3.4 The competitive environment – Five Forces Model

So far, the concern has been with broad aspects of the environment. Porter argued that, for most organisations, there is a set of external influences that are more immediate, and which they are likely to be able to affect directly by their own actions. This is the immediate or **competitive environment**, which directly influences the capability of an organisation to position itself more or less effectively against its rivals. As explained in Section 2.8, Porter proposed a 'Five Forces' approach, which is a structured means of examining the environment of an organisation so as to provide an understanding of the forces at work

These five competitive forces jointly determine the intensity of competition and profitability of a company and reflect the underlying structure of the market. They are shown in the diagram below.

Porter's five competitive forces

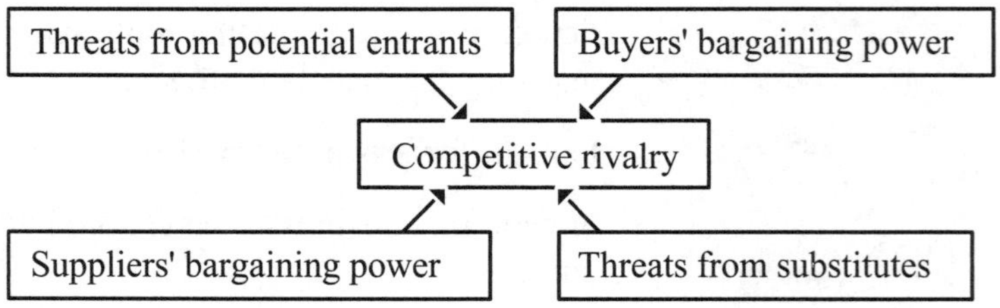

Essentially this model determines the level of competition an organisation is facing by assessing the extent to which the five forces are relevant.

KEY POINT

The five forces include the:

- threat from new entrants;
- bargaining power of buyers;
- bargaining power of suppliers;
- threat from substitute products;
- extent of competitive rivalry.

The threat from potential entrants -- new entrants into a market will bring extra capacity and intensify competition. This will affect the organisation in the following ways:

- An increase in supply usually leads to lower prices.
- The new entrant threatens the market share of existing companies.
- Existing companies will often face increased costs either through competition for supplies or by increased spending on items such as marketing in order to protect market share.

The ease with which new entrants can enter the business segment is largely determined by the extent of the barriers to entry.

The bargaining power of buyers – do the buyers of the product have the power to depress the supplier's prices? Buyers are powerful in any of the following circumstances:

- The buyer is a relatively large company or represents a large proportion of the supplier's business.
- The supply of the product is standard (particularly if quality is standard as well).
- There are few switching costs from one supplier to another.
- The buyer's profit margins are tight.
- Backward integration is a possibility i.e. the buyer could buy or establish his own supplier.
- The buyer has full knowledge of all suppliers

The bargaining power of suppliers – is very closely linked in with the issues of buyer power. The extent of the power of the suppliers will be affected by the concentration of suppliers, the degree to which products can be substituted by the various suppliers and the level of importance attached to the buyer by the supplier.

The threat from substitute products – if there are similar products that can be used as substitute, then the demand for the product will increase or decrease as it moves upwards or downwards in price relative to substitutes. Threats can come from:

- an alternative product – especially when there are many brands available, often with little to distinguish one from another;
- a different industry – customers may switch to a product in a different market that has similar qualities;
- customers who may decide they do not want to buy the product or service from anyone. For example, they may decide to give up smoking cigarettes.

The extent of competitive rivalry – the most competitive markets will be affected by the previously discussed four forces. However, they will also be affected by:

- the number of competitors and the degree of concentration;
- the rate of growth of the industry;
- the exit costs. If they are high, firms may be willing to accept low margins so as to stay in the industry.

Barriers to entry

As we have noted, the threat from new entrants will depend on the strength of the barriers to entry and the likely response of existing competitors to a new entrant. Barriers to entry are factors that make it difficult for a new entrant to gain an initial foothold in a market.

They include:

- Economies of scale – in the type of industry where unit costs decline significantly as volume increases, a new entrant will be unable to start on a comparable cost basis.
- The patterns of distribution or access to distribution channels may be restricted – if there are only certain outlets for a product it is harder to break in to the market.
- Capital requirements – in some industries the initial capital requirements are prohibitive. This would apply, for example, in the supermarket sector or rail transport.
- Likely retaliation from existing producers – they can use advertising, patents and trade secrets.
- Government legislation.
- The 'learning curve' phenomenon could put new entrants at a cost disadvantage.

Using Porter's model

Porter's model may be used to help clarify the overall business strategy. The model provides a framework to discuss the interrelationships between the five forces. A change in one of the five forces can have an impact on another. Imagine a scenario where a technological breakthrough makes entry into the industry much easier. If the industry is earning above average profits, new firms are likely to enter. This in turn could make rivalry more intense, and may well feed through to the buyers who are now able to play one firm off against another.

The main role of the model is to provide a framework to discuss areas that can yield competitive advantage. The advantages may be in defending the organisation against the forces or by attacking and influencing them in its favour. Management should use the model to determine which of the forces poses a threat to the future success of the organisation. By ranking these threats in terms of intensity and immediacy, the most critical can then be considered in terms of how different strategies can be used to gain advantage or avoid disadvantage.

This theory is often used to judge the attractiveness of an industry. Using it, an organisation can decide whether to enter into a new industry or exit from the current industry in which it operates. For example, consider the global car manufacturing market. The defining characteristics are the following:

- **Power of buyers** – high, because buyers can change cars very easily and often show little brand loyalty.
- **Degree of competitive rivalry** – intensive, because there is already overcapacity in the car manufacturing business; margins are often squeezed to very low levels.

Both of the above factors show that involvement in the car manufacturing industry is not particularly attractive. Many manufacturers are trying to diversify into other areas. Those choosing to remain in the industry may try to reduce the power of buyers through attempting to differentiate their product.

When all five of the forces are strong, the profitability of the market or industry would be expected to be low, regardless of the products or services being produced. On the other hand, weak forces permit higher prices and above average market profitability. Organisations can influence the five forces through the strategies they pursue. However, some innovations can lead to a short-term advantage which, when every participant in the market is forced to follow suit, can result in the whole industry being worse off. For example, the first organisation to advertise on the television may gain an increase in market share but when everyone else follows and there is a stalemate, the only winners are the advertising agencies and the television companies.

Activity 5

What factors are likely to limit or reduce the level of profitability of a medium-sized, family-owned firm in travel and tourism that arranges packaged holidays for clients travelling to the sunshine and sandy beaches of the Mediterranean?

Feedback to this activity is at the end of the chapter.

3.5 The internal environment = resources

Inevitably, organisations that are performing successfully in competitive industries are achieving this success because of the way they are deploying their resources, using highly productive systems and skilled motivated staff to reduce operational costs and create competitive advantage. As environmental situations change, so too organisations must consider how their product/market operations – and their underlying resource activities – must also change. The internal appraisal of the organisation's resource position (a **resource audit**) is a key prerequisite for making informed choices on organisational change. It should indicate:

- the capability (or otherwise) of the organisation to exploit present and future environmental opportunities;

- the ways in which resources might be changed to create competitive advantage and to improve the organisation's wealth-producing capacity.

Resources include all assets, capabilities, organisational processes, information, knowledge, etc. controlled by a firm that enable it to create and pursue effective strategies. The resource audit can be a starting point in understanding strategic capability. It identifies the resources available to an organisation, their productivity, flexibility, balance and effect on internal politics. Productivity performance involves a ratio measurement of effectiveness over efficiency (output over resource input) and these measurements should be compared with industry norms, specific competitors, market conditions and targets. The audit also notes how the resources fit the strategy, how powerful they are in dealing with the external environment, their strengths, weaknesses and distinctive abilities. Finally, the analysis deals with how value can be added to the organisation.

Strategic misfits can be avoided if the analysis is thorough. The organisation that introduces new technology but fails to prepare the workforce and management for its efficient use, through communication, training and modified rewards has not thought its strategy through. The classic misfit seems to occur when tradition meets innovation. Customers may want variety and regular product/service modifications but the organisation's technology may still be designed to produce one standard model or it may prefer to maintain its previously effective bureaucratic forms.

Activity 6

Briefly describe four key areas that might be assessed in the resource audit.

Feedback to this activity is at the end of the chapter.

3.6 The resource-based view of the firm

The resource based view emphasises **developing capabilities before plans**. It enables strengths or weaknesses to be examined in terms of the criteria for establishing sustainable competitive advantage. For example, such a framework forces managers to assess whether or not claimed strengths actually matter in the marketplace i.e. do they provide value to customers. There are many examples of firms that brought unique resources to market and yet failed because these perceived strengths did not actually matter to customers. A classic case in point is the difficulty encountered by Euro Disney in Paris. The company had access to several strengths such as its group of cartoon characters, its reputation and its well-honed skills in theme park management but, unfortunately, Disney's core strengths did not enable the creation of as much value in Europe as they had elsewhere.

KEY POINT

Advantage-creating resources must meet four conditions – value, rarity, inimitability and non-substitutability.

One of the principal insights of the resource-based view is that not all resources are of equal importance or possess the potential to be a source of sustainable competitive advantage. Much attention has focused, therefore, on the characteristics of advantage-creating resources. Barney (1991) proposes that advantage-creating resources must meet four conditions – namely, value, rareness, inimitability and non-substitutability.

1. *Value* – obviously a resource must be valuable to be strategic – it must have the capacity to improve the organisation's efficiency and effectiveness.

2. *Rarity* – a resource is strategic to the extent that it is rare and in high demand. Hence a supermarket chain that has tied up the prime locations in a city has an advantage.
3. *Inimitability* – the resource must not only be valuable and rare but also difficult to imitate. Patents and trademarks of course ensure this. Otherwise, and in the long run, perhaps the best protection is afforded by intangible relationships, systems, skills and knowledge.
4. *Substitutability* – a resource may be rare and inimitable and yet not strategic if competitors can find a substitute for what it can do.

Value to customers is an essential element of **competitive advantage**. Therefore, for a resource to be a potential source of competitive advantage, it must be valuable or enable the creation of value. In the words of Barney (1991), it must permit the firm to conceive of or implement strategies that improve its efficiency and effectiveness by meeting the needs of customers. This implies that, though resources may meet other conditions, if they do not enable the creation of value, they are not a potential source of advantage.

The inability of competitors to duplicate resource endowments is a central element of the resource-based view. For example, organisations offering services (such as advertising agencies and investment banks) may find that their only unique resources are certain key individuals which places them in a vulnerable position as these resources are mobile and may be lured away by competitors. Rather than the indiscriminate lists provided by SWOT analyses, resources should be categorised according to ease of duplication by competitors. Broadly speaking intangible resources and capabilities are more difficult to duplicate and provide a more meaningful basis for strategy development.

Even where resources are clearly identified and understood their imitation may be prevented through the legal system of property rights. Resources such as patents, trademarks and copyrights may be protected through intellectual property laws and competitive advantages may accrue from other regulatory activities such as the granting of operating licences.

The resource-based view of the organisation enables an understanding of the resources that underpin the alternative positioning strategies it might choose to pursue, making it possible to identify a matching resource set and identify 'resource gaps' that may need to be filled. For example, the pursuit of a low price strategy is considered to necessitate resources such as cost control systems, Total Quality Management (TQM) processes, and skills in procurement and information systems. In contrast, a positioning strategy based on superior quality is believed to require a quite different resource set including market sensing, quality control and assurance, brand and reputation, and supply chain management, while a positioning strategy based on rapid innovation requires skills in the areas of new product/service development, R&D, technical skills and creative skills. In short, for any positioning strategy a firm might choose to pursue in the marketplace, it is possible to identify a matching resource set, which furthermore allows firms to identify 'resource gaps' that may need to be filled.

3.7 Porter's value chain

For an organisation to develop its strategy, it must know its **strategic capability**. This can be assessed by carrying out a resource analysis. Traditionally this has consisted of identifying the strengths and weaknesses of the various resources and the way they are deployed. Porter's value chain concept identifies the links between activities and the value of these activities.

This approach is based on the premise that the organisation's capability is related to the way resources are used and controlled, rather than the resources *per se*.

Porter's central thesis is that resources should be arranged to enhance least cost production or differentiation strategies (as discussed in Section 2.8).

Porter's value chain

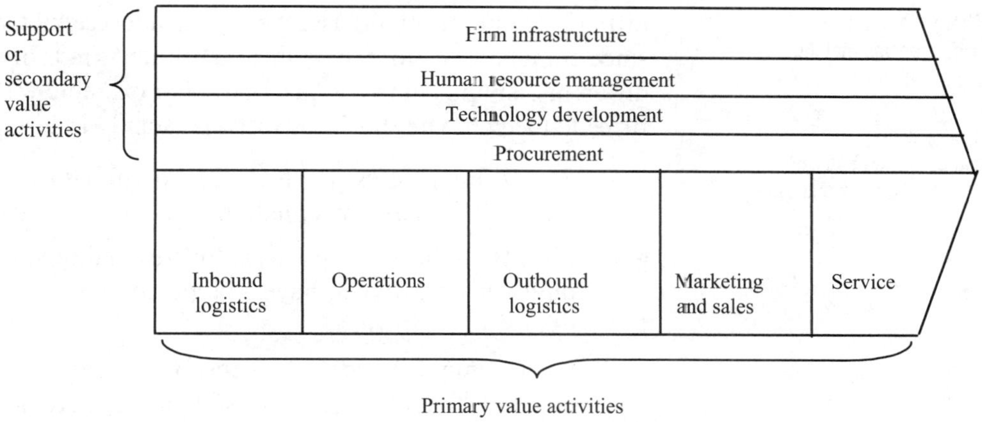

KEY POINT

Five primary value activities:

1 Inbound logistics
2 Operations
3 Outbound logistics
4 Marketing and sales
5 Service.

Porter groups organisational activities into five primary areas:

1 **Inbound logistics** – are the activities concerned with receiving, storing, and distributing the inputs to the organisation system (materials handling, stock control, transport, etc)

2 **Operations** – transforming inputs into final products/services (machining, packing, assembly, testing and equipment maintenance)

3 **Outbound logistics** – collecting, storing and distributing final products (for tangible products this includes order processing, warehousing, stock control, distribution and vehicle scheduling. In the case of services it may be more concerned with arrangements for bringing customers to the service if it is in a fixed location e.g. theatre, sports event)

4 **Marketing and sales** – activities that attract customers to purchase (includes sales administration, advertising, selling, channel selection, pricing and promotion)

5 **Service** – activities that ensure that customers enjoy their purchases by providing installation, training, maintenance, repair and breakdown assistance, etc.

All of these primary activities are linked to the secondary or support activities.

One of the notable features of value analysis is that it recognises that an organisation is much more than a random collection of machinery, money and people. These resources are of no value unless they are organised into structures, routines and systems, which ensure that the products or services that are valued by the final consumer are the ones which are produced. The organisation must assess how the resources are **utilised** and **linked to competitive advantage**.

3.8 Core competencies

Allied to the notion of developing capabilities is that of distinctive competencies – those features of the organisation that differentiate it attractively in the eyes of the customer.

There are two kinds of competencies that the organisation should aim to develop – distinguishing competencies and threshold competencies.

KEY POINT

There are two kinds of competencies that the organisation should aim to develop – distinguishing competencies and threshold competencies.

Distinguishing competencies can give the organisation some kind of competitive advantage or allow it to exploit new opportunities. They should be difficult to imitate, otherwise, the organisation cannot sustain its advantage since competitors will imitate them. Different kinds of companies will stress different distinguishing competencies. For example we might imagine three firms in the computer business software supply industry.

- Firm A might stress the high level of after-sales service that it provides for its customers. This might be especially attractive to first-time buyers.
- Firm B might stress that its software is tailored to individual needs. This might be attractive to buyers prepared to pay extra for non-standard types of business software.
- Firm C might stress the low cost of its software. This might appeal to buyers who require standard software and are operating on a limited budget.

Each of the three firms above has different competencies that distinguish it from its competitors. Any strategy followed by the firm should aim to build on these competencies. For example, Firm A might suffer if it tried to save money by recruiting low cost after-sales staff who could not deliver the same service levels as previously.

Threshold competencies are a different concept. These refer to areas in which an organisation must do well in order to keep up with its competitors. In the example of the software companies above, threshold competencies would include ensuring that programs perform the required function, that they are error-free and that they are not too expensive.

Note that Firm A will probably try to keep its software price below a certain level or customers will buy from elsewhere in spite of the quality of after-sales service. Similarly, Firm C may have a basic level of customer support as long as it does not add substantially to costs.

Summary

- The rational model of strategy formulation involves three stages: strategic analysis, strategic choice and strategic implementation. Simon argues that 'bounded' rationality is more common in practice.
- Other methods of strategy formulation include emergent strategies, entrepreneurial strategies, imposed strategies, logical incrementalism, and adaptive strategies.
- Organisations can be analysed in terms of system theory.
- Professor Michael Porter emphasises five forces in relation to competitive advantage: the intensity of competitive rivalry; the threat of new entrants; the threat of substitutes; the bargaining power of suppliers; the bargaining power of buyers.

- Strategic analysis includes external environmental analysis (e.g. PESTLE analysis, examining Political, Economic, Social, Technological, Legal and Ecological factors) and internal capability analysis.
- The resource-based view of the firm focuses on developing capabilities before plans. Strategic capability depends on:
  - advantage creating (valuable, rare, inimitable, unsubstitutable) resources;
  - use and control of resources through the value chain to enhance least-cost production or differentiation strategies (Porter);
  - the development of core (distinguishing, threshold) competencies.

Having completed your study of this chapter you should have achieved the following learning outcomes.

- Explain the process of strategy formulation.
- Apply tools for strategic analysis appropriately.
- Evaluate competitive situations and apply this knowledge to the organisation.

Self-test questions

1 Outline the three stages of the rational model. (1.2)

2 What is bounded rationality? (1.3)

3 What advantages does Ansoff give for the systematic planning process? (1.4)

4 How do emergent strategies develop? (2.2)

5 Describe strategy making in entrepreneurial mode. (2.3)

6 How does the systems model portray decision making? (2.7)

7 List the PESTLE factors. (3.3)

8 List Porter's five forces. (3.4)

9 What are the characteristics of advantage-creating resources? (3.6)

10 Describe the two types of core competency. (3.8)

Multiple-choice questions

Question 1

John's manager criticises the rational model. Which of following comments is not a criticism of the model?

A It is unrealistic to distinguish between goals and the possible strategies to achieve them. In practice, managers confuse the two.

B The approach does not try to identify and review all the potential strategies available to the organisation.

C It is hard to imagine a strategic planner carefully sifting through every possible option to achieve predetermined goals.

D At best, the formulation of strategy is a process of evaluating a few slight extensions to existing policies.

Question 2

Logical incrementalism is seen as the middle way of strategic management. Three of the following describe its main characteristics and one is following a rational model. Which is the rational model?

A Managers have some notion as to where the organisation should be.

B It is a continuous process of making present risk-taking decisions with the greatest knowledge of their futurity.

C Managers deliberately keep their decisions small scale.

D Strategy is best described as a learning process.

Question 3

Which one of the following statements does not describe an open system?

A A system that has a dynamic relationship with its environment from which it receives various inputs, which it transfers into outputs.

B An entity, which consists of interdependent parts which influences and is influenced by its environment.

C A system that is connected to, and interacts with, its environment.

D A system that does not communicate with its environment.

Question 4

What type of strategy calls for being the low cost producer in an industry for a given level of quality?

A Cost leadership

B Cost focus

C Differentiation

D Differentiation focus

For the answer to these questions, see the 'Answers' section at the end of the book.

Exam-type questions

Question 1: Tub plc

Tub plc was founded in the early 1980s by two brothers. As employees in their father's home-decorating business they became aware of the opportunities available in the growing home improvement and DIY markets. Spotting a gap in the middle price range of the market for bathroom and kitchen fittings, they set up a company to manufacture these items. The demand for their products outstripped their ability to supply, and they expanded rapidly. Most of this expansion was financed from retained profits but, as they happened to be located in an area of economic decline, they qualified for a state grant towards the cost of their new premises.

In 1987, the company changed its status to a public quoted company. By 1995 Tub plc employed in excess of 1,200 personnel and had organised itself around 8 operating companies covering the different products and sales activities of the Group. Some of these sold directly to housing developers, some to major retail DIY multiples and one of the companies coordinated the Group's export operations.

Each company had its own independent board of directors on which the brothers sat with one vote each. The brothers could be out-voted and in fact had been at various times in the past. The senior management believed in decentralisation, arguing that it promoted enterprise and that it was easier for small companies to grow than for larger ones to do so. The reasoning here was that the Managing Director could concentrate on the demands of the core business and would not have to worry about the Group and its problems.

Despite competition from larger and longer-established rivals. Tub plc has consistently outperformed them. It has invested heavily in new technology, automating processes wherever possible. It has developed good relationships with its suppliers and developed just-in-time purchasing and production systems. It is also able to deliver its products within 48 hours of orders being placed. It has progressive human resource management policies in place.

It produces a good-quality product at a reasonable price. Retailers are said to like Tub plc because the company's products allow the retailer the best yield in profit per square foot.

The market for the products that the company produces has become steadily more sophisticated. When the company was first established it sold bathroom and kitchen fittings and now it also sells whole kitchens and bathrooms. The market for the products is becoming increasingly saturated as new entrants enter the market. At the present time the company has no new products coming on stream and its research and development function is tiny and confines itself to modifying existing products for what is a difficult overseas market.

Required:

(a) Identify the key issues involved in formulating the corporate strategy of a company like Tub plc. **(10 marks)**

(b) How would you go about setting the business strategy of the various operating companies within the Tub Group? **(10 marks)**

(c) In what ways might the strategies of the organisational functions within each of the operating companies contribute to the overall strategy? **(5 marks)**

(Total: 25 marks)

Question 2: Cuddles Limited

Cuddles Limited is a garment manufacturer based in Nottingham in the United Kingdom producing clothing for babies and infants. The company is owned and managed by Richard, whose wife, daughter and two sons are all working in different capacities within the firm.

The company's small range of garments is being sold successfully to retail clothing outlets specialising in baby and infant wear. Richard has ambitions of growing his company substantially over the next few years.

Required:

(a) What general environmental factors are likely to influence Cuddles Limited? **(9 marks)**

(b) What are the competitive forces that the company is going to face as Richard attempts to achieve his ambitions? **(10 marks)**

(c) What competitive strategies can Cuddles Limited adopt to achieve and sustain its need for growth? **(6 marks)**

(Total: 25 marks)

For the answers to these questions, see the 'Answers' section at the end of the book.

Feedback to activities

Activity 1

Bounded rationality is the limited ability of individuals to understand the full complexity of any given issue.

Activity 2

The rational model of strategy management i.e. the management of deliberate strategies, has three elements.

- Strategic analysis – what is the organisation's strategic position?
- Strategic choice.
- Strategic implementation – planning how the chosen strategy will be implemented.

The concept of emergent strategies holds that a strategy can develop from patterns of behaviour, or from consistency in the types of decisions it makes. Emergent strategies are not thought out before being realised. They are a reaction to circumstances.

Activity 3

Strategy as plan: Clearly deliberate. A plan, and the actions necessary to carry it out, must be consciously devised. Should actual behaviour deviate from planned behaviour, various contingency plans and feedback mechanisms will route actions back to those intended.

Strategy as ploy: Clearly deliberate. It implies that customers, markets, rivals and the capabilities of the strategist's own company are understood sufficiently well that actions can be devised and implemented to gain an advantage over a rival.

Strategy as pattern: Emergent. The consistent behaviours that could be mistaken for logical decisions might have routes that are quite different. Entrepreneurial and innovative companies frequently argue that their strategies for the next few years will, in practice, be determined by things that they haven't yet thought of.

Strategy as position: Mostly deliberate. Writers such as Michael Porter, who have written much on the subject, generally argue that strategy is about achieving a desired position in the market place. However, some writers, such a Mintzberg, point out that often positioning happens by accident as well as design.

Strategy as perspective: Deliberate. Perspective implies that the environment is scanned, and the results pondered, in a systematic way. However, such writers as Gerry Johnson use the word paradigm to describe the more subjective and emergent factors that go into making up a perspective.

Activity 4

The firm's market is shrinking. There is an absolute fall in the number of school leavers. Moreover, it is possible that the increasing proportion of school leavers going to higher education will mean there will be fewer who can afford Fun 'n' Sun's packages. That said, a higher disposable income in the population at large might compensate for this trend. People might be encouraged to try destinations other than Fun 'n' Sun's traditional resorts if these other destinations are publicised on television.

Activity 5

Applying Porter's Five Forces Model to analysing the firm's competitive position which directly affects profitability, the following are examples of the likely factors:

Competitive Rivalry: The firm is a small player in a market dominated by well-resourced, vertically integrated multinational operators such as Thomas Cook and others. It will find it very difficult to achieve reasonable margins in the face of such intense competition. It is also likely to have a limited product range and be unable to offer a 'one-stop' service to its clients.

Substitute Products: It is possible for customers to arrange their own holidays rather than have them packaged. Although the price is likely to be higher than a package, the advance of internet technology is making it easier and cheaper for individuals to make their own arrangements.

Suppliers' Bargaining Power: The firm's large rivals will have a stronger position with the hotels and airlines owing to their greater purchasing power. Some of these rivals are vertically integrated and are therefore their own suppliers.

Threats from Potential Entrants: The threat of other small entrants just like this firm is always present. However, the barriers to entry posed by the large multinational players as a result of the economies of scale they enjoy is a deterrent to new entrants unless they establish a specialised service, for example, customised holidays.

Buyers' Bargaining Power: If the customers are individuals, they have a choice of travel outlets. If the customers are retail travel outlets, these outlets have more power over the firm relative to the firm's rivals who may have their own outlets.

Overall, the above analysis indicates that the firm may well be in an unprofitable position. It is a small player in a market dominated by strong, large organisations who enjoy economies of scale. The firm's margins are likely to be constantly under pressure and its costs continuously escalating if it tries to increase its share of a very competitive market.

Activity 6

Financial resources – this consists of constructing a series of accounting ratios to measure profitability, growth and liquidity, and then comparing them with earlier results and also with results of other firms in similar circumstances.

Profitability – might include an analysis of sales and profit involving sales mix, pricing strategy, discount facilities, and an assessment of the returns on total assets employed. Costs obviously have important implications for profitability and, therefore, determination of operational costs and internal efficiency is also required.

Product range – involves the determination of the profit contribution of each product in relationship to the resources it utilises. It is also necessary to pay particular attention to market trends to ascertain whether in the product mix, certain products need upgrading whilst others require phasing out.

Human resources of the organisation – an analysis will ensure that personnel are suitably motivated and that adequate facilities are available for appropriate staff development.

Chapter 3

STRATEGY AND STRUCTURE

Syllabus content

- The relationship between strategy and organisational structure.
- Transaction cost view of the firm (e.g. Coase and Williamson) and its implications for organisational structure.
- Ecological perspective on the firm.

Contents

1 Organisational structure

2 The basic structural forms

3 Mintzberg's organisational configurations

4 The adaptive organisation

5 Transaction cost view of the firm

6 Ecological perspective on the firm

1 Organisational structure

1.1 The links between strategy and structure

Through organisational structure, the organisation:

- allocates the organisation's resources;
- assigns tasks to employees;
- instructs employees about the organisation's rules, procedures and expectations;
- collects and transmits information.

The nature of the organisation and its strategy will indicate the most appropriate organisational levels for different functions and activities and the formal relationship between them. Regardless of how well it may have been conceived, a strategy without effective organisation of human resources is doomed to sub-optimise, if not fail completely. Since strategies can only be implemented by and through people, the manner in which human resources are co-ordinated through hierarchical and lateral assignments of responsibility and authority becomes a central management challenge.

The impact of IT will also have a significant impact on the structure, management and functioning of the organisation because of the effect it has on patterns of work, the formation and structure of groups, the nature of supervision and managerial roles. Computer-based information and decision support systems influence choices in design of production and/or service activities, and may influence the centralisation or decentralisation of decision-making and control systems.

New technology has resulted in fewer management levels because it allows employees at clerical/operator level not only to check their own work, but to take on a wider range of functions.

The influences that have a bearing on organisational structure and design include:

- the types of problems the organisation has when constructing strategies;
- a consideration of whether it is operating in a stable environment or in a highly complex or changing environment;
- the diversity of the organisation. The needs of a multinational are different from those of a small company;
- the technology;
- the type of ownership.

Because of all of these different influences, it is not possible to have a simple set of rules that can prescribe organisational structures and systems. The structure of the organisation is only a skeleton on which the flesh of the strategy can be hung and, unfortunately, the structure in itself will not ensure the success of the strategy, although an inappropriate choice of structure could impede success.

Developing the flesh on the structure consists of three elements:

(i) *organisational configuration* – matching the detailed structure with the context in which the organisation is operating;

(ii) *centralisation/decentralisation* – where the responsibility for operational and strategic decision-making should lie;

(iii) *management systems* – how the systems relate to the structure and influence the behaviour of people.

1.2 Fundamentals of structuring

Lawrence and Lorsch claim that the process of structuring consists of two basic processes, which they term differentiation and integration.

DEFINITIONS

In the context of organisational structure: **Differentiation** is:

'the state of segmentation of the organisation into sub-systems, each of which tends to develop particular attributes in relation to the requirements posed by its relevant external environment'.

Integration is 'the process of achieving unity of effort among the various subsystems in the accomplishment of the organisational tasks'

Differentiation can be defined as 'the state of segmentation of the organisation into sub-systems, each of which tends to develop particular attributes in relation to the requirements posed by its relevant external environment'.

Differentiation consists of vertical differentiation – establishing a hierarchy; and horizontal differentiation – setting up various departments. Differentiation must occur to achieve economies of scale, including:

- technical economies (machine utilisation and labour specialisation);
- managerial economies;
- financial and marketing economies; and
- risk spreading economies.

Integration is 'the process of achieving unity of effort among the various subsystems in the accomplishment of the organisational tasks'.

Integration consists of both co-ordination and control. Integration is essential for utility of direction – towards the common goal.

1.3 Classifying organisation structure

KEY POINT

The organisational structure specifies the mechanism to accomplish the tasks and programmes.

Organisational structure can be described in terms of lines of authority and communication. It specifies the mechanism to accomplish the tasks and programmes. An important issue for the organisation is whether the proposed strategy will fit into the existing structure or whether a new one will be required.

When planning an organisation structure, the basic intention must always be to make sure that the formal structure itself does not frustrate the main aim of organisation, which is to arrange the work so that people may perform it in the most effective way.

An organisation chart shows the relationship between all the different parts of the business. At a more detailed level it shows the relationships between staff at each level i.e. the reporting lines within the organisation.

There are many ways of classifying organisation structure.

A common analysis views organisation structures that develop in response to the size of the organisation. There is thus:

- a small business structure;
- a functional structure (which arises when a small business structure develops beyond the small stage);
- a divisional structure (which arises when an organisation grows by diversification into many different products or regions);

- a matrix structure (which is designed to combine the virtues of the divisional and functional structures).

Which structure should an organisation choose? If the organisation is trying to compete by lowering costs, a functional structure might be more appropriate. For an organisation trying to differentiate a product, a product structure is probably more suitable.

KEY POINT

The span of control means how many people report to a given manager.

The organisation should also consider the span of control of its managers. The span of control means how many people report to the manager. If the number is small, it is worth asking whether that manager is actually needed. If it is large, the manager cannot effectively oversee all the different activities that are happening.

The nature of the environment in which the organisation is operating will also make a difference. Generally, product-based structures are more flexible. They are more suitable in a dynamic or complex environment where organisations have to be adaptable. It is important also to consider not only the position now, but also what it might be in the future. If a company may be making acquisitions in the future, then adopting a divisional structure now will make the acquired companies easier to assimilate.

2 The basic structural forms

2.1 Small business structure

KEY POINT

Basic structural forms include:

- small business structure;
- functional structure;
- product and geographical;
- structure;
- divisional structure;
- matrix structure.

Also known as the entrepreneurial structure, this has the great advantage of simplicity so that the owner/manager can adjust employee tasks to the latest opportunity. This is illustrated below:

Small business structure

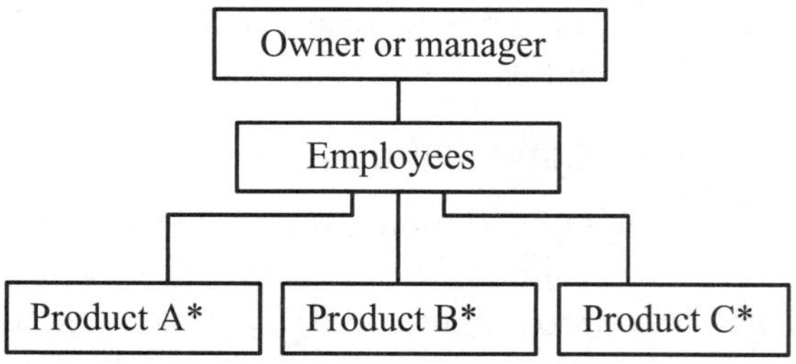

*(Although, throughout, the term 'product' is used to describe the output of a business, this section could apply equally well to companies that produce only 'services'.)

This type of business produces a single product, or a related group of products, and the owner, or manager, is responsible for strategic and operational management. Thus, it is a discrete, self-contained and largely self-controlled business unit. It is equivalent to a strategic business unit in a divisionalised organisation.

2.2 Functional structure

The functional structure is usually the next stage in the development of a business, and is illustrated below:

Functional structure

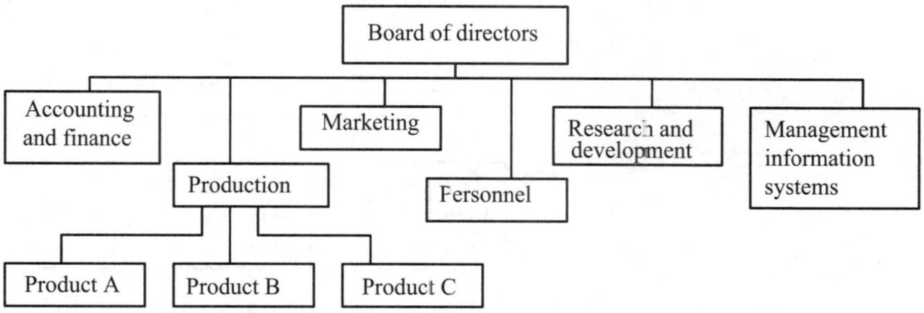

Planning is divided between the corporate and functional levels, with strategic planning being decided at board level and being executed at the functional level.

Activity 1

What would you expect to be the advantages and disadvantages of functional organisation?

Feedback to this activity is at the end of the chapter.

2.3 Product and geographical structure

As the number of products produced by an organisation increases, functional design at all levels of the organisation may not be appropriate. In a multi-product organisation, such as Heinz (the food processing company), a product orientation is used as a modification of the functional structure. This structure establishes each product, or group of products, as an integrated unit within the framework of the company. The main functions of production, sales, people and finance are apportioned to the relative products. So each product group could have its own specialist of accounting personnel, technical, etc. Such an organisation allows considerable delegation by top management and clear profit accountability by division heads.

The advantages of product divisionalisation are as follows:

- The focus of attention is on product performance and profitability. By placing the responsibility for product profitability at the division level, they are able to react and make decisions quickly on a day-to-day basis.
- It encourages growth and diversity of products, for example, by adding additional flavours, sizes, etc. to capture other segments of the market. This, in turn, promotes the use of specialised equipment, skills and facilities.
- The role of general manager is encouraged with less concentration upon specialisation. This promotes the wider view of a company's operations – 'the helicopter ability' highly prized by John Harvey-Jones and others.

Product divisionalisation is generally to be preferred over, say, geographic divisionalisation when the product is relatively complex and requires high cost capital equipment, skilled operators and significant administrative costs. This is the situation in the car industry, farm machinery manufacture and electronics industry.

With geographic divisionalisation, the enterprise is organised by regions or countries. The major, international accountancy firms tend to follow this structure. A possible road transport company structure is outlined below:

Geographic structure

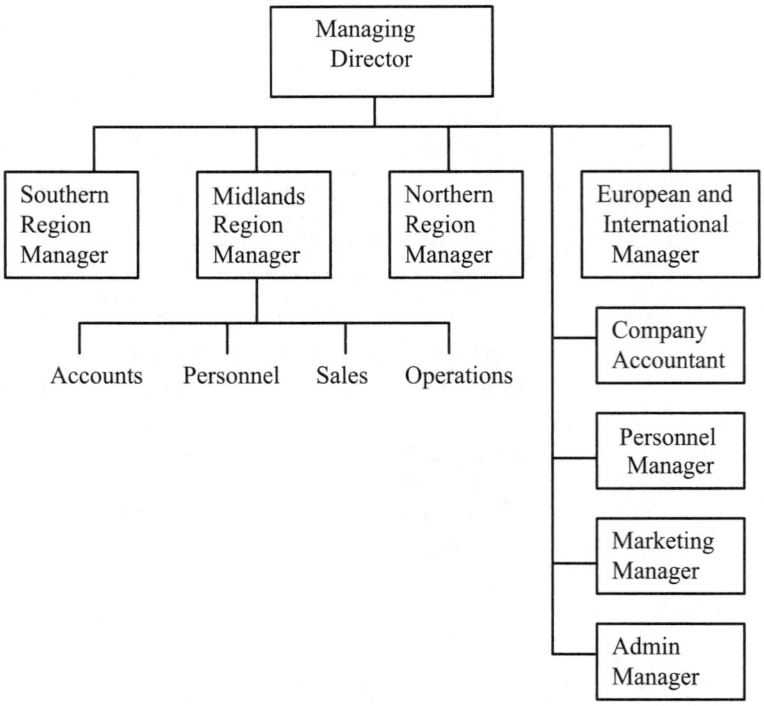

Carried to completion, the geographic division becomes a relatively complete administrative unit in itself. The geographic unit can itself be organised by function or product. The effect of the geographic division at company level is to draw a territorial boundary around these basic components.

2.4 Divisional structure

Where the functionally structured business grows by diversification, the above structure will be inappropriate, and the divisional structure illustrated below is likely to be adopted:

Divisional structure

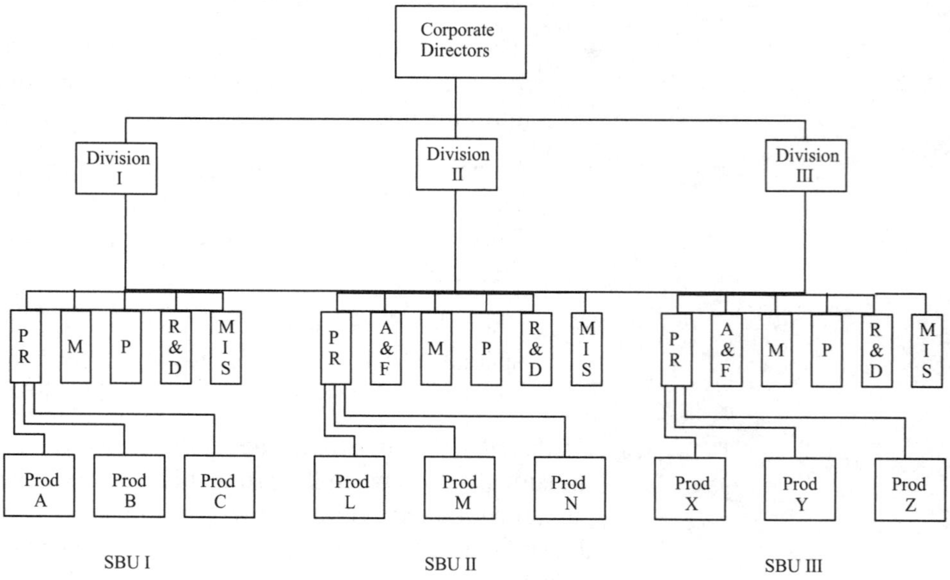

Each division is now responsible for its own functions in relation to a related group of products. Thus, each division may be regarded as a Strategic Business Unit (SBU).

Strategic planning in this environment becomes a complex hierarchical process:

- Corporate strategic planning takes place at central board level.
- Divisional planning is concerned with developing a portfolio of products.
- Operational planning is at the functional level within divisions.

KEY POINT

A holding company (group) structure is a radical form of divisionalisation, where subsidiaries are separate legal entities.

The holding company (group) structure is a radical form of divisionalisation. Subsidiaries are separate legal entities. The holding company can be an organisation with a permanent investment or one that buys and sells businesses. In its most extreme form, a holding company is really an investment company. It may simply consist of shareholdings in a variety of individual, unconnected business operations over which it exercises little or no control.

An example of a holding company structure is shown below. Central corporate staff and services may be very limited. The essential differentiating feature for a holding company is the extent of the autonomy of the business units, particularly over strategic decisions. The advantages that a holding company can offer are based on the idea that the constituent businesses will operate to their best potential if left alone, particularly as business environments become more turbulent.

Holding company structure

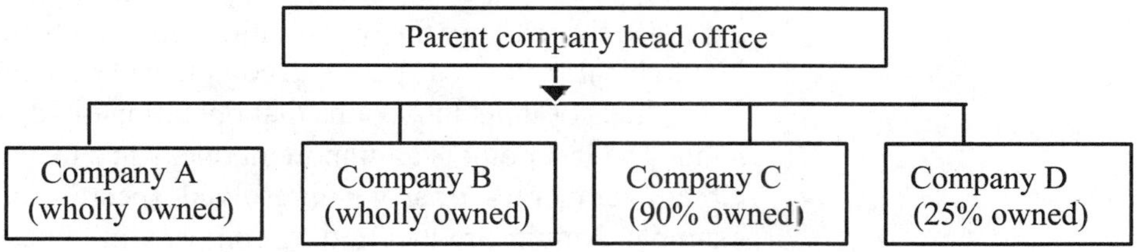

There are other organisational advantages and disadvantages of the holding company structure. For example:

- the organisation does not have to carry the burden of a high central overhead, since the office staff of the parent is likely to be quite small;
- the holding company can spread the risk over many business ventures;
- divestment of individual companies is easy.

2.5 Matrix structure

KEY POINT

Matrix structures (often used for project teams) provide integration of functional activities across 'vertical' boundaries.

The division of work and methods of grouping previously discussed tend to be relatively permanent forms of structure. With the growth in newer, complex and technologically advanced systems it has become necessary for organisations to adapt traditional structures in order to provide greater integration of a wide range of functional activities. Attention has been given, therefore, to the creation of groupings based on project teams and matrix organisation. Members of staff from different departments or sections are assigned to the team for the duration of a particular project, such as the design and development, production and testing of a new product; or the design and implementation of a new system or procedure. (Project teams are discussed further in Chapter 9.)

The matrix structure may be appropriate where there are at least two significant criteria for success. For example, a multinational company produces three sets of product ranges (Product A, Product B and Product C) and sells the product in three geographical areas (Europe, U.S.A. and South America).

The management of each product range is equally important, as is the responsiveness to the needs of the different geographical areas. The product managers and area managers have equal weight. Thus the manager of the U.S. area must liaise with the managers of Product A, B and C but does not have authority over them or vice versa.

Matrix structure

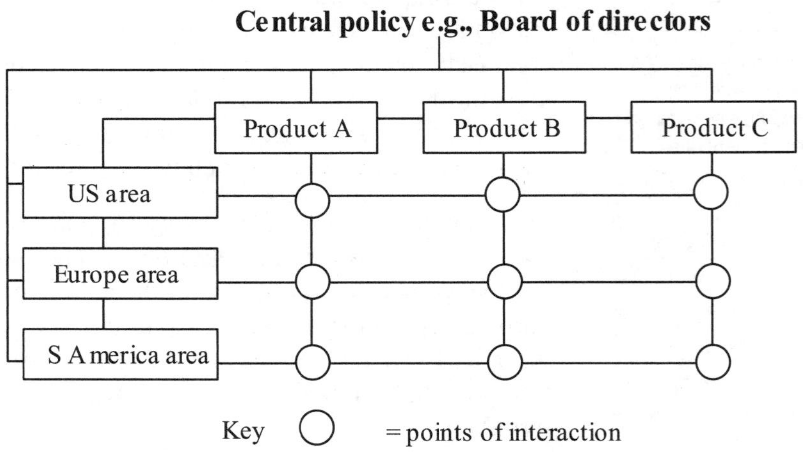

The objective in the matrix organisation is to capitalise on combinations of expertise that exist in the organisation, but which are stifled by normal hierarchical structures. This is accomplished by **horizontal groupings** of individuals or units into teams that operationally deal with the strategic matter at hand. The last point is an important one, since matrix groupings often reflect either a temporary, or as yet unresolved, specific strategic commitment. For example, a multi-product trading company might establish an export research group to study international markets. Or an aerospace firm might establish a unique product group (e.g., special alloy turbine blades) for a limited-duration government contract.

Of course, the matrix structure suffers from problems of dual authority, among others, but it can creatively serve the needs of strategic change that otherwise might be constrained by more traditional structures.

Advantages of matrix structures

- Retains functional economies and product co-ordination.
- It is organic – open communications and flexible goals.
- Improved motivation through:
  - people working participatively in teams;
  - specialists broadening their outlook;
  - encouraging competition within the organisation.

Disadvantages of matrix structures

- Higher administrative costs.
- Conflict between functional and product managers leading to individual stress arising from:
  - threat to occupational identity;
  - reporting to more than one boss;
  - less clear expectations.

Activity 2

Outline four alternative organisation structures suitable for multinational organisations.

Feedback to this activity is at the end of the chapter.

2.6 Intermediate structures and structural variations

Few organisations adopt a pure structural type; the skill is in blending the structure to the organisation's circumstances. There is a whole range of 'shades of grey' between these pure types of structure e.g. a company may move from a functional structure to a divisional structure by a series of smaller incremental changes.

Problems first arise within the functional structure as new products/markets compete for resources. Initially these conflicts might be resolved by pushing the decision upwards until a sufficiently senior manager makes the decision. Problems are dealt with by manipulating methods of control and operation rather than by structural changes.

As the new products/ markets become more important and create competition for resources, it may be necessary to create interdepartmental liaison roles: for example, a committee or a temporary taskforce may be set up to advise on priorities. This may lead to either permanent teams of co-ordinators or special co-ordinating jobs (the product manager is a good example). Another step, which may prove necessary to maintain the functional structure, is the creation of departments with the sole function of co-ordination. Ultimately, the organisation will divisionalise as the diversity increases and the 'costs' of maintaining the functional structure become unacceptably high.

It is also common to adopt a mixed structure to address such problems as a functional structure with subsidiaries. The main business, which employs the majority of employees, might have a functional structure, with more peripheral business interests organised as divisions or subsidiaries. The converse of this is the company that is divisionalised except for certain key functions which remain at the centre and which have responsibilities across all the divisions.

2.7 Structural types in multinational companies

The basic form of structure for the multinational is the retention of the 'home' structure and the management of overseas subsidiaries through direct contact between the manager of the subsidiary and the chief executive of the parent company. This is most common in single-product companies or where the overseas interests are relatively minor. Beyond this simple structure the critical issue is the extent to which local independence or responsiveness should take precedence over global co-ordination. The different types of multinational structure are shown in the diagram below:

KEY POINT

Different types of multinational structure include:

- international divisions;
- international subsidiaries;
- global product companies;
- transnational corporations.

Multi-national structures

Global co-ordination ↓ / Local independence and responsiveness →	Low	High
Low	International diversions	International subsidiaries
High	Global product companies	Transnational corporations

- **International divisions** – here the home-based structure may be retained at first, whether functional or divisional, but the overseas interests are managed through a special international division. The international subsidiaries will draw on the products of the home company and gain advantage from this technology transfer. The disadvantage is a lack of local tailoring of products or technology. Such structures tend to work best where there is a wide geographical spread but quite closely related products.
- **International subsidiaries** – are geographically based and operate independently by country. In these companies virtually all the management functions are nationally based, allowing for higher degrees of local responsiveness. The control of the parent company is likely to be dependent on some form of planning and reporting system and perhaps an ultimate veto over national strategies, but the extent of global co-ordination is likely to be low.
- **Global product companies** – represent a move away from the international divisional or subsidiary structure to an integrated structure. Here the multinational is split into product divisions, which are then managed on an international basis. The logic of such an approach is that it should promote cost efficiency (particularly of production) on an international basis, and should provide enhanced transfer of resources (particularly technology) between geographical regions.
- **Transnational corporations** – are structures that attempt to combine the local responsiveness of the international subsidiary with the advantages of co-ordination found in global product companies. The key lies in creating an integrated network of interdependent resources and capabilities. Each national unit operates independently, but is a source of ideas and capabilities for the whole corporation. National units achieve global scale through specialisation on behalf of the whole corporation. The centre manages a global network firstly by establishing the role of each subsidiary and then by sustaining the culture and systems to make the network operate effectively.

3 Mintzberg's organisational configurations

3.1 Building blocks

KEY POINT

Mintzberg argues that structure exists to co-ordinate the activities of different individuals and work processes.

Mintzberg argues that the organisation structure exists to co-ordinate the activities of different individuals and work processes. The nature of co-ordination changes with the increasing size of an organisation. In small organisations, mutual adjustment is sufficient but as organisations increase in size increased reliance is placed upon standardisation as a means of co-ordination.

Mintzberg's ideas on the building blocks and co-ordinating mechanisms, which make up the detailed configuration of the organisation are shown in the diagram below.

KEY POINT

Mintzberg's building blocks include the strategic apex, middle line and operating core, plus the technostructure and support staff.

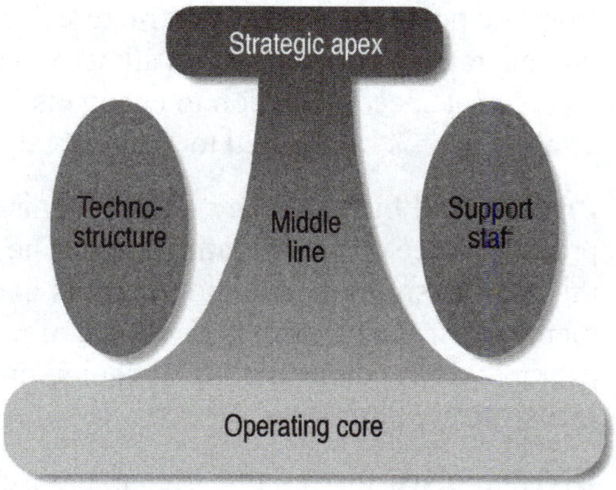

Mintzberg's organisational components

Strategic apex – higher levels of management.

Technostructure – provides technical input that is not part of the core activities.

Operating core – members involved in producing goods and services.

Middle line – middle and lower-level management.

Support staff – support that is not part of the operating core.

Whilst Mintzberg suggests the above five parts as an analytical tool, in practice there are several linking mechanisms at work:

- A formally determined hierarchy of decision levels, power and responsibility.
- A formal flow of information around the organisation.
- An informal communication network, the 'grapevine'.
- Formal work constellations whereby sections of the organisation set up and operate formal co-ordinating mechanisms such as working parties and committees.
- A system of ad hoc decision processes whereby the organisation responds in a particular manner when it faces a problem. The aim is to define the problem and find a solution to what may be a unique problem.

3.2 Configurations

The importance and relative size of these building blocks will vary with organisations, the configuration chosen to support the organisation's strategies depending on the mix of building block and co-ordinating mechanism.

Mintzberg discusses six configurations, covering the environment, the type of work and the complexity of tasks facing the organisation. These are outlined below:

- **Simple structure** – corresponding to the entrepreneurial organisation. The strategic apex – possibly consisting of a single owner-manager in a small business – exercises direct control over the operating core, and other functions are pared down to a minimum. There is little or no middle line, and technostructure and support staff are also absent. The fact that co-ordination is achieved by direct supervision means that this structure is flexible, and suited to cope with dynamic environments.
- **Machine bureaucracy** – just as the simple structure is based on predominance of the strategic apex, so the machine bureaucracy arises from the power of the technostructure. The emphasis is on regulation: bureaucratic processes govern all activities within the organisation. This means that speedy reaction to change is impracticable, and this arrangement is best suited to simple, static environments.
- **Professional bureaucracy** – this organisational structure arises from the predominance of the operating core. The name is appropriate, because this type of structure commonly arises in organisations where many members of staff have a high degree of professional qualification (for example the medical staff in a hospital or the analysts and programmers in a software developer).
- **Divisionalised form** – this is characterised by a powerful middle line in which a large class of middle managers each takes charge of a more or less autonomous division. Depending on the extent of their autonomy, managers will be able to restrict interference from the strategic apex to a minimum.
- **The 'adhocracy'** – refers to a complex and disorderly structure in which procedures and processes are not formalised and core activities are carried out by project teams. This structure is suited to a complex and dynamic environment.

  There are two types of adhocracy:

  - *operating adhocracy* – innovates and solves problems directly on behalf of its clients. Admin work and operating work are blended together (consultancy firm, advertising agency);
  - *administrative adhocracy* – undertakes projects to serve itself, so it has its own operating core (research department, hi-tech companies).
- **Missionary organisations** – are organisations formed on a basis of a common set of beliefs and values shared by all workers in the organisation. Firm belief in such norms implies an unwillingness to compromise or change, and this means that such organisations are only likely to prosper in simple, static environments.

Activity 3

Describe Mintzberg's simple structure and sketch the structural configuration.

Feedback to this activity is at the end of the chapter.

The key differences between Mintzberg's organisational configurations are shown below:

Mintzberg's organisational configurations

	Environment	**Internal factors**	**Key building block**	**Key co-ordinating mechanism**
Simple structure	Simple/ dynamic	Small Young Simple tasks	Strategic apex	Direct supervision
Machine bureaucracy	Simple/ static	Large Old Regulated tasks	Technostructure	Standardisation of work
Professional bureaucracy	Complex/ static	Professional control Simple systems	Operating core	Standardisation of skills
Divisionalised	Simple/static Diverse	Very large Old Divisible tasks	Middle line	Standardisation of outputs
Adhocracy	Complex/ dynamic	Young Complex tasks	Operating core Support staff	Mutual adjustment
Missionary	Simple/ static	Middle-aged Simple systems	Ideology	Standardisation of norms

If we take a system that is a mass production process with a large work force, we can illustrate what the structure might look like using Mintzberg's structural configuration.

Mintzberg's model in a large mass-production system

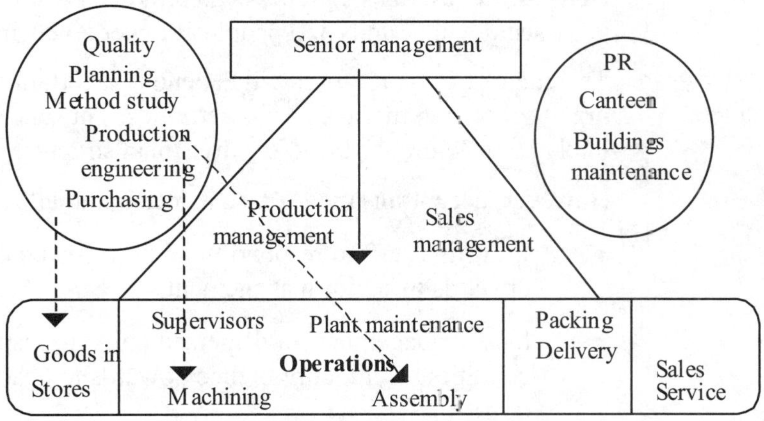

4 The adaptive organisation

4.1 Stability or flexibility

Flexibility is one of *the* hot issues in both strategic and human resource management. How can organisations co-ordinate and control their activities efficiently (to ensure unity of direction and controlled performance) – and at the same time retain the ability to respond swiftly to constant changes in the business environment: new technologies, new competitors, customer demands and consumer trends?

The push towards structural flexibility basically involves increasing managers' ability to:

- Delegate decision-making authority and initiative to units and levels of the organisation closest to the customers, supply chain and/or local marketplace. (We will discuss this under the heading of 'centralisation and decentralisation' below.)
- Structure decision-making, communication and the deployment of labour/skills in such as way as to be able to respond flexibly to changing conditions and demands. (We will discuss this under the heading of 'organic and mechanistic structures' below.)
- Vary the size and deployment of the workforce in line with variations in work demands, in order to maintain a 'lean' workforce. (We will discuss this under the heading of 'the shamrock organisation' below.)

4.2 Centralisation and decentralisation

DEFINITIONS

Centralisation is 'a condition where the upper levels of an organisation's hierarchy retain the authority to take most decisions.'

Delegation describes a process whereby the **authority** to make specific decisions is passed down to units and people at lower levels in the organisation's hierarchy.

One issue in flexibility is the level at which decisions are made.

'**Centralisation** is a condition where the upper levels of an organisation's hierarchy retain the authority to take most decisions.' (John Child)

Delegation describes a process whereby the **authority** to make specific decisions is passed down to units and people at lower levels in the organisation's hierarchy.

The choice of organisation will depend to a certain extent on the size of the organisation and the scale of its activities. Thus the small business structure is likely to be centralised, and the divisional structure is likely to be decentralised.

However, decentralisation is also a decision to allow:

- front-line staff to respond flexibly to customer demands without reference upwards to senior management;
- local management (of dispersed units) to respond flexibly to local market conditions without reference upwards to head office.

Advantages of centralisation include:

- Co-ordinated decisions and better management control, therefore less sub-optimising.
- Conformity with overall objectives – goal congruence is more likely to be achieved.
- Standardisation e.g. variety reduction and rationalisation
- Balance between functions, divisions, etc – increased flexibility in use of resources.

- Economies of scale – general management, finance, purchasing, production, etc.
- Top managers become better decision makers, because they have proven ability and they are more experienced.
- Speedier central decisions may be made in a crisis – delegation can be time-consuming.

Research shows that **centralisation of strategic decisions** and **delegation of tactical and operating decisions** can be very effective.

Disadvantages of centralisation include:

- Those of lower rank experience reduced job satisfaction.
- Frequently, senior management do not possess sufficient knowledge of all organisational activities. Therefore, their ability to make decisions is narrowed and delegation becomes essential.
- Centralisation places stress and responsibility onto senior management.
- Subordinates experience restricted opportunity for career development toward senior management positions.
- Decisions often take considerable time. This restricts the flexibility of the organisation, as well as using valuable time.

Slower decision-making impairs effective communication. Such communication problems may affect industrial relations.

4.3 Organic and mechanistic structures

In a classic management study, Burns and Stalker evaluated the role of different organisational structures in achieving particular strategies. Their result, surprising to some at the time, was that there was no intrinsic advantage to one structural form over another. At a crude level, companies that needed to be responsive to market and technological changes adopted flexible, or organic structures, while those who specialised in stable, cost focused industries tended to adopt hierarchies, called mechanistic structures. In general, firms that adopted the appropriate form for their market tended to perform rather better than those that had adopted contrary ones, although there were important exceptions.

- Organic structures (based on the analogy between an organisation and a living organism) are characterised by a network structure of communication and control: people co-ordinate their activities by interaction with each other. Communication is multi-directional, crossing hierarchical and functional barriers. Decisions are taken by those best placed, and most knowledgeable, to take them – rather than on the basis of closely defined role and job descriptions. The focus is on outputs/results, rather than internal processes or jobs. Organic structures are flexible and adaptive, 'regrouping' swiftly to cope with dynamic operating environments.
- Mechanistic structures (based on the analogy between an organisation and a machine) are characterised by a strictly defined hierarchy of authority, formal communication channels, job/role descriptions and so on. In other words, they are classic bureaucracies: stable, efficient and well-suited to slow-changing operating environments.

4.4 The shamrock organisation

Several writers have suggested 'core-periphery' models of the firm, in which a stable, permanent core of full-time staff are supplemented at periods of peak demand by a peripheral source of part-time, temporary and sub-contracted labour.

Charles Handy (1989) put forward a 'shamrock' or 'cloverleaf' model, with four 'levels' or components.

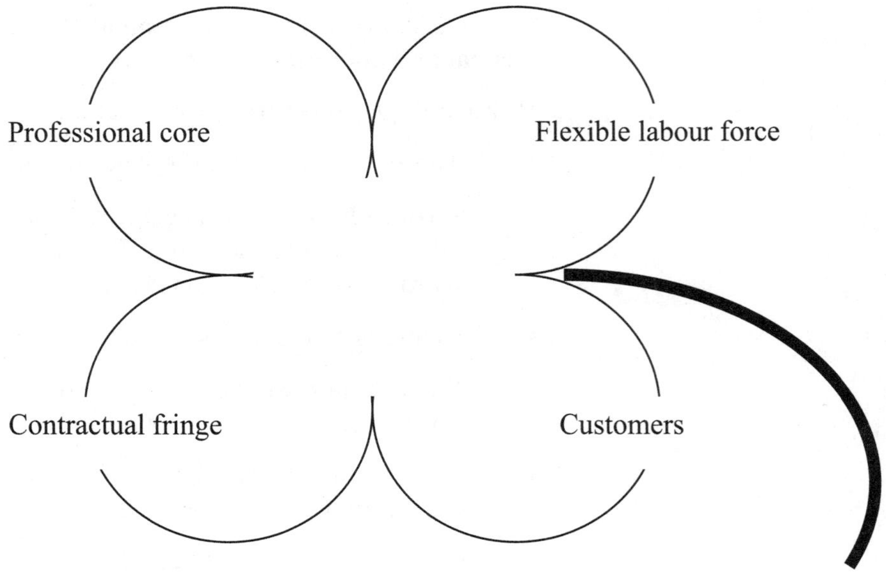

- The **professional core** are permanently employed staff who provide the core competencies and distinctive knowledge base of the organisation.
- The **flexible labour force** are temporary and part-time workers who can be deployed, when required by peaks in demand (e.g. seasonal tasks or projects).
- The **contractual fringe** are external providers (consultants, sub-contractors and freelancers) who can undertake non-core activities and/or provide specialist services more economically than the organisation could arrange internally. Many organisations now **outsource** activities such as IT, logistics, maintenance, call-centre management and so on.
- **Customers** are a fourth cluster, to whom the organisation may be able to 'sub-contract' some tasks. Information and communication technology (such as the Internet) has allowed sales, service and supply to be conducted on a 'self-service' basis: booking tickets, downloading music/books, getting on-line help and so on. (Even low-tech equivalents, such as home-assembly furniture, enable the organisation to devolve activities to customers and save costs.)

Organisations are increasingly seeking to be lean at the core – where activities are important to their competitive strategy – while maintaining access to a full range of flexibly deployed services at the periphery.

4.5 Ad-hocracy and beyond

As Mintzberg's concept of 'ad-hocracy' (Section 3.2) suggests, complex and dynamic environments are creating ever more loosely formed and adaptable structures. We will look at the concept of **virtual organisations** – and other **network** forms – in Chapter 4.

5 Transaction cost view of the firm

5.1 Transaction costs – Coase

One of the choices that a business faces is whether to carry out a process itself or whether to buy in the results of that process. In a classic article in 1937, Nobel Prize winner Ronald Coase first posed the following related questions:

- 'When will a transaction be carried out within a single firm rather than by two separate firms transacting in the market?'
- 'If the market mechanism improves efficiency, why do so many of the activities take place outside the price system?'
- Taken to an extreme, he questioned 'Why do firms exist?'

Coase pointed out that a large proportion of the total use of resources takes place within firms. Thus, it has deliberately been withheld from the price mechanism – the market system – in order to be co-ordinated administratively instead. Coase's answer was because there must be costs to using the market – traditional theory disregarded what he called transaction costs, i.e., the time, work and other resources used in order to enter into contracts and manage firms and similar institutions. His relatively simple – but, as it turned out, highly viable – thesis was that a firm arises if the costs of achieving a certain use of resources are lower when carried out administratively as compared to purchases and sales on the market. If it did not cost anything to enter into contracts, then there would be no need for firms.

He argued that a firm would expand until the cost of organising an extra transaction within the firm equalled the cost of carrying out the same transaction in the market.

DEFINITION

Transaction costs are the expenses incurred by allowing some activity to be undertaken outside the organisation.

Transaction costs are the expenses incurred by allowing some activity to be undertaken outside the organisation and arise from the effort that must be put into specifying what is required and subsequently co-ordinating delivery and monitoring quality. If the product or service is a standard design, then specification will be straightforward and the transaction costs will be low. But unfortunately, with sophisticated products and services there needs to be a great deal of negotiation between the organisation and its supplier.

A number of kinds of transaction cost have come to be known by particular names:

Search and information costs are costs such as those incurred in determining that the required good is available on the market, who has the lowest price, etc.

Bargaining costs are the costs required to come to an acceptable agreement with the other party to the transaction, drawing up an appropriate contract, etc.

Policing and enforcement costs are the costs of making sure the other party sticks to the terms of the contract, and taking appropriate action (often through the legal system) if this turns out not to be the case.

Transaction costs arise because of:

- mutual interdependence between upstream and downstream units in the value chain;
- inability to write complete contracts;
- factors that prevent complete contracting include:
  - bounded rationality – refers to the limits on the capacity of individuals to process information, deal with complexity and pursue rational aims;
  - difficulties in specifying/measuring performance e.g. terms like 'normal wear and tear' may have different interpretations;
  - asymmetric information – one party may be better informed than another who cannot acquire the same information without substantial costs;
  - uncertainty and complexity;
- incentives to cheat on the contract e.g. request a higher price if demand unexpectedly increases, demand a lower price if the contract is to be renewed, cheat on quality to increase profit margins.

5.2 Oliver Williamson's 'transaction cost theory'

Organisations choose between two methods of obtaining control over resources: the ownership of assets (hierarchy solutions – decisions over production, supply, and the purchases of inputs are made by managers and imposed through hierarchies) and buying-in the use of assets (the market solution – individuals and firms make independent decisions that are guided and co-ordinated by market prices). Williamson classifies these transactions into those that support co-ordination between multiple buyers and sellers, i.e., market transactions, and those supporting co-ordination within the firm, as well as industry value chain, i.e. hierarchy transactions. The decision is based on a comparison of the transaction costs of the two approaches.

Transactions have three dimensions that determine the costs associated with them:

- uncertainty – the more uncertain the environment the harder it is to write effective long-term contracts and the more likely vertical integration is;
- the frequency with which the transactions recur; and
- asset specificity – the extent to which the transacting firms invest in assets whose value depends on the business relationships remaining intact. The greater the specificity of the assets involved, the greater the likelihood that a transaction will take place within the firm.

DEFINITION

Asset specificity has been defined as the extent to which particular assets are only of use in one specific range of operations.

These factors translate into 'make-or-buy' decisions: whether it is better to provide a service from within the organisation, with hierarchical co-ordination, or from outside the organisation, with market co-ordination.

Williamson argues that it is the third dimension, the degree of asset specificity, which is the most important determinant of transaction. The more specific the assets are to a transaction then, all other things being equal, the greater will be the associated transaction costs and the more likely that the transaction will be internalised into a hierarchy. Conversely, when the productive assets are non-specific the process of market contracting is the more efficient because transaction costs will be low.

Asset specificity

An asset is said to be transaction-specific if its value to a given transaction is greater than its value in its best alternative use. The greater the gap between these two values, the greater the degree of specificity of the asset. Williamson has suggested six main types of asset specificity:

- Site specificity – suggests that once sited the assets may be very immobile.

  For example, a car components manufacturer locating a components factory near to a large customer's manufacturing plant.

- Physical asset specificity – when parties make investments in machinery or equipment that are specific to a certain transaction these will have lower values in alternative uses.

  For example, the car components manufacturer above invests in dedicated machinery to make bespoke components for just one manufacturer. Should the contract be lost, these components may have to be adapted for sale elsewhere.

- Human asset specificity – occurs when workers may have to acquire relationship-specific skills, know-how and information that is more valuable inside a particular transaction than outside it.

  For example, a consultant may have to acquire detailed knowledge of a client's in-house developed systems but this knowledge may not be useful on other clients.

- Brand name capital specificity refers to becoming affiliated with a well-known 'brand name' and thus becoming less free to pursue other opportunities.

  For example, an actor may become 'typecast' in a particular role or show.

- Dedicated asset specificity entails investments in general-purpose plant that are made at the behest of a particular customer. The specificity here refers to committing funds to a specified transaction that might have been used elsewhere.

- Temporal specificity – arises when the timing of performance is critical, such as with perishable agricultural commodities where a farmer may struggle to find alternative processors at short notice.

KEY POINT

Firms develop whenever the costs of transactions through markets exceed the costs of organising and co-ordinating production within firms.

5.3 Implications for organisational structure

Firms develop whenever the costs of transactions through markets exceed the costs of organising and co-ordinating production within firms. Their boundaries and structures depend on these relative costs and their changes over time. When transaction costs are high, market mechanisms fail and hierarchical characteristics become preferable.

This has the following implications for organisational structure:

1 Vertical integration and restructuring – firms should sell off up-stream or down-stream business units if they can be provided at lower transaction costs by the market.

2 Virtual organisations – rather than just out-sourcing non-core activities such as cleaning, some organisations have tried to out-source areas such as production and warehousing. A more detailed analysis of such 'virtual' organisations is carried out in Chapter 4.

3 The role of IT – as information technology continues its rapid cost performance improvement, firms will continue to find incentives to co-ordinate their activities electronically using networks. It follows too that electronic markets are more efficient forms of co-ordination for certain classes of product transactions. Utilising cheap co-ordinative transactions, interconnected networks and easily accessible databases, economic theory predicts that a proportional shift of economic activity from single-source sales channels to electronic markets is likely to occur, as lower co-ordination costs favour electronic markets. An evolution from manufacturer-controlled value chains to electronic markets can be anticipated.

6 Ecological perspective on the firm

6.1 Change in organisations

KEY POINT

There are three theories of organisational change.

- population ecology;
- rational adaptation;
- random transformation.

There are three theories that explain organisational change:

- **Population ecology** – where most of the variability in organisational structures comes about through the creation of new organisations and organisational forms and the replacement of old ones.
- **Rational adaptation** – where organisational variability reflects designed changes in strategy and structure of individual organisations in response to environmental changes, threats, and opposition.
- **Random transformation** – when organisations change their structures mainly in response to endogenous processes, only loosely coupled with the desires of organisational leaders and with the demands and threats of environment.

Survival and failure of firms are a key interest in organisation theory. The rational perspective supposes that companies containing the appropriate characteristics survive whilst market forces drive those companies out that do not exhibit some particular features. This view assumes that organisational structures can adapt through the actions of decision makers. In contrast, population ecologists Hannan and Freeman argue that adaptation to the environment occurs at the population level, with organisations replacing other organisations when conditions change. They claim 'high levels of structural inertia in organisational population can be explained as an outcome of an ecological-evolutionary process.' They say that organisations rarely succeed at making changes in strategy and structure in response to environmental changes because the organisations are subject to inertial forces and when they do adapt their structures, it is often too slow to successfully react to environmental changes.

Since the simplest measurable quantity for adaptability is survival, most population ecologists have focused on mortality rates. Some factors leading to higher mortality rates are:

- liability of newness (newer firms more likely to fail);
- liability of smallness (smaller fail more often than bigger);
- density dependency (more likely to fail at founding if lots of competing organisations have the same type).

KEY POINT

The ecological perspective focuses on how the population of firms changes over time, as unfit firms are forced out of existence by selection (competitive) pressures.

6.2 Population ecology

There are two issues that are important to the ecology approach.

- First, the single organisation is not the appropriate unit of analysis. The focus is on populations. Selection pressure forces some firms out of the population. In this way, the composition of the population changes. Put differently, the population adapts to the environmental changes by selecting the firms within the population that are not fitting. This view explains how a population of inert firms can adapt to the changes in the business environment.
- Second, the organisational ecology approach stresses the analogy between the natural populations and the human social organisations. Applying the analogy from biology to organisational populations identifies something similar to the genetic code. Organisational ecologists find this in what they call the blueprint of a firm. It consists of those structures, rules and procedures that are unlikely to change over the firm's life span. Thus, the blueprint is closely connected with the idea of inertia. According to the ecology approach, the imprinted initial conditions at the start up determine to a large extent the organisation's lifelong structures i.e. their initial structures define the subsequent development.

Hannan and Freeman state that the most important issues in applying the evolutionary-ecological theories to organisations concern timing of changes. The ability for an organisation to learn and adapt to environmental changes is only useful if the response time is fast enough. An organisation can be continually changing only to find out that the environment has already shifted to yet another state that requires a different structure.

6.3 Concept of inertia

There are a number of constraints that restrict organisational adaptation and create inertia. The internal constraints for organisational change include the sunk costs, the information problems, and the existence of internal policies and established agreements about rules and procedures. External constraints are legal barriers, fiscal limitations, and costs of securing legitimacy and political support from external forces.

The pivotal argument in the ecology view is the assumption of inert firms. That is for two reasons. First, the organisations face internal and external constraints. They do not adapt to environmental change, at least not with the same pace as the market conditions alter. Second, ecologists assume that structural change involves less reliable performance and less accountable action. Reliability is the power to create consistent quality products repeatedly. Accountability is the ability to rationally account for their actions. Since market forces favour reliability and accountability, which presumes stable, rational structures, selection pressure drives transforming firms out of the markets and increases the share of the inert companies. Thus, the emergence of inert firms is a result of selection.

6.4 Emerging in an ecological perspective

We can now explain how some specific organisational forms emerge in an ecological perspective. The variation appears mainly through differences across firms at founding (start up) stage. The permanent processes of entry and exit in which the firms appear randomly with different organisational characteristics reveal the only source of variety. Since selection favours the reliability and accountability of companies, some few particular imprinted structures are more persistent towards the forces of selection. The firms with those adhered structural features remain in the market. They dominate the industrial population they belong to. Other firms cannot adapt the relevant features since the attempt to change reduces the company's reliability and accountability. Thus, those firms survive that have by chance the right organisational features at the stage of entry. Only through this mechanism, the firm populations contain different organisational forms to a certain extent. The ecology approach emphasises the selection of accountability and reliability but not the selection of particular characteristics. Organisational features are more or less a by-product of reliable and accountable firms.

Summary

- There is a two-way influence between organisational strategy and organisational structure.
- Basic structural forms include: small business structure; functional structure; product and geographical structure; divisional structure (including holding company structure); and matrix structure.
- Organisational structure influences the level of centralisation in decision making.
- Mintzberg analyses organisational configurations in terms of five building blocks: strategic apex; technostructure; operating core; middle line; support staff.
- Transaction cost theory (Coase and Williamson) influences organisational structure. Firms select either hierarchy solutions or market solutions.
- The transaction cost view of the firm (e.g. Coase, Williamson) and its implications for organisational structure.
- Ecological perspective on the firm.

Having completed your study of this chapter you should have achieved the following learning outcome.

- Evaluate different organisational structures.

Self-test questions

1 List four different types of organisational structure. (1.3)

2 What levels of planning are associated with the divisional structure? (2.4)

3 Explain the advantages and disadvantages of a matrix structure. (2.5)

4 What structural difficulties are faced by multinational companies? (2.7)

5 Name the two types of adhocracy, according to Mintzberg. (3.2)

6 Explain the difference between centralisation and decentralisation. (4.2)

7 What are the four leaves of the 'shamrock' organisation? (4.4)

8 What are transaction costs? (5.1)

9 How do organisation forms emerge, in an ecological perspective? (6.4)

Multiple-choice question

Question 1

Organisation charts are used to give an impression of the structure of the organisation. Only three of the following are represented in diagrammatic form on the chart. Which is the odd one out?

A The units (departments) into which the organisation is divided and how they relate to each other.

B The structure of authority, responsibility and delegation in the organisation.

C The number of employees at each level.

D The formal communication and reporting channels of the organisation.

For the answer to this question, see the 'Answers' section at the end of the book.

Exam-type questions

Question 1: Resources and transactions

'Asset specificity' is a term used within Transactions Cost Theory. It has been defined as the extent to which particular assets are only of use in one specific range of operations. It has further been suggested that asset specificity falls into six categories: site specificity, physical asset specificity, human asset specificity, dedicated asset specificity, brand name capital specificity and temporal specificity.

Supporters of resource-based views of strategy contend that a firm's sustainable competitive advantage is generated from its possession of unique assets that cannot be easily imitated by other firms. These unique assets have been called core competencies or distinctive capabilities.

Network organisations have been defined as those which are reliant on relationships with other organisations to carry out their work.

Required:

(a) Briefly explain what transaction costs are and how resource-based views of strategy can be used for competitive advantage. Interpret the six categories of asset specificity by explaining what they mean. **(15 marks)**

(b) Discuss whether analysis of transactions cost has any influence on the increase in numbers of network organisations. **(10 marks)**

(Total: 25 marks)

Question 2: Gensup plc

Gensup plc has been formed from the acquisition by a major distributor – Universal Sales plc (Unisal) – of three manufacturing businesses – A Ltd, B Ltd and C Ltd. This occurred following discussions among the shareholders of A Ltd, B Ltd and C Ltd regarding the problems and opportunities facing their companies. An approach was made to Unisal, as a result of which it has acquired all three businesses.

As part of the reorganisation that followed the acquisition, Gensup has established a joint research and development centre for the manufacturing units. Corporate planning, management services, finance functions and group purchasing of common raw materials have been centralised at the head office of Gensup.

Universal Sales plc (Unisal) – this was an internationally established distribution company specialising in the worldwide distribution of products and components to the engineering industry. Its customers included those of A Ltd, B Ltd and C Ltd.

Unisal had a number of distribution centres in countries where demand was strong. The distribution managers liaised directly with contract customers. The distribution centres were also a base for the sales force. Sales persons focused on particular types of customer, such as manufacturers of cars or power plant, to which they sold a wide range of products. Marketing was co-ordinated at head office.

The shares of Unisal were traded on various stock exchanges. The acquisition leaves the former owners of A Ltd, B Ltd and C Ltd as minority shareholders in the quoted company, Gensup plc.

Manufacturing – A Ltd, B Ltd and C Ltd were all private limited companies. A Ltd manufactured aluminium rods and wire. B Ltd manufactured copper rods and wire. C Ltd manufactured plastic rods and thread. The manufacturers all produced their products using continuous processes with a relatively small number of production workers, most of whom were unskilled. These continuous processes required large, expensive manufacturing plants. Packaging of the output and distribution were on a batch basis. Their main raw materials were ores, raw chemicals, water and electric power. These raw materials represented a large part of the cost of the finished product. Many new sources of ore and chemicals have become available from Eastern Europe.

Maintenance, purchasing, quality control, and R&D were important functions, with skilled and professional staff. Directors who were not shareholders managed them

The market – there were numerous competing companies in the industry, operating either in a similar way or as part of larger groups. The market of A Ltd, B Ltd and C Ltd was exclusively in the United Kingdom. It consisted of a large number of engineering companies, which used the products in their own conversion processes.

During the last few years amalgamations and takeovers have reduced the number of customers, but changing economic conditions have also opened considerable export potential for A Ltd, B Ltd and C Ltd. Unfortunately the companies did not have the staff or expertise to take advantage of the opportunities.

Total quality control policies among the customers have meant that quality specifications and ordering procedures have become much more sophisticated, requiring substantial expenditure to meet customers' demands.

Required:

(a) Identify and explain the structural forms that might be appropriate for Gensup. **(10 marks)**

(b) Explain, with reference to the information provided in the scenario, the advantages and disadvantages of each structural form identified. **(15 marks)**

(Total: 25 marks)

For the answer to these questions, see the 'Answers' section at the end of the book.

Feedback to activities

Activity 1

Advantages of functional organisation:

- Pooling of expertise, through the grouping of specialised tasks/staff.
- Avoids duplication of functions and enables economies of scale.
- Facilitates management and control of functional specialists (suited to centralised organisations).

Disadvantages:

- Creates 'vertical' barriers between functions, which may affect work flow (creating co-ordination problems) and information flow (creating communication problems).
- Focuses on internal processes/inputs – rather than outputs: quality and customer satisfaction through a horizontal value chain.

Activity 2

The following organisational structures would be suitable for a multi-national company.

International divisional structure – this structure consists of a centralised parent company in one country and functions such as sales and marketing, production, distribution and research and development are established in the various countries where the company has divisions.

Geographical structure – this structure follows on from the international divisional. In this instance the company is divided up into regions. The long-term strategic plan is formulated by headquarters; the short-term decisions/strategic plan are taken care of in the region. If the region is large, further sub-division may take place (e.g. by product).

Product-based structure – here, the regions will not be based on geographical area but on products. The divisions are given responsibility for profits. The regions, although defined by products, may be split down into more manageable sub-divisions by geographical area.

Matrix structure – this structure aims to balance product needs and geographical needs. Functional reporting may also be introduced making the structure more complicated.

Activity 3

Simple structure is characterised, above all, by what is not elaborated. Typically, it has little or no technostructure, few support staff, a loose division of labour, minimal differentiation among its units, and a small managerial hierarchy.

Coordination in the **simple** structure is effected largely by direct supervision. Specifically, power over all of the important decisions tends to be centralised in the hands of the chief executive officer. Thus, the strategic apex emerges as the key part of the structure; indeed, the structure often consists of little more than a one-person strategic apex and an organic operating core.

Chapter 4

CONCEPTS IN STRATEGIC MANAGEMENT

Syllabus content

- Translating strategy into business (e.g. formation of strategic business units, encouragement of entrepreneurship inside organisations).
- Contemporary issues in business management (e.g. alliances, demergers, virtual organisations, corporate social responsibility and business ethics).

Contents

1 Translating strategy into business

2 Entrepreneurship

3 Strategic Business Unit (SBU)

4 Contemporary issues in business management

5 Virtual organisations

6 Non-growth strategies

7 Corporate social responsibility and business ethics

1 Translating strategy into business

1.1 Strategy identification and selection

Strategic management involves decisions concerning what a company might do, given the opportunities in its environment; what it can do, given the resources at its disposal; what it wants to do, given the personal values and aspirations of key decision makers; and what it should do, given the ethical and legal context in which it is operating. A firm needs a well-defined sense of where it is going in the future and a firm concept of the business it is in.

KEY POINT

McNamee identified seven fundamental strategies:

- Recovery strategy
- Non-growth strategy
- Corrective strategy
- Neutral strategy
- Growth strategy
- Risk reducing contingency strategy
- Reduction strategy.

It is assumed (following McNamee) that there are seven fundamental strategies, each one comprising the heart or base of a company's new strategic initiative. Each is planned to meet specific objectives or needs and encompasses other secondary strategies.

1 **Recovery strategy** – is about the management of crisis. The organisation will become insolvent unless appropriate management actions are taken to effect turnaround in the financial performance.

2 **Non-growth strategy** – a company might pursue a non-growth strategy if it saw its non-economic objectives as more important than its economic objectives (given a certain minimum level of profit), although a non-growth strategy does not imply a lack of attention to economic objectives. Strictly speaking, a non-growth strategy means no growth in **earnings**. This does not necessarily mean no growth in **turnover** – if margins are falling, turnover will need to increase to maintain the same level of earnings.

3 **Corrective strategy** – although there is no overall growth (or negative growth occurs) the company will shift its product-market positions, it will employ its resources in different fields and it will continue to search for new opportunities. In particular it will aim to correct any weaknesses it has discovered during its appraisal.

4 **Neutral strategy** – this is adopted where there is no significant deviation from the past strategy i.e. the goals achieved, the organisation's activities and its current competitive position are satisfactory.

5 **Growth strategy** – the use of resources to achieve high growth objectives is the most common form of business strategy and is present in most companies, at least to the extent of specific product/market involvement. Attacking with a new market entry; defending a market from competitive attack; funding long-range research for major technological innovation; and diversifying into high-margin markets are all examples of high growth strategy.

6 **Risk reducing contingency strategy** – a company faces risk because of its lack of knowledge of the future. When it evaluates a project, it will at best be able to forecast that 'if event A happens we shall have such and such a return, but if event B happens we shall lose £x million'. The extent of the risk it faces can be revealed using performance-risk gap analysis, where forecasts of the outcome in n years' time take into account not only the likely returns but also the probability of achieving various returns less than the likely level.

7 **Reduction strategy** – involves the curtailment of some activities e.g. when there is a planned cutback or retrenchment in the overall level of business activities – sales, range of markets served or products offered, geographical scope or decrease in the total assets of the company.

Governing the choice between strategic options should be the notion of competitive advantage. The organisation has to identify unique opportunities for itself in its chosen area. It has to identify particular characteristics within its approach to individual product markets that will give it a strong competitive position.

It might go for a large market share that would enable it to dominate particular markets and define the conditions of competition in them, for instance, as regards pricing policy. It might pursue technological dominance, looking for breakthrough products or a new manufacturing technology that would give it a technological edge over the competition. It might go for a better quality of product and service or the organisation might choose to combine some of these.

1.2 Innovative capability

Invention is the act of creating or producing through the use of imagination, while innovation is the commercial exploitation of an invention. An innovation may be a new product or a new way of producing the product. It may be a new service or a new way of organising the delivery of a service. It may be a change in the way the organisation is structured or a change in the way employees are recruited.

Most organisations need to be innovative and need to have the ability to create new or improved products or processes and enter new markets. Innovation and entrepreneurial attitudes are best nurtured in a climate that permits and actively encourages new ideas and new ways of doing things. People must be trusted and given the control and opportunity to make things happen. Managers must allow more interaction between employees within and between work groups. The creation of a more permissive climate encourages ideas and information to flow and new perspectives on problems and opportunities to be developed. Conflict must be contained and channelled constructively to find new and better ways of achieving results. This process helps managers anticipate change and plan for it.

2 Entrepreneurship

2.1 Role of entrepreneurship in business growth and development

DEFINITION

An entrepreneur is 'someone who introduces new technical and organisational solutions to old problems, an innovator who introduces new products processes, new organisational arrangements'.

According to Buchanan and Huczynski, an entrepreneur is more than one who founds businesses: he is: 'someone who introduces new technical and organisational solutions to old problems, an innovator who introduces new products processes, new organisational arrangements. A person with the entrepreneurial spirit has what is called 'executive drive', a need to do a good job and a need for recognition.'

Smith claims that owner managers can be arranged along a continuum whose polar positions are occupied by what he terms the 'craftsman entrepreneur' and the 'opportunistic entrepreneur'. The latter is far more orientated towards and capable of growth than the former, and it is therefore the opportunists whom Governments and the large companies find appealing.

According to Deeks, the owner manager and the professional manager possess different characteristic skills as follows:

Small organisation entrepreneur	Large organisation manager
• adaptive • diagnostic • exploitation of change; opportunities • tactical facility • pragmatic use of techniques as aid to problem solving • social skill applied on a social basis • consequence mitigating decision making	• predictive • prognostic • control of change • strategic facility • co-ordination and control specialists • manipulative skills applied largely on an interpersonal basis • event shaping decision making

Entrepreneurship can be encouraged within the economy e.g. lower tax rates and incentives can boost investment in smaller business start ups. However, the main source of finance remains the banks and in the past they have been unhelpful in aiding new businesses.

2.2 Entrepreneurship within large organisations

Organisations can only achieve their goals and objectives through the co-ordinated efforts of their members. The nature and extent of employees' expectations vary widely, as do the ability and willingness of the organisation to meet them. Organisations have expectations and requirements that may be in conflict with an individual's expectations. One of the main contradictions of organisational life is the maintenance of individuality and self-responsibility alongside the creation of co-operation and conformity. Employees are expected to work with others and obey but at the same time to show evidence of creativity and independence.

A successful company is one that is outward looking, and has accepted the reality of constant change and the necessity to review its product-market policy continuously. It places emphasis on vigorous initiative, always looking to the future towards new markets, innovative products, better designs, new processes, improved quality and increased productivity. It has a management style and structure designed for innovation in which employees are stimulated to think and act innovatively, which recognises potential entrepreneurs and ensures that everyone welcomes changes for the better. The company might require people to work in cross-disciplinary teams with employees becoming more involved in the development of new products or processes, to move around and experiment with fresh ideas or to brainstorm various issues.

Mintzberg described an entrepreneurial strategy as one where intentions exist as the personal, unarticulated vision of a single leader, and so are adaptable to new opportunities.

There is obviously a link between the creative and the entrepreneurial organisation and much depends on the structure adopted to encourage innovation and creativity. Burgelman feels that this structure should be based on the strategic importance of new business to the organisation and how related that business is to the organisation's current activities. This premise leads to nine organisational designs for entrepreneurship.

Organisational designs for entrepreneurship

Operational relatedness	Strategic importance: Very important	Uncertain	Not important
Unrelated	Special business unit	Independent business unit	Complete spin off
Partly related	New products department	New venture division	Contracting
Strongly related	Direct integration	Micro new venture department	Nurturing and contracting

Activity 1

How can managers encourage innovation and entrepreneurial attitudes within their workforce?

Feedback to this activity is at the end of the chapter.

3 Strategic Business Unit (SBU)

3.1 What is it?

DEFINITION

A strategic business unit (SBU) is a semi-autonomous unit within an organisation, which undertakes to design, produce, market, deliver and support a product or closely related products (or services).

In recent years, many companies have decided that a complex, functional organisational structure is not an efficient way to organise activities so they have re-engineered according to processes or strategic business units (called SBUs as a way of managing the complexity of growth and encouraging creativity. A **strategic business unit** is a semi-autonomous unit within an organisation. It is usually responsible for developing its own business strategies, its own budgeting, new product decisions, hiring decisions, and price setting. An SBU is treated as an internal profit centre by corporate headquarters.

According to Porter, a strategic business unit is a relevant entity for business strategy formulation. It can be defined as a collection of activities that are performed to design, produce, market, deliver, and support a product or closely related products (or services). An SBU is a business unit that represents a strategically distinct business (industry) and encompasses products and services where the sources of competitive advantage are similar. There may be related industries that provide services sharing customers, technologies, or channels, but they have their own unique requirements for competitive advantage.

The characteristics of a viable SBU include:

- unique business mission;
- definable set of competitors;
- integrative planning done independently;
- responsible for resource management in all areas;
- large enough but not so large as to become bureaucratic.

3.2 Central strategic planning and strategic business units

In large organisations the traditional central strategic planning system can become unmanageable if there are many products and markets involved. With so many activities, it becomes extremely difficult for strategic planners to conceptualise the total and plan, co-ordinate and integrate the range of diversity into coherent strategies. The danger is that strategies can be added without firm direction or meshing. This situation lends itself to an organisation structure based on SBUs.

An SBU will ensure that a certain product or service is promoted and handled as though it were an independent business. It preserves the attention and energies of a manager and staff, whose job is to guide and promote that product or product line. And as we have noted, each SBU has its own distinct set of competitors, and its own strategic plan. It might also have its own mission.

It is an organisational technique for preserving the entrepreneurial attention and drive, so characteristic of the small company. In fact, it is an excellent means of promoting entrepreneurial behaviour, which is likely to be lacking in the larger organisation.

3.3 The strengths of SBUs

KEY POINT

Peters suggests that successful organisations will be flatter, have more autonomous units, be oriented toward differentiation, be quality and service conscious and much faster at innovation and use highly trained, flexible people as a means of adding value.

Tom Peters in *Thriving On Chaos* writes about the need for companies to accept management revolution. He asserts that future successful organisations will be:

- flatter (have fewer layers of organisation structure);
- populated by more autonomous units (more local authority to introduce and price products/services);
- oriented toward differentiation, producing high value-added goods and services, creating niche markets;
- quality and service conscious;
- much faster at innovation; and
- users of highly trained, flexible people as the principal means of adding value.

In short the principal **benefits of an effective SBU decision-making structure** are that it will:

- define the company according to the markets it serves – one SBU per market. (In the same way that a small company always does);
- enable a complex and dynamic environment to be divided into relatively small more manageable segments;
- be a fast, responsive, flat, semi-autonomous decision unit;
- provide the capability for the development of strong expertise and experience, business intelligence and decision making ability within narrow areas of business activity;
- exercise the potential of managers at a lower level;
- develop general management ability, versatility and flexibility;
- reduce corporate management overload;
- give status to the separate units, and thus promote a competitive spirit, creativity, participation and motivation of all levels of staff and managers in general;

- sharpen responsibility and accountability and generally improve financial control.

3.4 Problems with SBUs

An organisation comprising SBUs has built-in structural inefficiencies; it is less efficient in terms of coping with inter-dependence, integration and co-ordination. Corporate management must be aware of these in-built problems and take steps to resolve them by achieving a sensible balance of resources, the integration of separate strategies and careful monitoring. Other problems include:

- the mushrooming of service costs because of duplication;
- a need for specific types of management information by each separate SBU;
- a build-up of bureaucracy;
- inefficiencies arising from possible parochialism;
- the reluctance of central management to relinquish control over day-to-day activities.

However, it is a general view of commentators that the benefits of SBUs outweigh the potential problems.

4 Contemporary issues in business management

4.1 Alternative methods of strategic development

KEY POINT

Methods of strategic development include:

- internal development;
- acquisition;
- joint development or alliances.

Our discussions on strategic options so far have been concerned with the generic basis (cost leadership, focus and differentiation) on which organisations might sustain competitive advantage and the alternative directions in which they might develop. For each of these alternative directions there are three different potential types of method of development to choose from:

- internal development;
- acquisition;
- joint development or alliances.

4.2 Internal development – organic growth

Where a company operates in a market with a good prospect for growth, it can grow organically either by exploiting existing product or service market opportunities or by diversifying.

However, because existing products have a finite life, a strategy of organic growth must include plans for developing new products and strategies, new capabilities and competencies – the company must be innovative. Even stability requires innovation because an organisation cannot rely on its existing products/services and markets forever. Because tastes, life styles and fashions change, an organisation that wants to maintain its sales and profits must develop or replace the products or services in decline.

For many organisations internal development – or organic growth – has been the primary method of strategic development, especially with products that are highly technical in design or method of manufacture. This is because the process of development is seen as the best way of acquiring the necessary skills and knowledge to exploit the product and compete successfully in the market place.

A parallel argument applies to the development of new markets by direct involvement.

Although the final cost of developing new activities internally may be greater than by acquiring other companies, the spread of cost may be more favourable and realistic, especially for small companies that may not have the resources available for major investment.

4.3 Growth by merger or acquisition

A merger is the coming together of two organisations, often of a broadly similar size. Negotiations are usually friendly because the merger is deemed to be mutually beneficial.

In contrast, an acquisition is the purchase of one company by another and a takeover is a hostile acquisition – where the directors of the target company do not wish their organisation to be acquired.

Advantages of mergers and acquisitions

Acquisition has some significant advantages over internal growth:

- High speed access to resources – this is particularly true of brands; an acquisition can provide a powerful brand name that could take years to establish through internal growth.
- Avoids barriers to entry – acquisition may be the only way to enter a market where the competitive structure would not admit a new member or the barriers to entry were too high.
- Less reaction from competitors – there is less likelihood of retaliation because an acquisition does not alter the capacity of the competitive arena.
- It can block a competitor – if Kingfisher's bid for Asda had been successful it would have denied Walmart its easy access to the UK.
- Asset valuation – if the acquiring company believes the potential acquisition's assets are undervalued it might undertake an asset stripping operation.

Disadvantages of mergers and acquisitions

There are some disadvantages associated with this method of growth:

- There is bound to be a cultural mismatch between the organisations – a lack of 'fit' can be significant in knowledge-based companies, where the value of the business resides in individuals.
- Disposal of assets – companies may be forced to dispose of assets they had before the acquisition. The alliance between British Airways and American Airlines was called off because the pair would have had to free up around 224 take-off and landing slots to other operators.
- Risk – of not knowing all there is to know about the business it seeks to buy.

Activity 2

List all the possible motives you can think of for a company attempting to acquire the ownership of more, or all, of another company.

Feedback to this activity is at the end of the chapter.

4.4 Growth by joint development

KEY POINT

Joint development is an option for companies that have no resources or capabilities for future expansion.

Joint development is seen as an attractive way forward for companies that do not have resources or capabilities needed for future expansion. This does not mean that the firms involved will be small. It is common to find large companies undertaking joint development where the costs and risks of a project are high, such as construction and pharmaceuticals.

The term joint development covers a range of possible arrangements including:

- Networks – loose associations of companies that co-operate for mutual advantage. Many biotechnology companies share resources through such arrangements. Of paramount importance is the ability of the network to learn together. Network or virtual organisations are discussed in more detail in Section 5 below.
- Licences and franchises – where other firms undertake part of the value creation process under contractual arrangements.
- Joint ventures – where assets are formally integrated and jointly owned.

4.5 Strategic alliances

DEFINITION

A strategic alliance can be defined as a co-operative business activity, formed by two or more separate organisations for strategic purposes.

A strategic alliance can be defined as a co-operative business activity, formed by two or more separate organisations for strategic purposes, that allocates ownership, operational responsibilities, financial risks, and rewards to each member, while preserving their separate identity/autonomy. It is a long-term collaboration bringing together the strengths of two or more organisations to achieve strategic goals. For example, IBM formed links with Ricoh for distribution of low-end computers. This allowed them to move into the Japanese market quickly, inexpensively and with a relatively high prospect for success. It can also help result in improved access to information and technology. Strategic alliances can take many forms, from loose informal agreements, partnerships, and formal joint ventures to contracting out services to outside suppliers.

As was noted with SBUs, some organisations are trying to retain some of the innovation and flexibility that is characteristic of small companies. They are balancing between bureaucracy and entrepreneurship by forming strategic alliances (closer working relationships) with other organisations. Some organisations are using strategic alliances to extend their reach without increasing their size. Others are motivated by the benefits associated with a global strategy, especially where the organisation lacks a key success factor for some market. This may be distribution, a brand name, a selling organisation, technology, R&D or manufacturing capability. To remedy this deficiency internally would often require excessive time and money.

The ability of a business to become a global player depends on a number of factors. Some companies service niche markets, which are protected from global competition. In many cases, however, it is necessary to enter into strategic alliances of some sort in order to become a global operator.

5 Virtual organisations

5.1 Introduction

DEFINITION

A virtual organisation consists a group of companies, acting as one company to fulfil a need in the marketplace.

A virtual organisation consists of a group of companies, acting as one company to fulfil a need in the marketplace. These companies collaborate, share skills, information, products, services, etc in order to meet the goal of customer fulfilment.

A virtual organisation is thus an association constructed from both administratively and geographically distributed business units or organisations which has rejected the traditional work patterns of bringing people to one location for a fixed period, and organising them into departments and functions.

The growth in computing power and networks has encouraged information to be distributed instantly within and beyond the organisation. This facility can be used to transform the organisation's structure, scope, reporting and control mechanisms, workflows, products and services.

For an international company operating worldwide, the creation and transformation of knowledge is paramount. In this environment, the 'virtual organisation' structure promotes cross-border alliance and a network of organisations designed to: share technology or facilities; agree on common standards; or exploit a particular market opportunity. Such an enterprise is, by definition, flexible, dynamic and responsive.

Its aim is to provide an organisational solution to problems posed by the uncertainties arising from increasingly intense global competition. Along with increasing reliance on information and communication technology (ICT), the idea of the virtual organisation emphasises:

- the decentralisation of control;
- the creation of more flexible patterns of working;
- a greater empowerment of the workforce;
- the displacement of hierarchy by teamworking;
- the development of a greater sense of collective responsibility; and
- the creation of more collaborative relationships among co-workers.

The key element in supporting the transformation is IT. This is mainly through the systems that facilitate co-ordination and communication, decision-making and the sharing of knowledge, skills and resources. Information systems can reduce the number of levels in an organisation by providing managers with information to manage and control larger numbers of workers spread over greater distances and by giving lower-level employees more decision-making authority. It is no longer necessary for these employees to work standard hours every day, nor work in an office or even the same country as their manager. With the emergence of global networks, team members can collaborate closely even from distant locations. Information technology permits tight co-ordination of geographically dispersed workers across time zones and cultures. Different companies can join together to provide goods and services.

5.2 Examples of virtual organisations

The key question in building a virtual organisation is deciding which activities and assets to outsource or 'buy-in' ('market solutions') and which to perform in-house and own directly ('hierarchy solutions'). The answers to these issues can give rise to the following examples:

- Outsourcing core activities – many firms outsource non-core activities such as catering and cleaning but virtual organisations may outsource areas such as production and warehousing.

  Many Internet companies are examples of this approach – Amazon being perhaps one of the best known on-line retailers. Amazon operates its website but relies on external book publishers, book warehouses, couriers and credit card companies to deliver the rest of the customer experience. These partners are also expected to provide Amazon with information on, for example, stock availability, delivery times, promotional material, etc. The customer feels that they are dealing with one organisation not many.

- Contract staffing – many firms use temporary staff in operations to deal with busy periods, but virtual organisations may extend this to lawyers, systems experts, HR managers, etc. The idea is to reduce staff levels to a small level of core employees. Handy's Shamrock approach discussed in Chapter 3 is relevant here.

- Asset ownership – many firms lease vehicles and buildings but virtual organisations may extend this to IT facilities, office equipment, specialist machinery, etc.

- Office space – most firms have offices to work from. Proponents of virtual organisations see offices as unnecessary overheads and encourage staff to work from home. As mentioned above, the key determinant is the IT system used to ensure good communication between different parties. This could include video conferencing, discussion forums, email, virtual organisation portals, remote access to company intranets and extranets as well as conventional telephone calls.

Most virtual organisations have an operating core:

Virtual or network organisation

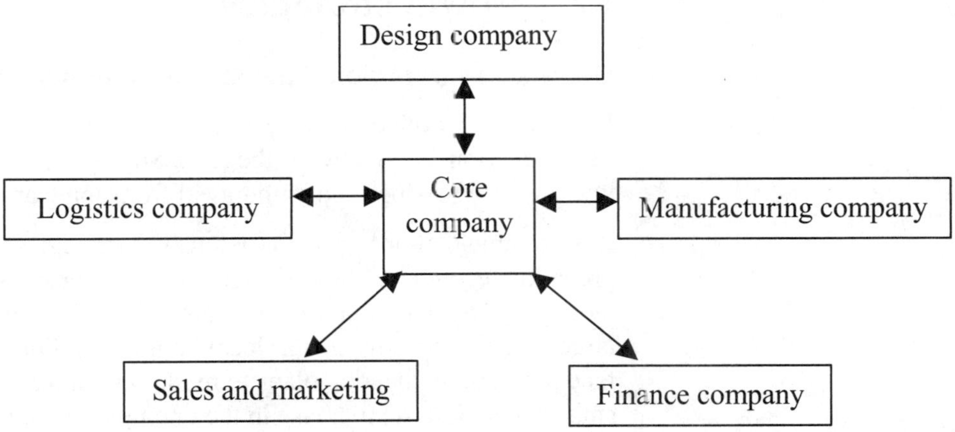

Activities tend to be managed by self-organising project teams. This enables flatter structures to be used, and gives greater spans of responsibilities to individuals. Fewer activities will be attempted in-house, allowing the company to specialise in only those activities that add value.

5.3 Virtual organisation as process

Virtual organisation requires a different way of perceiving the world by those who wish to participate in it. There are four key characteristics of virtual organisation as process.

1. First, virtual organisation entails the development of relationships with a broad range of potential partners, each having a particular competency that complements the others.

2. Second, virtual organising capitalises on the mobility and responsiveness of telecommunications to overcome problems of distance.

3. Third, timing is a key aspect of relationships, with key players using responsiveness and availability to decide between alternatives.

4. Last, there must be trust between players separated in space for virtual organisation to be effective.

5.4 Transaction costs

The concept of transactions costs was discussed in Chapter 3. Activities are brought in-house if the transaction cost of using the market is too high. The rise in virtual organisations can thus be explained by arguing that such transaction costs must be lower than they used to be:

- IT has reduced transaction costs – for example, CIM approaches trigger automatic orders to suppliers.

- Increased mutual trust has reduced the transaction costs of monitoring and controlling suppliers.

An alternative approach would be to argue that the internal costs of a hierarchical solution are higher than previously thought:

- Some firms have concluded that the costs of internal control are higher than expected, particularly if viewed using an opportunity costing approach – what is the cost of not using resources such as managerial time elsewhere?

6 Non-growth strategies

6.1 Defensive strategies – demergers and divestment

When we think of strategies we assume that the organisation is intent on growth. This is obviously not always the case. Strategic decision-making may therefore involve 'downsizing' and withdrawal from some areas of business.

It is possible that non-growth (defensive) strategies are adopted because of the prevailing economic climate. Some large companies are confronted by anti-monopoly legislation or are constrained by public opinion. They might have too large an effect on a particular local population. For example, a company might face pressure to abandon plans to modernise and automate, since that would cause too serious an increase in the unemployment rate in the locality. In addition, there is a debate about the quality of life, as opposed to continued economic growth, which calls into question some of the fundamental philosophies of large companies. Thus the company cannot always be guided by purely economic motives.

Apart from the external pressures, there may be internal reasons for deciding on a non-growth strategy. It might be that once the company gets above a certain size, management problems rise out of proportion to the growth in size. Owner-managers might prefer to keep their firms at a size which they personally could control comfortably, rather than have to appoint other managers or raise outside capital with perhaps the eventual risk of losing control of their organisations. Defensive strategies include demergers and divestment.

6.2 Demergers

DEFINITION

A demerger is where a company, instead of selling a major subsidiary, will spin that company off as a separate listed company.

A demerger (sometimes called unbundling) is the opposite of a merger. It is where a company, instead of selling a major subsidiary, will spin that company off as a separate listed company or where a set of SBUs are split off from the parent and the parts then exist separately. On the day the demerger becomes effective, shareholders will own two shares, one in the existing company and one in the new company.

An example of a demerger is the split of ICI into two separately quoted companies. The name ICI was retained for the chemicals, paints and explosives divisions, while the new name Zeneca was given to the pharmaceuticals, agrochemicals and seeds. The rationale was to enable each company to respond better to economic circumstances and to the shifts and rationalisations likely to come in the international chemical market.

A demerger is appropriate if the sum of the values of the two companies after the split is greater than the value of the single company before the split.

Demerging would appear to fit strategically when:

- an organisation has become too large and unwieldy;
- there is little synergy between the SBUs;
- management is fettered by the constraints imposed by the parent;
- funding becomes easier when each component of the demerger can act independently when seeking funds;
- the organisation feels that the business would be more valuable if it were to operate independently;
- it allows businesses to supply former competitors.

6.3 Divestment

DEFINITION

Divestment is the process of disposing of part of an organisation's activities, and usually the assets and personnel that relate to it, or pulling out of certain product or service market areas.

Divestment is the process of disposing of part of an organisation's activities, and usually the assets and personnel that relate to it or pulling out of certain product or service market areas. One motive for doing so might be simply an opportunistic attempt to make a swift profit. Another reason might be a strategic decision to focus management effort on core activities while disposing of areas that distract from the core activities or are vulnerable. The most common reason is to rationalise an enterprise as a result of a strategic appraisal. This could mean deciding to concentrate on its core business and sell off fringe activities, or to sell off subsidiaries where performance is poor or where growth prospects are not good.

Management buyout

This latter point is well illustrated in the particular type of divestment known as a management buyout. This term describes the case where a strategic business unit (SBU) is sold off, not to another company, but to the existing management team, who become owners as well as managers in the newly hived-off entity.

This procedure has many advantages.

- The people most likely to make a success of the business – and hence to agree a high price for purchasing it – are the managers who are already intimately familiar with its products, markets, strengths, weaknesses, etc.
- The investment return demanded by the new owner managers may be less than is required by the head office of a mammoth organisation in which the SBU is just a very small part.
- Managers can put in some of their own capital, but may very likely attract investment also from venture capital providers.

Several variants of a management buyout may be identified and are listed below.

- **Management buyout** – strictly these occur where the executive managers of a business join with financing institutions to buy the business from the entity which currently owns it. The managers may put up the bulk of the finance required for the purchase.
- **Leveraged buyout** – these occur where the purchase price is beyond the financial resources of the managers and the bulk of the acquisition is financed by loan capital provided by other investors.
- **Employee buyout** – this is similar to the above categories but all employees are offered a stake in the new business.
- **Management buy-in** – this is where a group of managers from outside the business make the acquisition.
- **Spin-out** – similar to a buyout but the parent company maintains a stake in the business.

Liquidation

A more severe form of divestment is liquidation, which is the selling off or voluntary winding up of an organisation and is preferable to a compulsory liquidation. However, it is a difficult policy to adopt as top management does not notice that crises are developing and often makes light of them when they do occur in the hope that they will go away. This option would be preferable if the organisation's only alternative is bankruptcy. Liquidation represents an orderly and planned means of obtaining the greatest possible cash for an organisation's assets.

7 Corporate social responsibility and business ethics

7.1 Business ethics

KEY POINT

Business ethics are concerned with truth and justice.

Business ethics are concerned with truth and justice and have a variety of aspects including:

- the expectations of society;
- fair competition;
- advertising;
- public relations;
- social responsibilities;
- consumer autonomy;
- corporate behaviour in the home country, as well as abroad.

The two factors which have the strongest bearing on ethical standards in management, are **public disclosure** and **publicity**, and the increasing **concern** of a public that is better informed.

These two factors are supported by government regulations and education to increase the standard of professionalism among business managers.

7.2 Ethics at three levels

Ethical issues regarding business and public sector organisations exist at three levels:

1. At the **macro level**, there are issues about the role of **business** in the national and international organisation of society. These are largely concerned with the relative virtues of different political/social systems, such as free enterprise, centrally planned economies, etc. There are also important issues of international relationships and the role of business on an international scale. Unfortunately, in a world of multinationals, where competition is now international, the standards of ethics vary from nation to nation.
2. At the **corporate level**, the issue is often referred to as corporate social responsibility and is focused on the ethical issues facing **individual corporate entities** (private and public sector) when formulating and implementing strategies.
3. At the **individual level**, the issue concerns the behaviour and actions of **individuals within organisations**. Handy cites the problem where an organisation's standards of ethics may differ from the individual's own standards. For example, what is the responsibility of an individual who believes that the strategy of their organisation is unethical?

7.3 The nature of social responsibility

Business ethics are concerned with how an organisation interacts with *all* its stakeholders. **Social responsibility** is the branch of business ethics that is concerned with the interaction of the organisation with its secondary stakeholders.

DEFINITION

Social responsibility describes the duties an individual or an institution has towards the wider community or society.

The term **social responsibility** is used to describe the duties an individual or an institution has towards the wider community or society. Naturally, there are usually rights and privileges associated with carrying out these duties of an individual or an institution, but the main concern in the present context is the scope and fulfilment of those duties.

Philosophers have argued about the nature of these duties for thousands of years, but the following consistencies emerge:

- It is wrong to treat others in ways that you would not wish them to treat you.
- Others should be treated with respect and allowed their dignity.
- It is wrong to withhold assistance where this would not harm the giver.

Naturally, these are rather simplistic, but carry the essence of the nature of social responsibility. They are not merely 'nice' things, in themselves, but essential for the maintenance of a fair society overall.

Activity 3

A visitor to a factory notices that a machine operator is using the machine without the safety guard in place. What are the visitor's social obligations?

Feedback to this activity is at the end of the chapter.

In a business and accounting sense, social responsibility is concerned with what economists term 'externalities' – costs not absorbed in the product or service and not paid for directly by the customer but borne by the wider community e.g. the smoke emissions generated by a power station. The cost of not cleaning up the emissions falls on the wider public through increased air pollution giving rise to illnesses and acid rain damage to forests and buildings.

Three key areas of social responsibility can be identified:

1 **Environmental issues** – includes all forms of pollution, such as air pollution from cars, water pollution killing fish and pesticide overuse destroying wildlife.

2 **Exploitation** – is often concerned with the treatment of people in poorer countries, who typically have little power and who are not protected by health and safety legislation.

3 **Sustainability issues** – affect future generations and are extremely important. One highly publicised issue here is the enhanced greenhouse effect; the warming of the Earth due to the industrial production of carbon dioxide and other gases. Where companies are directly exploiting the world's natural resources – through mining or oil extraction, for example – the concern of pressure groups is that irreplaceable resources are being squandered.

An organisation's social responsibilities can generate various types of behaviour:

- **Social obligations** – the organisation meets its social obligations by conducting its business within the legal constraints imposed by society, i.e. obeying the law.
- **Social responsibility** – the organisation meets the prevailing social norms, values, and performance expectations of society.
- **Social responsiveness** – the organisation anticipates the emergence of problems that may be the result of organisational activities. (Certain oil companies may take this approach.)

7.4 Why be socially responsible?

There are two schools of thought about an organisation's social responsibilities.

1 Milton Friedman maintains that the only responsibility of business is to make as much for its owners as it can. He took the view that 'the business of business is business and companies should leave it to legislators to pass laws against socially irresponsible acts and to consumers to vote with their purses against socially irresponsible companies'. This view is based on the argument that a business is an economic institution whose legitimate function is economic performance, not social activity.

The business arguments for social responsibility include:

- Saving energy and recycling resources in many cases will lead to lower overheads, which consequently will help profits.
- Acting in a socially responsible way will often attract favourable publicity for a company, which may be used as a source of competitive advantage against rivals. For example, The Body Shop's stance against animal testing and support for third world producers has increased its attractiveness.

- Increasingly consumers are becoming more concerned for the environment and therefore increasingly purchase goods from more ethical sources. For example, in the UK there has been an increase in the attractiveness of those supermarkets, which sell non-genetically modified (GM) foods, leading to a decline in sales in those companies.

2 The alternative view of social responsibility is that a business must play an active social role in the society in which it functions. Many businesses are large and powerful economically, which often means their decisions can have a major impact on:

- the environment e.g. pollution;
- utilisation of public goods and services e.g. roads, bridges, law and order, etc;
- consumers e.g. monopoly situations in terms of control of markets;
- employment opportunities and working conditions;
- economies of specific regions and the whole country.

7.5 Social and ethical objectives

Few organisations would put profits and growth at the top of their corporate objectives ranking list nowadays because there are so many other issues to be taken into account. Not only are there doubts as to whether profits and growth are desirable ends in themselves, there are also doubts about their practicality. Other new factors are measures such as pollution control, conservation of natural resources and avoidance of environmental disfigurement by companies. Companies are now developing a social conscience, even at the cost of lower profits.

It is management's job to cover the demands placed on an organisation by public opinion and attitudes, and legal and political pressures, into opportunities for future growth and innovation. Under this heading there may well be objectives relating to:

- preservation and improvement of the environment;
- consumer protection, and the avoidance of socially undesirable activities;
- improvement of conditions of work and social services for employees;
- participation in local activities;
- ensuring that plans for expansion, rationalisation or other major changes are carried out without adverse effects on employees or on the community.

Companies also tend to accept employee pressure where it appears to be moving towards legitimate aspirations. Employees are offered opportunities for job satisfaction and personal development, but the most significant moves seem to be in the direction of peripheral benefits such as pension schemes and welfare activities. The emphasis on employee aspirations is so strong that many companies sanctify them by their elevation to the status of objectives.

Summary

- McNamee identifies seven fundamental strategies: recovery, non-growth, corrective, neutral, growth, risk reducing and reduction strategies.
- Many firms operate through strategic business units (semi-autonomous profit centres).
- Methods of strategic development include organic growth, growth by merger or acquisition, growth by joint development, strategic alliances, and virtual organisations.
- A non-growth strategy may involve demerger or divestment.
- Increasingly, it is recognised that organisations have social and ethical responsibilities that must be observed even when profit maximisation is the prime objective.

Having completed your study of this chapter you should have achieved the following learning outcome.

- Discuss concepts in contemporary thinking on strategic management.

Self-test questions

1 What is the difference between a non-growth strategy and a neutral one? (1.1)

2 What type of characteristics does a small organisation entrepreneur display? (2.1)

3 How did Mintzberg describe an entrepreneurial strategy? (2.2)

4 Describe the characteristics of an SBU. (3.1)

5 Give three characteristics of future successful organisations according to Peters. (3.3)

6 What is the difference between a merger and an acquisition? (4.3)

7 Why do organisations form strategic alliances? (4.5)

8 What is divestment? (6.3)

9 Give three examples of key social responsibility issues. (7.3)

Multiple-choice question

Question 1

Which of the following is *not* a feature of virtual organisation?

A Use of ICT to connect remote collaborators

B Development of collective responsibility

C Centralisation of management control and decision-making

D Flexible patterns of working

For the answer to this question, see the 'Answers' section at the end of the book.

Exam-type questions

Question 1: Classes of strategy

(a) It is recognised in most industrialised, commercial and institutionalised organisations that there are three principal classes of strategy:

- growth;
- corrective; and
- contingency.

You are required to:

(i) explain and compare the three classes; **(5 marks)**

(ii) describe the methods that may be used to secure the objectives of a growth strategy. **(10 marks)**

(b) The profits of C Accessories Ltd have risen over the past 20 years by an average of 10% per annum although, because the company is a major supplier of components to the automotive industry, there have been peaks and troughs. During the period of growth in the automotive industry, C Accessories Ltd's increased profits came from increased sales. More recently such increased sales and profits have stemmed mainly from obtaining a bigger share of a somewhat reducing market.

In recent years many new products have been introduced: currently there are 30 products, as against 15 five years ago. Over the 20-year period the number of customers has fallen from 15 to five, one of whom takes a little over half of C Accessories Ltd's output.

You are required to critically appraise the company's present strategy and recent development, and state your views on its future. **(10 marks)**

(Total: 25 marks)

Question 2: Pharmaceutical companies

Scientists from various countries in the world have researched into and achieved success in mapping the genetic code of human beings. It is considered that this research may identify how serious life-threatening diseases develop. It is believed that this will lead to improved treatments and in time removal of these diseases altogether. Eventually this may result in the Directors of world-class pharmaceutical suppliers facing a conflict of interests. These conflicts may arise because of the need to satisfy the demands of their shareholders in terms of maximised long-term wealth and also the need to discharge social responsibilities by developing treatments which eventually may render its products redundant.

Required:

Discuss the ethical implications of this research for major world-class pharmaceutical companies. In your discussion, comment on how the Directors might reconcile conflicts between satisfying the demands of shareholders and discharging their social responsibilities. **(25 marks)**

For the answers to these questions, see the 'Answers' section at the end of the book.

Feedback to activities

Activity 1

To create the climate that will encourage and reward innovation, managers must do the following things.

- Set clear objectives and spell out the freedom to achieve them.
- Offer recognition and reward for creative behaviour and for tasks well done.
- Encourage new ideas and be willing to listen to subordinates' suggestions.
- Permit more interaction between employees within their own work group and between work groups.
- Accept and allow for failure.

Managers must promote and encourage the following attitudes and motivations.

- The desire for responsibility and accountability for results.
- The willingness to take moderate risks in an attempt to achieve high performance.
- Self confidence and the willingness to make judgements.
- Future orientation to search for and anticipate future opportunities and plan for their successful exploitation.
- The willingness to organise work and obtain resources to achieve goals. Entrepreneurs want to get the job done efficiently.

Activity 2

Area	Among possible aims are to:
General:	• obtain joint synergy; • buy management talent; • buy time while the strategy of the acquiring company develops.
Marketing:	• preserve the balance of market power; • control spheres of influence of potential competitors; • break into a new market (perhaps export or beachhead); • take advantage of joint marketing synergies (for example by way of rationalisation of distribution, advertising, sales organisation and sales costs in general); • reposition markets and products; • obtain the reputation or prestige of the acquired company; • take over 'problem child' products; • obtain a critical mass position.

Area	Among possible aims are to:
Manufacturing:	• acquire technical know-how; • amalgamate manufacturing facilities to obtain synergies (economies of scale, group technology, shared research, rationalisation of facilities and working capital, and so on); • extend manufacturing involvement (for example the provision of field maintenance services).
Procurement of supplies:	• control spheres of supply influence; • safeguard a source of supply for materials; • obtain operating cost synergies; • share the benefits of the suppliers' profitability.
Financial:	• acquire property; • acquire 'cash cow' organisations; • obtain direct access to cash resources; • acquire assets surplus to the needs of the combined businesses and dispose of them for cash; • obtain a bigger asset backing; • improve financial standing (market price and earnings per share); • speculative gain purposes.

Activity 3

There is no legal reason why the visitor should involve himself or herself. However, doing nothing would violate all three principles of social responsibility. In the first place, it is reasonable to suppose that the visitor would prefer to be told of an unsafe action were the position reversed. Bringing it to the operator's attention will not inconvenience or harm the visitor in any way. By acting politely, there is no reason why the affair should lead to embarrassment or loss of dignity.

Note that with a social obligation, there is no obvious penalty if no action is taken. However, society would be much the worse if everyone did so.

Chapter 5

CULTURE AND CORPORATE GOVERNANCE

Syllabus content

- The determinants, importance and role of organisational cultures and ways to improve the effectiveness of an organisation.
- Introduction to corporate governance, including stakeholders and the role of government.

Contents

1 Determinants of culture

2 The importance and role of culture

3 Improving the effectiveness of an organisation

4 Corporate governance

1 Determinants of culture

The term 'culture' is used to encompass the sum total of the beliefs, knowledge, attitudes of mind and customs to which people are exposed in their social conditioning. It is the glue that unconsciously binds members of a group and guides their actions. The culture of an organisation has the potential for providing a competitive advantage and managers who fail to understand the culture of their organisation will find that successful strategic management is difficult to achieve.

Corporate governance is about the relationship between companies and their shareholders, particularly the balance of power between directors and investors. The board of directors in the UK has four principal roles: accountability, supervision, direction and executive action.

1.1 The concept of culture

Business strategies rest on two pillars. There is the tangible business situation – the environment of competitive pressures, the firm's reputation and its technology, level of capital employed and so on. The other is the people in the firm – how they think and feel, organise and are led and how they use their intellect and imagination. This human aspect is often referred to as corporate culture.

DEFINITION

Organisational culture has been defined as 'the commonly held and relatively stable set of beliefs, attitudes, values and norms that exist throughout an organisation'.

There is no shortage of definitions of organisational culture. It has been described, for example, as 'the dominant values espoused by an organisation' and 'the basic assumptions and beliefs that are shared by members of an organisation'. As it relates to organisations, culture is the general pattern of behaviour, shared beliefs and values that members have in common. Culture can be inferred from what people say, do and think. It reflects the underlying assumptions about the way work is performed and what behaviour and actions are encouraged and discouraged.

Handy describes culture as the 'way things are done around here'.

In every organisation there has evolved, over time, a system of beliefs, values, norms of behaviour, symbols, myths and practices that are shared by members of the organisation. The key elements can be shown in a diagram:

Elements of culture

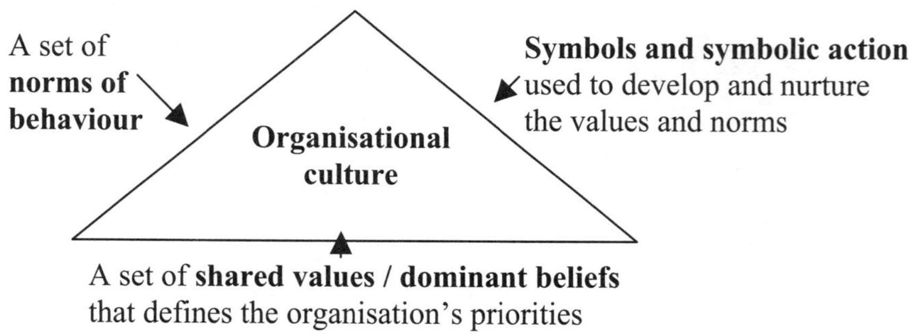

Shared values or dominant beliefs – these underlie the culture by specifying what is important and need to be shared by everyone in the organisation so that they are reinforced and widely accepted. Examples of shared values include a belief in the importance of people as individuals, a management style and an operational focus, such as guaranteeing delivery on time.

Norms – guide people's behaviour, suggesting what is or is not appropriate. The commitment to shared values must be strong enough to develop norms of behaviour or informal rules, which influence the decisions and actions throughout the organisation. For example, in a 'quality service' culture, fellow workers would informally police sloppy work that affects the product or service, without reliance on formal systems.

Symbols or symbolic actions – there are many examples of persistent, consistent and visible symbols and symbolic actions that make up an organisation's culture. These include role models, activities and the organisation's unique roots established by the personal style and experience of the founder and the original mission, e.g. the concept of entertainment developed by Walt Disney includes rituals and other examples such as recruitment techniques, eating lunches and giving impromptu awards.

1.2 Major determinants of culture

KEY POINT

Major determinants of organisational culture include: technology; leadership and the power structure; market factors; the ownership, history, age and size of the organisation; and the environment.

Major determinants of organisational culture include the following:

Technology – can have a profound effect on work patterns and thus on culture. The more complex the technical system, the more elaborate and professional the support staff. The way in which co-ordination between individuals and groups is exercised determines the appropriate form of organisation and thus significantly affects the culture. The more formalised the work the more bureaucratic the operations and thus the more similar they would be e.g. an oil refinery would probably be operated in a very similar way all over the world.

Leadership and the power structure – have a considerable impact and a particularly powerful force is the make-up of the senior management team. The greater the external control exerted on an organisation (e.g. by head office or government), the more centralised and formalised its structure.

Market factors – those most significant to success will tend to be reflected in the make-up of the board of directors of an organisation. For example, a company with an IT director on its board is likely to see information as more important than one that doesn't.

Ownership and history of the organisation – the organisation's founder might have set up a strong set of values and assumptions and even after he or she has retired, these values have their own momentum. Businesses in which the owner is 'hands-on' are likely to have a different culture from those where ownership is divorced from management. An organisation that has only experienced success will have a view of life completely different from a company that has suffered job losses and loss of market share.

Organisational age and size – the older and larger an organisation, the more formalised its behaviour and the more likely it is to be bureaucratic. The larger an organisation, the larger the size of its average unit and the more specialised the jobs and units within it. Each specialisation is likely to be accompanied by an appropriate culture, and thus various cultures will flourish in the organisation.

Environment – the more dynamic an organisation's environment, the more its culture needs to be one that supports flexibility. The more complex an organisation's environment, the more decentralised its structure is likely to be, with a consequent development of cultural diversity.

1.3 Culture and structure

KEY POINT

Handy describes four types of organisational culture:

- Zeus – the power culture
- Apollo – the role culture
- Athena – the task culture
- Dionysus – the person culture.

Harrison and later Handy (in *Gods of Management*) suggests that organisation cultures can be grouped into four basic cultural types, characterised by the concentration of power and hierarchy, the relationship of the individual to the organisation and the centrality of tasks of the individual.

The power culture – Zeus (the god representing the power culture) is a dynamic entrepreneur who rules with snap decisions. This culture tends to rely on a central figure for its strength and has lines of communication which not only radiate out from this centre but link side ways across the organisation. This may be expressed as a web. The boss sits in the centre, surrounded by ever widening circles of intimates and influence. There are few procedures and rules of a formal kind and little bureaucracy.

The dominant influence of the centre results in a structure that is able to move quickly and respond to change and outside threats. This culture is often found in small entrepreneurial organisations but will frequently break down as they grow since the web is more difficult to maintain with size. As might be expected attempts to implement a structured system into this culture are likely to be vigorously resisted both on the grounds of constraining flexibility and unnecessary cost.

KEY POINT

Role culture is equivalent to bureaucracy.

The role culture – Apollo is the god of the role culture or bureaucracy and is perhaps the most readily recognised and common of all the cultural types. Everything and everybody are in their proper place. There is a presumption of logic and rationality. It is based around the job or role rather than the personalities and is epitomised by what we tend to think of as the traditional hierarchical structure.

This kind of culture is best suited to an environment that is relatively stable and a large-sized organisation. Because of the focus on the role this culture tends to be impersonal, and by implication restrictive, suppressing individuals' attempts at any improvements. It doesn't take much thought to work in a role culture. Change is therefore relatively slow and is often only brought about by fear. Although it can adapt, this ability is restricted and a 'role culture' will have problems in surviving a dramatic change. Examples include the civil service and ICI.

KEY POINT

Task culture is concerned with the continuous and successful solution of problems.

The task culture – Athena is the goddess of the task culture, where management is basically concerned with the continuous and successful solution of problems. Performance is judged in terms of results and problems solved.

Although a structure exists it is flexible and capable of being formed and reformed depending upon the task in hand. The organisation is therefore more loosely bound than the role model. Power and respect come from individual knowledge rather than rank or position. People describe their positions in terms of the results they are achieving. A net that can pull its cords this way and that and can regroup at will illustrates this culture. This also means that resources are easily obtained from all parts of the organisation. These cultures are suited to organisations that are concerned with problem solving and short-term one-off exercises – often found in rapidly changing organisations, where groups are established on a short-term basis to deal with a particular change.

Structurally this culture is often associated with the matrix structure. Examples: market research organisations, entertainment industry, computer software design.

KEY POINT

Person culture is built around individuals.

The **person culture** – Dionysus is the god of the existential culture – the person culture (a structure and a culture built around individuals). Although not a common culture for an entire organisation to be based on, it is none the less found in small areas of large companies. The culture is that of educated and articulate individuals – specialists who have come together because of common interest – solicitors, academic researchers, consultants etc. They may use some common office services but generally operate independently. In some instances, a key individual heads a support team of different skills. An example is a barrister in chambers.

Policy makers who have spent their career in, say, a role-orientated culture are likely to develop future policy accordingly. Culture influences what the executive group attends to, how it interprets the information and the responses it makes to changes in the external environment. It is a significant contributor to strategic analysis and the development of strategy. Since culture influences what other members of the organisation attend to, how they interpret this information and react, it is a significant determinant of the success of strategic implementation. Culture influences the ability of the organisation both to conceive and to implement a new strategy.

Activity 1

Name the following types of orientation (or culture):

(a) where the organisation is dominated by a single powerful figure;

(b) where the organisation serves the person;

(c) where there is a strong emphasis on close role definition and the features of bureaucracy are largely present;

(d) where the focus is on task and goal accomplishment.

Feedback to this activity is at the end of the chapter.

1.4 Strategy creation and culture

What kind of culture does an organisation have at present? Miles and Snow propose that by looking at past strategic choices and the dominant culture within an organisation, the likelihood of a new strategy fitting with the current culture can be assessed.

KEY POINT

Miles and Snow identified four distinctive cultural types of organisation: defenders, prospectors, reactors, analysers.

They identified four, distinctive cultural types – *defenders*, *prospectors*, *reactors*, *analysers* – categorised by their approach to innovation and to risk.

Defenders are organisations in which the managers are experts in their organisation's limited area of operation but tend not to search outside their current areas for new opportunities. These organisations have cultures whose stories and rituals reflect historical continuity and consensus. Decision taking is relatively formalised. Organisations implementing a defender strategy need to be efficient and emphasise low costs by maintaining the position of current products. Systems tend to be centralised, emphasising cost efficiency and formal planning.

Prospectors are organisations where the dominant beliefs are more to do with results. They continually search for market opportunities, regularly experimenting with potential responses to emerging environmental trends. An organisation pursuing a prospector's strategy needs to be creative, innovative, flexible, and decentralised and have an emphasis on new product development using ad hoc measures.

Analysers are organisations that exhibit both defender and prospector characteristics. They try to balance risk and profits by using a core of stable products and markets as a source of earnings to move into innovative prospector areas. Analysers follow change, but do not initiate it. An analyser strategy requires simultaneous emphasis on improving operations in the current business and encouraging creativity, innovativeness, flexibility, and decentralisation in new businesses.

Reactors are organisations in which managers are impotent in the face of the change and uncertainty they perceive. Arguably, they do not have a strategy, either deliberate or emergent, at all, unless it is simply to carry on living from hand to mouth, muddling through. Their attributes tend to vary significantly over time.

2 The importance and role of culture

2.1 The organisational iceberg

KEY POINT

Organisations can be seen as having overt, formal aspects on the tip of the iceberg and covert, behavioural aspects hidden underneath.

In their book *Organisational Behaviour*, Hellriegel, Slocum and Woodman suggest that one way to recognise why people behave as they do, is to view an organisation as an iceberg. 'What sinks ships is not always what sailors can see, but what they can't see.'

They portray an organisation as having overt, formal aspects on the tip of the iceberg and covert, behavioural aspects hidden underneath.

- The formal aspects (the visible bits) include aspects such as organisational design, financial resources, customers, technology, formal goals, rules and regulations.
- The covert, behavioural aspects (the hidden bits) include attitudes, personalities, conflict, informal team processes and political behaviour.

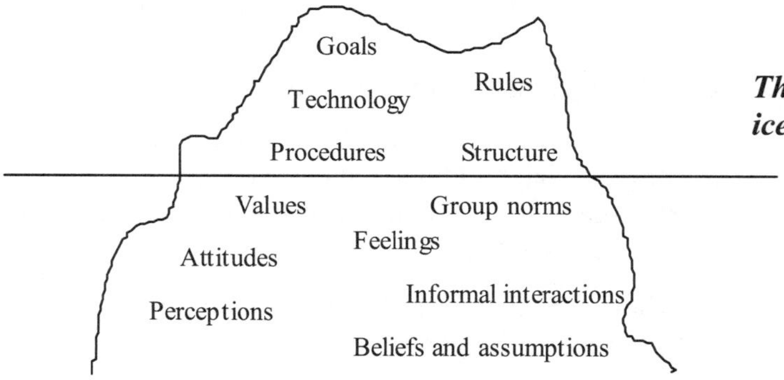

The organisational iceberg

There are four types of icebergs:

- the ones you can see and basically know what they are doing;
- the ones that are half above the water, which means there is still a little bit of mystery, but you have a good idea of what is coming;
- the one that is just below the water level and you only have a general idea of the effect it will have;
- the one that is well below the surface, which you cannot anticipate and you have no idea what it will do.

The managers who can understand the potential effect of the iceberg well below the surface will go a fair way down the journey to success.

The pervasive nature of culture, in terms of 'how things are done around here' and common values, beliefs and attitudes, will have a significant effect on organisational processes such as decision-making, design of structure, group behaviour, work organisation, motivation and job satisfaction, and management control.

2.2 The role of culture

KEY POINT

A culture defines identity and creates boundaries.

First and foremost, a culture defines identity. It communicates a corporate and professional membership to employees within the company and to outsiders. It creates boundaries as to 'This is the way we do things here, not everywhere else'. People in an organisation with a defined culture live and breathe this culture whether they are at work, at home, or at play.

Within an organisation managers can do more than simply understand the culture and work within it. They have the power to alter it.

The beliefs are the manifestations of the deeper aspects of culture. It is easy to see and describe them and relatively easy to alter them through managerial action. For example, managers can change reward systems to promote certain behaviours and can impose sanctions to prevent others. But this is only altering behaviour and specific behaviour at that; it does not alter more fundamental attitudes.

An appreciation of the beliefs is likely to provide insights into the underlying values, and it may be appropriate to use these insights in order to alter the values. If questioning what drives this behaviour unearths the underlying values, then more fundamental change might be possible.

2.3 The importance of culture

Schein suggests that organisational culture is even more important today than it was in the past. Increased competition, globalisation, mergers, acquisitions, alliances, and various workforce developments have created a greater need for:

- coordination and integration across organisational units in order to improve efficiency, quality, and speed of designing, manufacturing, and delivering products and services;
- product innovation;
- strategy innovation;
- process innovation and the ability to successfully introduce new technologies, such as information technology;
- effective management of dispersed work units and increasing workforce diversity;
- cross-cultural management of global enterprises and/or multi-national partnerships;
- construction of hybrid cultures that merge aspects of cultures from what were distinct organisations prior to an acquisition or merger;
- management of workforce diversity;
- facilitation and support of teamwork.

In addition to a greater need to adapt to these external and internal changes, organisational culture has become more important because, for an increasing number of corporations, intellectual as opposed to material assets now constitute the main source of value. Maximising the value of employees as intellectual assets requires a culture that promotes their intellectual participation and facilitates both individual and organisational learning, new knowledge creation and application, and the willingness to share knowledge with others. Culture today must play a key role in promoting:

- knowledge management;
- creativity;
- participative management;
- leadership.

3 Improving the effectiveness of an organisation

3.1 The concept of excellence

A simple distinction can be drawn between strong and weak cultures. A strong culture is marked by the organisation's core values being both intensely held and widely shared. On the other hand, weak cultures show a lack of uniformity and limited commitment. Some writers, noticeably Peters and Waterman in their book *In Search of Excellence*, have suggested that a strong organisational culture is a key factor in determining organisational effectiveness.

The main aspects of culture in 'excellent' companies are as follows.

(a) **A bias for action** – an urgency to produce and complete results rather than analyse obstacles to action. A positive attitude of 'what can we do now' rather than a negative attitude of 'what is preventing us'.

(b) **Hands-on, value driven** – showing a commitment to the organisational values.

(c) **Close to the customer** – a continuous pursuit to understand the customer's needs and improve the quality offered. Peters and Waterman see improving quality as a motivating force for workers as well as affording opportunities for employees to be innovative. Their concern for quality and customer needs must exist in all functions at all levels.

(d) **Stick to the knitting** – no evidence of conglomerate diversification.

(e) **Autonomy and entrepreneurship** – teams and individuals are encouraged to establish their own targets for improvement. An element of competition is regarded as invigorating. This self-improvement drive encourages innovation and a culture based on customer satisfaction.

(f) **Simple form, lean staff** – uncomplicated structures without large numbers of employees at head office.

(g) **Productivity through people** – staff must be treated as intelligent contributors, who are individually valuable and capable of 'extraordinary effort'. Sir John Harvey-Jones in his experience at ICI states that he never ceased to be surprised at the exceptional results that motivated people were capable of achieving.

(h) **Simultaneous tight-loose properties** – tight controls and detailed rules were replaced by common understanding and acceptance of the main guiding values of the organisation. Clearly this philosophy affects a company's recruitment, training and promotion standards and is not attainable overnight. Rather, there is a steady change in the balance between control and trust.

Although a strong organisational culture is a key factor in determining organisational effectiveness, can it be concluded that a strong culture is always desirable? The first point that needs to be made is that the content of the culture must match the objectives and the environment of the organisation. A strong innovative culture, for example, will only work well if the company wishes to innovate and is operating in a dynamic environment. Strong cultures will always be more difficult to change than weak ones. A strong culture might be based on values that are not compatible with organisational effectiveness; for example, certain loyalties may restrict the process of change. Problems can clearly arise in a merger or acquisition situation where two conflicting organisational cultures are brought together.

Though a strong culture may be a liability, the potential benefits should not be forgotten. A strong culture increases commitment to the organisation and the consistency of behaviour of its members. Having a clear mission and agreed values about the means of pursuing it removes ambiguities and can replace the need for more formal controls. An appropriate culture, as Peters and Waterman suggest, can be a crucial factor in determining levels of performance, both for the organisation and for the individual.

An inappropriate culture may be the reason for a company's poor performance. A good example is a public sector organisation about to be privatised. The attitudes of the staff may not be those required to survive in the competitive world in which the organisation will find itself.

Activity 2

What are the potential drawbacks of a strong culture?

Feedback to this activity is at the end of the chapter.

3.2 The influence of the leader

The link between leadership and culture is very strong. Several researchers have shown the personality of the leader is at least as strong an influence on strategy and structure decisions as the environment, technology or any other of the factors commonly associated with strategic decisions.

The culture of the organisation takes much of its nature from leadership, but leaders cannot change a culture by decree. Much of a leader's style is communicated through symbols and rituals, which become part of the cultural web. Peters listed several symbol acts of a leader that can communicate and energise culture change more effectively than any statement of intent, mission statement or other managerial devices.

- *Use of time*: The leader's stated aims will be contrasted with what he or she spends time on. For example, an attempt to energise and empower lower levels of the organisation will fail if the leader spends no time actively encouraging and supporting activities with those levels. Time spent solely telling middle managers what to do communicates all the wrong signals to both middle and junior levels.

- *Use of language*: An idea can be expressed in many different ways, and the leader can do much to influence the way that people interpret and react to events. On a mundane level, the word challenge seems different to the word problem, yet both can refer to the same thing. On a grander scale, language can be used to highlight issues by making them more emotional in some way.

- *Meetings, agenda and minutes*: There are generally too many things to talk about at any meeting, so the leader must assert priorities. Where the leader is attempting a culture change, it is necessary to ensure that the new behaviours are highest on the agenda. For example, having a new policy of customer service means nothing if key meetings never reach the topic in the agenda.
- *Settings*: The leader can do much to influence activity by manipulating the physical spaces and symbols. When Japanese managers take over a British plant, they usually close down the directors' car park and canteen immediately. They arrive at work early, and park their cars next to the gate so that workers will see that their seniors are working longer hours. They take their lunch in canteens with everyone else, and attempt to mix. The symbols are clear to everyone; hard work and teamwork are considered more important than status.

In addition to the above, it is also worth noting that many leaders communicate their purpose to the organisation by variety of actions, such as posting themselves to minor jobs for a short period. This has the secondary effect of improving the quality of management information, as they experience things rather than read performance indicators.

4 Corporate governance

4.1 Introduction

DEFINITION

The Cadbury Committee described **corporate governance** as 'the system by which companies are directed and controlled'.

Corporate governance is a concept, which was introduced in the early 1990s. It was described by the Cadbury Report, as *'the system by which organisations are directed and controlled'.* It can be defined as the way the management of a firm is influenced by many stakeholders, including owners/shareholders, creditors, managers, employees, suppliers, customers, local residents and the government. It is about the way in which corporations (incorporated businesses) are run and who should control them. It is also about the process of governing (running or managing) – how decisions are to be taken and, if by vote, who has the right to vote. Different economies have systems of corporate governance that differ in the relative strength of influence exercised by the stakeholders.

KEY POINT

Four main roles of a board of directors in the UK are:

- accountability;
- supervision;
- direction;
- executive action.

Boards of Directors in the UK have four main roles, which are:

- **accountability** – recognising responsibilities to those making a legitimate demand to know what the organisation is doing and intending to do;
- **supervision** – monitoring and overseeing management performance;
- **direction** – formulating the strategic direction of the organisation in the long term;
- **executive action** – involvement in implementing strategy.

The principal problem of corporate governance is how the providers of capital can ensure that the directors act in their interests. The laws relating to company reporting and auditing have developed in order to answer this problem by delineating the relationships between the directors, the auditors and the shareholders. The three-way relationship between directors, auditors and shareholders has been developed and changed over time, often in response to events such as major corporate collapses due to fraud and other problems.

4.2 Principles of good corporate governance

In recent years, some high profile business frauds and questionable business practices in the UK, the US and other countries have led to doubt being cast on the integrity of business managers. Many large organisations are multinational or trans-national which means that they impact on citizens of several countries across the globe. If things go wrong, they will affect many countries, albeit some more severely than others. This has led to scrutiny of corporate governance and a desire for governments to tighten the regulation around corporate governance further.

Essentially, the pressure for improvements in corporate governance has been based on the view that senior executive directors have enormous powers, and in some cases these can be exercised to promote the self-interests of the director rather than in the interests of the company's shareholders (and other stakeholders).

The degree to which corporations observe basic principles of good corporate governance is an increasingly important factor in investment decisions. Of particular relevance is the relationship between corporate governance practices and the increasingly international character of investment. International capital markets enable corporations to access funds from a much larger pool of investors. Countries with high standards of corporate governance practices are more likely to attract international capital. Although there is no single model for good corporate governance, it is affected by the relationships among participants in the governance system, which are subject to law and regulation, market forces and voluntary adaptations.

The OECD (Organisation of Economic Co-operation and Development) has carried out work among member countries, and identified some common elements, which underlie good corporate governance.

KEY POINT

The OECD Principles of Corporate Governance cover five sections:

- The rights of shareholders
- The equitable treatment of shareholders
- The role of stakeholders
- Disclosure and transparency
- The responsibility of the board.

The OECD Principles of Corporate Governance cover five sections:

- **The rights of shareholders** – the corporate governance framework should protect and facilitate the exercise of shareholders' rights.
- **The equitable treatment of shareholders** – the corporate governance framework should ensure the equitable treatment of all shareholders, including minority and foreign shareholders. All shareholders should have the opportunity to obtain effective redress for violation of their rights.
- **The role of stakeholders** – the corporate governance framework should recognise the rights of stakeholders as established by law and encourage active co-operation between corporations and stakeholders in creating wealth, jobs, and the sustainability of financially sound enterprises.
- **Disclosure and transparency** – the corporate governance framework should ensure that timely and accurate disclosure is made on all material matters regarding the corporation, including the financial situation, performance, ownership, and governance of the company.
- **The responsibility of the board** – the corporate governance framework should ensure the strategic guidance of the company, the effective monitoring of management by the board, and the board's accountability to the company and the shareholders.

These principles can be used by a nation state to design its own corporate governance rules. Auditors may use them to assess the adequacy of any corporate governance regime in the absence of more immediate standards.

4.3 Corporate governance and stakeholders

By their nature large incorporated businesses are usually owned by one group of people (the owners or shareholders) whilst being run by another group of people (the management or the directors). This separation of ownership from management creates an issue of trust. The management have to be trusted to run the company in the interest of the shareholders and other stakeholders. If information were available to all stakeholders in the same form at the same time, corporate governance would not be an issue at all. Armed with the same information as managers, shareholders and creditors would not worry about their money being wasted on useless projects; suppliers would not worry about the customer not fulfilling its part of a supply agreement; and customers would not worry about a supplier firm not delivering the goods or services agreed.

Looking at conventional firms, management will usually have an informational advantage over other stakeholders and hence the need for corporate governance. Good corporate governance means governing the corporation in such a way that the interests of the shareholders are protected whilst ensuring that the other stakeholders' requirements are fulfilled as far as possible. For example, it means that the directors will ensure that the company obeys the law of the land while still remaining in business.

The purpose of the corporate governance structure is to specify the distribution of rights and responsibilities among different participants in the corporation, such as the board, managers, shareholders and other stakeholders, and spell out the rules and procedures for making decisions on corporate affairs. By doing this, it also provides the structure through which the company objectives are set, and the means of attaining those objectives and monitoring performance.

However corporate governance has wider implications and is critical to economic and social well being, firstly in providing the incentives and performance measures to achieve business success, and secondly in providing the accountability and transparency to ensure the equitable distribution of the resulting wealth. The significance of corporate governance for the stability and equity of society is captured in the broader definition of the concept offered by the World Bank: 'Corporate governance is concerned with holding the balance between economic and social goals and between individual and communal goals. The governance framework is there to encourage the efficient use of resources and equally to require accountability for the stewardship of those resources. The aim is to align as nearly as possible the interests of individuals, corporations and society.'

(We discussed the related issue of **corporate social responsibility** in Chapter 4.)

4.4 The role of Government

The broad aims of corporate governance at a political level include the following:

- Creating a framework for the control of large, powerful companies whose interests may not coincide with the national interest.
- Controlling multinationals, which can dominate the local economy.

- Ensuring that companies are answerable to all stakeholders, not just to shareholders.
- Ensuring that companies are run according to the laws and standards of the country and are not in effect states within states.
- Protecting investors who buy shares in the same way as investors are protected who buy any other financial investment product, such as insurance or a pension.

Increased disclosure has been seen as one of the main methods of increasing the interest of shareholders and thus encouraging them to act as a proper check on the managers of the company. Its effectiveness, however, depends on the willingness of shareholders to exercise their influence rather than selling their shares.

Although shareholders were the original focus of corporate governance, current thinking recognises a corporation's obligations to society generally in the form of stakeholders. Corporate governance is therefore concerned with such issues as:

- effectiveness and efficiency of operations;
- reliability of financial reporting;
- compliance with laws and regulations;
- safeguarding of assets.

Summary

- An important analysis of organisational culture distinguishes between power culture, role culture, task culture and person culture.
- An increasingly competitive environment makes it important to foster a suitable organisational culture. Peters and Waterman analyse the factors necessary in the pursuit of excellence.
- Corporate governance is the system by which companies are directed and controlled. The need for effective corporate governance is underlined by principles laid down by the OECD.

Having completed your study of this chapter you should have achieved the following learning outcome.

- Explain the purpose and principles of good corporate governance.

Self-test questions

1 How does Handy define culture? (1.1)

2 Describe the role culture. (1.3)

3 What were the four cultural types that Miles and Snow identified? (1.4)

4 Why is culture important to organisational survival? (2.3)

5 What are the characteristics of a strong culture? (3.1)

6 How would you define corporate governance? (4.1)

7 What are the four main roles of the Board of Directors in the UK? (4.1)

8 Outline the five OECD Principles of Corporate Governance. (4.2)

Multiple-choice question

Question 1

Which of the following is least likely to be a strategy-critical area where it is very important to create a strong 'fit' with strategy?

A Organisation skills, capabilities, and structure

B Rewards and incentives

C Beliefs, attitudes, shared values, and ethics

D Policies, procedures, and support systems

For the answer to this question, see the 'Answers' section at the end of the book.

Exam-type question

Jetstreem

'I have worked for Jetstreem Limited for five years as a driver, delivering parts to its airline customers at Newport airport in the UK. Work is very important to me. I am a sociable person and feel that I understand my place in society through my work and the way others treat me. I enjoy my work, especially the friends I have made at work. The other delivery people are very supportive when we are working under pressure and the bosses seem not to understand the difficulties we have. The work is very stressful because we get many grumbles both from the customers and from the storemen in the company warehouse who see us as nuisances. We try to give the best service to the service managers of the airlines at Newport, and their engineers know that we try our best. Where we do meet opposition, though, is from our own bosses. They are always pressing us to cut corners, to save time and get more orders delivered on each journey, even if it means the customer is kept waiting and an aircraft is kept grounded longer whilst we deliver to other airlines. Often though I find myself adopting the attitudes to customers that the bosses take to me and my mates.

I had previously worked in Singapore for Cathay Pacific and they did things differently. They were a very good company. When I came here I had to learn a lot. One of the main differences I had to learn was that Jetstreem do not welcome delivery people using their own initiative in the way they did things. In Jetstreem, because things were done in a certain way in the past, then it must always be done that way in the future.'

Required:

Explain what is meant by the term 'organisational culture' and describe its principal characteristics. **(10 marks)**

For the answer to this question, see the 'Answers' section at the end of the book.

Feedback to activities

Activity 1

(a) Power orientation

(b) People orientation

(c) Role orientation

(d) Task orientation

Activity 2

Though Peters and Waterman stress the positive benefits of having a strong organisational culture there are also potential drawbacks:

(a) Strong cultures are difficult to change.

(b) Strong cultures may stress inappropriate values.

(c) Where two strong cultures come into contact, e.g. in a merger, then conflicts can arise.

(d) A strong culture may not be attuned to the environment e.g. a strong innovative culture is only appropriate in a dynamic, shifting environment.

Chapter 6

BASICS OF PROJECT MANAGEMENT

Syllabus content

- The definition of a project, project management, and the contrast with repetitive operations and line management.
- 4-D and 7-S models to provide an overview of the project process, and the nine key process areas (PMI) to show what happens during each part of the process.
- Stakeholders (both process and outcome) and their needs.
- Roles of project sponsors, boards, champions, managers and clients.

Contents

1 Project management

2 Project structures and frameworks

3 Project stakeholders

1 Project management

1.1 Definition of a project

The Association of Project Managers defines a project as:

- a human activity that achieves a clear objective against a time scale.

DEFINITION

A project is a temporary process, which has a clearly defined start and end time, a set of tasks and a budget, that is developed to solve a well-defined goal or objective.

A more detailed definition is:

- a project is a temporary process, which has a clearly defined start and end time, a set of tasks and a budget, that is developed to solve a well-defined goal or objective.

A project is considered to be a temporary process because once the end goal is achieved the project is completed. For this reason, the end point of a project or objective needs to be defined at the very beginning of the project to ensure completion.

A project differs from 'ordinary work' that is ongoing and has a mixture of many recurring tasks and more general goals and objectives.

Examples of projects include implementing a new business process, producing a new product, organising a wedding, or decorating the dining room.

Activity 1

Give some examples of projects ranging from simple to complex.

Feedback to this activity is at the end of the chapter.

1.2 Characteristics of a project

The following are the characteristics of a project according to Trevor Young in his book *The Handbook of Project Management.*

KEY POINT

Characteristics of a project:

- has specific purpose;
- is unique;
- focused on the customer;
- not usually routine;
- a series of activities;
- has time constraints;
- is complex;
- has cost constraints.

A project:

- has a specific purpose which can be readily defined;
- is unique, because it is most unlikely to be repeated in exactly the same way by the same group of people to give the same results;
- is focused on the customer and customer expectations;
- is not usually routine work but may contain some routine-type tasks;
- is made up of a series of activities that are linked together, all contributing to the desired result;
- has clearly defined time constraints – a date when the results are required;
- is frequently complex because the work may involve people in different departments, and even on different sites;
- has cost constraints which must be clearly defined and understood to ensure the project remains viable.

When an activity can be classified as a project it falls within the scope of project management.

1.3 The project lifecycle

Projects can be divided into several phases to provide better management control. These phases are collectively known as the project lifecycle.

The project lifecycle

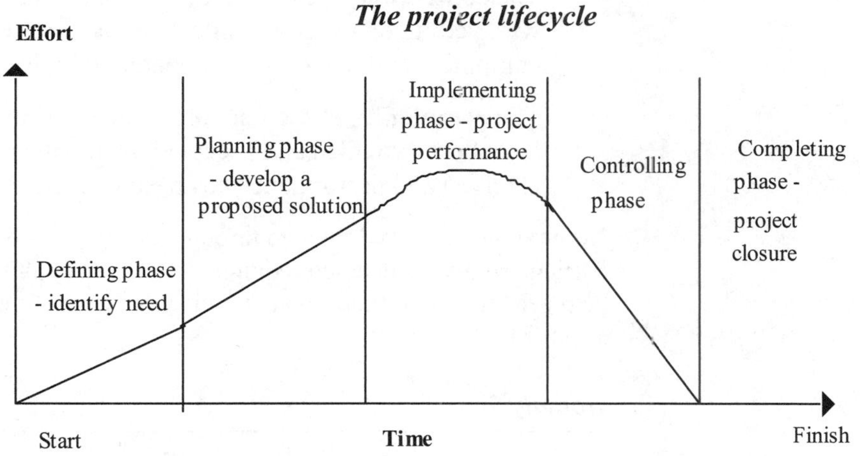

As shown in the diagram, resource use is low at the start of the project, higher towards the end and then falls away rapidly as the project comes to the end.

Risk and uncertainty are highest at the start of the project and the probability of successfully completing it are at their lowest. As the project progresses, the likelihood of successful completion increases.

The stages in the lifecycle are:

- The **defining** or **initiation** phase – involves identification of a need, opportunity or problem. This process will form the basis for the organisation to establish its own requirements and find out whether they are achievable.

  At this stage the feasibility study will be undertaken and a decision made whether or not to proceed. If the project is to be undertaken, then the project team will be brought together and a project initiation document ('PID') prepared. The PID is discussed in more detail in Chapter 7.

- The **planning** phase – will result in the submission of proposals to the customer by the organisations that want to perform the project. The proposals will be evaluated and the most appropriate solution chosen. A feasibility study and cost benefit analysis is generally used in the option evaluation process.

  The project manager responsible for conducting the feasibility study would normally consider:

  Performance / quality: will the project satisfy performance criteria which have been determined? Basically this means will it do the job it is designed to do?

  Cost: is this within the budget set by the organisation or within the capabilities of the organisation to finance it? How do the alternatives compare?

  Timing: are there specific constraints on timing and is it possible to complete the project within these constraints?

  Effect on the organisation: is it feasible in the context of the organisation?

The customer and contractor will then sign a contract.

- The **implementing** phase – is the actual performance of the project, resulting in the accomplishment of the project objective.
- The **controlling** phase – involves monitoring and controlling the project, with vetting on progress, milestones achieved or missed, costs of equipment and manpower compared to budget.
- The **completing** phase – involves the confirmation that all the deliverables have been provided and accepted, all payments have been made and received and performance has been evaluated and appraised.

Note: Some projects do not go through the simple process outlined above. Particularly where detailed requirements are difficult to establish, the lifecycle may be repeated several times in an iterative manner before an acceptable solution is achieved.

Activity 2

Use a personal example, such as a holiday, to describe the stages of the project lifecycle.

Feedback to this activity is at the end of the chapter.

1.4 What is project management?

Project management is much more than the tasks carried out by a project manager. It is a combination of the roles and responsibilities of individuals assigned to the project, the organisational structure that sets out clear reporting arrangements and the set of processes to deliver the required outcome. It ensures that everyone involved knows what is expected of them and helps to keep cost, time and risk under control.

DEFINITION

Project management may be defined as 'the application of knowledge, skills, tools and techniques to project activities in order to meet or exceed stakeholder needs and expectations from a project'.

It can be defined as 'the application of knowledge, skills, tools and techniques to project activities in order to meet or exceed stakeholder needs and expectations from a project'. It is concerned with the allocation of resources in the most effective manner, and ensuring the following:

- the right people at the right time;
- the correct sequence of activities;
- adherence to the project timetable;
- adoption of a formal project plan.

Experience has shown that projects are inherently at risk – through overrunning on time and cost and/or failing to deliver a successful outcome. Such failures are almost invariably caused by:

- poor project definition by the project's owner, perhaps because of insufficient consultation with stakeholders or their failure to be specific about requirements and desired outcomes;
- lack of ownership and personal accountability by senior management;
- inadequately skilled and experienced project personnel;
- inadequate reporting arrangements and decision-making;
- inconsistent understanding of required project activities, roles and responsibilities.

Project management helps to reduce and manage risk. It puts in place an organisation where lines of accountability are short and the responsibilities of individuals are clearly defined. Its processes are clearly documented and repeatable, so that those involved in the project can learn from the experiences of others

1.5 Project management versus line management

A project has important management differences when compared to managing a typical functional department with its continuous, standardised, repetitive work providing an on-going service on essentially a never-ending basis e.g. human resource management or management accounting.

KEY POINT

Project management is different from line management because of:

- its one-off nature;
- strong attention to schedule;
- temporary team assignments.

The key differences between line management (so called because there is a clear line of responsibility) and project management include:

- the one-time nature of projects;
- the strong attention to schedule that is a feature of projects; and
- the temporary and/or partial nature of team assignments.

In contrast a project is a singular task, and project management is simply the management of that task and the resources that are attempting to achieve specific objectives within set timescales and budgets. Examples of a singular task include: constructing a bridge, putting a man on the moon, building a submarine, organising a wedding, developing a piece of courseware, etc.

2 Project structures and frameworks

2.1 Introduction

A project is like a journey; it has a beginning and an end and is undertaken with specific objectives. To have a successful journey or project we need a road map, which indicates what project management sub-processes and activities need to be done, and when.

All projects, regardless of their size, complexity or industry, require a set of defined disciplines for the project to be effectively managed and brought to a successful conclusion. We use models either to gain an overview of the project or to keep the project on track and to reduce the risk of failure. In this section we will be looking at the McKinsey 7S model, Appreciative Inquiry (AI), the Project Management Body of Knowledge (PMBOK) and we briefly introduce the key processes of PRINCE 2.

2.2 McKinsey's 7S model

KEY POINT

The McKinsey 7S model describes Strategy, Structure, Systems, Staff, Skills, Style and Shared Values.

The 7S framework for managers outlines seven distinct factors ideally involved in managing an organisation – Strategy, Structure, Systems, Staff, Skills, Style, and Shared Values.

The McKinsey 7S model (shown below) is used to identify all the areas that make up an organisation.

The 7-S model

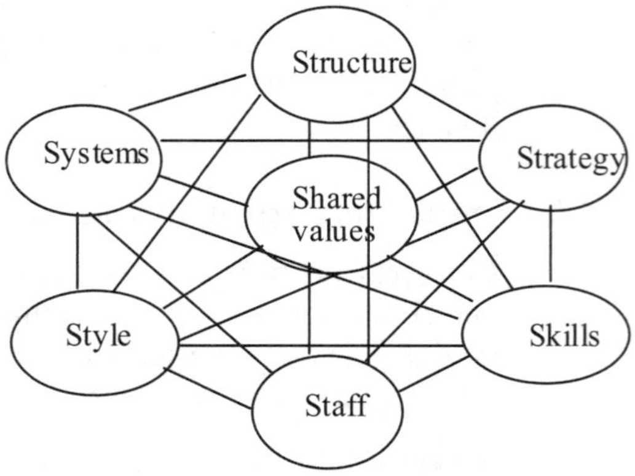

The model can be used as a tool for analysing an organisation's strengths and weaknesses or as a more detailed analysis of the critical success factors for a project. A key emphasis of both is to see how each of the 7Ss inter-relate – changing one can impact the others.

In the context of project management, the constituent parts of the 7S model are:

Strategy – this refers to how the project fits into the organisation's strategic plans, in terms of competitive strategy, expansion plans, resource plans, etc.

Structure – this refers to how the project will be organised within the formal structure of the overall organisation (e.g. division of tasks, responsibility and authority, degree of hierarchy, presence of internal market, extent of centralisation or decentralisation, process based, levels of support, functional delineation of duties, etc.).

Systems – this includes manual and automated systems, procedures, tools and processes that direct the performance of work, including how information moves around the organisation. Key issues for project management could include an analysis of which systems the project will use/impact, whether they need to be changed, whether existing systems deliver the standards of quality required, etc.

Staff – staffing issues are always a key factor in successful project management. (e.g. motivation, group management, abilities, working conditions, staffing levels required to achieve timescales, career advancement, attitude toward and of the staff, etc)

Style – this refers to how key managers behave in order to achieve the organisation's goals. It can also include the 'cultural' style of the organisation. A key issue is thus ensuring that the style of management adopted within a project is consistent with the underlying cultural mix.

Skills – this refers to the distinctive capabilities of key personnel or the organisation as a whole. For a project a key issue lies in ensuring that the organisation has the skill required to deliver the required level of performance/quality. A more strategic view involves looking at how the project will enhance such skills.

Shared values – these are the guiding beliefs as to why the organisation exists, the significant principles or guiding concepts that an organisation instils as values in its members.

2.3 The 4-D model of Appreciative Inquiry (AI)

A traditional Appreciative Inquiry is based on four steps:

1 Discover
2 Dream
3 Design
4 Deliver

KEY POINT

Appreciative Inquiry is based on four steps (the AI 4-D Cycle) – Discover, Dream, Design and Deliver.

Appreciative Inquiry (AI) is an approach to organisational development and change. It is based on the premise that every organisation is dynamic in nature. It therefore has the ability to intentionally move in the direction of its focus. So if an organisation sees only its problems, deficits, or weaknesses, that is what it tends to reflect; whereas, if it seeks to discover, value and highlight the best of what already exists in order to collectively imagine and dream about what it might become, it opens itself to limitless possibilities for positive sustainable change. The key then to creating organisational change is as simple as knowing where to direct the organisation's attention.

The AI 4-D cycle

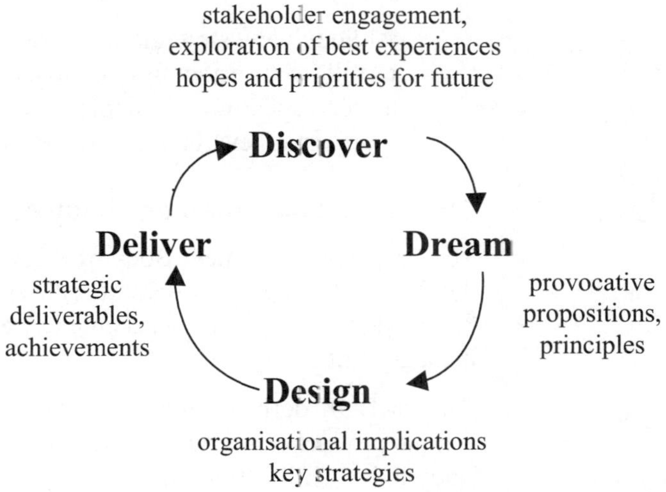

1 Discover

In the first stage, a series of questions is set to stimulate the discovery of excellence and achievement in an organisation. For example, questions might include: 'What have we got to build on?' 'What works best around here?' 'Can you describe a time when you think the team/organisation performed really well?', 'What were the circumstances during that time?' 'When are you most proud to be associated with the team/organisation?' 'What's the best possible outcome for you; how best may organisational strengths be employed?' 'Who will be impacted by change in/out of the organisation; who needs to be engaged to make it work?

2 Dream

During the 'Dream' phase ('imagining what might be'), a future vision is developed based on the common themes that surfaced through the examination of past excellence. The group develops a picture of the ideal future, grounded in the organisation's reality. What could the world look like if our moments of exceptional success were the norm? The process provides people with the opportunity to exercise their imaginative competence based on their best experiences, their core human values, their appreciation of interdependencies and their collective goodwill.

3 Design

Questions relate to what would be ideal, how we can make it work and what conceptual, behaviour, and operational changes we need to make.

Hard work is willingly undertaken here as concept teams, project teams, task forces and working parties form voluntarily to work through 'making it happen'. Through consensus, short and long-term goals are developed to achieve the dream based on what the model calls a 'provocative proposition'. Examples of provocative propositions are 'In eight months we will have a fully functional membership database that is fully accurate and is the key to tracking, managing and forecasting superior customer service needs.'

4 Deliver

The 4D cycle evolves through 'Design' to the 'Deliver' phase. This is the action planning and execution stage. Strategies and plans are put in place to meet the goals of the provocative proposition, and roles and responsibilities are assigned. Reflection on key measures of effectiveness, ways of knowing, recognising and acknowledging what has been achieved, are encouraged.

Although any strategic or operational planning methodology can be used, to follow AI principles you must maintain a positive mindset and involve a broad spectrum of people throughout your organisation. It also involves monitoring, evaluation and feedback.

2.4 The Project Management Body of Knowledge (PMBOK)

The Project Management Body of Knowledge (PMBOK), which is adopted by the Project Management Institute (PMI), is a collection of processes and knowledge areas generally accepted as best practice within the project management discipline.

DEFINITION

The Project Management Body of Knowledge (PMBOK) is a collection of processes and knowledge areas accepted as best practice within the project management discipline.

The PMBOK defines a **project** as 'a temporary endeavour undertaken to create a unique product or service' and defines **project management** as 'application of knowledge, skills, tools, and techniques to project activities in order to meet or exceed stakeholder needs and expectations from the project.' It then goes on to discuss the context in which the project is managed, such as project phases and life cycle, project stakeholders, organisational influences, key general management skills needed by the project manager, and the various socio-economic influences on the project.

After defining and setting the stage for project management, the PMBOK provides a description of the project management process and key knowledge areas. The high-level processes defined include:

- **Initiating processes** – recognising that a project or phase should begin and committing to do so.
- **Planning processes** – devising and maintaining a workable scheme to accomplish the business need that the project was undertaken to address.
- **Executing processes** – co-ordinating people and other resources to carry out the plan.
- **Controlling processes** – ensuring that project objectives are met by monitoring and measuring progress and taking corrective action when necessary.

- **Closing processes** – formalising acceptance of the project or phase and bringing it to an orderly end.

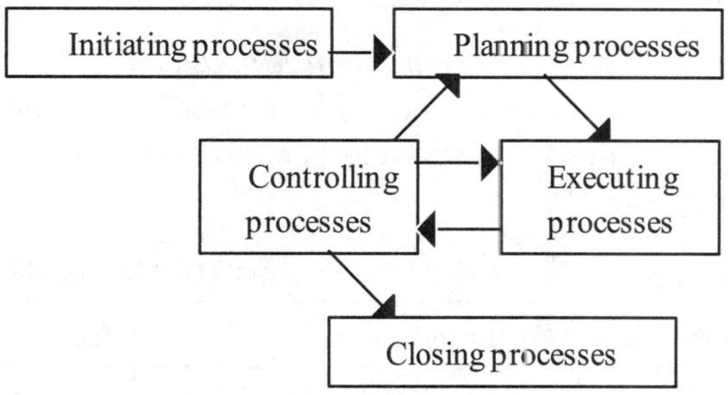

High-level processes

Processes overlap and interact throughout a project or phase. Processes are described in terms of:

- inputs (documents, plans, designs, etc);
- tools and techniques (mechanisms applied to inputs);
- outputs (documents, products, etc).

Within each high-level process, the document defines the various sub-processes such as core processes (activity planning and resource planning) and facilitating processes (risk management and team development).

The PMBOK describes nine Project Management Knowledge Areas:

1 *Project Integration Management* – processes for ensuring that the various elements of the project are properly coordinated.

2 *Project Scope Management* – processes for ensuring that the project includes all the work required and only the work required to complete the project successfully. Before commencing a project, it is vital to define and control what is or what is not to be included as projects may involve a few work tasks or many thousands.

3 *Project Time Management* – processes for ensuring timely completion of the project. All projects are finite, and time ranks as one of the main limits.

4 *Project Cost Management* – processes for ensuring that the project is completed within the approved budget. All projects must have a budget.

5 *Project Quality Management* – processes for ensuring that the project will satisfy the needs for which it was undertaken. As a project manager, a common pitfall is to get buried in day-to-day operations and forget about your real goals – to meet the project's goals with appropriate quality.

6 *Project Human Resource Management* – processes required to make the most effective use of the people involved in the project. Managing and allocating resources is an integral role of the project manager, and leading and managing people on projects is no exception.

7 *Project Communications Management* – processes required to ensure timely and appropriate generation, collection, dissemination, storage, and ultimate distribution of project information. Critical links among people, ideas, and information are necessary for success in projects. Everyone involved in projects must be prepared to send and receive communications and must understand how the communications they are involved in as individuals affect the process as a whole.

8 *Project Risk Management* – processes concerned with identifying, analysing and responding to project risk. Risk management is a continuous process that starts at the initiation of the project and proceeds until the project is completed.

9 *Project Procurement Management* – processes for acquiring goods and services from outside the performing organisation. The acquisition of goods and services is a vital process to facilitate the project's scope of work.

These overlap the five high level processes as follows:

	Initiating	***Planning***	***Executing***	***Controlling***	***Closing***
Integration Management		Project plan development	Project plan execution	Integrated change control	
Scope Management	Initiation	Scope planning Scope definition		Scope verification Scope change control	
Time Management		Activity definition Activity sequencing Activity duration estimating Schedule development		Schedule control	
Cost Management		Resource planning Cost estimating Cost budgeting		Cost control	
Quality Management		Quality planning	Quality assurance	Quality control	
Human Resource Management		Organisational planning Staff acquisition	Team development		
Communications Management		Communications planning	Information distribution	Performance reporting	Administrative closure
Risk Management		Risk management planning Risk identification Qualitative risk analysis Quantitative risk analysis Risk response planning		Risk monitoring and control	
Procurement Management		Procurement planning Solicitation planning	Solicitation Source selection Contract administration		Contract closeou

3 Project stakeholders

3.1 Outcome and process stakeholders

> **KEY POINT**
>
> Outcome stakeholders have an interest in seeing the project's outcomes achieved.
>
> Process stakeholders have an interest in how the project is conducted.

We discussed organisational stakeholders in Chapter 1.

'Satisfy stakeholders!' is the project manager's mantra. For successful projects, it is not enough to deliver on the customer's demands; projects have to meet all stakeholder expectations. Identifying stakeholders is a primary task because all the important decisions during the initiation, planning and execution stages of the project are made by these stakeholders.

Stakeholders are those individuals or groups who will be affected by the project. There are essentially two types of stakeholders:

- outcome stakeholders have an interest in seeing that the project's objectives are achieved; whilst
- process stakeholders have an interest in the way in which the project is conducted.

Many stakeholders are both outcome and process stakeholders. They could include senior managers whose business areas are directly or indirectly involved, the end users (including customers outside the organisation), suppliers and partners.

It is important to identify all stakeholders – not just the obvious stakeholders such as the project sponsor and project manager. In a larger sense, anyone who participates in the project (process) or is impacted by its results (output) is a stakeholder. Each stakeholder has an essential contribution to make and all stakeholder expectations need to be met. The contribution made by different people to the project is the principal criterion for identifying stakeholders.

Effective project organisation facilitates management of the stakeholders' interests, including the resolution of conflicting objectives and representation of end-users who may not be directly involved in the project. Stakeholders' interests can be managed through user panels providing input to the requirement specification. For larger projects, there is usually a project board, with a senior individual nominated to represent the stakeholders' interests

3.2 Project sponsor or organisation

> **KEY POINT**
>
> The term 'project sponsor' is a generic term given to the source of the project manager's authority.

The organisation is responsible for project selection and the approval of the project budget. The term 'project sponsor' is a generic term given to the source of the project manager's authority. He or she may be the owner, financier, client or their delegate. The sponsor acts as agent of the organisation to ensure that the project achieves the objectives set by the organisation (such as cost, quality and time). The sponsor is also responsible for reporting progress to the organisation and supporting the project manager.

The project sponsor, of course, remains a key stakeholder. The role accrues most profitably to the stakeholder who:

- stands to gain the most if the project succeeds;
- stands to lose the most if the project fails; and
- controls the resources, or has the means to control the resources, necessary to deliver the project.

The success of the sponsor role (and hence the project) is dependant, in part, on the extent to which these attributes coincide in one person. This is one reason why projects in which the sponsor is forced to use 'free' internal resources have less chance of success – the sponsor lacks adequate leverage to control these resources.

It is the sponsor's responsibility to control the project budget and ensure that the organisation's needs are met. This entails being responsible for the control of the project within the organisation, and providing a channel of communication between the project manager and senior management to report on progress and future developments.

Often a project involves change – a state that invariably meets with resistance. It is for this reason that the support of senior management is required. Ideally the project sponsor needs to be someone with sufficient authority to be able to progress the project in the face of difficulties and who has sufficient personal interest in the project to see it through. The project sponsor:

- agrees project outcomes;
- authorises definition of project;
- controls provision of resources;
- ensures delivery of project;
- promotes project at high level;
- owns project risks and resolves major problems.

3.3 Project owner

The project owner is responsible for financing the project. He or she is the person for whom the project is being carried out and consequently will be interested in the end result being achieved and the needs/requirements met.

3.4 Project customer/user

KEY POINT

The user group should, ideally, consist of at least one user from each of the departments affected by the proposals.

These are the individuals or groups that will use the end product, process or service produced by the project. The user group should, ideally, consist of at least one user from each of the departments affected by the proposals, as well as the project manager and team leader/s. This group is an ideal forum for users to express their concerns; to highlight problems affecting users as the system develops; for solutions to be explored; for obtaining user feedback. Although its role is advisory, management generally accept the merits of responding to the issues raised.

3.5 The project steering committee

This committee would typically consist of representatives from the user departments who are members of the user group; the project team leaders; the project manager and members of senior management who are responsible for either the staff or the functional areas affected by the project. The role of the steering committee is to:

- facilitate the discussion of user concerns in a forum where recommended courses of action can be provided due to the presence of senior level staff;
- review the project's current position in terms of time, resources, costs and scope;
- analyse the likely reason and impact of any departure from the plan, and evaluate alternative remedial action;

- recommend modifications to the project, with a view to remedy current or anticipated departures, or to take into account adjustments in the users' requirements from the system;
- provide advice with regard to the formulation of policy relating to the operation of the information system within the organisation at all levels.

Activity 3

A steering committee is formed to monitor and control the feasibility study for the introduction of a management information system in a medium sized company. Who might be a member of this committee?

Feedback to this activity is at the end of the chapter.

3.6 Vendors and specialists

In any project, many of the components of the solution may be bought in from suppliers or vendors. These individuals and organisations will have an interest in the project as they see it as a source of profit, and they will therefore want to ensure that they supply the right product or service and are paid on time.

Most complex projects enlist the help and support of specialists from within the organisation. These individuals and groups will each have their own objectives, and may not see the project as their first priority. Typically, specialists come from human resources (personnel), purchasing, production, IT, quality control and engineering.

3.7 Project manager and project team

The project manager is the person who takes ultimate responsibility for ensuring the desired result is achieved on time and within budget. He or she will co-ordinate a project from initiation to completion, using project management and general management techniques.

The project team consists of individuals brought together purely for the purpose of undertaking a specific project. The size of the team and the period of their existence will be determined by the nature of the project.

With large development projects, there may be several leaders, each responsible for a part of the project team and reporting to the project manager. The team leader will typically be responsible for:

- planning and organising the work of the team members on a regular basis (daily/weekly);
- constantly supervising the activities of each individual team member;
- providing advice or taking appropriate decisions in the case of technical difficulties;
- co-ordinating and overseeing intercommunication between user departments and other project teams;
- reporting to the project manager and/or user group and, where problems have been encountered, providing advice on feasible solutions;
- reporting back to the team members any modifications to the project resulting from decisions made at a more senior level;
- supervising the implementation of any changes to the planned activities or schedules resulting from control activities.

3.8 Project champions and agents of change

Project success relies on the project manager's ability to implement change. In order to do this he/she must enlist a team that is responsible for, and capable of, making that change happen.

A project champion – someone who grasps the benefits of and is enthusiastic about the project – can be one of the most critical elements of any project team. He or she:

- has the vision to get the project going;
- pushes for a project to be accepted where there are competing priorities;
- keeps things going when difficulties arise.

The project champion is often a senior customer (user) who wants a particular capability or a senior supplier (technician) who wants to try out the latest 'toy'.

If these people are too senior to work on the project team directly, they will help enlist champions to represent them and so will be no less vocal and visible in their support of the project and its goals.

Change agents are those people in the business that have the expertise that the project team requires to successfully deliver the project and will ensure that all of the requirements of the business are met. They are the people that will assure that the end-users' expectations are met. They are the conduit to the end-user community, and should form the core delivery team when it comes to delivering the product to the ultimate users.

3.9 Role of key stakeholders in the project

Project stakeholder management is an important discipline. The benefits of using a stakeholder-based approach are that:

- You can use the opinions of the most powerful stakeholders to shape your projects at an early stage. Not only does this make it more likely that they will support you, their input can also improve the quality of your project.
- Gaining support from powerful stakeholders can help you to win more resources – this makes it more likely that your projects will be successful.
- By communicating with stakeholders early and frequently, you can ensure that they fully understand what you are doing and understand the benefits of your project – this means they can support you actively when necessary.
- You can anticipate what people's reaction to your project may be, and build into your plan the actions that will win people's support.

Stakeholder analysis (discussed in Chapter 1) is the first stage of this, where you identify and start to understand your most important stakeholders. List all the people and/or groups who are affected by the project or the outcomes of the project in any way. Try to work out the nature of their interest and their perspective on the project (how they are likely to view it). Having done this try to work out their importance to the project (stakeholders are important if they can have a big impact on the success of the project – e.g. they control the budget). The next stage is to prioritise them by power and interest, and to plot this on a Power/Interest Grid (see Section 6.2 of Chapter 1).

Stakeholder planning is the next step, to get an understanding of how you need to manage your stakeholders. This could mean looking at ways of keeping them informed about progress, undertaking further research to understand their perspective more accurately or changing the way the project is designed or performed in order to keep them happy

You might start with a Stakeholder Planning Sheet. This is a table with the following column headings:

Stakeholder Name
Power
Interest
Key Issues
Current Status – Advocate, supporter, neutral, critic, blocker
Desired Support – High, medium or low
Desired Project Role (if any)
Actions Desired (if any)
Messages Needed
Actions and Communications

Using this table, you can work through a planning exercise using the steps below:

- Update the planning sheet with information from the stakeholder analysis, in the 'Power' and 'Interest' columns.
- Work out **what you want from each stakeholder**: think through the levels of support you want from them and the roles you would like them to play (if any). Think through the actions you would like them to perform. Write this information down in the 'Desired Support', 'Desired Project Role' and 'Actions Desired' columns.
- Identify the **messages you need to convey** given any potential barriers (identified in the 'Key issues' column). Typical messages will show the benefits to the person or organisation of what you are doing, and will focus on key performance drivers such as increasing profitability or delivering real improvements. (This is part of the process of stakeholder marketing, discussed in Chapter 10.)
- Identify **actions and communications**. With the time and resource you have available, identify how you will manage the communication to, and the input from, your stakeholders. Focus on the high-power/high-interest stakeholders first, and use the power/interest grid strategies: keep your best supporters on-board; win over or neutralise sceptics; where you need the active support of people who are not currently interested in what you are doing, engage them. Where appropriate, let people know as early as possible of any difficult issues that may arise, and discuss with them how you can minimise or manage any impact.

Good stakeholder management helps you to manage the politics that can often come with major projects. It helps you win support for your projects and eliminates a major source of project and work stress.

Summary

- Projects go through a lifecycle involving the following phases: defining; planning; implementing; controlling; completing.
- Control of projects can be improved by the use of structured frameworks such as the McKinsey 7S model or the appreciative inquiry model.
- The project management body of knowledge is a collection of processes and knowledge areas generally accepted as best practice.
- Project managers must attempt to satisfy the objectives of both outcome stakeholders and process stakeholders.

Having completed your study of this chapter you should have achieved the following learning outcomes.

- Identify a project and its attributes.
- Apply suitable structures and frameworks to projects to identify common management issues.
- Produce a basic outline of the process of project management.
- Identify the characteristics of each phase in the project process.
- Demonstrate the role of key stakeholders in the project.
- Identify stakeholder groups and recommend basic strategies for the management of their perceptions and expectations.

Self-test questions

1 How does a project differ from ordinary work? (1.1)

2 Draw a simple project lifecycle diagram. (1.3)

3 Distinguish project management from line management. (1.5)

4 Identify the constituent parts of the 7S model. (2.2)

5 What are the four stages in the Appreciative Inquiry cycle? (2.3)

6 Describe three of the nine project management knowledge areas. (2.4)

7 Explain the differences between an outcome stakeholder and a process stakeholder. (3.1)

8 What is a project champion? (3.8)

Multiple-choice questions

Question 1

The McKinsey 7S model has three hard and four soft Ss. The four soft ones are:

A Systems, Staff, Skills and Style

B Skills, Style, Structure and Systems

C Staff, Skills, Strategy and Shared Values

D Staff, Skills, Style and Shared Values

Question 2

A traditional Appreciative Inquiry is based on the following four steps (the AI 4-D Cycle):

A Discover, Dream, Define and Deliver

B Define, Dream, Design and Deliver

C Discover, Dream, Design and Deliver

D Discover, Define, Design and Deliver

For the answer to these questions, see the 'Answers' section at the end of the book.

Exam-type question

Project management

A colleague of yours at work, Jill Jackson, has asked you for some advice. She is the project manager in charge of introducing the new information system that is planned this year and is aware that project management techniques will need to be used.

Required:

(a) In a memo to Jill, list the features which distinguish project management from 'line' or 'business as usual' management. **(10 marks)**

(b) Highlight the management problems she is likely to face. **(10 marks)**

(Total: 20 marks)

For the answer to this question, see the 'Answers' section at the end of the book.

Feedback to activities

Activity 1

Examples of projects and project objectives could include:

- arranging a dinner party;
- organising a holiday;
- hosting a conference;
- designing and producing a brochure for publicity;
- building an extension to a house;
- modernising a factory;
- designing and implementing a computer system;
- re-building a city after a tornado.

Activity 2

Using a holiday, we can describe the stages of the project lifecycle.

- **Identify the need** – you have been working hard and feel a holiday will make you feel better. A friend has suggested visiting a place that is very interesting archeologically.
- **Develop a proposed solution** – pick up brochures from the travel agents, look on Teletext and sites on the Internet to find a suitable venue. Check that the prices, times, modes of travel, health and political restrictions are all favourable. Buy a travel guide and note the places of interest. Check that the holiday chosen fulfils all the objectives and then book it at the best price available. Start planning the other aspects of the holiday – the clothes, passport, excursions and luggage.
- **Project performance** (including the monitoring and control) – go on holiday and, whilst enjoying yourself, make sure that the travel arrangements and accommodation are as expected and all the planned trips can be achieved within budget.
- **Project closure** – return home, evaluate and appraise the holiday and get back to work to pay for the next trip.

Activity 3

Membership is bound to vary in accordance with the kind of project involved but the steering committee might include the information director or a senior IS staff member, accountants for technical financial advice relating to costs and benefits and a senior user manager as well as representatives from the user departments who are members of the user group; the project team leaders; the project manager and members of senior management who are responsible for either the staff or the functional areas affected by the project.

Chapter 7

TOOLS FOR PROJECT MANAGERS

Syllabus content

- Key tools for project managers (e.g. Work Breakdown Structure, network diagrams [Critical Path Analysis], Gantt charts, resource histograms, establishment of gates and milestones).

Contents

1 Project management tools

2 Network analysis

1 Project management tools

1.1 Types of project management tools

A project manager has a range of project management tools available to assist with the planning and control of individual systems projects. These tools have been refined and developed over the years, but they are all designed to improve the effectiveness of the project management process.

Based on the five-stage process outlined in the previous chapter, the main tools available to managers are as follows:

Project stages

Managerial stages and tools and techniques

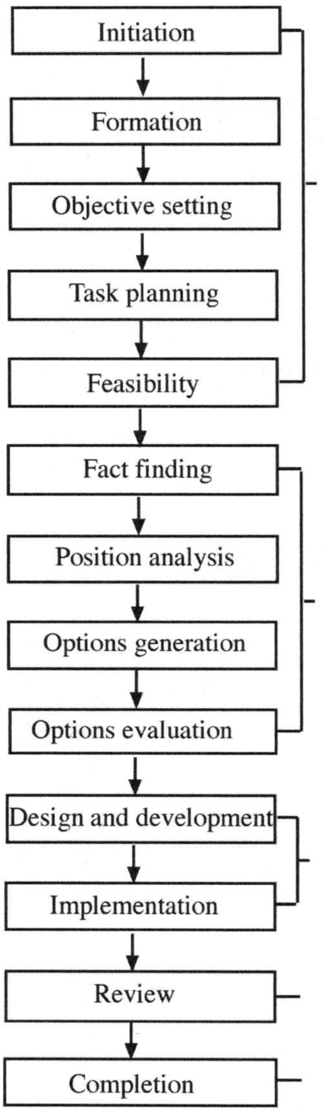

1. Initiation stage

Project initiation document
Work breakdown structure
Cost breakdown structure
Budget schedule
Task list
Network diagram
List of resources
Feasibility study - cost-beneft analysis

2. Planning stage

SWOT analysis
Scenario building
NPV
Work breakdown structure
Gantt charts
Critical path analysis
PERT
Resource histogram

3. Implementing stage

Budget report
Progress report

4. Controlling stage

Cost analysis

5. Completing stage

Completion report
Post completion audit

KEY POINT

Some project management tools:

- Project initiation document
- SWOT analysis
- Work breakdown structure
- Budget
- Gantt chart
- Resource histogram
- Network analysis/ critical path analysis.

The **project initiation document** (or PID) – sometimes called a **statement of work** or **project charter**. This is a formal document listing the goals, constraints and success criteria for a project. When all the stakeholders in a project have agreed the document, it will be referred to as a means of resolving disagreements about the project as it progresses.

SWOT analysis – outlining the strengths, weaknesses, opportunities and threats facing the project.

Work breakdown structure (WBS) – a breakdown of the 'work' involved in the project into smaller and smaller parts, until the project consists of a series of 'work packages', which can be put into the project plan as activities.

Budget – showing the proposed expenditure for each month of the project. This will be updated as the project progresses with the actual expenditure and the reason for any variances.

Gantt charts – showing the activities of a project as a bar chart with the start and finishing times clearly identified.

Resource histogram – a stacked bar chart showing the number and mix of staff required over the duration of a project.

Gates and milestones – partitioning the project into identifiable and manageable phases

Network analysis/critical path analysis (CPA) – breaking down a project into its constituent activities, and presenting these activities in diagrammatic form.

We will look at each of these in turn

1.2 Project initiation document

KEY POINT

A PID should contain at least the following sections:

- Purpose statement
- Scope statement
- Deliverables
- Cost and time estimates
- Objectives
- Stakeholders
- Chain of command.

The project initiation document (PID), sometimes called a 'statement of work' or 'project charter', is a formal document listing the goals, constraints and success criteria for the project – the rules of the game. The PID, once written, is subject to negotiation and modification by the various stakeholders of the project. Once they formally agree its content it becomes the document that is referred to in the case of any disagreement later as to precisely what the project was intended to achieve. According to Eric Verzuh, a PID should contain at least the following sections:

- **Purpose statement**. This explains why the project is being undertaken.
- **Scope statement**. This puts boundaries to the project by outlining the major activities. It is important to include this section in order to prevent 'scope creep', where additional activities are added during the project making achievement of the cost and time objectives totally impossible.
- **Deliverables**. What are the main outcomes expected from the project? Deliverables tend to be tangible elements of the project, such as reports, assets and other outputs.
- **Cost and time estimates**. Even at this early stage, it is a good idea for the project team to have some feel for the organisation's expectations in terms of the project budget. These estimates will necessarily be modified later in the project, but are necessary to give a starting point for planning.
- **Objectives**. A clear statement of the mission, critical success factors and **milestones of the project.**

- **Stakeholders**. A list of the major stakeholders in the project and their interest in the project.
- **Chain of command**. A statement (and diagram) of the project organisation structure

The PRINCE methodology (see next chapter) also favours the use of a PID, and suggests the content should include the following:

Terms of reference

Acceptance criteria

Project organisation and responsibilities

Outline project plans

Detailed plan for the first stage of the project

A statement of the business case for the project

An assessment of the business risks associated with the project

Product descriptions

Project issues

Whichever of these structures are used for the PID, and they are very similar, the document should be signed off by all the stakeholders before any further work commences.

1.3 SWOT analysis

SWOT analysis is a commonly used business planning tool. Although often carried out on an organisation as part of the strategic planning process, it can be used at the early stages of a project, to assess the starting position, or as part of a periodic report to the project sponsor to summarise progress and raise issues.

The **internal appraisal** should identify:

- **Strengths** – the organisation's strengths that the project may be able to exploit. These are the things that are going well (or have gone well) in the project e.g. the skills that are prized, major successes, parts of the project that are well received by the users or were completed early.
- **Weaknesses** – organisational weaknesses that may impact on the project. These are things that are going badly (or have gone badly) in the project e.g. the skills that are lacking, major failures, parts of the project that are poorly received by the users or were completed late.

The **external appraisal** should identify:

- **Opportunities** – events or changes outside the project (elsewhere in the organisation or its business environment) that can be exploited to the advantage of the project (such as growth in market demand, or new technological possibilities).
- **Threats** – events or changes outside the project (elsewhere in the organisation or its business environment) that should be defended against e.g. competitors' actions, declining economy, legislation, etc.

The four parts of the SWOT analysis are shown in the diagram below.

Strengths	**Weakness**
- The things that are going well (or have gone well) in the projects - The skills that are prized - Major successes - Parts of the project that are well received by the users or were completed early.	- The things that are going badly (or have gone badly) in the projects - The skills that area lacking - Major failures - Parts of the project that are poorly received by the users or were completed late.
Opportunities - Events or changes outside the project (elsewhere in the organisation or its business environment) that can be exploited to the advantage of the project - Things likely to go well in the future.	**Threats** - Events or changes outside the project (elsewhere in the organisation or its business environment) that should be defended against - Things likely to go badly in the future.

Activity 1

The internal and external appraisals of SWOT analysis will be brought together and it is likely that alternative strategies will emerge. Which technique from the following list will management probably adopt?

(a) Major strengths and threats can be exploited.

(b) Major strengths and profitable opportunities can be exploited.

(c) Major weaknesses and opportunities can be developed into strategies.

(d) Major weaknesses and strengths will be identified to find alternative strategies.

Feedback to this activity is at the end of the chapter.

1.4 Work breakdown structure to identify resource needs

KEY POINT

Work breakdown structure identifies the stages of a project beginning with the whole project, and then continually breaking down the work until the smallest unit can be identified.

Work breakdown structure (or WBS) is a hierarchical ('family tree') view of the way a project is structured: in other words, a formal version of a project outline. It is produced by:

- identifying the key elements;
- breaking each element down into component parts;
- continuing to break down until manageable **work packages** (tasks or activities) have been identified. These can then be allocated to the appropriate person.

This exercise is the best way of discovering the work that must be done, as well as determining the resources required. The sequencing of tasks and the priorities and pitfalls also become more apparent as the project is broken down. Note, however, that this is *not* a schedule: a WBS is constructed before developing any kind of project time line.

The set of plans or forms produced from the work breakdown structure can then be used for:

- Defining and controlling scope – scope management is the most common project management problem. Organisations need the WBS as a basis of configuration management.
- Communicating responsibilities – this provides the framework for subsequent delegation of effort.
- Estimating, allocating, and accumulating cost – the project team can capture and budget cost in each work package, and the intermediate levels of detail.
- Performance management – work is managed at the work package level, so the project manager can verify the acceptability of work.
- Risk management – work packages provide inputs to risk identification as well as a way to assign responsibility to risk. The WBS itself provides a framework for describing all project risk.

Here is an example of work breakdown structure for a house-building project.

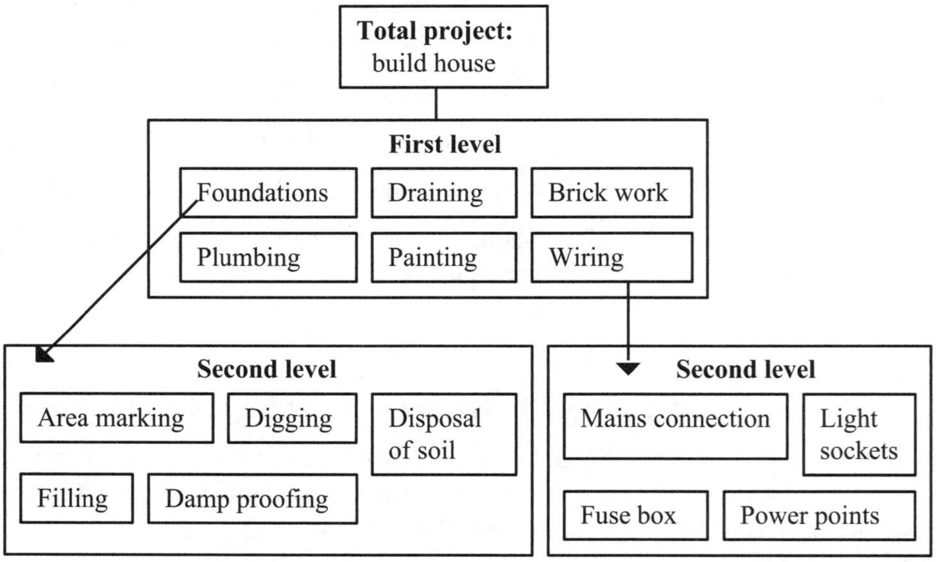

The process of work breakdown continues until the smallest possible sub-unit is reached. Digging the foundations for example would be analysed so that number of labour hours needed, and hence the cost, could be determined.

Where projects require sub-contractors there may be a problem in estimating correctly, especially for the type of contract where fixed penalties are difficult to enforce if the estimates are wrong e.g. bricklayers on a building project.

Collecting estimates from the members of the project team can also be fraught with difficulties. If labour time is requested there is the possibility that the person asked wants to please the project manager and therefore estimates optimistically, understating the amount of time needed to complete the task.

There is the opposite problem where the person asked is over-cautious and estimates too high by building in a cushion in case of problems.

Unless extra costs are built into the estimate, problems can arise from:

- design faults;
- an increase in prices over the project's life;
- material or component failure;
- production errors;
- resource delivery delays.

When all the estimated costs have been collected, projections on future inflation built in and allowances are made for errors in the project team's estimation of time, the estimated total project cost can be calculated.

1.5 Costing and budgeting

KEY POINT

Work breakdown structure can be used to produce the cost breakdown structure – a complete list of every item that can be classed as expenditure.

The normal approach to project costing is to use the work breakdown structure in order to produce the cost breakdown structure (CBS) at an increasing level of detail. This CBS will be a complete list of every item that can be classed as expenditure.

Project costs can be analysed into:

- direct costs, including labour and materials;
- indirect costs, including rent, light, heating and other overheads.

The various costs identified with each part of the work breakdown structure will be collected to provide a useful cost analysis for the various business functions and also to be a mechanism for controlling costs.

Another methodology for cost planning, called the C/SPEC, combines the work breakdown structure, the organisation breakdown structure (labour, sub-contractors, materials, overheads, etc) and the cost breakdown structure. This would have to be done using a computer, because of the three dimensions.

It is very common for a project budget to be constructed as shown below. The use of a spreadsheet package for project budgeting makes variance analysis and financial control much easier.

Month	1	2	3	4	5	6	7	8	9	10	11	Total
Salaries	420	285	662	850	122	453	411	502	850	421	409	5385
Materials	0	125	0	0	1000	250	400	325	100	125	800	3125
Overheads	180	55	320	123	249	402	111	122	451	123	201	2337
Sub-con.	0	200	200	200	200	0	0	560	560	250	0	2170
Total	600	665	1182	1173	1571	1105	922	1509	1961	919	1410	13017

Such a budget can, of course, be shown as a histogram for immediate visual impact, as shown below:

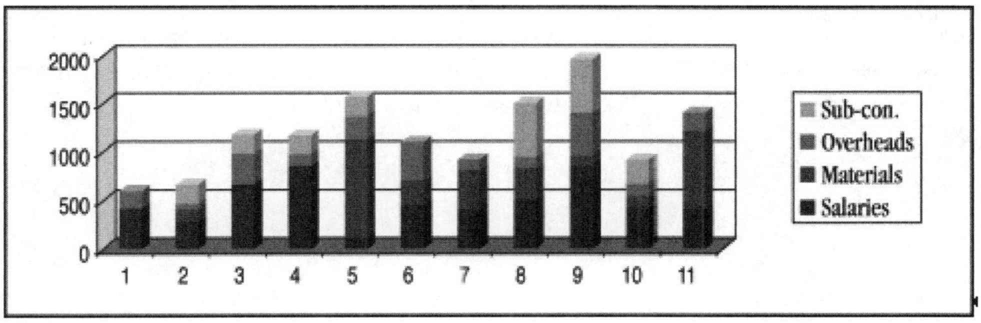

Activity 2

Sketch the outline of a work breakdown structure for recruiting a person to fill a vacancy in the organisation.

Feedback to this activity is at the end of the chapter.

1.6 Gantt charts

The ideal project reporting system is a mixture of graphics and tables. One form of graphical presentation that is commonly used as a part of network analysis is the Gantt chart.

KEY POINT

A Gantt chart is a kind of horizontal bar chart where the length of the bar represents the duration of the activity.

A Gantt chart is a kind of horizontal bar chart where the length of the bar represents the duration of the activity as in the figure below. When a Gantt chart is used to help in the control of a project, two bars are used to represent each activity – one the planned duration and the other the actual duration.

In this example, the programming took longer than expected, but extra resources are put into program testing to enable the project to be put back onto course.

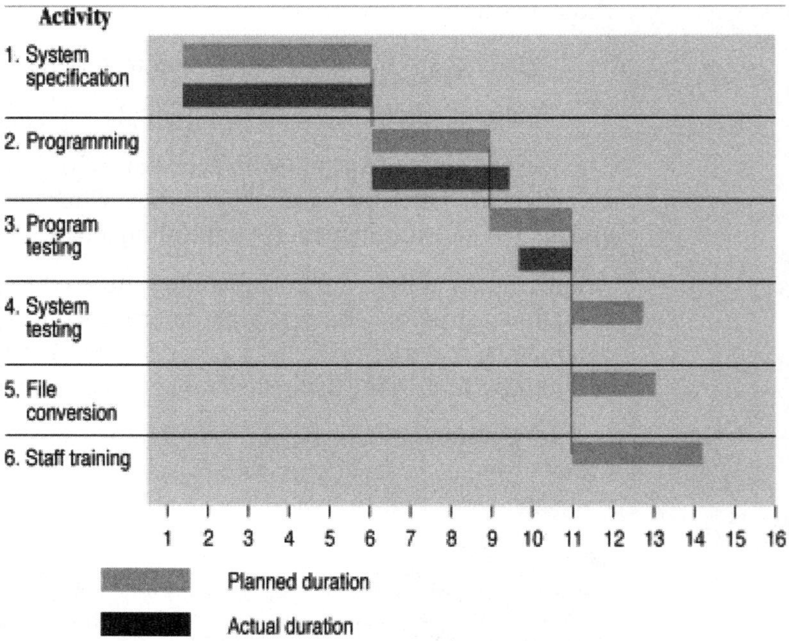

1.7 Resource histograms

KEY POINT

A resource histogram is used to plan and control the human resource requirements of the project.

A resource histogram is simply a stacked bar chart showing the number and mix of staff over the duration of the project. It is used to plan and control the human resource requirements of the project.

If we know how many project staff are required to perform each activity in a project, and also what skills are required, this information can be added to a plan Gantt chart as shown below.

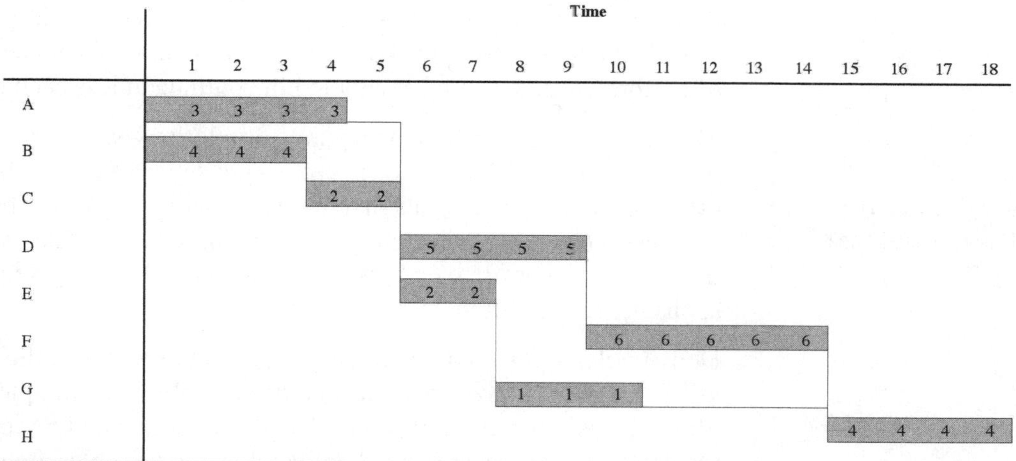

	1	2	3	4	5	6	7	8	9	10	11	12	13	14	15	16	17	18
Project manager	1	1	1	1	1	1	1	1	1	1	1	1	1	1	1	1	1	1
Analysis	6	6	6	4	1	2	2	2	2									
Programmers						4	4	3	3	5	5	5	5	5	3	3	3	3
Total Staff	7	7	7	5	2	7	7	6	6	7	6	6	6	6	4	4	4	4

The **resource histogram** for this project can now be constructed as follows:

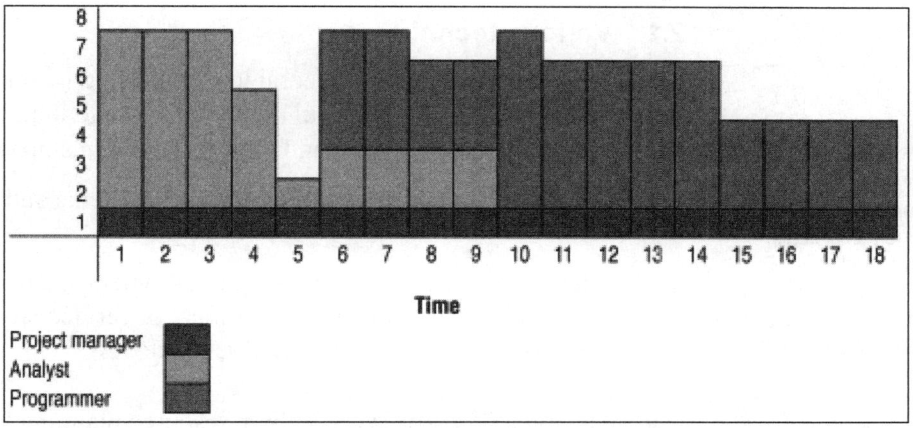

For a simple project such as this, the resource histogram seems to show very little. For a more complex project, however, this is a useful manpower-planning tool. A project manager might use a resource histogram to help with decisions as to when to schedule non-critical activities.

In organisations made up of a series of projects, each with their own complex resource requirements, the project histograms may be consolidated into one for the whole organisation. This will allow decisions to be taken about recruitment, retraining and redundancy.

1.8 Gates and milestones

DEFINITION

Gates are tests which must be passed at key points in the project, in order to indicate that the products and processes are on track.

Gates are significant completion events or quality milestones, placed at key points in the project lifecycle. Gates assess either the quality of the products produced so far, or the adequacy and completeness of the process to date, and a gate can only be 'passed' if the products or process meet a predefined performance standard. Gates may take the form of technical reviews, risk assessments, completion of documents, demonstrations or test cases, or project audits. Gates are identified in a project's plan/schedule, and a gate review is required to formally 'pass' each gate.

If, at a gate review, the gate's criteria have not been met, it is possible that a significant change in project direction may need to take place to address the lack of performance. The project should not continue unless each gate is passed.

KEY POINT

Milestones are important checkpoints or interim goals for a project.

Milestones are important checkpoints or interim goals for a project. In order to monitor and control progress in a project, a series of project milestones will be established. They are points in a project, which provide an absolute measure of progress. Generally, milestones are the completion of tasks or stages of the project with clear 'deliverables' (tangible items that are given to the users or sponsor), such as a report.

Deliverables signal and document the accomplishment of the milestone. Each milestone should have an associated deliverable. For example, testing may be identified as a specific milestone. The documenting and reviewing of the test results would be the associated deliverable. Deliverables are an important element to assessing the status of the project and the quality of the work.

Milestones allow the time spent on a project to be controlled more effectively, as it is easy to compare the actual time of milestone achievement with the planned time.

2 Network analysis

2.1 Various techniques

KEY POINT

Network analysis refers to various techniques adopted to plan and control projects that are complex and consist of interrelated activities. It emphasises the sequence of events and the activities to co-ordinate them.

Network analysis is a general term, referring to various techniques used for planning projects by breaking them down into their component activities and showing those activities and their interrelationships in the form of a network.

The analysis emphasises the sequence of events and the activities to co-ordinate them.

It has been used very effectively in all types of activities associated with strategy implementation, such as: new product or service launches, acquisitions and mergers, plant construction and relocation.

This type of analysis can help in resource planning by:

- breaking down the programme of implementation into its constituent parts by activity, making it easy to build onto the value chain analysis;
- helping to establish priorities by identifying the activities that others depend on;
- representing a plan of action, where the implications of changes or deviations in the plan can be examined.

KEY POINT

Critical path analysis determines the most important activities in relation to the time allocated.

There are two major groups of techniques in network analysis:

- **Critical path analysis** (CPA) – the critical path indicates the most important activities in relation to the time allocated. Used as an integral component of planning and control this provides the basis for allocation of resources to various tasks by dividing the project into specific jobs done, who will undertake them, and the respective target dates.
- **Programme evaluation and review techniques** (PERT) – allows uncertainty about the times of each activity in the network to be considered.

Network analysis provides these advantages to management:

- Identification of both the duration and the critical path.
- Provision of an analytical device for any project which has an introduction (start) time and a finishing point.
- Progress control is emphasised.
- An early indication is given of crises in the project.
- The technique stresses and encourages careful appraisal of activities and stages of projects on the part of managers.

2.2 Steps used in critical path analysis

A project can be defined as being a series of activities designed to achieve a specific objective, and which has a definite beginning and a definite end. For network analysis to be of use, the project must be capable of being split into a number of discrete activities, which relate together in a logical and well-defined manner.

Critical path analysis involves the breaking down of a project into its constituent activities, and the presentation of these activities in diagrammatic form.

The following steps are used in CPA:

- **Analyse the project** – the project is broken down into its constituent tasks or activities. Once this has been done, the way that these activities relate together is examined. This enables the planner to ascertain which parts of the project need to be completed before others can begin.
- **Draw the network** – the sequence of these activities is shown in diagrammatic form called the network diagram.
- **Estimate the time and cost** – the amount of time that each activity will take is estimated. Where appropriate, the cost is also estimated.
- **Locate the critical path** – the chain of operations that determine how long the overall project will take is determined.
- **Schedule the project** – the analysis is used to develop the most efficient and cost-effective schedule, if necessary with any alternative way of completing the project being analysed.
- **Monitor and control the progress of the project** – use the schedule and any progress charts that have been drawn up to monitor progress of the plan.
- **Revise the plan** – the plan is modified to take account of eventualities and problems that occur during the progress of the job.

2.3 Drawing the network diagram

Drawing a logic diagram is a skill requiring practice and ingenuity, and for major projects may require two or three attempts before a satisfactory network or diagram is completed. Computer packages are often used to carry out this process, cutting drastically the time taken.

The following diagram represents the sequence of activities involved in *turning on the television and selecting a channel to watch*; larger diagrams can be used to represent situations that are more complicated.

This diagram is called a **network** and represents the whole project.

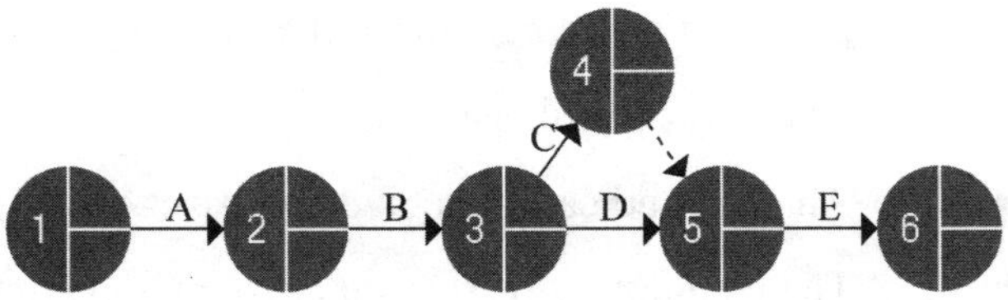

KEY POINT

In a network:

- Straight lines connecting circles represent tasks that take time or resources; these lines are called activities.
- The circles are called events, and represent a point in time.

Each of the straight lines connecting the circles represents a task that takes time or resources; these lines are called **activities**. The arrowheads show the direction of the activity.

The circles are called **events**, and represent a point in time. Each event represents the beginning of an activity, and/or the completion of an event. Event 3 represents the point in time when activity B has been completed, and activities D and C begin.

The dotted line connecting events 4 and 5 is called a **dummy activity**. Dummy activities do not take any time or resources, and are drawn in to make the diagram clearer, and they ensure that none of the rules or conventions for drawing diagrams is breached.

The activities represented in the diagram are shown in the table below. The network contains the assumption that you will use both the TV guide and review television programs on the TV at the same time, while trying to find a program to watch.

Choosing a TV program

Activity	Description	Immediate preceding activities
A	Find TV guide	-
B	Turn on television	A
C	Review channels on television	B
D	Review programs in TV guide	B
E	Select program to watch	C, D

The network was drawn using the rules and conventions explained below.

2.4 Rules for drawing a network

KEY POINT

Rules for drawing a network:

- one point of entry;
- each activity has one preceding and one following event;
- activities can share same tail or head, but not both use a dummy);
- an event does not happen until all activities into it are complete;
- all activities must contribute to forward progression (no loops or danglers).

1 A complete network should have only one point of entry – the start event, and one point of exit – the finish event.

2 Every activity must have one preceding event (the **tail)**, and one following event (the **head)**.

3 Several activities may use the same tail event, and several the same head event, but no two activities may share the same head and tail events. Thus the following diagram would not be allowed as part of a network:

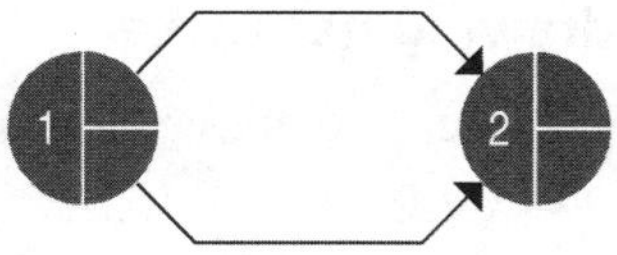

Instead, a dummy activity is used, so the correct version of the above would be either of the following two diagrams:

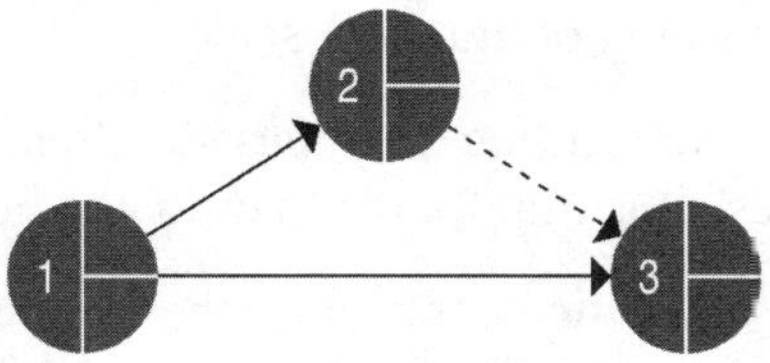

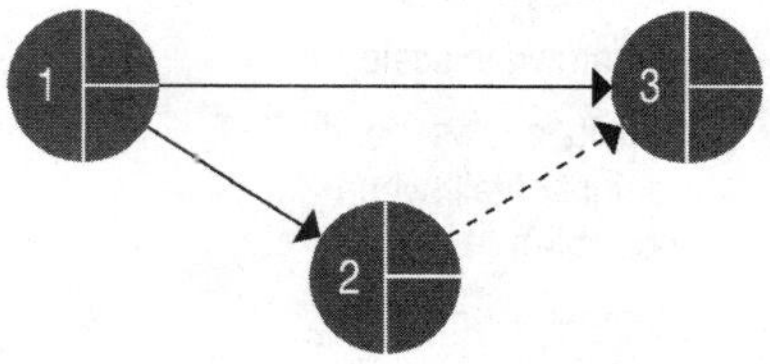

4 An event does not happen until all activities into it are complete. In the network for selecting a TV program for example, event 5 is not complete until both of the activities C and D are complete. You cannot choose the TV program you want to watch until you have reviewed the alternatives in the TV guide and on the television.

5 **Loops** are not allowed. You cannot have a series of activities leading from an event that lead back to the same event. The essence of drawing a network is that it represents a series of activities moving on in time. Neither of the two following diagrams is allowed:

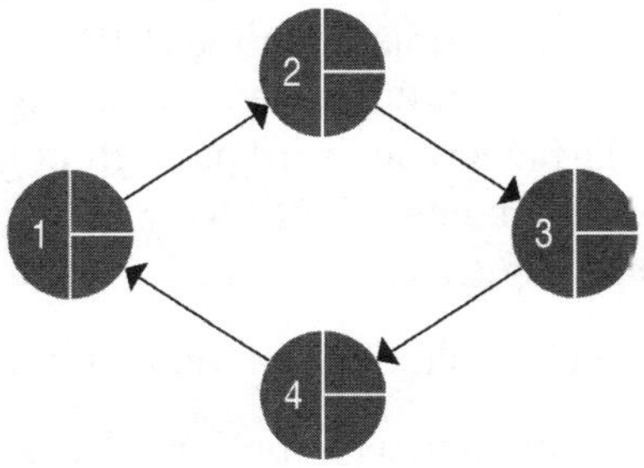

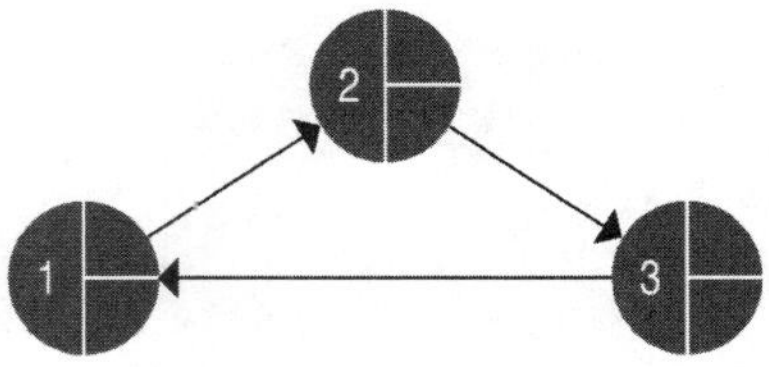

6 **Danglers** are not allowed. All activities must contribute to the progression of the network or be discarded as irrelevant.

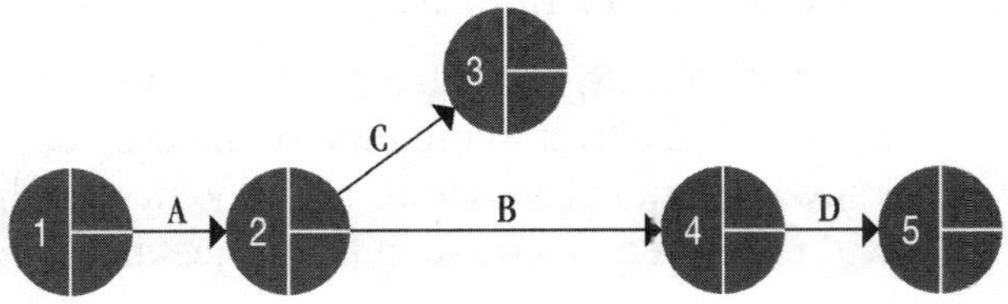

The dangling activity should only be included if it contributes to the progress of the project, in which case it should link to the end event as in the following diagram:

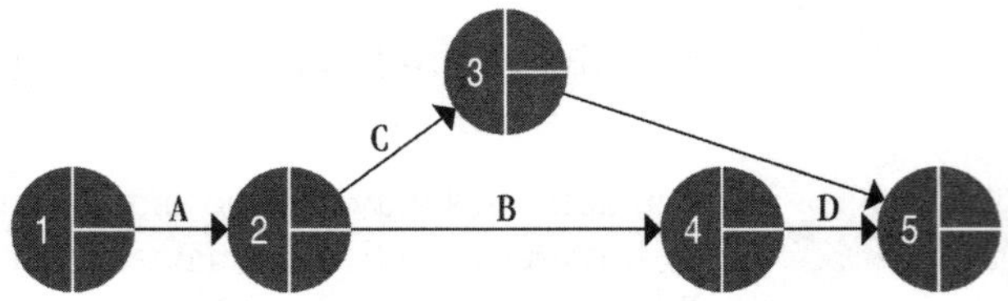

2.5 Conventions for drawing networks

KEY POINT

Conventions for drawing networks:

- go from left to right;
- not drawn to scale;
- activity arrows: head to right of tail (when possible);
- number events or nodes so an activity moves from lower number to higher;
- avoid crossing lines.

In addition to the rules described above, certain conventions are followed for the sake of clarity and conformity.

- Networks proceed from left to right – the start event is at the left hand side of the diagram, and the end event at the right hand side.
- Networks are not drawn to scale.
- Arrows representing activities should have their head to the right of their tail unless it is impossible to draw the network in that way.
- The 'activity' line connecting the event symbols shows the time taken to complete an activity. Each activity line is referenced.
- Events or nodes should be numbered so that an activity always moves from a lower numbered event to a higher one. this convention is relatively easy to accomplish in a simple network but in a complex network it may be necessary to number in tens to allow for extra activities to be added without the need for a complete renumbering of the whole diagram.
- The left hand side of the event symbol details the earliest start time (EST), which is the earliest time at which an activity can begin. ESTs are entered during a 'forward pass' through the network; in other words, once all the event symbols have been plotted we work from left to right through the network, entering ESTs as we go. The right hand side of the event symbol details the latest finishing time (LFT), which is the latest time an activity can finish without the project exceeding its estimated duration. LFTs are entered during a 'backward pass' through the network; in other words, once we have entered ESTs we work back through the diagram from right to left entering LFTs as we go.
- Lines that cross should be avoided if possible.
- The start event may be represented as a line instead of a circle, particularly when several activities may begin at the start point.

2.6 Finding the critical path

KEY POINT

The critical path through a network is the chain of activities whose times determine the overall duration of the project.

Activities on the critical path are known as critical activities.

The critical path through a network is the chain of activities whose times determine the overall duration of the project. Activities on the critical path are known as critical activities, and any increase in the duration of a critical activity will result in an increase in the project duration.

Finding the critical path is a routine task to identify the longest path in a network. In the network diagram below, there are two possible paths from the start event to the end event: namely ABE and CDE. The time taken is 26 days for ABE and 18 days for CDE. Because path ABE takes the longest time, it is called the Critical Path.

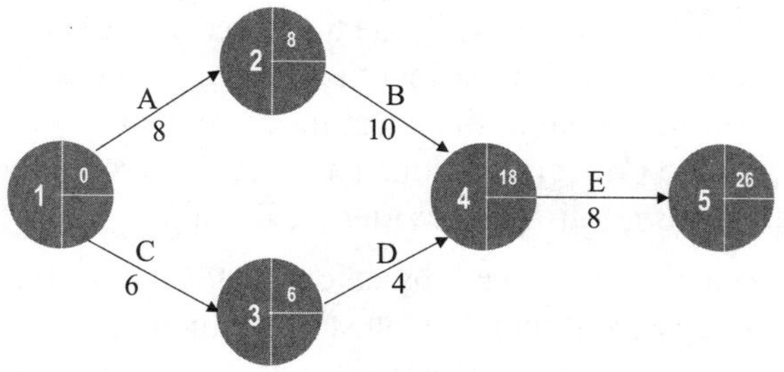

The basic technique of finding the critical path is as follows, taking each node in turn:

Event 1 is the starting event, reached after time 0. Event 2 is reached after activity A, and therefore the earliest it can be reached is after 8 days. Event 3 can be reached after 6 days. Event 4 can be reached either through activity D from event 3, or via activity B from event 2. The earliest it could have been completed is via the longer of these two paths, i.e. 10 days from event 2. Activity E cannot begin until event 4 is completed, i.e. after activity B is completed. Even though activity D has been completed 8 days before B, E must wait.

Information concerning the time for each of the activities in the network is recorded in the events at the end of each activity. The top right of each event records the earliest finish time (EFT) for each activity that is the working from left to right, the quickest time that an event can be finished. For example, activity A takes 8 time units, so the top left of event 1 shows a 0, the start of the network, and event 2 shows 8. Similarly, activity B takes 10 time units to go from event 2 to 4, making the earliest finish time at event 4 of 18. The earliest finishing times for other events can be calculated in the same way.

Event 4 has an earliest finishing time of 18, not 10 (activity C plus D) because both activities B and D must be complete by this event. The activity with the later finishing time is always included, otherwise this activity would still be running when the event occurred.

The next process is the backward pass. The bottom right of the event records the latest finishing time. This is the latest time an event can finish in order to reach the end of the network when the last activity finishes.

The latest finish time for 5 is the same as the earliest time – 26 days. This is always the start point for calculating the backward pass: the final event has the same earliest and latest times.

The latest finish time (LFT) for each of the previous events is obtained by subtracting the activity durations from the preceding events along the backward route, taking the minimum value where there is more than one route back into an event.

The LFT for event 4 = 26 – 8 = 18 days

The LFT for event 3 = 18 – 4 = 14 days

The LFT for event 2 = 18 – 10 = 8 days

The LFT for event 1 = the minimum of 8 – 8 = 0 days (from 2), and 14 – 6 = 8 days (from 3).

Event 3 has a latest finish time 8 greater than the earliest start time. A delay of up to 8 days would not affect the total project duration. The other events have earliest times equal to the latest times, and so any delay in reaching them would increase the project duration. These events are on the critical path. The critical path therefore follows activities A, B and E.

The critical path is found by calculating earliest times first by means of the forward pass, and then the latest times by means of the backward pass. Events whose earliest time equals their latest time are by definition on the critical path. The critical path should be traceable from the start event through to the end event.

2.7 Calculating the float

KEY POINT

Spare time for an activity is called its float.

Some activities in a project, like C above, have spare time, so that when delays occur on those activities, the overall project duration may not be affected. This spare time is called the **float**. In a typical project, only about 20% of operations are critical, so the other 80% have a float time. All activities on the critical path have, by definition, zero float time; delaying those activities will have the effect of increasing the overall time for the project.

Calculation of the float can be illustrated using the same network:

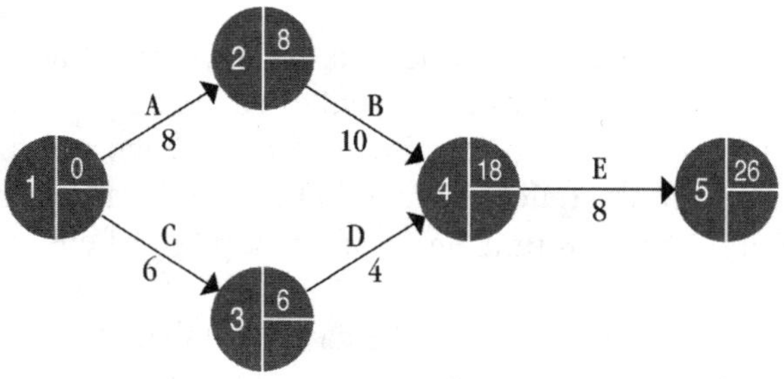

The critical path goes through events 1, 2, 4, 5 – or activities A, B, E. There is no float time on those activities. You know there is no float because the start and finish times at each event are the same.

KEY POINT

Total float = Latest finish time – Earliest start time – Activity duration

The float time on activities can be obtained from the formula:

Total float = Latest finish time – Earliest start time – Activity duration

Float for C = 14 – 0 – 6 days = 8 days

Float for D = 18 – 6 – 4 days = 8 days

The Float for C is therefore the latest finish time of 14 (from event 3) less the earliest finish time of 0 (from event 1) less the duration of the activity of 6. This gives a float of 8. In other words, as long as activity C reaches event 3 by time day 14, the network can still be completed. Activity D will take 4 and activity E 8 time days to reach the last event of 5 by time day 26.

Similarly, D has a float of 8, (event 4 latest finish time of 18 less event 3 earliest start time of 6 less activity duration of 4). As long as activity D reaches event 4 by time unit 18, again the network can be finished.

KEY POINT

The float is used to identify whether any delay in starting or carrying out an activity will cause a delay in the project completion time.

The float is used to identify whether any delay in starting or carrying out an activity will cause a delay in the project completion time.

A delay in either activity C or D of up to 8 days will not cause an increase in the project time, but if there is a delay in activity C, the earliest start time for D will be delayed, reducing its float. The two floats are not independent of each other; when calculating a float, a check must be made to identify progress from previous activities, as late running activities will limit the floats of subsequent activities.

The example above has been made very simple, to demonstrate the principles. A real development project is likely to have far more activities, with more complicated dependencies between them. However large the project, and however many parallel activities there may be, the principles of calculating forward and backward passes is exactly the same, and so are the principles for deriving the critical path, and amount of float on all non-critical activities.

Activity 3

Your manager has just told you what a work breakdown structure does and you need to explain this to your project team. Which one from the following list will *not* be included in your explanation?

(a) Identifies the work that must be done in the project.

(b) Determines the resources required.

(c) Sequences the work done, to allocate resources in the optimum way.

(d) Determines the minimum possible duration of the project.

Feedback to this activity is at the end of the chapter.

2.8 Benefits of network analysis

The following are the main advantages afforded by using critical path methods:

- **Easier visualisation of relationships**. The network diagram that is produced shows how the different tasks and activities relate together, making it easier to understand a project intuitively, improving planning and making it easier to communicate details of the project plan to interested parties.
- **More effective planning**. CPM forces management to think a project through thoroughly. It requires careful and detailed planning, and the discipline imposed often justifies its use even without the other benefits.
- **Better focusing on problem areas**. The technique enables the manager to pinpoint likely bottlenecks and problem areas before they occur.
- **Improved resource allocation**. Manpower and other resources can be directed to those parts of the project where they will have the most effect in reducing cost and speeding up the completion of the project. Overtime can be eliminated, or confined to those jobs where it will do the most good.
- **Studying alternative options**. Management can simulate the effect of alternative courses of action. They can also gauge the effect of problems in carrying out particular tasks and can, therefore, make contingency plans.
- **Management by exception**. CPM identifies those actions whose timely completion is critical to the overall timetable, and enables the leeway on other actions to be calculated. this makes it possible for management to focus their attention on the important areas of the project.
- **Improved project monitoring**. By comparing the actual performance of each task with the schedule, a manager can immediately recognise when problems are occurring, can identify when those problems are important and can take the appropriate action in time to rescue the project.

One of the most significant benefits of network analysis is that it enhances management's ability to monitor the project as it is being carried out. After the project has been analysed, a series of charts, diagrams, graphs, narratives and tables are drawn up. These can be used as a reporting system that will identify immediately a critical activity that is out of control, or a non-critical activity that has used up its float.

Once problems have been identified, extra resources can be brought in or transferred between activities. Managers are thus in a better position to correct the situation before the problems become insoluble.

Summary

- A project is launched on the basis of a project initiation document and a project scope statement.
- There will always be trade-offs between time, cost and scope: the project triangle.
- SMART objectives are specific, measurable, attainable, realistic and time-limited.
- Risk and uncertainty arise from measurement errors, lack of data, and the underlying variability of complex natural, physical, social and economic situations.

Having completed your study of this chapter you should have achieved the following learning outcome.

- Distinguish the key tools and techniques that would need to be applied in the project process, including the evaluation of proposals.

Self-test questions

1. Identify the most commonly used project management tools. (1.1)
2. What are deliverables? (1.2)
3. Explain what a WBS does. (1.4)
4. How would project costs be analysed? (1.5)
5. Describe a Gantt chart. (1.6)
6. Briefly describe a project milestone. (1.8)
7. What are dummy activities in a network diagram? (2.3)
8. What is the float? (2.7)

Multiple-choice question

Question 1

In a critical path network, the EST (earliest start time) is established by:

A working backwards from the project deadline

B subtracting activity duration from the LST (latest start time)

C working forwards from the start event, adding activity durations

D adding activity duration to LFT (latest finish times).

Exam-type questions

Question 1: Drawing networks

Identify the errors of logic and the departures from convention in the following diagram:

(10 marks)

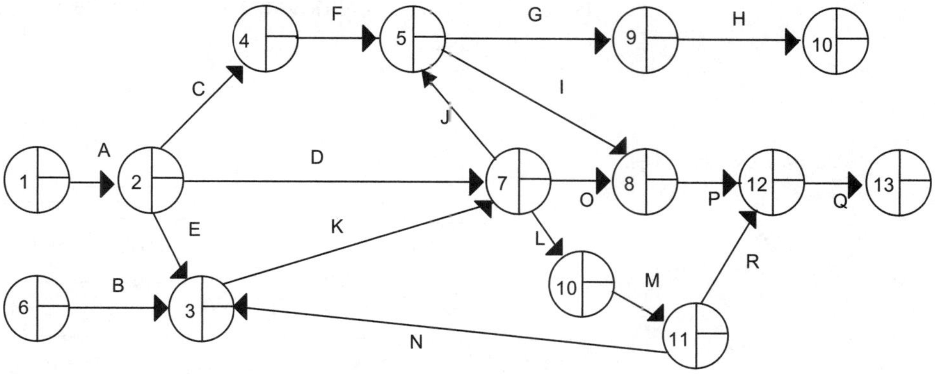

Question 2: Finding the critical path

Draw a network and find the critical path for the following project:

Activity	Preceding activity	Duration (mins)
A	-	4
B	A	2
C	B	10
D	A	2
E	D	5
F	A	2
G	F	4
H	G	3
J	C	6
K	C, E	6
L	H	3

(10 marks)

For the answers to these questions, see the 'Answers' section at the end of the book.

Feedback to activities

Activity 1

The technique that management will probably adopt is (b): Major strengths and profitable opportunities can be exploited.

Activity 2

Below is a work breakdown structure for the recruitment of a new person to fill a vacant post.

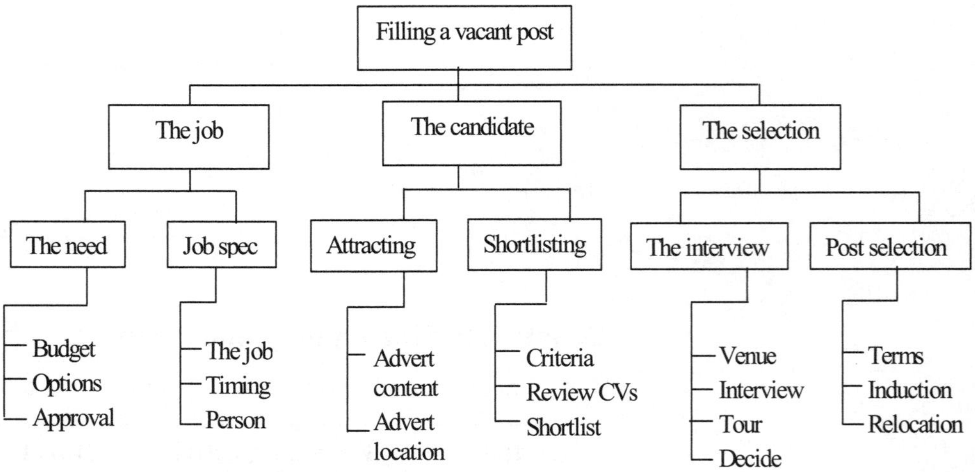

Activity 3

(d) (Determines the minimum possible duration of the project) will not be included in your explanation.

Chapter 8

PROJECT METHODOLOGIES AND PLANNING

Syllabus content

- Evaluation of plans for projects.
- The key processes of PRINCE2 and their implications for project staff.
- The role of determining trade-offs between key project objectives of time, cost and quality.
- Managing scope at the outset of a project and providing systems for configuration management/change control.
- The production of basic plans for time, cost and quality.
- Scenario planning and buffering to make provision for uncertainty in projects, and the interface with the risk management process.

Contents

1 Project management methodologies and systems
2 The project initiation stage
3 Strategy and scope for a project
4 Management of configuration, change and risk
5 The project planning stage

1 Project management methodologies and systems

1.1 Introduction

There are many formal project management methodologies that combine a framework or approach with a set of project tools and guidelines. Some are 'proprietary' approaches developed by consulting firms and software houses whilst others are in the public domain. They vary in scale and complexity but all are based around a small core of common sense principles.

KEY POINT

Common project management methodologies and systems include:

- PRINCE2
- JISC infoNet
- PMBOK
- Microsoft Project ®.

- A methodology that is commonly used in the public sector is PRINCE2 (PRojects IN Controlled Environments). This is the methodology approved by government for public sector projects and was originally designed to aid the development and implementation of information systems.
- The JISC infoNet method pares down PRINCE2 to the bare bones of a framework suitable for managing any project.
- The Project Management Body of Knowledge (PMBOK) recognises five basic process groups and nine knowledge areas typical of almost all projects. The basic concepts are applicable to projects, programs and operations (as discussed in Chapter 6).
- Microsoft Project® is one of the more commonly used project management software tools.

1.2 The key processes of PRINCE 2

PRINCE2 (PRojects IN Controlled Environments, version 2) is a process-based approach for project management providing an easily tailored, and scaleable method for the management of all types of projects.

PRINCE 2: Overview

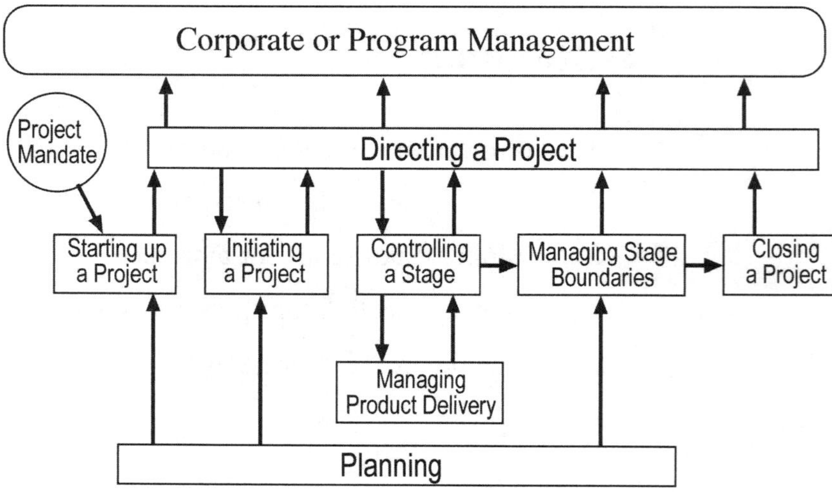

As a formal method, PRINCE 2 is based on a common set of project management principles which, when adhered to, will increase the probability of a successful outcome to the project. Successful projects are those where the following basic areas or activities are implemented and managed effectively:

- formally starting or initiating the project;
- establishing an organisational structure around the project;
- using a structured planning method;

- applying project control techniques;
- managing the stages of the project;
- executing the project tasks and activities;
- assessing and managing risks that could impact on the project;
- formally closing the project.

Successful project management is aided by a stepped, logical approach, which addresses each of the above areas.

Completing some of the processes may seem somewhat heavy going and bureaucratic, but they have been devised as a means of ensuring that the correct amount of detail is applied to the key elements of the project. Lack of attention to detail in projects can lead to expensive time and cost overruns or serious failure in terms of the quality of project deliverables.

The key stages of project management

Starting up a Project (SU)
This is the first process in PRINCE. It is a pre-project process, designed to ensure that the pre-requisites for initiating the project are in place. The process expects the existence of a Project Mandate which defines in high level terms the reason for the project and what outcome is sought.

Key aspects include:

- ensuring that all the information required for the project team was available;
- helping design and appoint the Project Management Team;
- creating the Initiation Stage Plan.

Initiating a Project (IP)
Key aspects include:

- ensuring a firm and accepted foundation to the project prior to commencement of the work;
- getting agreement to the commitment of resources for the first stage of the project;
- enabling the Project Board to take ownership of the project.

Managing Stage Boundaries (SB)
Here, the project should be broken down into stages. Managing stage boundaries ensures that all deliverables planned in the current Stage Plan have been completed as defined before authorising the next stage.

Controlling a Stage (CS)
This process describes the monitoring and control activities of the Project Manager involved in ensuring that a stage stays on course and reacts to unexpected events.

The PRINCE2 methodology encourages the firm to set up cycles consisting of:

- authorising work to be done;
- gathering progress information about that work;
- watching for changes;
- reviewing the situation;

- reporting;
- taking any necessary corrective action.

In addition there should be the on-going work of risk management and change control.

Managing Product Delivery (MP)
This process ensures that the recommendations are acceptable to all parties and that they deliver the quality and user benefits wanted.

Closing a Project (CP)
The purpose of this process is to execute a controlled close to the project. The PRINCE2 approach is to check whether objectives have been achieved and to put forward a plan of action to resolve problems.

Implications for project staff

All project management methodologies identify a standard set of processes common to all types of project and offer guidance and support on the execution of these processes. The PRINCE2 method is flexible and adaptable for any type and size of project, and offers an excellent management foundation for any member of staff

Each process is defined with its key inputs and outputs together with the specific objectives to be achieved and activities to be carried out. A properly implemented structured project management approach is necessary to organise, plan and control all business undertakings. PRINCE 2 provides those responsible for planning and managing projects with a structure, which will help them without imposing too great an overhead, or stifling creativity. Senior managers' needs are also addressed by providing the structure for a suitable decision support environment

1.3 The JISC infoNet method

The JISC infoNet method pares down PRINCE2 to the bare bones of a framework suitable for managing any project. As with any project management framework there is a certain amount of core documentation required. This is essential in order to define and manage the project and measure its success.

The diagram below shows the main components of the JISC infoNet project management methodology. Some elements, namely Project Start-up and Project Closure, occur only once. The remaining elements, Planning, Managing and Controlling, form an iterative cycle that may repeat many times before the project is complete.

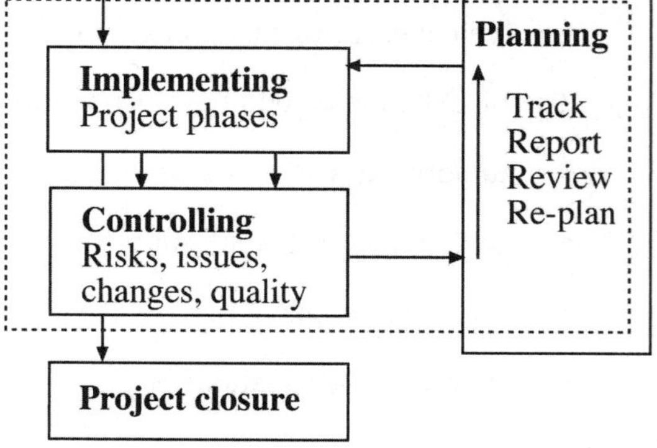

JISC infoNET: overview

2 The project initiation stage

2.1 Project initiation

> **KEY POINT**
>
> The PID lists the goals, constraints and success criteria for the project.

The project initiation document, 'statement of work' or 'project charter' was discussed in Chapter 7 (see Section 1.2). It is subject to negotiation and modification by the various stakeholders of the project and once they formally agree its content it becomes the document that is referred to in the event of any disagreement later.

Projects originate from someone attempting to resolve a problem or seeing an opportunity to do something new. Unfortunately, it is not always clear what the problem is and not all ideas result in a viable project. A reality test needs to be applied to eliminate those that are obviously not viable. The production of a project initiation document (PID) during the initial stages of the plan will establish the scope and overall mission of the project. More importantly, it will explain the terms of reference which will provide a framework for review over the course of the project.

Terms of reference will topically include:

- Details of the work to be performed.
- The cost of the work and a mechanism for costing specification changes.
- The deadlines for various stages of the project.
- Involvement of client staff and contracting staff; specification of expertise to be available. Who does what?
- Quality control issues, testing and acceptance.

It is very important that the terms of reference be documented in language that is clearly understood by all members of the project team. Having clear parameters in writing will allow the project to proceed with certainty, and reduce the risk of disagreements later.

2.2 Project definition

Clear and accurate definition of a project is one of the most important actions you can take to ensure the project's success. The clearer the target the more likely you are to hit it. Defining a project is a process of selection and reduction of the ideas and perspectives of those involved into a set of clearly defined objectives, critical success factors (or 'key success criteria') and evaluated risks.

> **KEY POINT**
>
> The main elements of a project definition include:
>
> - purpose;
> - goals;
> - beneficial gains.

The way to define a project is to ask a standard set of questions. They fall into the categories given below.

The purpose (or mission) – this is the reason for doing the project and is a statement of its overall aims, expressed in the most general of terms.

- What is the project about in broad terms?
- Who wants it done and why?

The goals – these are the targets we want to meet.

- What is it we want to achieve and when do we want to achieve it?
- What are our specific aims and why are they essential to the project?
- What gates and milestones will be used to monitor and control progress towards these goals?

The **beneficial gains** – this is how the organisation will gain. Here we define the performance criteria and set our quality standards for the project.

- How will things be different if the project is successfully completed?
- Is there a clear need and can it be quantified?
- Who will benefit, how will they benefit and what will they gain?
- Do the beneficiaries agree about the need and the proposed solution?
- Is the project to identify that need and/or that solution?
- How will they react to that solution?
- What are the alternatives?
- Are those alternatives more or less acceptable (satisfactory)?

A **fitness for purpose checklist** is a means of checking that all the variables are covered:

- ❑ Is the business need clearly stated?
- ❑ Have the benefits been clearly identified?
- ❑ Are the reason for and benefits of the project consistent with the organisation's strategy?
- ❑ Is it clear what will define a successful outcome?
- ❑ Is it clear what the preferred option is?
- ❑ Is it clear why this is the preferred option?
- ❑ Where there is an external procurement is it clear what the sourcing option is?
- ❑ Is it clear why this is the preferred sourcing option?
- ❑ Is it clear how the necessary funding will be put in place?
- ❑ Is it clear how the benefits will be realised?
- ❑ Are the risks faced by the project explicitly stated?
- ❑ Are the plans for addressing those risks explicitly stated?

3 Strategy and scope for a project

3.1 Strategy

Projects generally arise for strategic or efficiency reasons, that is, to improve the competitive advantage of an organisation or improve its productivity. The business case is used to obtain management commitment and approval for investment in the business change project. It provides a framework for the planning, management and ongoing viability of the project. To ensure the strategic fit of the project the organisation needs to be clear about the following:

- description of the business need and its contribution to the organisation's business strategy;
- objectives;
- why it is needed now;

- key benefits to be realised;
- critical success factors and how they will be measured.

It almost goes without saying that all large projects need to fulfil a strategic purpose. Yet many projects are undertaken at a tactical or even operational level without considering the overall strategic vision of the organisation.

Strategic evaluation of a systems implementation usually starts with a single fundamental question. 'How does this system benefit the organisation's primary clients?' If you do not ask this question prior to implementation it follows that the answer to it during evaluation might be less than clear.

The following diagram shows how we might integrate the system into the organisation. We use the example of an educational institution, where the main clients to be served are the learners.

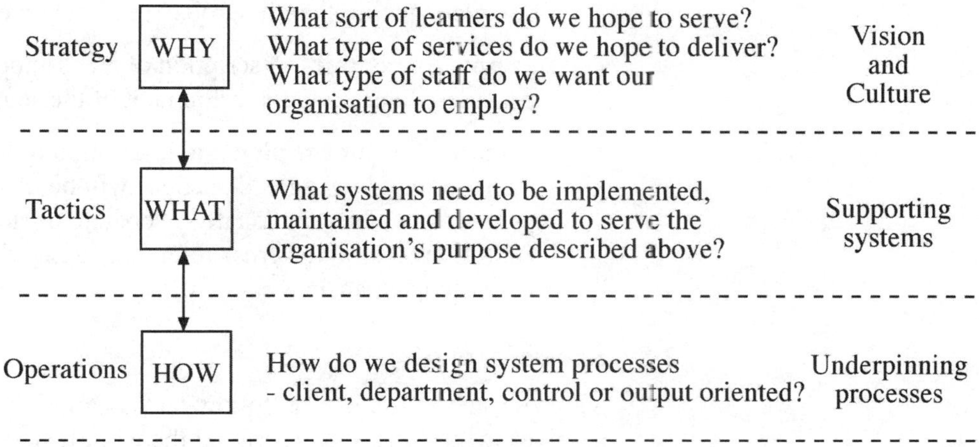

A **strategy** is a course of action created to achieve a long-term goal. However, project managers cannot 'do' a goal or strategy. They break down processes, analyse them, set objectives and then drive hard to achieve them. An **objective** is the object or aim of an action. It implies an explicit direction for the action to take and a specific quality of work to be accomplished within a given period of time.

3.2 Scope statement

Proper scope management is critical to the success of any project, especially in terms of time and money. And one of the first tasks of any project manager is to develop a written scope statement.

The aim of the scope statement is to document and justify the proposed solution. This is sometimes also called a **concept brief** or **project proposal**. It determines whether the project is a single/discrete entity or part of a larger programme of work. Scope provides a common understanding of the project for all stakeholders by defining the project's **overall boundaries**. Scope can be defined in terms of processes, internal entities, systems, customers, and outside entities, data, functionality that will (or will not) be part of the project. It names major activities clearly enough to define what the project will and won't do; lists major activities that are critical to success of the project, but beyond the scope of the project; and defines a project's place in a larger scenario

The scope statement eliminates any confusion or ambiguity that might still exist after considering the project's goal, objectives and high-level deliverables statements. Poorly defined scope leads to changes in collected project accomplishments (**scope creep**). These changes inevitably lead to increased work effort, which in turn causes project delays, cost overruns, poor team morale and/or customer dissatisfaction. Clearly defined scope will crystallise realistic stakeholder expectations. Additionally, a clear statement of scope is the foundation for defining a change management strategy. Using a change management process, changes to scope can be managed, rejected, or deferred in a disciplined manner.

This scope statement forms the basis for agreement between customer and supplier and will be the basis for all project related decisions It should include the following information:

- **Strategy** – an overview of the customer's business needs in relation to the project and the business need the project was undertaken to address.
- **Product of the project** – a summary of the project deliverables.
- **Project objectives** – will be quantifiable in terms of time, money and technical quality that the project must achieve to be considered successful.
- **Supporting detail** – description of all assumptions and constraints considered during the development of the scope statement.
- **Scope management plan** – a description of how the project scope will be managed and how agreed changes will be incorporated into the project deliverables. There is usually a separate document describing the change control process and a cross reference to that document should be included in the scope management plan.

3.3 Scope definition

Scope definition is a natural follow on task after writing the scope statement. It involves identifying and describing the work that is needed to produce the product of the project in sufficient detail to ensure that:

- the project team understands what it must do;
- all of the reasonably knowable project work has been identified;
- appropriate management controls can be applied.

This means subdividing the project deliverables into smaller components. The work breakdown structure (discussed in Chapter 7: see Section 1.4) is an absolutely essential project management technique, providing a foundation for all planning and execution activities.

3.4 Project objectives and basic plans for time, cost and quality

The project objectives are the anticipated result or final outcome and must be clearly understood at the outset.

KEY POINT

From our list of specific goals for the project we must develop a set of measurable objectives that will confirm that we have reached certain project milestones (or way points) including the final one of project completion.

These objectives will tell us if we have met our goals and to what standard. From our list of specific goals for the project we must develop a set of measurable objectives that will confirm that we have reached certain project milestones (or way points) including the final one of project completion.

The measurable objectives (when achieved) demonstrate the extent to which the beneficial gains have been achieved, the goals have been met, and the purpose of the project has been achieved.

Project objectives are usually defined in terms of scope, schedule and cost and the management of them is often a delicate balancing act, as the various objectives normally conflict with one another.

Time

There are two aspects to the time dimension of a project:

- an overall time constraint on a project (sometimes called a deadline) by when the project must be completed;
- a 'time budget' for the project. This is often expressed in terms of resource availability and measured in labour hours or worker days.

The time objective or schedule is the timetable of activities involved in achieving the project's objectives. It helps to plan for a firm delivery date, which will make the project viable and minimise disruption time, optimise cash flow and co-ordinate the availability of resources.

The time objective describes the deadlines or time constraints on the project. The implications of delivering the project late will vary depending on the nature of the project.

Project time management includes the processes and techniques used to ensure the timely completion of the project. It involves the development and management of the project work activities and the project schedule. As part of project planning in the definition phase, a detailed project schedule and work breakdown structure should be developed based on the proposals contained in the scope document and agreed to in the project contract.

As the project activities progress, you will see differences between planned and actual duration of activities begin to emerge. You will need to monitor and control changes to the schedule of activities as well as to the overall project, as discussed in chapter 10. Changes are made and communicated according to the project change control procedures and as agreed to with the client and other stakeholders.

Project scope

There are two aspects to the scope dimension of a project:

- a certain series of tasks or activities to be performed in reaching the project solution;
- an expected quality level associated with each task. It is also important that the tasks are performed well, and that the sponsor's quality expectations are met.

The aim of the scope objective is to ensure that the project's purpose is achieved, specify the work that must be done and specifically exclude work that is superfluous or otherwise unnecessary. The quality objective describes the quality the project is aiming at.

Developing the scope of the project means planning for quality. In project terms this means delivering a project, which satisfies the customer and is 'fit for the purpose'.

Quality management includes the activities and techniques used to ensure that all project activities and work products comply with all relevant standards, procedures and requirements. Evaluation and testing activities will contribute to overall quality of the package but do not constitute the whole quality management process. (This is discussed in Chapter 10.)

Cost

There are two aspects to cost:

- a budget available for project completion, which the project manager should not exceed without authorisation;
- the need, in most projects, to prove that the benefits of the project exceed the costs.

The project cost is based on the budget, which includes an estimate of the resources that will be used in the project.

Costs and resources include people, equipment and money. They may be internal or external and include suppliers, contractors, partners, statutory bodies, governments, banks, loans, grants, expert opinion (lawyers, accountants, consultants), etc. Generally, organisations are reasonably good at estimating or obtaining estimates for the use and costs of external resources and, if need be, they can obtain the opinion of an expert (another cost). Where they often fail is in estimating the cost of the use of their internal resources, particularly people.

The cost objective indicates how much we are willing to spend on the project. This usually involves cash, but it is worth thinking about other costs such as staff time and impact on other projects. For instance it might be acceptable for a very important project to use up the staff effort allocated to other projects, so the price of success in one area is failure in others.

Project cost management includes the processes used to ensure that the project is completed within the approved budget. The resources and budget required for the project are proposed in the scope document and agreed to in the project contract. This is further detailed as part of project planning in the definition phase. The contract should set the points for review of the project budget (and project schedule). Budget and schedule reviews (also discussed in Chapter 10) are necessary especially when the requirements, design and content of the product are going to be iteratively defined.

In all subsequent project phases and after each development cycle, cost management involves the confirmation of resources (people, equipment and materials) and estimation of the budget needed to complete project activities for the phase/cycle.

On small projects, the processes of determining resources, estimating and budgeting cost may be viewed and conducted as a single process. On larger projects, these may be quite distinct and the skills and resources applied to these processes may be vital for the project's success. Although project cost management is primarily concerned with the cost of the resources needed to complete project activities, you may need to also consider the effect of project decisions on the eventual cost of using the project product. Certain design decisions or limited testing may result in increased cost to the end user's operating costs.

3.5 Trade offs between key project objectives

KEY POINT

Every project has constraints. The primary ones are the trade off between time, cost and scope – which also impact on quality.

Every project has constraints. The primary ones are the trade off between time, cost and scope, often referred to as the 'project triangle'.

This is a standard project management idea, used to ask the question 'If things go wrong do we go over budget, deliver late or do less (or do it less well)?'

For example, a change to the specification that increases its scope will logically require that either the timescale is extended or that resources are added to cater for the new parts of the specification in the same timescale. Conversely, a reduction in timescale will logically require that either the specification is reduced in scope or that resources are added to complete the same amount of work in less time.

Microsoft has linked quality with scope, time and cost. Their online web site *Assistance for Microsoft Project 2000*, illustrates 'The Quality Triangle' as shown below:

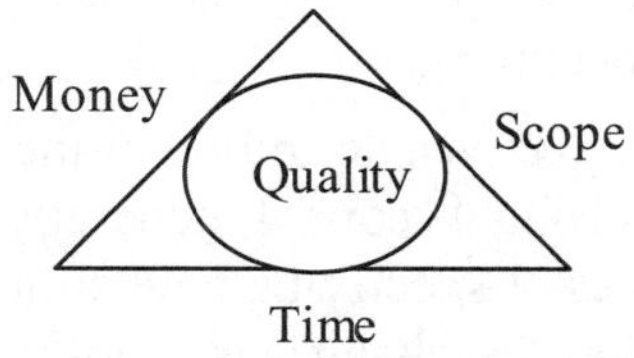

The quality triangle

As Microsoft explains it: quality, a fourth element, is at the centre of the project triangle. Changes you make to any of the three sides of the triangle are likely to affect quality. Quality is not a side of the triangle; it is a result of what you do with time, money, and scope.

3.6 SMART objectives

Objectives should be **SMART** (**S**pecific, **M**easurable, **A**ttainable, **R**elevant, **T**ime-bounded).

Specific – an objective must be specific with a single key result. If more than one result is to be accomplished, more than one objective should be written. Just knowing what is to be accomplished is a big step toward achieving it.

Measurable - an objective must be measurable. If possible, state the objective as a quantity. Some objectives are more difficult to measure than others are. However, difficulty does not mean that they cannot be measured.

Attainable – an objective must be attainable with the resources that are available.

Relevant– the objective should be central to the goals of the organisation. The successful completion of the objective should make a difference.

Time-bounded – the objective should have a clear time horizon or scheduled completion date.

4 Management of configuration, change and risk

4.1 Management of configuration

KEY POINT

Management of configuration provides a mechanism which can be used to track changes to project products.

Management of configuration provides a mechanism, which can be used to track changes to project products and as such keeps track of product versions. For example, multimedia products are very often made up of a large number of files. Each component is produced in various stages or versions, again increasing the file numbers. A significant challenge is to ensure that you can identify each component, as well as different versions of the same component, to ensure that different 'builds' of the product incorporate the right version of the components.

This is achieved through effective configuration management, which includes a change control procedure and a file naming convention. The configuration management procedures and techniques are determined as part of project plan development during the definition phase and are carried out as an ongoing project management activity.

4.2 Management of change

As a project is a dynamic process, it is unrealistic to assume that requests for changes will not occur. These changes will originate from changes in the user requirement and/or difficulties in realising the user specification in practice.

One of the most effective methods of dealing with the need to amend projects is to have a project change procedure. Although this procedure will not remove all risks, it will enable some changes to be made to the project with minimal disruption and slippage occurring.

The change management plan is a definition of the formal process for making changes to the project's original scope. It generally involves redefining existing objectives and deliverables or specifying new project objectives and deliverables. The procedure for changes is as follows:

Change requests should be assigned a **change priority classification code** based on a set of standards. Possible priority codes might be: critical; high importance; medium importance; low importance.

After the change request evaluation, the project manager schedules **a change decision meeting**. Participants in the change decision meeting include the project sponsor(s), the change review committee or board members, the project manager, user management, and the originator of the change request.

The project manager presents the proposed change and the results of the evaluation, including a copy of the proposed revised project plan illustrating the impact of the change. The requestor may speak on behalf of the change (if necessary) and the evaluators may defend their evaluation (if necessary). The project manager acts as a neutral observer. The project manager gets involved only if the evaluation indicates that the proposed change would have a **significant impact** on the project – increasing costs, schedule, or project risk.

KEY POINT

The later into a project that a change is made, the more difficult it will be to accommodate that change, and the greater will be the expense of that change.

The later into a project that a change is made, the more difficult it will be to accommodate the change, and the greater will be the expense of that change.

A change management procedure for a project will normally involve the following activities:

- **Identifying the need for change** – this may arise from many sources including user input, technical difficulties with implementing part of the project, time or cost efficiencies identified by the project team, etc. Any change will be discussed with the project manager initially.
- **Change recommendation** – a more formal explanation of the change is produced, stating clearly the need for the change, what the change will be, and the costs and benefits associated with the change.
- **Feasibility of change** – the project manager and senior members of the project team will check that the change is actually possible in terms of technical and social feasibility.
- **Steering committee approval** – when the case for a change has been checked, the change document will be placed before the steering committee for discussion, and approval if the change is accepted.
- **Project sponsor approval** – major changes will also require the authorisation of the project sponsor and possibly the board or similar decision-making body of the organisation.
- **Amending project plan** – the project plan will be amended to take account of the change. Deadlines and costs will be revised.
- **Make change** – the change is actually carried out and, where necessary, tested to ensure that there are no conflicts with other sections of the project.

KEY POINT

Change management activities:

- identify need for change;
- make recommendation;
- check feasibility of change;
- get steering committee approval;
- get project sponsor approval;
- amend plan;
- make change.

The change management plan should describe the following elements:

- initiating a change request;
- logging and tracking change requests;
- assigning change requests for analysis and recommendation;
- implementing change request resolution actions (acceptance, delayed acceptance or rejection of change request);
- how accepted changes will be integrated into the project control documents (schedule and task plan, risk management plan, acquisition plan, etc.);
- roles and responsibilities in the change management process.

The last step is to communicate the change management plan to all project team members and stakeholders. Well-documented change request descriptions, resolutions and action plans are key to successful change management.

4.3 Management of risk

Management of risk arise from measurement errors, lack of data, and the underlying variability of complex natural, physical, social, and economic situations.

All projects require a degree of risk management, but the effort expended will depend on the size and scope, including outcomes, customers, outputs, work and resources. Larger projects involving significant investment and/or major outcomes require formal and detailed risk management activities on an ongoing basis. This occurs during the *initiation phase* of the project. It is also conducted throughout the project to ensure that changing circumstances are tracked and managed.

DEFINITION

Risk is defined as 'the chance of exposure to the adverse consequences of future events'.

Risk is defined as 'the chance of exposure to the adverse consequences of future events'. **Risk management** comprises risk assessment (identifying and analysing risk) and risk control (taking steps to reduce risk, provide contingency and monitor improvements). The processes are iterative throughout the life of the project and should be built into the project management activities.

Processes of risk management

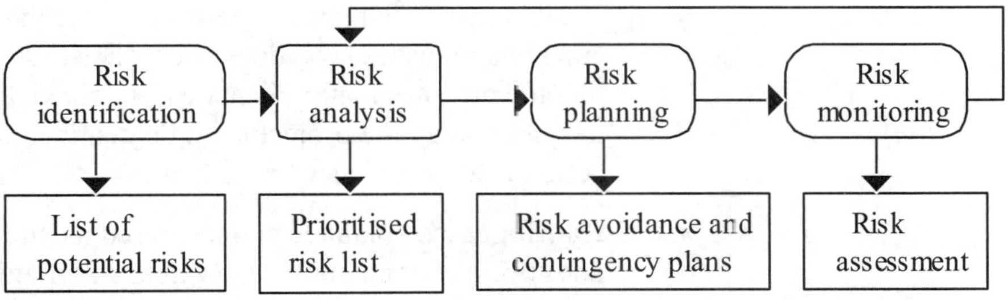

Risk identification

Before risks can be properly managed, they need to be identified Once the project has received approval to proceed, risk identification is usually done initially by involving key stakeholders. Brainstorming sessions to identify and clarify the main risks, which may prevent the project achieving its stated outcomes, are one way of doing this.

Risk analysis

Risks can be analysed and evaluated according to the likelihood they will occur and whether their level of seriousness/impact will be low, medium or high if they happen. From this, a priority listing for action can be developed.

The potential risks involved in undertaking a project can be presented in a tabular format as set out below. A typical risk assessment table is likely to run to many rows.

Risk	Odds	Impact	Management approach/mitigating actions	Warning signs
Skills				
Inability to recruit suitably qualified staff.	Low	Med	Ensure remuneration is appropriate to skill level.	Low numbers and poorly qualified applicants.
Retention of staff.	Med	Med	Motivation via contractual terms, good job design, good working environment and personal development. Consider retention clauses in contract for key staff.	Low morale. High turnover.
Management				
Necessary facilities not available.	Med	High	Accommodation available to project is currently limited. There could be implications for future of project if additional functionality is required and appropriate accommodation is not available to support it.	Delay to work plans caused by lack of facilities.
Failure to get all parties to share same understanding of purpose.	Low	High	Definition of stakeholder needs and clear plan with well-defined deliverables. Use of sound project management methodology.	Differing views on forward plan. Confused messages in draft publications.

Risk avoidance and contingency plans

Risk mitigation actions reduce the chance that a risk will be realised and/or reduce the seriousness of a risk that is realised. There are two broad types of risk mitigation or treatment activities:

- **Preventative** – planned actions to reduce the likelihood a risk will occur and the seriousness if it does occur. For example, if an identified risk is that the project's major clients will not have the technical expertise to use the technology the project is implementing, an appropriate preventative action is to provide technical training.
- **Contingency** – planned actions to reduce the seriousness of the risk, if it does occur. For example, a possible action in response to the previous risk might be that ongoing technical support and advice is provided to the client organisation once the technology is implemented.

Risk mitigation should be cost-efficient and effective. Conscious decisions need to be made regarding the wearing of certain risks as opposed to the costs of mitigation.

Recording risks

You will need to maintain a risk log or register. This should rec

- a description of the risk;
- the likelihood of the risk occurring;
- the potential impact of the risk;
- the risk owner;
- details of mitigating actions to be taken;
- identification of any early warning signs that indicate the risk is about to occur;
- details of any contingency plans where applicable.

Monitor and review

Risk management is not a one-off activity. Risks should be monitored throughout the project as their likelihood or impact ratings may change or new risks may emerge.

Since stakeholders can have a significant impact on decisions made, it is important that their perceptions of risk be identified and documented with the underlying reasons for the perceptions understood and documented. Communication and consultation with all key stakeholders should be an ongoing process and not just part of the initial identification and analysis process. It can be tied in with the overall communication strategy for the project and need not be a separate activity.

Activity 1

The identification of risk involves an overview of the project to establish what could go wrong and the consequences. What sorts of questions need to be asked to accomplish this?

Feedback to this activity is at the end of the chapter.

5 The project planning stage

5.1 PRINCE 2

Planning is essential – it helps to:

- communicate what has to be done, when and by whom;
- encourage forward thinking;
- provide the measures of success for the project;
- make clear the commitment of time, resources (people and equipment), and money required for the project;
- determine if targets are achievable;
- identify the activities the resources need to undertake.

Three main types of planning are required within PRINCE projects:

- **Project planning** – This is required in order to provide an overview of the whole project.
- **Stage planning** – Plans for each stage need to be prepared. These are produced towards the end of the previous stage. Plans are considered at end stage assessment meetings. This enables the assessment of the previous stage of the project and consideration of plans for the new stage.
- **Exception planning** – This type of planning is used when there are signs that the project is slipping behind schedule or is deviating from budget or quality targets.

5.2 Detailed planning

Planning without a system such as PRINCE 2 involves defining the resources to complete the project, devising a schedule and budget and negotiating with the project team the time and performance specifications required to achieve the objectives. A detailed plan is of value for three main reasons:

- The plan can be discussed with the project sponsor and users, to gain their agreement for the project to proceed.
- The plan will give a clear view to the project team of what is expected from them. This will improve their motivation level.
- The plan can be used as a basis for performance review.

The planning phase will result in the submission of proposals to the customer by the organisations that want to perform the project. The proposals will be evaluated and the most appropriate solution chosen. The SWOT analysis and scenario building will be part of the position analysis and fact-finding phase and a feasibility study with a cost benefit analysis is generally used in the option evaluation process. The customer and contractor will then sign a contract.

5.3 Evaluation of plans for projects

KEY POINT

Methods of evaluation include:

- examining existing records;
- structured observation;
- individual interviews;
- group interviews;
- expert opinion.

For planning to be meaningful and effective, evaluation must first be performed. A plan typically requires a needs assessment, a vision, a goal or goals, objectives or action steps, and measurement to determine the significance, worth, or quality of the undertaking so that what has been learned can be incorporated into future behaviour, service, or plans.

Project staff may already be collecting information through their normal procedures. By modifying current procedures or simply examining the data in a different way, key evaluation questions might be answered. This is known as examining existing records.

Structured observation is another evaluation technique. The observer(s) can focus on project setting, nature of interactions, program or service activities, user behaviours, unplanned results or activities, informal interactions and other aspects of projects, programs, and services.

Individual interviews are more formal with development of a set of structured questions consistently asked of key persons. Individual interviews can be conducted either face-to-face or by telephone.

Group interviews such as focus groups, nominal groups, and work groups can be effective evaluation techniques when staff feel group interaction is likely to increase the quality of data or when they believe this will reach a broader base of interviewees.

Expert opinion happens when the project manager solicits the evaluation of a professional or a panel of professionals.

Evaluation is as necessary during the implementation of a plan through to its conclusion as it was at the outset.

5.4 Position analysis

Following the investigation of the current situation, and indeed at any stage of the project, the project manager might decide to review the key issues relating to the project in terms of progress to date and external factors.

The most popular tool used for this type of assessment is the SWOT analysis, and it is common for project managers to produce SWOT analyses on a regular basis for discussion with the project sponsor or steering committee. (SWOT analysis was covered in Chapter 7: see Section 1.3.)

5.5 Fact finding

Once the project plan is agreed, it will be necessary for the project manager and team to carry out a full investigation into the current situation. This will often begin with a fact-finding exercise to establish the different views of stakeholders regarding the project.

During fact finding a number of methods can be used to help the project team identify the current situation and collect views and opinions. They include:

- interviews with project stakeholders;
- the preparation and circulation of questionnaires, and the analysis of responses;
- the observation of organisational facilities and activity;
- the review of documents such as procedures or technical literature.

Once the fact-finding is complete, it is important that the project team keep a written record of their findings. There are two reasons for this:

- The record will provide evidence that can be referred back to during later stages of the project.
- The documents will form a record of the starting point of the project. This will allow the project team to demonstrate exactly what changes and improvements they have made as a result of the project.

5.6 Options generation

At this stage of the project, the team must identify all of the available options using the internal strengths identified and the results from the fact-finding investigation. A number of approaches are available to help with the identification.

- The project team and some stakeholders may hold an informal meeting to discuss all of the options available.
- Brainstorming is an exercise commonly used in business to identify options. At the early stages of brainstorming it is essential that no idea, however ridiculous, be discarded. It is only as the session develops that the less realistic solutions are discarded. In this way the team can benefit from the discussion of radical and unconventional ideas, some aspect of which can be incorporated into the final solution.

- It is very common for project teams to seek the advice of consultants when generating and evaluating options. Business consultants bring a wealth of experience to a brainstorming meeting, and are often able to identify good solutions or to point out possible pitfalls.

5.7 Options evaluation

DEFINITION

Evaluation is: 'The systematic acquisition and assessment of information to provide useful feedback about some object.'

Evaluation has been defined as: 'The systematic acquisition and assessment of information to provide useful feedback about some object.'

Once a 'short-list' of options has been generated, each of them must be evaluated using some reasonably objective bases. A range of **feasibility study tools** (discussed in Section 5.9 below) can be applied to each of the options in order to determine the optimal approach. It may be useful for the project team to seek the views of potential users as to the desirability of each of the options on the shortlist.

Proposals may have been submitted by various product/service providers – for example, in the case of a project to design or implement a new computer system.

All proposals should be evaluated to determine whether they satisfy the basic requirements: a matrix of **requirements** versus **offerings** is a helpful tool in the comparison of proposals.

If the organisation does not have personnel technically qualified to perform the evaluation of the proposals, it may consider using an external consultant, who may be able to apply specific experience to the evaluation of techniques proposed, as well as provide an objective and credible point of view. A written report from the consultant regarding the proposals, the selection process, and recommendations for contracting can serve as a valuable starting point for approval and negotiation.

5.8 Scenario planning and buffering

Scenario analysis and planning are used to forecast the occurrence of complex environmental events. They are concerned with the evaluation and selection of strategies and make managers aware of environmental uncertainties. They are part of the organisation's management of risk. It is important to note there is no best scenario, rather managers must 'bet' on the most probable.

Scenarios describe in detail the sequence of events that could plausibly lead to a prescribed future state. They identify factors that are likely to affect the organisation, and they assess implications of future conditions for corporate objectives and performance. Scenario analysis usually leads to the development of best-case, worst-case, and most-likely scenarios. Each scenario represents a different set of assumptions about external and internal factors.

For example, a power-plant contractor that executes projects in the Middle East might identify risks including natural events (a sand storm), technical events (a test failure), partner events (a supplier not delivering), financial events (a guarantee falling through) or political events (a local power broker's resistance). Each identified risk would be assigned a probability, and then methods such as scenario evaluations or simulations would be used to estimate potential impact and to prioritise risks. Handling the risks could mean avoiding them, taking preventive action or simply accepting them as a nuisance. Preventive action could mean inserting buffers (or slack) at strategic points in the critical path and setting control limits for taking corrective action.

Activity 2

What is meant by project planning, and who should be involved in the process?

Feedback to this activity is at the end of the chapter.

5.9 Feasibility study

KEY POINT

Four dimensions of project feasibility:

- technical feasibility;
- economic feasibility;
- social feasibility;
- ecological feasibility.

The requirements will be clearly defined and set out in a statement, outlining what is expected of the project or product. It is a statement of the reason for what is being done or developed. It is not a specification with detailed characteristics and size or performance criteria. It gives the customer and the project team an opportunity to agree that the requirement is appropriate and meets the organisational needs and objectives.

Once the requirements have been identified, potential projects can be investigated to examine their feasibility. The primary objective of the feasibility study is to identify the key technical and performance objectives that the project must achieve and to ensure that the technology exists to achieve these targets. The study must also determine the cost of achieving these targets. This cost information is fed into the economic feasibility assessment. Four issues are particularly important:

- technical feasibility;
- economic/financial feasibility;
- social feasibility;
- ecological feasibility.

Technical feasibility is the matching of the project requirements to the performance that can be achieved from available material, technology and processes. In terms of a new computer system, say, technical feasibility may be evaluated by consideration of the following factors:

- ability to support a number of users;
- response times required;
- ability to process a certain number of transactions within a time constraint;
- capacity to hold a certain number of records on line;
- networking with distant locations.

Economic feasibility – the project must provide a benefit to the organisation. Economic feasibility will be assessed through a process of cost benefit analysis. Costs will include:

- capital costs for purchasing assets e.g. equipment plus any additional costs of installation and maintenance;
- revenue costs for purchases other than assets e.g. consultancy, conversion and training, staff salaries, stationery and financing costs.

The benefits may be as a result of:

- direct cost savings;
- increased capacity;
- improved quality of product or service;
- competitive edge;
- improved decision-making.

Social or operational feasibility – this type of feasibility is concerned with ensuring that the project fits with the business and social organisation of the company. The new project may require new skills and attitudes. The feasibility study must assess whether the current employees have such skills and, if they do not, whether they can attain these skills and the cost of attaining them (for use in economic feasibility). Redundancies may be necessary and the feasibility study should assess both the direct and indirect costs of such a programme.

Ecological feasibility considerations may be stimulated by health and safety legislation. Products that are ecologically sound and less harmful to the environment will lessen the chances of customers switching to alternatives. The project feasibility should consider the raw material input, the production processes and the disposal of the product at the end of its life.

Summary

- Key project methodologies include PRINCE2, JISC infoNet, and PMBOK.
- A project is launched on the basis of a project initiation document and a project scope statement.
- There will always be trade-offs between time, cost and scope: the project triangle.
- SMART objectives are specific, measurable, attainable, relevant and time-bounded.
- Risk and uncertainty arise from measurement errors, lack of data, and the underlying variability of complex natural, physical, social and economic situations.

Having completed your study of this chapter you should have achieved the following learning outcomes.

- Identify methodologies and systems used by professional project managers.
- Identify the strategy and scope for a project.
- Produce a basic project plan, recognising the effects of uncertainty and recommending strategies for dealing with this uncertainty, in the context of a simple project.

Self-test questions

1. What are the main components of the JISC infoNet method? (1.3)
2. List the probable content of the terms of reference for the project. (2.1)
3. What information should be included in the project scope statement? (3.2)
4. List typical stages in a change management procedure. (4.2)
5. What headings might be used in a risk assessment table? (4.3)
6. List four techniques used in evaluation of project plans. (5.3)

Multiple-choice questions

Question 1

The risk management planning process is:

A identify and classify risk, monitor risk, analyse risk and respond to risk

B analyse risk, identify and classify risk, monitor risk and respond to risk

C monitor risk, identify and classify risk, analyse risk and respond to risk

D identify and classify risk, analyse risk, respond to risk and monitor risk.

Question 2

Configuration management is:

A a means of monitoring and controlling emerging project scope against the scope baseline

B the production of a scope statement

C the creation of the work breakdown structure

D a mechanism to track budget and schedule variances.

For the answer to these questions, see the 'Answers' section at the end of the book.

Exam-type question

Feasibility study

The managing director of a distributor of motor accessories is convinced that the retail outlets to which they sell see them as a 'staid and stodgy' organisation and that new computer systems could help change that image by the production of new look invoices and reports for the outlets. This is despite the fact that there are currently no substantial problems with the existing computer systems. So convinced is he that he calls in the information technology manager and asks him to briefly analyse the situation and report back in person a week later. The IT manager duly returns as requested to report that most users who have substantial contacts with the computer systems are happy with them. The IT department staff agree that the technology is readily available to update the systems. The IT manager himself is of the opinion that just because it can be done, it doesn't mean it should be done.

However, the managing director requests that a feasibility report be produced, and you are asked to carry out the preceding feasibility study.

(a) How would you assess the feasibility of this project? **(6 marks)**

(b) Outline the likely contents of a formal feasibility study report for the managing director. **(8 marks)**

(c) Assuming that the managing director decides to proceed with the project, discuss the various fact-finding techniques you might now make use of to collect all the necessary information about the existing system and the new requirements. **(11 marks)**

(Total: 25 marks)

For the answer to this question, see the 'Answers' section at the end of the book.

Feedback to activities

Activity 1

The type of questions include:

What are the sources of risk?

What is the likelihood of the risk presenting itself?

To what extent can the risk be controlled?

What are the consequences of that risk presenting itself?

To what extent can those consequences be controlled?

Activity 2

Project planning is the arrangement of the activities required to achieve the project objective. The first part of this stage is the establishment and agreement of the project objectives. This means determining exactly what the project aims to achieve. The next stage is to determine what activities or tasks need to be undertaken to achieve the objective.

The project plan articulates exactly what needs to be achieved, how it is to be achieved, by whom and at what time in the project's life. It is a benchmark against which actual project results can be compared and monitored. If the comparison of actual versus plan indicates a deviation, then corrective action needs to be taken.

It is important that the planning stage involves the members of staff who will be working on the project. These people will be in the best position to know what activities will be needed, how they will be performed and how long they will take. In addition, by encouraging team participation in planning, it is more likely that they will become committed to achieving their activity targets.

Chapter 9

MANAGING THE PROJECT TEAM

Syllabus content

- Organisational structures, including the role of the project and matrix organisations, and their impact on project achievement.
- Teamwork, including recognising the life cycle of teams, team/group behaviour and selection.

Contents

1 Project structure

2 Building and managing the project team

1 Project structure

1.1 Basic stakeholder hierarchy

A project is much like an organisation in that it has a hierarchical set of relationships. This hierarchy is put in place for two main reasons:

- to create a structure of authority so everyone knows who can make decisions; and
- to create a series of superior-subordinate relationships so each individual or group has only one 'boss'.

The stakeholder hierarchy *(adapted from Gido & Clements, 1999)*

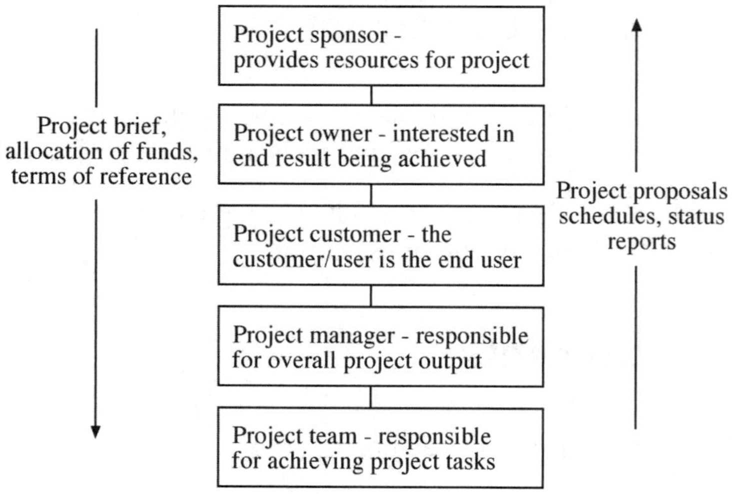

We discussed the roles of all these stakeholders in Chapter 6 (see Section 3).

1.2 PRINCE structure

Organisation is a key element of the PRINCE method and a structure is defined which provides management of the project for its whole duration, and represents the interests of the major stakeholders. The organisation structure identifies project roles, the experience and training needed, lines of authority, reporting and communication. It defines the responsibilities of the user and higher management, how and when they are involved, as well as the roles of the project team. It describes how the user keeps in touch on a day-to-day basis with the entire development.

Within PRINCE, responsibilities are defined in terms of roles, rather than individuals. Assignment of roles to individuals is a decision for each project to take according to size, how many user areas are involved and the availability of resources. The same individual may be assigned to more than one role, to different roles at different stages of the project, or more than one person may share a role.

The basic PRINCE project organisational structure is illustrated below (arrows indicate accountability).

PRINCE project structure

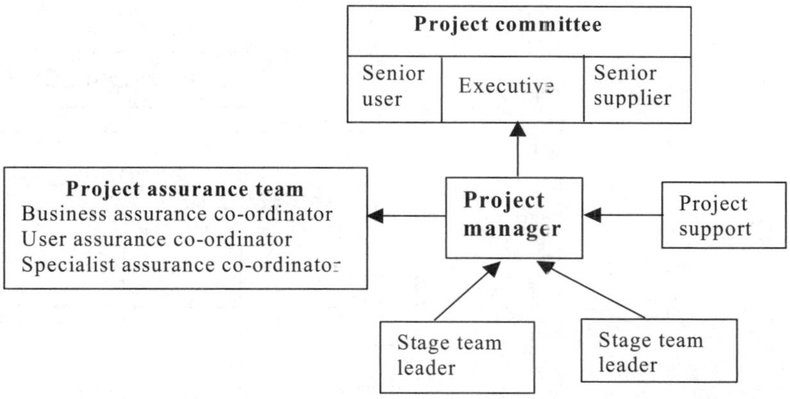

KEY POINT

The PRINCE structure defines the roles of:

- project committee
- project manager
- team leader
- project assurance
- project support.

The PRINCE guidance specifies quite precisely the roles and responsibilities of each member of the project organisation.

Project committee (sometimes called a project board) – provides senior input to the management of the project. This committee carries overall responsibility for the success or failure of the project. The members must be of sufficient seniority to be able to secure the resources needed by the project manager to manage the project.

Project manager – is given authority, within certain tolerances, by the committee to manage the project on a day-to-day level. He or she reports regularly to the committee, keeping them informed of progress and highlighting any problems he/she can foresee.

Team leader (sometimes called stage team leader) – manages parts of projects, focus on schedule, quality and cost targets. There may be one or more team leaders involved in a project. The project manager delegates responsibility to team leaders to produce the project products.

Project assurance – provide an independent view of how the project is progressing. In PRINCE2, there are three views of assurance: business, user and specialist. Each view reflects the interests of the project committee members.

Project support – is an optional set of roles. A project support office, if provided, undertakes administrative activities required to keep the project going. These activities will typically include arranging meetings, updating project plans on project planning software, and filing project documents. For smaller projects, existing administrative and clerical staff in the organisation can fulfil this role.

1.3 Project and matrix organisation

The various bases of organisation at the corporate level were discussed in Chapter 3.

Project organisation is the creation of a unit with responsibility for all aspects of project development. Features include:

- integration of project and functional resources;
- business functions carried out within projects and along functional lines;
- two-dimensional supervision, with project members reporting to a project manager as well as to their (functional) line manager.

Professional, technical and administrative staff are co-opted for the duration of the project.

Note that this implies a form of **matrix organisation**:

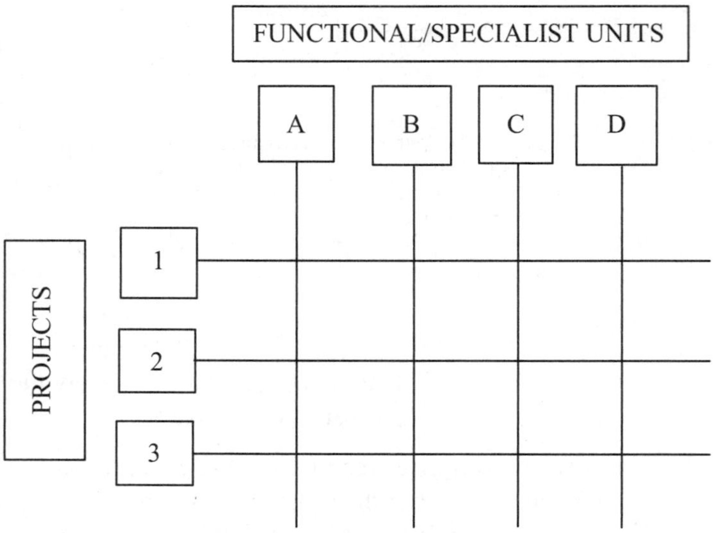

Which employees are borrowed is negotiated by the project manager with functional department heads. The choice is usually based on the availability of personnel and the qualifications demanded by the project. Sometimes, department heads are reluctant to release competent personnel. However, most recognise that having staff representatives on the team protects departmental interests, and offers potential for staff learning and development.

KEY POINT

One problem with matrix organisation is that project members have two bosses.

One problem with matrix organisation is that project members have two bosses. They are responsible to the stage leader/manager for work assignments, yet their permanent supervisors retain jurisdiction over personnel matters such as salary and promotions. The two bosses may clash in values and objectives, with the project member caught in between. Such potentially explosive situations can be defused if, before the team is constituted, ground rules are negotiated between the project manager and functional heads regarding shared authority and responsibility over project members.

However, the essence of project management is that it cuts across, and in a sense conflicts with the conventional organisation structure, with its 'vertical' boundaries between specialist functions.

Because a project usually requires decisions and actions from a number of functional areas at once, the main interdependencies and the main flow of information in a project are not vertical but lateral. Projects are characterised by exceptionally strong lateral working relationships, requiring closely related activity and decisions by many individuals in different functional departments.

Teams gain when people share their knowledge, and this is an important contributor to project success. As an example, when one project team learns a new technique, which adds to their performance, they are able to use it to increase their performance on the next project. However, if they are to share that learning, every project team in the organisation will improve next time. Adopting a matrix organisation for project teams ensures people 'swap' teams regularly and therefore spread their experience. It leads to improved working practices, cross fertilisation of ideas and thinking, and facilitates the development of new ideas and implementation of changing technology. In addition, it has a direct effect on the development of younger team members, helping them be better performers and become the experts of the future.

KEY POINT

The main impact a matrix organisation has on project achievement is its high task and objectives orientation, flexibility, creativity and innovative capacity.

The main impact a matrix organisation has on project achievement is its high task and objectives orientation, flexibility, creativity and innovative capacity.

Matrix organisation:

- Allows a project manager to cut across vertical organisational divisions.
- Involves functional departments and is responsive to their needs because representatives are on the project staff.
- Has access to the resources in all functional departments (on a negotiated basis).
- Provides a departmental 'home' for project personnel to return to after the completion of the project.
- Does not permanently disrupt organisational sub groupings or the continuity of seniority, fringe benefits, and so on.

2 Building and managing the project team

2.1 What is a team?

DEFINITION

Teams have been described as collections of people who must rely on group collaboration if each member is to experience the optimum of success.

Teams have been described as collections of people who must rely on group collaboration if each member is to experience the optimum of success. Teams are groups of people who show the following characteristics:

- they share a common goal, and are striving to get a common job done;
- they enjoy working together, and enjoy helping one another;
- they have made a commitment to achieve the goals and objectives of the project by accomplishing their particular portion of the project;
- they are very diverse individuals having all kinds of different disciplinary and experiential backgrounds who must now concentrate on a common effort;
- they have great loyalty to the project as well as loyalty and respect for the project manager, and have a firm belief in what the project is trying to accomplish;
- they have attained a team spirit and a very high team morale.

To ensure that the group is truly an effective team working toward the same goals and objectives, the team members must have an overpowering reason for working together. They must need each other's skills, talent, and experience in order to achieve their mutual goals. Helping team members to achieve this goal is a key responsibility of the project manager.

2.2 Project team selection

KEY POINT

A team is a small number of people with diverse, yet complementary backgrounds, skill sets, and capabilities who are committed to a common purpose, clearly defined performance goals, and an approach for which they hold themselves mutually accountable.

A team is a small number of people with diverse, yet complementary backgrounds, skill sets, and capabilities who are committed to a common purpose, clearly defined performance goals, and an approach for which they hold themselves mutually accountable.

As a project manager, one of the most important steps is the selection and recruitment of a project team.

For some projects, the manager may have a team 'forced' on them, or may inherit a team from a previous project manager. If this is the case, little can be done to change the team membership. However, if a project manager is able to select a team, this can be a major determinant of the success of a project.

Simply accepting a team member because of their functional specialism and availability is not sufficient. Team members should see that being part of a project team is a privilege, and a formal set of recruitment interviews will help to reinforce this view.

At the recruitment stage, the project manager should consider asking candidates the following:

- What is their relevant technical experience?
- Have they any specialised knowledge relevant to the project?
- Have they worked in project teams before?
- Have they other departmental or project commitments?
- When do these commitments end?
- Can they commit to the project full-time?
- Do they get on well with others?
- Do they like working alone?
- What do they seek to gain from the project?
- Is their line manager in agreement with their joining the team?

KEY POINT

Effective team working is essential for the success of a project and it is important to foster this through regular meetings to establish team cohesion.

The project team is likely to be made up of a range of staff with different skills and experience. Effective team working is essential for the success of a project and it is important to foster this through regular meetings to establish team cohesion, helping to develop a team which is integrated, has common objectives and positive group dynamics. The ideal project team will achieve project completion on time, within budget and to the required specifications. They will do all this with the minimum amount of direct supervision from the project manager.

The project team should include everyone who will significantly contribute to the project, both managerial and non-managerial people, whether they are full-time or part-time. It will obviously include all of the technical people responsible for the project's efforts toward research, design, development, procurement, production, and testing. It is less obvious which of the many supporting and service functions involved with the project should be represented on the project team. However, representatives from other supporting groups such as quality control, finance, and logistics should be sought when their function is vital to the project or is desired by the customer.

2.3 Managing the project team

Once the project is under way, it is one of the project manager's major responsibilities to motivate, develop and manage the work of the project team. In large projects, it is the team that does the work, while the manager, although responsible for the quality of the work, does little of it and concentrates on managing others.

The project manager must pay attention to two particular characteristics of each team:

- Each project is a complete entity, and unique in terms of experiences, problems, constraints and objectives.
- The members of the team concerned may well have not worked together as a group on any previous occasion.

The style of management for the team must be the relevant approach aimed at the creation of the appropriate internal team environment, or, in other words, team climate. Some large organisations provide the team with initial status by providing it with all the necessary support and resources, such as office accommodation, a budget, support secretarial staff, and so on. Other organisations simply appoint a leader, authorised by the board to appoint team members and acquire resources at his or her own discretion.

The planning and controlling of the team activities are vital aspects of management in that a major project cost lies in the fact that team members are not undertaking their own tasks but have been taken from these temporarily. It is essential that there should be an unambiguous statement of:

- *the project objective(s)* – what is to be achieved?
- *the project approach, methods* – how is it to be achieved?
- *the location of activities* – where is it to be achieved?
- *the allocation of responsibilities* – what is to be done by whom?
- *the project budget* – at what cost?

2.4 Project team development – Tuckman

All groups or teams have a **lifecycle**. They do not perform optimally straight away – particularly if the members are new to each other.

B W Tuckman has formulated four stages of team development:

KEY POINT

Tuckman's four stages in the group lifecycle:

- Forming
- Storming
- Norming
- Performing.

(i) **Forming** – members are trying to gauge their own acceptance, their acceptance of others, who will take charge, roles people will take etc. At this initial stage, the team members are no more than a collection of individuals who are unsure of their roles and responsibilities until the project manager clearly defines the initial processes and procedures for team activities, including documentation, communication channels and the general project procedures. The project manager must then provide clear direction and structure to the team by communicating the project objectives, constraints, scope, schedules and budget.

(ii) **Storming** – sooner or later, any team which is going anywhere much has to address this conflict stage and get all the differences out in the open. As tasks get underway, team members may try to test the project manager's authority, preconceptions are challenged, and conflict and tension may become evident. Conflict may be about goals, leadership, work methods, relationships, hierarchy etc. Some matters will cause arguments, others may be resolved peacefully. Generally some disagreement will be aired and resolved and the group moves on. Storming results in agreed processes, and styles of interpersonal relationship e.g. level of trust and openness. The conflict resolution skills and the leadership skills of the project manager are vital at this stage and he or she needs to be more flexible to allow team members to question and test their roles and responsibilities and to get involved in decision-making.

(iii) **Norming** – means agreeing who is doing what and establishing modes of behaviour etc. At this stage the norms under which the team will operate and team relationships become settled. Project procedures are refined and the project manager will begin to pass control and decision-making authority to the team members. They will be operating as a cohesive team, with each person recognising and appreciating the roles of the other team members.

(iv) **Performing** – once this final stage has been reached the team is capable of operating to full potential. Progress is made towards the project objectives and the team feels confident and empowered. The project manager will concentrate on the performance of the project, (in particular the scope, timescales and budget) and implement corrective action where necessary.

All teams do not automatically follow the four stages in this sequence. For example, a team where a large number of the members have worked together previously or have a much greater knowledge of the technical aspects of the problem will tend to arrive at the performing stage quickly. Unfortunately, each time a member changes (leaves, gets promoted or has job re-defined) the team lifecycle is likely to get knocked back a stage or two. Of course, not all teams pass through all the stages - some get stuck in the middle and remain inefficient and ineffective.

The implications of the Tuckman model:

- Duration and intensity of the stages vary.
- Teams must progress through the early stages to reach the performing stage.
- Teams can fixate at one of the first three stages.
- Regression to a previous stage can occur.
- Understanding the stages helps keep a team from over-reacting to normal problems.

Activity 1

What do you think happens within a team when:

(a) it has been performing effectively for a while?

(b) a project team comes towards the end of its task and faces being disbanded?

Feedback to this activity is at the end of the chapter.

2.5 Team roles – Belbin

KEY POINT

Belbin identified eight team roles:

- Chair
- Shaper
- Plant /innovator
- Monitor/evaluator
- Resource investigator
- Organiser/company worker
- Team worker
- Completer/finisher.

Belbin developed the concept of team roles, with everybody having their own preferred role(s). These are not **functional roles** (e.g. accountant, marketing person, IT person) but **process roles**: the roles people fill in the functioning and maintenance of the team; in the processes of ideas generation, discussion, decision-making, conflict resolution and so on. Belbin describes eight process roles (below) which a team must fill, plus that of the subject specialist (expert). Precise terminology can vary, but these headings can be used to consider how the team manages to cover the roles as a 'simple' starter.

- **Chair** (co-ordinator and social leader) – is self-confident, controlled and has a capacity for treating all members on their merits and a strong sense of objectives.
- **Shaper** (gives drive and impetus) – is highly-strung, outgoing and dynamic with a readiness to challenge any ineffective behaviour.
- **Plant/innovator** (ideas person) – is individualistic and serious-minded with genius and imagination.
- **Monitor/evaluator** (stopping over enthusiasm, missing key points) – is sober, unemotional and prudent and is noted for judgement, discretion and hard-headedness.
- **Resource investigator** (delicate external negotiations) – is extrovert, enthusiastic, able to rise to a challenge, curious and has contacts and networks.
- **Organiser/company worker** (implementer – turns ideas into practical action) – is conservative, dutiful, hard working, and self-disciplined and has organisational ability and practical common sense.
- **Team worker** (defuses friction) – is mild and sensitive with an ability to build team spirit and solve disputes.
- **Completer/finisher** (progress chaser) – is a conscientious perfectionist with a capacity to follow through.

It is not necessary for one individual to take on one role, as roles can be shared or individuals in smaller groups can take on more than one role, but it is important that all the roles are covered.

Adaptors and innovators

Professor Michael Kirton, in his adaptation/innovation theory, suggests that there is a spectrum of creative style, illustrating the different ways in which individuals approach bringing about change or problem-solving. Adaptors are at one end and innovators are at the other. Adaptors prefer 'to make improvements in existing ways of doing things' and innovators prefer 'to do things differently'.

Among many other characteristics, the adaptor is likely to:

- prefer improvement of existing structures over mould-breaking change;
- be methodical and prudent;
- put a high value on being efficient within a system;
- be interested in solving problems rather than looking for them.

By contrast the innovator is likely to:

- prefer mould-breaking change to improvement of existing structures;
- be seen as undisciplined and reckless;
- put greater value on thinking up new skills than on implementing them;
- enjoy seeking out problems.

Adaptors approach problem solving from the inside, and innovators from the outside, in relation to the status quo.

2.6 Difficulties or blockages in team working

There are many aspects of the team process, which might be impeding its effectiveness. Blocks to effectiveness include:

- objectives that are unclear or not accepted by the team members;
- a lack of trust or support;
- unsound working procedures;
- inadequate review of performance;
- problems with performance – it is slipping but no one knows why;
- decisions once made remain unimplemented;
- team members are unresponsive or apathetic to the needs of the team or of the project;
- team meetings are unproductive, full of conflict, and demoralising;
- team members withdraw into their own areas of responsibility and avoid co-operation;
- problem-solving activity, like 'constructive conflict', is avoided;
- poor motivation and apathy;
- schedule slippages, quality problems and consequent cost escalations develop.

2.7 Team building

When a new project is started, there is a great need to get everyone on the project team going in the same direction and aimed at accomplishing the same project goals. Basically the problem is that everyone on the project team sees the project in terms of their own particular discipline and background, and they will tend to go in different directions, often sub-optimising in their solution of project problems. The project manager must get the individual team members to view the project from the 'big-picture' perspective, and to concentrate on overall project goals.

Woodcock suggests that to achieve a successful team, the following nine aspects of its functioning and performance must have taken place.

1 Clear objectives and agreed goals.

2 Openness and confrontation.

3 Support and trust.

4 Co-operation and conflict.

5 Sound procedures.

6 Appropriate leadership.

7 Regular reviews.

8 Individual development.

9 Sound inter-group relations.

If any one, or more, of these key aspects of team performance is not developed, the team may fail to achieve its full potential. The responsibility for team building falls squarely on the shoulders of the project manager, for he or she is the only person in the position of being able to ensure that team building occurs and that it is effective.

2.8 The role of the project leader

KEY POINT

Team-building interventions are directed towards four areas: diagnosis, task accomplishment, team relationships and team organisation.

Team-building interventions are directed towards four areas:

- **diagnosis** – involves open discussion by the group to uncover problems that are affecting their performance
- **task accomplishment** – involves agreement on what the team exists to do, what can be achieved and how it should be accomplished
- **team relationships** – involves identifying the role expectations and responsibilities of the team members, examining what the leader expects from the group and what the group expects from the leader
- **team organisation** – is the process of selecting the best team to achieve the identified goals and determine the roles and responsibilities of each member selected.

The role of the leader in team building is to satisfy task, group and individual needs. Professor Adair's action-centred leadership model singles out the responsibilities of the group/team leader.

KEY POINT

The core responsibilities of the team leader are to:

1 achieve the task;

2 build and maintain the team;

3 develop each individual member.

The basic idea behind his theory is that the leader of any group or team has to strive constantly to achieve three major goals while at the same time maintaining a position as an effective leader:

1 The first goal considers the *task needs* – the manager ensures that the purpose (completion of the task) is fulfilled. This entails defining the objectives, aims and goals, etc. The main tasks could include setting standards, allocating jobs and controlling the work. Other leadership skills required include problem solving and decision-making, promoting involvement and commitment, evaluating ideas and performance, negotiating and resolving conflicts.

2 The second goal is a similar consideration of the *group needs* – until the task is completed the group has to be held together: the manager must maintain team spirit and build morale, concentrating on team-building, developing interdependence and keeping the members of the group well informed.

3 The third goal is to consider *individual needs* and motivate, develop and support individuals. Each member of a group or team has individual needs and the manager should try to find out what they are and work towards satisfying them within the group's needs.

Essentially, the model proposes that the three areas of need are interlinked and that an effective leader integrates them and sees that all needs are met. The functions to do this are shown below:

Task functions	Team functions	Individual functions
• Achieving the objectives of the work group • Defining group tasks • Planning the work • Allocating resources • Organising duties and responsibilities • Controlling quality and checking performance • Reviewing progress	• Maintaining morale and building team spirit • Developing work methods so the team functions cohesively • Setting standards and maintaining discipline • Setting up and maintaining systems of communication • Training the team • Appointing subordinate leaders	• Meeting the needs of the individual members of the group • Attending to personal problems • Giving praise and status • Reconciling conflicts between group needs and individual needs • Developing the individual

To achieve all this, the project leader will need the following skills:

- leadership skills;
- communication skills;
- negotiation skills;
- delegation skills;
- problem-solving skills;
- change-management skills.

2.9 Communication

KEY POINT

Communication tools for the project manager include:

- job/task descriptions;
- checkpoint meetings and reports;
- notice boards;
- appraisals;
- newsletters.

One of the keys to success in project management is creating and maintaining a communication structure within the project team. There are a number of communication tools that the project manager can use:

Job/task descriptions – giving each team member a clear written statement of their responsibilities, goals and performance measures will improve their motivation level and provide a framework for performance review.

Checkpoint meetings and reports – the PRINCE methodology recommends a regular, often weekly, meeting between the project team members and the project manager. At this meeting, any issues can be raised and dealt with in a fairly relaxed environment. The proceedings are often minuted and reported to the steering committee or project sponsor.

Notice boards – if the project team have an office, a notice board can be used for team-related correspondence. If the organisation has an intranet, an electronic bulletin board can be established.

Appraisals – if the project extends over months or even years, the team can have regular appraisals by the project manager.

Newsletters – the project team can publish and distribute a weekly or monthly newsletter, either in hard copy form or by e-mail.

2.10 Human resource management issues

Many of the major issues in project management arise because of the conflicting objectives of the various project team members. Among the most common reasons for conflict are the following:

- unclear objectives for the project;
- role ambiguity within the project team;
- unclear schedules and performance targets;
- a low level of authority given to the project manager;
- remote functional groups within the project, working almost independently;
- interference from local or functional management;
- personality clashes, or differing styles of working.

Most conflict arises from the interaction of individuals, and a good project manager must have the interpersonal skills to be able to manage conflict. (We discuss these in detail in Chapter 13.)

Summary

- Project stakeholders include the project sponsor, the project owner, the project customer, the project manager and the project team.
- The project team may be structured by means of a function organisation, a project organisation or a matrix organisation.
- In the development of a project team the work of Tuckman on formation of groups and of Belbin on the roles of group members is helpful.

Having completed your study of this chapter you should have achieved the following learning outcome.

- Identify structural and leadership issues that will be faced in managing a project team.

Self-test questions

1. Describe the PRINCE structure. (1.2)
2. What is the main impact a matrix structure has on project achievement? (1.5)
3. List four characteristics of teams. (2.1)
4. What are Tuckman's four stages of team development? (2.4)
5. What happens in the storming phase of the lifecycle of teams? (2.4)
6. Identify Belbin's team roles. (2.5)
7. List three blocks to team effectiveness. (2.6)

Multiple-choice question

Question 1

The PRINCE organisation structure shows three views of assurance. Which of the following does not fit?

A User assurance co-ordinator

B Executive assurance co-ordinator

C Business assurance co-ordinator

D Specialist assurance co-ordinator

For the answer to this question, see the 'Answers' section at the end of the book.

Exam-type questions

Question 1: Project management

What special problems arise in the management of projects, and how can they be overcome? **(10 marks)**

Question 2: Project processes

If a project is badly run then it is unlikely to gain the commitment of the people it needs for success. Poorly run projects fail to identify those whose commitment is needed to build the new system and as such individuals do not want to associate themselves with a project which is bound for failure.

Required:

Describe the conditions that are necessary to manage a successful information system project. **(10 marks)**

For the answer to these questions, see the 'Answers' section at the end of the book.

Feedback to activity

Activity 1

Later writers added these two stages to Tuckman's model.

(a) 'Dorming' happens when teams grow complacent about their performance. They may regress to self-maintenance functions, at the expense of the task. They may also become prey to 'group think': over-confidence in the cosy consensus of the group, leading to blinkered thinking.

(b) 'Mourning' happens when teams face disbanding. Members experience sadness and anxiety, and begin to withdraw from the group. The group begins to focus on evaluating its achievements, to give members closure.

Chapter 10

PROJECT CONTROL

Syllabus content

- Control of time, cost and quality through performance and conformance management systems.
- Project completion documentation, stakeholder marketing, completion reports and system close-down.
- The use of post-completion audit and review activities and the justification of their costs.

Contents

1 Project control systems

2 Control of time, cost and quality

3 Quality in the project environment

4 Project completion

1 Project control systems

1.1 Project control

DEFINITION

Project control is the continuous monitoring of the project for deviations from plan (time, cost, and quality) and the execution of corrective action.

Project control is the continuous monitoring of the project for deviations from plan (time, cost, and quality) and the execution of corrective action

A basic control system should have the following components:

- A plan – a statement of what is to happen.
- Observations – measurements of what is happening.
- Comparisons – between expectations and actual.
- Corrections – actions designed to re-direct what is happening back to what should happen.
- Updates – of forecasts and or plan as appropriate.

This involves scheduling, monitoring and controlling.

Scheduling

- Schedule the whole project at the beginning.
- Recognise interdependence of the parts.
- Identify the critical items early.
- Seek the best time and cost estimates.
- Modify and update the schedule.
- Bring all contributors into the scheduling process.

(We discussed planning, scheduling and objective-setting in Chapter 8.)

Monitoring

- Follow and monitor on a regular basis.
- Include all contributors in the monitoring process.
- Plan general alternatives for each contingency.
- Keep the goals and alternatives in mind.

A well-constructed plan with clear deliverables should make it very easy to track progress. The project manager should set up mechanisms whereby the team regularly reviews what tasks have been completed/delayed and what the impact is on the rest of the plan.

The diagram below shows a typical review loop indicating activities that occur once only, daily, weekly and at the end of each phase.

Project review loop

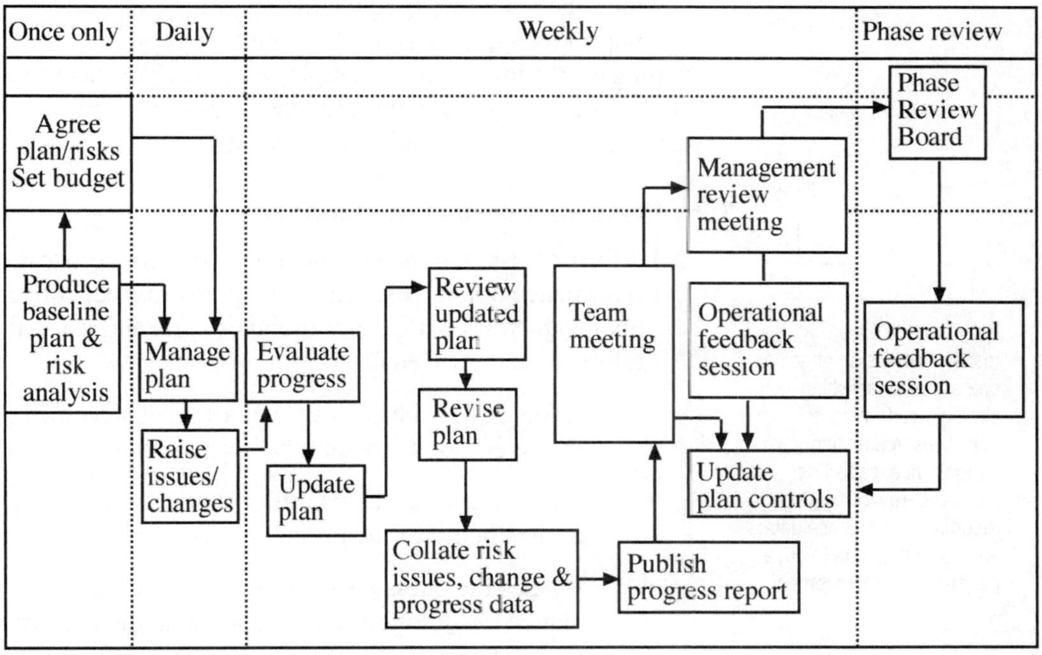

Phase boundaries are key points at which a number of aspects of the project can be reviewed:

- Is the business case for the project still valid?
- Is the project meeting its objectives?
- Has the risk situation altered?
- Should the project progress to the next phase?

For organisations using a PRINCE system, the project board is not involved in regular progress meetings. The task of monitoring progress is delegated to the project manager and the stage managers. It would be normal practice for the project manager, the project assurance team, the stage managers and the team leaders to meet on a weekly basis for a checkpoint meeting to report progress. On a less frequent basis, usually monthly, the project manager should prepare a highlight report for the members of the project board. This should report progress to date against the plan, highlight any significant problems encountered and contain an assessment of the work to come. The aim of this report is to keep the board members aware of the project status without an expensive meeting.

Controlling

- Take early corrective action when needed.
- Balance project effort.
- Look for where effort can be reduced.
- Make changes early rather than late.

Measurement of all relevant variables is important both for management information and also for the specification of 'what kind' and 'how much' corrective action is necessary. Corrective actions are 'management prerogatives' that are available to a manager based upon the type of organisation (hierarchical, matrix), the position of the project manager and the organisation culture.

Examples of corrective action include: 'fast tracking', 'crashing', adding additional resources (people, money, time, etc.), scope reduction, quality compromising, increasing risk, employee/contractor disciplinary actions (negative reinforcement), employee/contractor incentives (positive reinforcement), pep talks and other motivation, etc. Some corrective actions tend to be more tactical, and some more strategic.

1.2 Performance-based management

KEY POINT

Performance-based management is an ongoing process of establishing strategic performance objectives; measuring performance; collecting, analysing, reviewing, and reporting performance data; and using that data to drive performance improvement.

Performance-based management is an ongoing process of establishing strategic performance objectives; measuring performance; collecting, analysing, reviewing, and reporting performance data; and using that data to drive performance improvement.

- It focuses on the achievement of results deemed important by the project manager, not on the number of activities.
- It provides a mechanism for accurately reporting performance to the project board or the project sponsor.
- It takes the guesswork out of 'How are we doing?' because all work is planned and done in accordance with the performance objectives. The end result is an accurate picture of time, cost and quality performance.
- It brings all 'interested' parties into the planning and evaluation of performance.
- It provides a mechanism for linking performance to budget expenditures. At the beginning of the cycle, performance-based management provides a framework for showing what goals will be accomplished and what resources will be necessary to accomplish those goals. At the end of the cycle, it shows what was actually accomplished and what resources actually were used to achieve those results.

Thus, performance-based management takes the uncertainty out of budget allocations and provides an effective accounting for money spent. All actions, decisions, expenditures, and results can be easily explained, justified, and reported.

1.3 Project control systems

KEY POINT

The purpose of a project control system is to develop a plan of the work that is to be accomplished and to develop a system that monitors that plan and the performance of the work.

A **project control system** is simply a tool for the project manager. It enables recognition of problems before they become too difficult to solve. The essence is that it integrates the actual work to be done with the cost of doing the work and the time needed to do it. Its main objectives are to develop a plan of the work that is to be accomplished and to develop a system that monitors the plan and the performance of the work. This system must provide the information necessary so that the project team, company management, and the client can identify problem areas and initiate corrective action

The decision to introduce a formal control system and the selection of a specific system should be based largely on two aspects of the project:

- The risk involved – high-risk situations, where the probability of undesired outcomes is significant due to the complexity of the project, justify the investment in a formal, well-designed control system.
- The cost of the control system and its expected benefits – the cost of control should never exceed the expected benefits (i.e., savings) due to the control system.

How elaborate a system is depends on the size and scope of the task to be managed, as well as the size and distribution of the team working on it.

Large, lengthy and distributed projects are more likely to require elaborate, disciplined systems to ensure that all the pieces remain coordinated. Smaller projects may use a simple project control system, taking the form of weekly team meetings to discuss current status.

There are two key elements to the control of any project:

- milestones (clear, unambiguous targets of what, by when); and
- an established means of communication.

Communication and regular reporting are vital for monitoring progress, receiving early warning of danger, promoting cooperation, and motivating through team involvement.

For the project manager, the milestones are a mechanism to monitor progress; for the team, they are short-term goals. The milestones maintain the momentum and encourage effort; they allow the team to judge their own progress and to celebrate achievement throughout the project rather than just at its end.

The simplest way to construct milestones is to take the timing information from the work breakdown structure and sequence diagram. When you have guesstimated how long each sub-task will take and have added them together, you can identify by when each of these tasks will actually be completed. Another way is to construct more significant milestones. These can be found by identifying stages in the development of a project that are recognisable as steps towards the final product.

Earned value management (EVM) based systems of control (discussed later in this chapter) can then be used to combine effort measurements with milestone achievement to measure real progress.

2 Control of time, cost and quality

2.1 Introduction

The objective of planning, scheduling and control is straightforward – complete the project on time and within budget; maintain a high level of technical quality; conform to all applicable codes; reflect the client's scope, standards and other requirements; incorporate applicable professional standards and practice; be responsive; maintain an excellent working relationship with the client's representatives and others involved in the execution of the project; and continuously strive for technical excellence.

As discussed in Chapter 8, project performance typically involves a trade-off of several dimensions, specifically what is done (scope and quality) versus the resources used to do the work (time and cost).

The consumption of resources is usually measured. But also important are other factors that might affect the behaviour of those resources including the elements of risk and satisfaction. So a list of things that could possibly be measured includes:

- scope (percent complete);
- time (calendar);
- cost;

- risk;
- quality;
- satisfaction and attitudes of: project team; performing organisation; line management; benefiting organisation (customer); and other stakeholders (suppliers, collaborators, etc).

2.2 Time, cost and quality – performance measurement

Time and money, budgets and schedules are the most basic resources within which every project must operate.

Performance measurement is the integration of project work elements such as project schedules, project budgets, resource requirements and expenditures. Measurement can be based on the actual start or finish times of critical activities, the completion of milestones, or the timing of acceptance tests.

Once performance measures are selected, the information required to report the actual value of each performance measure must be defined. For example, the completion of a milestone may be reported at the successful completion of an acceptance test and the issuance of an appropriate report by quality control.

A control limit signifies the deviation of a critical success factor that has gone beyond acceptable limits. Control limits are set to assess the severity of deviations and deviations that are larger than a predetermined value are used to trigger corrective action.

KEY POINT

Control measurements may cover the following areas:

- cost;
- time;
- scope;
- functional quality;
- technical quality;
- client satisfaction.

Measurements can include:

- **Expenditure (cost) measures** – start with the establishment of budgets that refer to actual versus planned costs as defined in the project plan. As the project progresses, decisions regarding procurement, design, development, deployment etc, will be assessed with respect to their impact on expenditures. Actual expenditures will be compared to a baseline, and any variances will be reported to management for corrective action.
- **Schedule (time) performance measures** – refer to the timely completion of project deliverables as compared to a baseline schedule defined in the project plan. The schedules will identify all of the project's stages, phases, and activities assigned to each team member mapping them to a timeline that measures key milestones (dates) that are used to keep track of work progress. Avoiding schedule slippage is a key objective.
- **Scope performance measures** – are primarily concerned with product scope (the set of functions and features that characterise the product or service) and project scope (work that must be accomplished to deliver the product/service with the specified functions and features). Scope is measured based upon the degree of compliance of baseline product/service features and functions with proposed project deliverables (the means used for their delivery).
- **Functional quality** – refers to the quality or correctness of the products and/or services features/functions delivered as a result of the project. Functional quality can be measured by comparing the quality or correctness of the baseline product and services features/functions to the proposed project deliverables. It can also be measured using the number of product and service change requests made, approved, and effectively implemented or the number of critical, serious, and non-critical defects outstanding and resolved on a weekly basis.

- **Technical quality performance** – refers to the technical infrastructure that provides the foundation for product and service delivery. In the case of an IT project, such indicators as system availability, downtime, problem resolution, and response time and network utilisation would measure technical quality performance.
- **Client satisfaction measures** – include client perceptions on various aspects of achieving a high degree of client satisfaction with implementation support or with operational products/ services.

2.3 Earned value management (EVM)

Conventionally, project reporting is done separately with respect to scope, schedule and cost. This may sometimes obscure the true picture of the project status. The wrong perception of a project's status will eventually lead to incorrect decisions and actions resulting in project delays, or even worse, project failure. The status of a project cannot be determined just by looking at the schedule. Likewise, project status cannot be determined from cost alone.

For this reason, project control measurement needs to address the three parts in an integrated way where project performance or status at any point can be measured using a common unit of measure that applies to all three constraints.

The best available technique for this is earned value management (EVM), an integrated form of performance measurement that measures accurately the physical performance against detailed plan to allow for the accurate prediction of the final cost and schedule result for a given project.

It requires that the project's scope is fully defined and the baseline plan is put in place that integrates the scope with the authorised resources. These need to be within the identified time frame for performance.

KEY POINT

EVA involves calculation of three measurements:

- Budgeted cost of work scheduled (BCWS)
- Actual cost of work performed (ACWP)
- Budgeted cost of work performed (BCWP).

Earned value analysis (EVA) involves calculating three primary measurements for each activity or summary activity from a project's work breakdown structure (WBS).

1 **Budgeted cost of work scheduled (BCWS)** – also called the budget – is that portion of the approved total cost estimate planned to be spent on an activity during a given period. The total BCWS of each activity will make up the total budget of the entire project.

The BCWS values of activities A, B, and E in a hypothetical project for the first month are as follows:

Activity	Budgeted cost of work scheduled (BCWS)
A	4* £300 = £1,200
B	£3,000
E	4* £814 = £3,256
Total	£7,456

Thus the work content scheduled to be accomplished during the first four weeks of the project is budgeted at £7,456.

2 **Actual cost of work performed (ACWP)** – also called the actual cost, is total direct and indirect cost incurred in accomplishing work on an activity during a given period. This is the actual cost of the completed work. In the example, these costs are:

Activity	Actual cost of work performed (ACWP)
A	£1,500
B	£3,000
E	£2,900
Total	£7,400

As can be seen, a total of £7,400 was spent during the first four weeks to accomplish the work performed.

3 **Budgeted cost of work performed (BCWP)** – also called the earned value, is a measure of achievement or value of the work done.

In the example, 100% of activity A is accomplished. Therefore, its BCWP is equal to the total cost of activity A, which is £1,500. Similarly, for activity B, BCWP = £3,000.

For activity E, suppose two sevenths, or 28.6% of the work content (assume £5,700 total work content for activity E for the project) has been accomplished in the first four weeks. Then its BCWP = £5,700 × (2/7) = £1,629.

Activity	Budgeted cost of work performed (BCWP)
A	£1,500
B	£3,000
E	£1,629

The three measures BCWS, ACWP, and BCWP are the basis of the control analysis by which deviations in time and schedule are detected.

Schedule deviations

The difference between the budgeted cost of work performed (BCWP) and the budgeted cost of work scheduled (BCWS) indicates (in monetary units) the deviation between the work content performed and the work content scheduled for the control period.

If the absolute value of the difference is very small, then in terms of work content, the project is on schedule. A positive difference indicates that the project is ahead of schedule, and a negative difference implies that the project is late. Defining the schedule variance (SV) as the difference between BCWP and BCWS, we get:

Activity	BCWP – BCWS = SV
A	£1,500 – £1,200 = £300
B	£3,000 – £3,000 = £0
E	£1,629 – £3,256 = (£1,627)
Cumulative variance	– £1,327

Based on the SV values, we conclude that in activity A, the work performed is worth £300 more than what was planned for the control period; in activity B, the work performed is exactly equal to what was planned; and in activity E, the work performed is worth £1,627 less than what was planned for the period.

The cumulative variance is an indication in terms of work content performed, that the project is already late four weeks after its start. This measure, together with a simple critical path analysis, provides the means for tracking critical activities and for detecting overall trends in schedule performance.

Although the delay in non-critical activities may not cause immediate project delays, the fact that these activities are not performed on schedule means that the resources required to perform them will be needed in a later period.

This shift in resource requirements may cause a problem if the load on resources exceeds the available capacity.

The schedule delays detected by the earned value analysis should be monitored closely. When the delay extends beyond the control level, analysis of resource requirements should be initiated to test whether, due to resource limits, the entire project may be delayed.

Cost deviations

Deviations in cost are calculated based on the work content actually performed during the control period. Therefore, the cost variance (CV) is defined as the difference between the budgeted cost of work performed (BCWP) and the actual cost of work performed (ACWP).

A positive CV indicates a lower actual cost than budgeted for the control period, while a negative CV indicates a cost overrun.

The cost variance of activities A, B, and E for the first month of the example project is presented next.

Activity	BCWP – ACWP = CV
A	£1,500 – £1,500 = £0
B	£3,000 – £3,000 = £0
E	£1,629 – £2,900 = (£1,271)
Cumulative variance	–£1,271

Thus, based on the CV values, we can conclude that:

- Activities A and B are exactly on budget.
- Activity E, however, shows a budget overrun of £1,272, since the work performed on this activity was budgeted at £1,629 whereas the actual cost turned out to be £2,900.

Schedule and cost indices

The schedule variance and the cost variance are absolute measures indicating deviations between planned performance and actual progress, in monetary units.

Based on these measures, however, it is difficult to judge the relative schedule or cost deviation. A relative measure is important because a £1,000 cost overrun of an activity originally budgeted for £500 is clearly more troublesome than the same overrun on an activity originally budgeted for £50,000.

A schedule index (SI) and a cost index (CI) are designed to be proportional measures of schedule and cost performance, respectively.

The schedule index is defined as the ratio BCWP/BCWS. Thus an SI value equal to 1 indicates that the associated activity is on schedule. Values larger than 1 suggest that the activity is ahead of schedule, and values smaller than 1 indicate a schedule overrun.

The cost index is defined as the ratio BCWP/ACWP, implying that when CI equals 1, the activity is on budget. CI values larger than 1 indicate better-than-planned cost performance, and values smaller than 1 indicate cost overruns.

Following are CI and SI values for the example project after four weeks:

Activity	BCWP/BCWS = SI	BCWP/ACWP = CI
A	£1,500/£1,200 = 1.25	£1,500/£1,500 = 1
B	£3,000/£3,000 = 1	£3,000/£3,000 = 1
E	£1,629/£3,256 = 0.5	£1,629/£2,900 = 0.56

Activity A – these values indicate that during the control period, 25% more work was performed for activity A than planned (SI = 1.25) but at the exact cost budgeted for that work content (Cl = 1).

For activity B, the planned work content was performed at the planned cost.

For Activity E only half of the planned work content was performed (SI = 0.5). The planned cost of performing that work content was only 56% (Cl = 0.56) of the actual cost.

3 Quality in the project environment

3.1 Quality management

KEY POINT

The ISO defines quality as the 'totality of features and characteristics of a product or service which bear on its ability to satisfy stated and implied needs'.

For an organisation, **quality** means satisfying the customers' needs and expectations. There are many definitions of quality, from the simple and easy to remember 'fitness for use' (Dr J Juran, 1988) and 'conformance to requirements' (Dr P Crosby, 1979) to the longer definition given by the International Standards Organisation (ISO): 'the totality of features and characteristics of a product or service that bears on its ability to meet a stated or implied need'.

Japanese companies found the old definition of quality 'the degree of conformance to a standard' too narrow and consequently have started to use a new definition of quality as 'user satisfaction' or 'providing extraordinary customer satisfaction' (Wayne, 1983).

These definitions reflect two dimensions of quality: perceived quality and conformance quality.

- **Conformance quality** depends upon compliance with technical specifications and relates to the use of superior operations management to reduce waste, costs and increase uniformity.
- **Perceived quality** relates to the customer's expectations and experiences with the product. It is vitally important to ensure that the critical performance indicators set for quality match the two types together.

Quality management is concerned with getting things right. It may be critically important to drive out all possibility of errors, or it may be acceptable to take delivery of a product or service that is 'good enough'. For example, in construction it is essential that prefabricated components will fit together exactly when a building is constructed; quality in this context is about getting things right first time. However, for the design of a new e-business service, there may be a number of prototypes that gradually improve as understanding of the customer requirement increases – this is about achieving quality that is fit for purpose where it is recognised that perfection cannot be achieved in one step.

KEY POINT

Quality management is a systematic way of ensuring that the activities necessary to design, develop and deliver products and services which are more likely to be fit for their intended purpose, take place as planned and are carried out efficiently and effectively.

Quality management is a systematic way of ensuring that the activities necessary to design, develop and deliver products and services which are more likely to be fit for their intended purpose, take place as planned and are carried out efficiently and effectively.

There are three major aspects that require proactive management, namely:

- establishing what the business should be offering or doing;
- defining how it should be done;
- evaluating what can be done to improve the processes and service product offerings.

The third aspect helps to address 'perceived quality', as customers' views should be solicited; areas of complaint or disappointment will often relate to implied (rather than stated) needs.

3.2 Conformance management systems

A manufacturer is interested in the quality of the products that are produced, whereas consumers are interested in the quality of the products that they buy. Quality often means different things to different people but can generally be regarded as meaning that the product meets certain targets. For a light bulb, quality might mean that it works when we buy it, whilst for a packet of cornflakes quality might mean that we have over a certain minimum amount of cornflakes in the packet.

Conformance means that the material/product or service meets the customer's specifications and requirements. It is also the manufacturer's commitment that it meets specified standards. Conformance management systems focus on:

KEY POINT

Conformance management systems focus on:

- inspection;
- quality control;
- quality assurance.

- **Inspection** – complete, or 100%, inspection involves inspecting each item that is produced to see if it meets the desired quality level. This might seem to be the best procedure to meet quality targets but in fact it has a number of drawbacks - the main one being the expense. The alternative is to take a sample of a certain size from a batch (sometimes called *lot*) of items and operate 100% inspection on the sample.
- **Quality control** –is the technical activity and documentation to pursue the quality objectives. It regulates quality performance and prevents undesirable changes in the quality standards. Quality control is a process for maintaining standards and not for creating them. Standards are maintained through a process of selection, measurement and correction of work, so that only those products or services that emerge from the process meet the standards.
- **Quality assurance** – is a part of the overall management of the project. Quality assurance includes such things as developing Data Quality Objectives (DQO) and Quality Assurance Project Plans (QAPP).

Steps in the DQO process include:

- Define the problem to be resolved by the project.
- Determine what decision has to be made.
- Identify the type and amount of data that needs to be gathered.
- Use the most cost-effective plan that will meet the objectives.

Conformance is associated with traditional management where managers solve most of the problems and make most of the decisions. There has been an evolutionary shift to involvement, where employees have the opportunity to help solve problems and influence decisions and then on to empowerment, where employees and managers solve problems and make decisions that were traditionally reserved for higher levels of the organisation.

3.3 Total Quality Management (TQM)

DEFINITION

TQM is defined as 'managing the entire organisation so that it excels on all dimensions of products and services that are important to the customer'.

Total Quality Management (TQM) is one of the most important aspects of any organisation. It is defined as 'managing the entire organisation so that it excels on all dimensions of products and services that are important to the customer'. The three factors that are a part of TQM are:

- quality standards and specifications;
- cost of quality; and
- continuous improvement.

TQM is an integrated view of the quality function that emphasises the need for high quality and nil defects in all areas. It seeks to define the best available practice and quality in every aspect of the company's operations and creates an employee philosophy that expects high quality throughout.

As well as recognising the link between product quality and customer satisfaction, TQM also recognises that **product quality** is the result of **process quality**. As a result, there is a focus on continuous improvement of the company's processes. In turn this will lead to an improvement in product quality, and to an increase in customer satisfaction. Improvement cycles are encouraged for all the company's activities. This implies that all activities include measurement and monitoring of cycle time and responsiveness as a basis for seeking opportunities for improvement.

Continuous process improvement (CPI) is a never-ending effort to discover and eliminate the main causes of problems. It accomplishes this by using small-steps improvements, rather than implementing one huge improvement. The Japanese have a term for this called 'kaizen' that involves everyone, from the hourly workers to top-management. CPI means making things better.

Activity 1

Identify the areas where quality issues may be raised when applied to a service business such as a bank or restaurant.

Feedback to this activity is at the end of the chapter.

4 Project completion

4.1 Closing a successfully completed project

The final stages of a broadly successful project can be most rewarding. It is at this stage that people can finally see the realisation of plans and objectives. At the same time though, the 'tying up of loose ends' can be tedious and people can be more motivated to work on new projects. However, it is important that a project is satisfactorily completed.

KEY POINT

Elements involved in project finalisation:

- acceptance by client;
- review of outputs against goals;
- disbanding the team;
- post-completion review;
- closure by steering committee.

Essentially, successful project finalisation involves:

- **Acceptance of project outputs/deliverables by clients** – the outputs of the project should be successfully transferred to the project's clients or users. This should be planned well in advance and, preferably, in the initial project plans. It is important to ensure the clients or users will accept the hand-over date when the clients are given formal responsibility for the outputs/deliverables. Additionally, the project team should ensure there are facilities for ongoing maintenance or improvement of the outputs/deliverables and that the design of the product is adequately recorded.
- **A review of project outputs and outcomes against the formal goals of the project** – essentially, the project team should be able to illustrate that the project has delivered its planned outputs and that outcomes can reasonably be expected to flow from them. If it cannot, the project will not be completed successfully.
- **Disbanding the project team and 'tying up loose ends'** – it is important to ensure that all project activities are satisfactorily completed. It may help to produce ongoing checklists of outstanding work. There should be plans for releasing resources before the project is to be finalised, and project teams should be gradually wound down.
- **External post-completion review/audit** – for large projects, a post-completion review may be a useful way of identifying issues and concerns that may be relevant to other projects. Often projects that have radically gone wrong are audited, but many useful lessons can be gained from successful projects.
- **Formal closure by steering committee and disbanding the project steering committee** – the project steering committee cannot disband until the project's outcomes are seen as achieved, or the project is classed as unsuccessful. They are the group that formally closes the project.

Most texts recommend that a project closure meeting should be held at the end of the project. The objectives of the meeting are as follows:

- to bring the project to an orderly close;
- to confirm that all the planned work has been carried out;
- to check that all technical and quality issues have been resolved;
- to agree that all documentation required is available;
- to confirm that the project has been signed off;
- to review any lessons learned from the project for future reference.

A report is completed at the meeting, summarising the matters considered. This report is distributed to the steering committee and any other organisational stakeholders such as the director responsible for the project.

4.2 Closing an unsuccessful project

It is important to recognise that projects can be closed at any point during their lifecycle. Closing a successfully completed project can be challenging at the best of times, but closing a project that will probably not achieve its objectives can be seriously difficult, especially if considerable resources have already been expended on it. The project steering committee is ultimately responsible for closing down a project, whether it is successful or unsuccessful. Signs of an unsuccessful project that may need to be closed before being completed include:

- The project team is unable to meet major project milestones.
- The activities do not match with the stated objectives of the project.
- It is clear the clients will not accept the outputs and/or outcomes of the project.
- Key project team members leave the project.

For the project manager and team responsible, the decision to close an unsuccessfully completed project can be distressing and demoralising. They should remember that the reasons for project failure can be complex and varied, and that responsibility rarely rests entirely with one or two individuals. In this situation, it is important to ensure that project resources are appropriately redeployed. There should also be debriefing sessions for all those involved with the project and the group as a whole. In some cases, it may be useful to replace the project manager and/or other members of the project team with new people who can close down the project as quickly as possible.

4.3 Completion report

On project completion the project manager will produce the completion report. The main purpose of the completion report is to document (and gain client sign-off for) the end of the project. The report should include a summary of the project outcome. The assessment will include consideration of the following points:

- The project objectives and the outcomes achieved.
- The extent to which the required quality has been achieved.
- System efficiency during live operation compared with the agreed levels of performance.
- The cost of the system in comparison with budgeted cost, and explanations for variances.
- Comparison of actual time taken to complete the project with the budgeted time anticipated.
- The effectiveness of the management process.
- The significance of the problems encountered, and the effectiveness of the solutions generated to overcome them.

The completion report will also include provision for any on-going issues that will need to be addressed after completion e.g. a procedure for any 'bugs' that become apparent after a new software program has been tested and approved. Responsibilities and procedures relating to any such issues should be laid down in the report.

4.4 Post-completion audit

A post-completion audit is important because a project cannot be said to be successful until management is assured that all the benefits promised at the evaluation stage can be shown to have been subsequently realised.

KEY POINT

Main purposes of post-completion audit:

- checks whether benefits have been achieved;
- reduces the tendency towards over-optimism.

The audit should be conducted by staff experienced in appreciating the financial and/or production implications of the project and who are independent of the original commissioning team. Two purposes will be served.

- It checks whether benefits have been achieved and draws management's attention to unsuccessful projects.
- It reduces the tendency in many organisations to be over-optimistic with the data when presenting projects for evaluation.

The information will be presented in a report, which should contain the following:

- A summary that emphasises any areas where the structure and the tools used by management have been found to be unsatisfactory.
- A review of the end results of the project compared with the results expected. Reasons for any discrepancies between the two will be identified, preferably with suggestions as to how future projects could prevent these problems occurring again.
- A cost-benefit review comparing the forecast costs and benefits identified at the time of the feasibility study with the actual costs and benefits.
- Recommendations as to any steps that should be taken to improve the project management procedures used.

Lessons learnt that relate to the way the project was managed should contribute to the smooth running of future projects. A starting point for any new project should be a review of the documentation of any similar projects undertaken in the past.

4.5 Post-implementation review (PIR)

KEY POINT

Post-implementation review (PIR) is a formal review of a programme or project. It is used to answer the question: Did we achieve what we set out to do in business terms – and if not, what should be done?

Post-implementation review (PIR) is a formal review of a programme or project. It is used to answer the question: Did we achieve what we set out to do in business terms – and if not, what should be done? It should include the following elements:

1. **Project history description** – provide an executive overview of the solution selected to satisfy the project objectives. Briefly describe changes from the original design that occurred during the course of the project development. Incorporate a brief overview of the chronology of the project that highlights turning points in the development and implementation of the system.

2. **Cost history** – provide a set of accounts for the actual costs of the development of the project using the cost schedule formats as prepared for the project plan. Show a planned cost history that reflects the approved amendments and the updated schedules.

   Include a comparison of the costs, actual and planned, and explain the major differences. When explaining the variances, describe how the costs changed, describe the impact of those changes, and briefly describe what led to each change.

3. **Project management and systems development methodology** –describe the methodology used to develop the system. Include a description of which parts of the project management methodology were used and not used, and explain the impact of these decisions. Include comparisons of the initially planned dates for milestones and deliverables to the actual

delivery dates, and briefly explain the major differences in schedules. When explaining the variances, describe how the schedule changed, the impact of those changes, and what led to each change.

4 **Performance measures** – provide a list of the performance measures initially used to justify the project. Provide a comparison of the initial performance measures to the actual, realised performance measures for the system. Include a description of how the project changed the organisation and/or the delivery of services.

5 **Lessons learned** – describe the lessons learned during this project. These lessons will show the planning and development process improvements that can be used for future projects.

Include recommendations for improvements in the future. Describe the best practices identified in this project that should be repeated in the next project.

6 **Impact of the system** –briefly describe the general impact of the system on the managers, users, and customers. Provide executive management's feedback on the success of the system, the benefits realised, and the improvement in performance measures. Include user feedback on the success of the system, the benefits realised, and the improvement in performance measures

KEY POINT

The objective of the PIR is to ensure that the maximum benefit is obtained for the organisation through the business change that the project made possible, and to make recommendations if the benefits are not obtained.

The objective of the PIR is to ensure that the maximum benefit is obtained for the organisation through the business change that the project made possible, and to make recommendations if the benefits are not obtained.

PIRs are not a one-off exercise – a programme of business change may be in excess of ten years and the business system it supports may be in existence for an even longer period of time. The level of cost, risk and benefit delivered by the change must be reviewed periodically, following the first PIR. Reviews must be conducted in an open manner; organisations must be prepared to learn – to get the most value, reviews should be conducted openly and participants must be prepared to make constructive criticism. It is only in this way that real lessons will be learned or improvements to business processes and supporting infrastructure made.

The PIR process

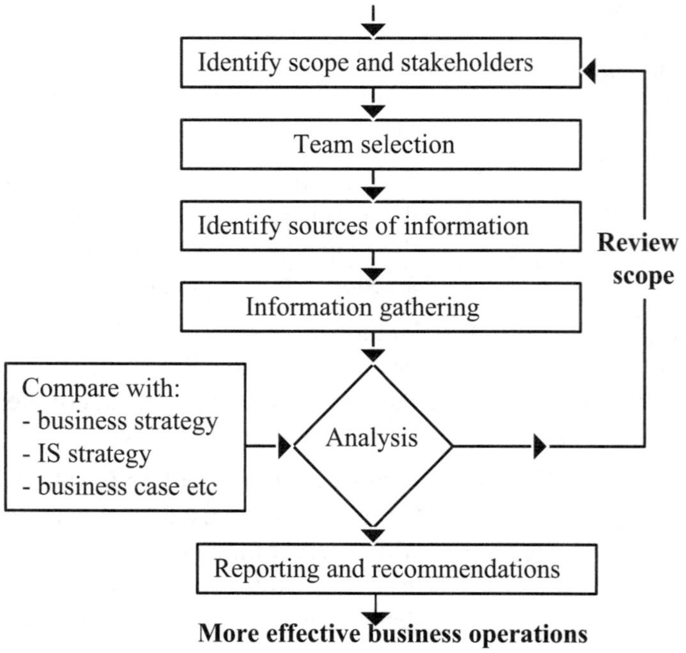

4.6 Stakeholder marketing

DEFINITION

Stakeholder marketing is described as 'establishing and maintaining mutually beneficial exchange relationships over time with all the stakeholders of the organisation'.

Stakeholder marketing is described as 'establishing and maintaining mutually beneficial exchange relationships over time with all the stakeholders of the organisation'.

Relationship marketing is an orientation that seeks to develop the relationship with customers (and other stakeholders) beyond a transaction or series of transactions, by:

- focusing on ongoing relationship and loyalty, through achieving consistent customer/stakeholder satisfaction;
- creating multiple points of contact and ongoing communication with customers/stakeholders:
- entering into dialogue (two-way information exchange) in order to create a partnership in shaping future exchanges to mutual benefit (e.g. through shared opportunity development or problem solving)

Projects are, by their nature, temporary structures and time-bounded processes. However, a **stakeholder relationship marketing** orientation suggests that the learning, contacts and communication/co-operation channels set up for a project need not be wasted. Such an orientation may imply management activities such as:

- Managing stakeholder expectations, interest and support (as discussed in Chapter 6) by conveying **marketing messages** throughout the project: emphasising benefits of the project outcomes; emphasising the stakeholders' value and contribution; soliciting feedback for performance adjustment and so on. (You should be able to see clear parallels with product/brand marketing to customers.)
- Involving stakeholders in the post-completion audit or review, particularly with regard to recommendations for future process improvements.
- Maintaining contact with stakeholders affected by implementation of the project (like after-sales service calls) to help with any teething problems, get feedback on any emerging issues, ensure ongoing satisfaction and so on.

Summary

- Systematic project control involves the tasks of scheduling, monitoring and controlling.
- Key elements in the control of a project are the establishment of milestones and means of communication.
- Control measurements may cover the areas of cost, time, scope, functional quality, technical quality and client satisfaction.
- Earned value analysis (EVA) involves calculation of three measurements: budgeted cost of work scheduled, actual cost of work performed, and budgeted cost of work performed.
- Conformance management systems focus on inspection, quality control and quality assurance.

- The process of finalising a project involves: acceptance by client; review of outputs against goals; disbanding the team; post-completion review; closure by steering committee.
- Once the project has been finalised, the processes of post-completion audit and post-completion review may be used.

Having completed your study of this chapter you should have achieved the following learning outcomes.

- Recommend appropriate project control systems.
- Evaluate, through selected review and audit, the learning outcomes from a project.
- Evaluate the process of continuous improvement to projects.

Self-test questions

1. What are phase boundaries? (1.1)
2. List the aspects of a project that can be measured. (2.1)
3. What does EVM stand for? (2.3)
4. Briefly define quality according to Juran and Crosby. (3.1)
5. How do conformance systems work? (3.2)
6. Outline three signs of an unsuccessful project. (4.2)
7. What is the difference between a post-completion audit and a post-implementation review? (4.4, 4.5)

Multiple-choice questions

Question 1

A periodic document (e.g. biweekly, monthly) detailing time, cost, and resource performance is called:

A an engineering change proposal (ECP)
B a status report
C a work authorisation
D the project charter.

Question 2

The final steps in the close-out phase generally lead up to:

A a project selection decision
B a redefinition of project requirements
C customer acceptance
D a final review of the deliverable by the engineering review board.

For the answer to these questions, see the 'Answers' section at the end of the book.

Exam-type questions

Question 1: Jim Ryan

Jim Ryan is general manager of the CityGo Bus Company. The company is currently one of the subsidiary companies and a regional operating division of a public corporation - the City Bus Corporation. As part of the privatisation strategy of the national government all the operating divisions of the City Bus Corporation have been separately sold by tender-based offer for sale. Some divisions have been acquired by private transport operators while the CityGo division has been acquired through a management buyout (MBO) led by the existing general manager of CityGo, Jim Ryan.

The CityGo Bus Company's computing systems were totally integrated into the City Bus Corporation's own systems and the newly privatised bus company must now implement its own financial systems. The privatisation timetable means that CityGo has only a few months to set up these new computer based systems.

The requirement will be for a project management process which can deal with tight timescales involving a complicated set of interrelated decisions and actions. CityGo management must realise that effective project planning and control needs different management skills from those required to run operational processes.

This is the immediate requirement, but in the longer term CityGo must put in place a strategy for managing information resources in ways which enable it to achieve a competitive advantage or at least competitive parity with other bus operators.

Required:

(a) In your role as a management consultant, write a memorandum to Jim Ryan describing five responsibilities of a project manager. **(10 marks)**

All projects include some risk: cost overrun, missed deadlines, poor outcome, disappointed customers and business disruption. Identification and management of risks is therefore important.

(b) Briefly describe how project risk is managed. **(10 marks)**

(c) Outline the areas that can threaten the success of a project and suggest ways of reducing those threats. **(10 marks)**

(Total: 30 marks)

Question 2: Managing project objectives

Scope, organisation, time, cost and quality are the five objectives that need to be managed in the successful completion of a project.

How is each objective planned and managed in practice? **(25 marks)**

For the answer to these questions, see the 'Answers' section at the end of the book.

Feedback to activity

Activity 1

The areas where quality issues in service businesses are raised include:

- customer expectations;
- the process by which the service is delivered;
- the attitudes and demeanour of the people giving the service;
- the environment of the service encounter.

Chapter 11

MANAGEMENT AND LEADERSHIP

Syllabus content

- The concepts of power, authority, bureaucracy, leadership, responsibility and delegation and their application to relationships within an organisation and outside it.
- The characteristics of leaders, managers and entrepreneurs.
- Management-style theories (e.g. Likert, Tannenbaum and Schmidt, Blake and Mouton).
- The advantages and disadvantages of different styles of management.
- Managing in different countries and cultures.
- Contingency approaches to management (e.g. Adair, Fiedler).

Contents

1 Authority and responsibility

2 Delegation

3 Power

4 Management and leadership

5 Theories of management style

6 Contingency approaches to management

7 Cross cultural management

1 Authority and responsibility

1.1 Introduction

The allocation of responsibilities, grouping of functions, decision-making, co-ordination, control and reward are all fundamental requirements for the operation of an organisation. The quality of its structure will affect how well these requirements are met.

Organisational structure means grouping people into departments or sections and allocating responsibility and authority or power. Authority and power flow downwards in a formal organisation, for example centralised structures maintain the power base at the corporate centre.

1.2 Nature of authority

DEFINITION

Fayol's definition of **authority** is 'the right to give orders and the power to exact obedience'.

Authority can be defined as the right that an individual has to require certain actions of others. It is the right to exercise powers such as hiring and firing or buying and selling on behalf of the organisation. Fayol defined authority as 'the right to give orders and the power to exact obedience'. He differentiated between official authority, which 'derives from office' and personal authority, which is 'compounded of intelligence, experience, moral worth, ability to lead and past services'.

It is necessary to distinguish between authority and power. Authority in an organisation is the right in a position to exercise discretion in making decisions affecting others. As such, it is one type of power. Power is a broader concept, which can be defined as the ability to influence the actions of others. So, it is quite possible to have authority without power (e.g. a weak and ineffective supervisor) or power without authority (e.g. a trade union shop steward). Three types of authority can be distinguished:

- **Formal authority** – where the organisation bestows the authority upon the individual by means of their job title and the reporting relationships specified.
- **Technical authority** – where the authority arises from personal skills or special knowledge or training. Here the authority exists only within the scope of that special knowledge or skill.
- **Personal, informal authority** – this authority is not recognised in any organisation chart. It exists because, without regard to the position they hold, the person is accepted as being particularly respected, or an elder citizen or is simply popular and recognised by colleagues as being efficient.

Administrative organisation creates superior/subordinate relationships and it is vital that these are properly defined and clearly understood. The right to use power should be sufficient to enable the proper discharge of duties assigned and the person should be held accountable for the proper use of power.

Organisations differ in the extent to which authority is relied upon as a means of achieving control or motivation. In the authoritarian or classical approach, great emphasis is placed upon formal relationships where communication upwards to the superior is discouraged; orders are given and obeyed, sometimes without question. Initiative and personal involvement with the allocated tasks are minimised. Current thinking favours a relationship in which the exercise of authority between a superior and their subordinate is replaced by personal influence through good leadership.

1.3 Legitimate authority

Weber's contribution to the study of the organisation was his interpretation of legitimacy. He identified two media by which commands are obeyed:

- **power** – the ability to force people to obey, regardless of their resistance;
- **authority** – where orders are voluntarily obeyed by those receiving them, and subordinates accept the ideas and directives from above because they are legitimate.

KEY POINT

Weber identified three grounds on which legitimate authority could exist – charisma, tradition and rational-legal.

Max Weber regarded an organisation as an authority structure. He was interested in why people obeyed commands and he identified three grounds on which legitimate authority could exist:

- **Charisma** – the individual has some special quality of personality. Structure and commands depend upon such inspiration. However, unless the leader has created an organisation that can survive without their physical presence, an inbuilt instability exists.
- **Tradition** – is authority based upon custom and practice. Status is largely inherited – e.g. father to son or mother to daughter, with a distinctly patriarchal/matriarchal attitude towards officials and subordinates.
- **Rational-legal grounds** – this is Weber's classic bureaucracy. It is rational because its means are expressly designed to achieve certain goals with maximum efficiency. It is legal because authority is exercised by means of a system of rules and procedures through the office, which an individual occupies. Weber's characterisation is the most technically efficient form of organisation possible, identified with precision, speed, knowledge, continuity, discretion, unity, strict subordination and minimisation of friction and material and personal costs.

1.4 Bureaucracy

KEY POINT

Bureaucracy (Weber) is a formal structure based on:

- hierarchical authority;
- defined duties;
- rules;
- technical competence;
- impersonality.

The bureaucratic model of Weber places great emphasis on formal relationships, where communication upwards to the superior is discouraged; orders are given and obeyed, sometimes without question – the superior has the *right to command* someone else and the subordinate has the *duty to obey* that command. Weber is credited with the concept of bureaucracy.

He stated that bureaucracies should have:

- clearly defined duties and responsibilities for all organisational members;
- hierarchically arranged staff with each member reporting to a superior and responsible for subordinates (except for those at the top or bottom of the structural pyramid);
- an elaborate system of rules governing the manner in which each official carries out their duties – decisions are recorded and preserved so as to constitute precedents to guide future decisions;
- officials who hold office on the basis of merit formally attested and subject to systematic selection and training (seniority and merit being considered to be the same) – this includes promotion by testing;
- all officials carrying out their duties without regard to any personal or family commitment, impartially and unemotionally – their authority is confined to official duties and they are motivated by a sense of duty and career prospects.

1.5 Authority relationships

There is a direct relationship between organisation structure and the pattern of authority. Many traditionalists made the assumption that authority relationships were synonymous with the organisation structure because they were concerned with the establishment of positions and the relationship between positions. Without authority various departments cannot become smoothly working units harmonised for the accomplishment of objectives. Authority relationships – vertical or horizontal – are the factors that make organisation possible. They facilitate departmental activities and bring co-ordination to an enterprise.

The organisational chart shows the formal relationships that exist between positions or offices in an organisation. The chart indicates positional authority – the authority to direct the activities of persons below in the line relationship based on the position which one occupies.

Positional authority is distributed hierarchically in that persons occupying positions at upper levels in the organisation have more power and exercise more control than those at successively lower levels. One of the functions of hierarchical authority is to provide predictability. The exercise of authority increases the probability of orderly, regularised behaviour. Authority relationships can be traced on an organisational chart by following the lines of an organisational chart downwards. Responsibility relationships can be traced by following those same lines upwards.

KEY POINT

Three types of authority relationship: line, staff and functional.

This view provides the basis for determining the authority and responsibility structure in the organisation. Three types of relationships exist – line, staff and functional.

Line authority – gives a superior a line of authority over a subordinate. It exists in all organisations as an uninterrupted scale or series of steps. The clearer the line of authority from the ultimate management position in an enterprise to every subordinate position, the clearer will be the decision-making and the more effective will be organisational communication. Line authority enables a manager to allocate work, direct and control subordinates and delegate authority. Line authority is a relationship in direct line or steps.

Staff relationship – the nature of the staff relationship is advisory. Individuals may offer specialist advice to others on certain technical matters. The person concerned may be an assistant to a manager, appointed to assist with the workload of a superior. He has no authority of his own, but acts in the name of his superior and on his authority.

Alternatively, an individual may be appointed to offer specialist information on computing or industrial relations, to managers in the line structure, but without the authority to insist that such advice is taken. Because these people are not in a line relationship, they do not constitute a level in the hierarchy.

Functional relationship – this type of relationship exists when a specialist is designated to provide a service, which the line manager is compelled to accept. Functional authority is a hybrid of line and staff authority and can be defined as 'the right which is delegated to an individual or a department to control specified processes, practices, policies or other matters relating to activities undertaken by persons in other departments'.

Examples are where a personnel manager has authority to dismiss a line manager's subordinate, or where a finance manager has authority to require timely reports from line managers.

1.6 Responsibility

DEFINITION

Responsibility is the liability to be called to account: the 'duty' to carry out an assigned task.

Responsibility is being accountable for the performance of specified duties or the satisfactory achievement of defined company objectives. It refers to the liability to be called to account for actions and results – the duty to carry out the assigned task. For example:

- A government in a democracy has a responsibility to the electorate.
- A board of directors has a responsibility to its shareholders
- A subordinate may have a responsibility to his or her superior.

The scope of responsibility must correspond to the scope of authority given. When people are given responsibility without the necessary authority, they are in the invidious position of being powerless to achieve the levels upon which their performance is being judged. Conversely, a person given authority without clear responsibility for achieving specified targets or without having to report to a more senior manager is in a position of false security.

Responsibility must be supported by authority and by the power to influence the areas of performance for which the subordinate is to be held responsible. Authority can be delegated readily, but many problems of delegation stem from failure to provide the necessary information and resources in order to achieve expected results, or from failure to delegate sufficient authority to enable subordinates to fulfil their responsibilities.

For example, if a section head is held responsible to a departmental manager for the performance of junior staff but does not have the authority to influence their selection and appointment, their motivation, the allocation of their duties, their training and development, or their sanctions and rewards, then the section leader can hardly be held responsible for their unsatisfactory performance.

To hold subordinates responsible for certain areas of performance without also conferring on them the necessary authority within the structure of the organisation to take action and make decisions within the limits of that responsibility is an abuse of delegation.

Similar problems will occur when responsibility and authority are not clear. When the organisation is doing something new or in a different way, the existing rules and procedures may be out of date or unable to cope with the new development. The managers may not have designed the organisation very well and various people may try to 'empire build'.

In large organisations, there may be real conflict between different departments. The organisation may need to change as it adapts to its environment.

The opposite of this situation – assigning responsibilities without corresponding authority – may also cause problems. The person is empowered to take decisions but is not held responsible for what results. An example of this is where the decision to appoint an employee to a line job may be taken by a person in the personnel department rather than by the line manager who will be responsible for that person.

2 Delegation

2.1 The nature of delegation

DEFINITION

Delegation is the process by which a person transfers part of their authority to a subordinate person.

Responsibility, authority and delegation are three inter-related terms. Delegation is the process of assigning tasks and granting sufficient authority for their accomplishment. The one to whom authority is delegated becomes responsible to the superior for doing the job, but the superior still remains responsible for getting the job done. Responsibility cannot exist without authority and vice versa.

Delegation is an important aspect of organisation and effective management. Without delegation, formal organisations could not exist. If there were no delegation, the chief executive would be responsible for everything and would be the only person with the authority to do anything; consequently nothing much would ever get done. Because management is the act of getting things done (accomplishing objectives) through the work of other people, it is obvious that management could not succeed without delegation. Of course, management could delegate completely the tasks, and the associated authority for planning, co-ordinating, controlling, organising and monitoring; to do so would be to abdicate the management role. Of necessity, however, the manager has to give some of the work to subordinates.

The basis of delegation is illustrated below showing how the subordinate is responsible to the manager for doing the job, the manager is responsible for seeing that the job gets done and the manager is accountable to the superior for the actions of subordinates.

Structure of authority, responsibility and accountability

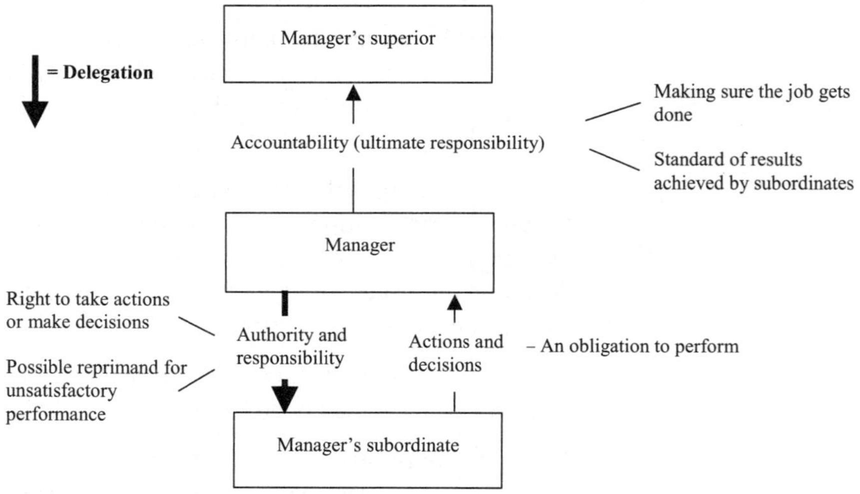

Note that **accountability** (ultimate responsibility) cannot be delegated. Managers have to accept responsibility for the control of their staff, for the performance of all duties allocated to their department or section and for the standard of results achieved.

Activity 1

In which example below does the assistant have the authority and ability to delegate to the operatives?

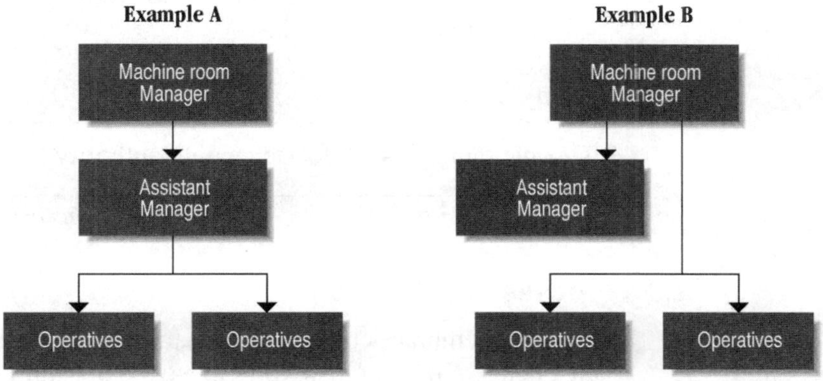

Feedback to this activity is at the end of the chapter.

2.2 Why delegate?

Rosemary Stewart in her book *Managers and their Jobs* stated that there are three questions that a manager should ask about any of their activities.

- Should it be done at all?
- If so, when should it be done?
- Should it be delegated?

Most frequently in her opinion, based on specified research, the manager will find some of their work ought to have been delegated. One of the conclusions at the end of her book is that few managers will have sufficient time unless they know how to delegate. They should have taught their subordinates what they can do without reference to the manager, what things they should tell the managers for information, when the subordinates should consult managers and at what times managers are available for discussion.

KEY POINT

Reasons for delegating authority:

- training;
- management succession;
- performance evaluation;
- relief of stress;
- job satisfaction.

The main reasons for delegating authority are:

- **Training** – by doing is acknowledged to be a very effective method. By delegating more and more and further and further down the line, and by insisting on full briefing and consultation between managers and subordinates, training becomes not a special process to be done at rare intervals, but a general day-to-day activity.
- **Management succession** – gives others a chance of acclimatisation. They not only need to get to know the routine but also to accustom themselves to the advantages and disadvantages of advancement.
- **Performance evaluation** – the virtue of gradually getting used to exercising authority is that a subordinate can be tested under actual conditions, before being permanently promoted. By regularly ensuring a free flow of delegation, there will be continuous trying and testing of persons, accepted as a matter of routine.
- **Relief of stress** – not just in the self-interest of managers is delegation valuable; it relieves pressure on them but its other advantages weigh heavier.

- **Job satisfaction** – the most valuable advantage of delegation is job satisfaction for subordinates. By ensuring that the mix of delegation is appropriate, some of the interesting jobs will be delegated and not only the tedium. By increasing employees' enjoyment in their jobs, employers can encourage better work.

Activity 2

List some more reasons for delegating authority.

Feedback to this activity is at the end of the chapter.

2.3 Process of delegation

KEY POINT

Many problems of delegation stem from failure:

- to provide necessary information and resources;
- to delegate sufficient authority for subordinates to fulfil their responsibilities.

Delegation embraces both authority and responsibility. Authority can be delegated readily, but many problems of delegation stem from failure to provide the necessary information and resources in order to achieve expected results, or from failure to delegate sufficient authority for subordinates to fulfil their responsibilities. Delegation is a process where a manager or supervisor:

- determines the results expected;
- allocates duties to subordinates;
- grants them authority to enable those duties to be carried out;
- holds them responsible for the completion of the work and achievement of results.

To delegate effectively managers must:

- define the limits of authority delegated to their subordinates;
- satisfy themselves that the subordinate is competent to exercise that authority;
- discipline themselves to permit the subordinate the full use of that authority without constant checks and interference.

2.4 The manner of delegation

There is no 'correct procedure' for delegation, and even if there were it would not be possible to become a good delegator by learning it. 'It is not what you do, it is the way that you do it.' Different manners of delegation could be:

- **Abdication** – at one extreme, it is not uncommon to leave everything to a junior, which is a very crude and usually ineffective method.
- **Custom and practice** – in some organisations it is customary to have work done by the age-old system whereby precedent rules. This method scarcely sounds progressive but it is common enough in the bureaucracies both of the Civil Service and major companies.
- **Explanation** – this more progressive way involves the manager in 'briefing' their subordinate along the lines of how the task should be done, without explaining too much because that could verge on actually doing the job. This is one of those cases when explanation is wanted – not too little and not too much – a fine balance that requires the art of management.

- **Consultation** – prior consultation was once quite novel in manager/union relations and also between managers and subordinates, but nowadays prior consultation is considered to be important and very effective. Another thing that has been realised by some, though not admitted by all, is that the middle grades of worker are immensely powerful; by contributing or withholding their co-operation they make the success of their seniors by no means automatic.

2.5 Accountability

In Section 2.1 of this chapter, we saw how (through delegation) authority flows down the chain from superior to subordinate, and how accountability flows back up the chain from subordinate to supervisor.

DEFINITION

Accountability is the obligation to give an account of the stewardship of the authority given, to a superior.

Accountability is the extent to which persons are answerable for their actions, the consequences of those actions and the measured effect on end results. It has three dimensions, which are, in order of importance:

- Freedom to act, which is measured by how much the person's performance is guided or controlled by his superior or by company policies or procedures. The less freedom a person has, the lower the evaluation of his/her job in this element.
- The impact on end results that a person's performance has. In banking for example, the impact of the performance of the manager is fundamental to the overall performance of the branch.
- The magnitude of the end result area primarily affected by the job. Clearly, any salesperson is evaluated by the orders expressed in money, and possibly contribution to profit terms, taken in a year.

Authority and accountability go hand in hand. A fair system means that managers or supervisors should be answerable for their actions. Just because a manager delegates a job to someone else, it does not mean the manager ceases to be accountable for the job being carried out. He or she is still accountable directly to higher or other authority for authority delegated and for tasks assigned to their direct reports.

3 Power

3.1 The nature of power

DEFINITION

Power is the ability to make someone do something they might otherwise not wish to do.

Power is the capacity to make someone act according to your own preferences: the potential to influence. As with leadership or management, power is a property of the relationship between the more and the less powerful. (In most organisations power will be unequally shared between the organisation's various stakeholders or coalitions.)

The exercise of power is a social process. A person's power depends, to a large extent, on the perceptions of others. So, although a leader may not have any formal authority, he or she may be able to assume power over others through their willingness to act as followers. Conversely, a manager may have formal authority but, having lost the respect of his or her staff, may be unable to exercise power or influence over them.

3.2 Sources of power

According to McGivering there are five sources/types of power, some of which are strongly linked to the position of the leader in the organisation:

Reward power – occurs when a person (or group of people, or company, etc.) has the capacity to offer or mediate rewards to others, e.g. promotions, recommendations, praise or answers to questions.

Coercive power – this enables a person to mediate punishments for others: for example, to dismiss, suspend, reprimand them, or make them carry out unpleasant tasks. Reward power and coercive power are similar but limited in application because they do not extend beyond the limits of the reward or punishment, which can be mediated. Such power is often diminished by a failure to exercise it.

KEY POINT

Power may derive from a number of sources – not just position (authority).

Legitimate power – is based on agreement and commonly held values which allow one person to have power over another person: for example, an older person, or one who has longer service or is seen to be charismatic. It normally arises from position and derives from our cultural system of rights, obligations and duties in which a 'position' is accepted by people as being legitimate.

Expert power – is based upon one person perceiving that the other person has expert knowledge of a given subject and is a recognised authority in a given situation; such knowledge may be theoretical but is more likely to be practical in its application.

Referent power – is based upon the identification with the person who has the resources, or the desire to be like that person. It could be regarded as 'imitative' power, which is often seen in the way children imitate their parents. It is not necessarily connected to the reward power or coercive power that parents may have over their children.

Psychologists believe that power is effective only when it is held in balance; as soon as power is used it gets out of balance because the person against whom it is used automatically resorts to some activity to try to correct the imbalance. This can occur through the coalition of weaker members as a defensive measure against authority or by a search for alternative relationships.

3.3 Power in channel relationships

We have already examined Porter's view on competitive forces and the power of buyers (in Chapter 2). In terms of channel relationships, power is the ability of one channel member to get another channel member to do something that might not otherwise have been the case. Considering the power bases as they relate to the five types of power:

Reward power – this would occur if the manufacturer offers some additional benefit for the performance of special acts by the other channel institution. The problem is that the positive effect of reward diminishes over time, and resentment can occur if, or when, the benefit it is withdrawn.

Coercive power – this would be represented by the manufacturer threatening to withdraw resources or terminate the marketing agreement between the two parties. It can be effective but will cause resentment, and may even result in retaliation by the channel institution.

Referent power – this would occur when the manufacturing concern is so highly respected that the channel institution is proud to be associated with it. Companies such as McDonald's, Marks and Spencer and IBM have high referent power and can exert influence over other channel members. Referent power is the most effective force of channel strength.

Expert power – this can be applied by the manufacturer who has special knowledge that is valued by the other channel institution. For example the manufacturer may provide expert training for the other channel member's sales-staff, or may have expert knowledge on the market and its customers. The manufacturer will need to continuously develop this attribute, because once the other channel member has acquired the expertise its power diminishes.

Legitimate power – this is wielded when a manufacturer requests an action in accordance with a contractual agreement. Thus Ford may demand that its dealers conform to an agreed level of spare-parts inventory. This power has force if its source is authentic, but it may have a time limit.

3.4 Power and other stakeholders

International and external stakeholders may also possess power, which helps them influence the organisation's strategy. (If you need to refresh your memory, see Sections 6.4 and 6.5 of Chapter 1.)

4 Management and leadership

4.1 Functions and characteristics of managers

DEFINITION

To manage means 'to bring about, to accomplish, to deal with problems, to control, to have responsibility for and to conduct.'

KEY POINT

Fayol listed the functions of management as planning, organising, commanding, co-ordinating and controlling.

To manage means 'to bring about, to accomplish, to deal with problems, to control, to have responsibility for and to conduct.'

Management is the process of designing and maintaining an environment in which individuals, working together in groups, efficiently accomplish selected aims.

Fayol listed the functions of management as follows:

- **Planning** – selecting objectives, and the strategies, policies, programmes and procedures for achieving the objectives either for the organisation as a whole or for a part of it.
- **Organising** – establishing a structure of tasks which need to be performed to achieve the goals of the organisation, grouping these tasks into jobs for an individual, creating groups of jobs within sections and departments, delegating authority to carry out the jobs, and providing systems of information and communication, and for the co-ordination of activities within the organisation.
- **Commanding** – giving instructions to subordinates to carry out tasks over which the manager has authority for decisions and responsibility for performance.
- **Co-ordinating** – harmonising the activities of individuals and groups within the organisation, which will inevitably have different ideas about what their own goals should be. Management must reconcile differences in approach, effort, interest and timing of these separate individuals and groups. This is best achieved by making the individuals and groups aware of how their work is contributing to the goals of the overall organisation.
- **Controlling** – measuring and correcting the activities of individuals and groups, to ensure that their performance is in accordance with plans. Plans must be made, but they will not be achieved unless activities are monitored, and deviations from plan identified and corrected as soon as they become apparent.

The classical ideas on management approaches have been, and still are, highly influential and of considerable relevance today but research in the past few years into the nature of the manager's task has produced many ideas. The manager in fact takes on a wider range of roles in pursuing the objectives of the organisation.

- A manager assumes responsibility to see that work is done effectively.
- A balance between the goals and needs of departments and individuals is needed and priorities have to be established.
- A manager works with and through other people at every level in an organisation in striving towards goals.

He or she must be:

- a *mediator* of disputes which may affect morale and productivity;
- a *politician*, using persuasion and compromise to promote organisational goals;
- a *diplomat*, representing the company at meetings within and outside the firm.

KEY POINT

Mintzberg classified the activities that constitute the essential functions of a manager's job and built up a model, which looked at three different roles: interpersonal, informational and decisional.

Mintzberg classified the activities that constitute the essential functions of a manager's job and built up a model, which looked at different roles.

These can be grouped under three categories to form an integrated view of what senior managers do (see diagram below). The three types of role are interpersonal, informational and decisional. Handy called these leading, administrating and fixing.

Mintzberg's managerial roles

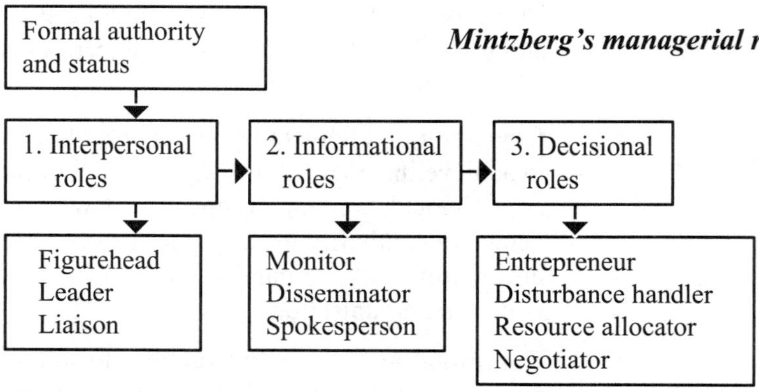

This approach to managing acknowledges the action-oriented, outward-looking and ritualistic aspects of managerial work as well as managers' strong preferences for verbal media in finding information.

Both the classical and the modern views of a manager point to the same characteristics. Managers deal with the physical resources of an organisation – its capital, the skills of the workforce, raw materials and technology. They resolve issues as they arise, do things right and work within defined policies. Although you could add many more to the following list of characteristics, we can say that a manager:

- concentrates on tasks;
- is an administrator;
- has specific competence;
- makes long-term plans and predictions;

- works with figures, calculated risks, checklists;
- formulates steps or actions based on analysis;
- has targets and is action-oriented;
- discusses and judges and sees the pros and cons.

4.2 The characteristics of a leader

Leadership is a means of directing. A leader's actions are devoted to helping a group achieve its objectives. Leadership is the ability of management to induce subordinates to work towards group goals keenly and with confidence.

To lead is 'to go in front, to show the way, to influence and guide in direction, course, action and opinions'. Typically, leaders are those rare people who can clearly see not only the details, but 'the big picture' as well. This is often referred to as vision. Good leaders value the input from trusted, knowledgeable subordinates, and usually actively seek out this input, especially before making momentous decisions. Given the choice between doing things *right*, i.e. according to rules and regulations, and doing the right *things*, leaders generally opt for the latter course of action. They are more likely to at least consider something new and different, particularly if it could result in producing a better product or service.

Leaders are also enthusiastic and have a tendency to engender the same level of enthusiasm in subordinates.

DEFINITION

Buchanan and Huczynski define a leader as 'someone who exercises influence over other people'.

Leadership is an interpersonal influence directed toward the achievement of a goal or goals.

Buchanan and Huczynski define a leader as 'someone who exercises influence over other people'. Another definition is: Leadership is an interpersonal influence directed toward the achievement of a goal or goals. Three important parts of this definition are the terms interpersonal, influence, and goal:

- **Interpersonal** – means between persons. Thus, a leader has more than one person (group) to lead.
- **Influence** – is the power to affect others.
- **Goal** – is the end one strives to attain.

Basically, this traditional definition of leadership says that a leader influences more than one person toward a goal.

KEY POINT

There are different viewpoints on leadership. It can be viewed as an attribute or a position, a characteristic or a style of behaviour.

There are different viewpoints on leadership. Some people think it is an attribute or a position; others think it is a characteristic of a person; and a third group think leadership is a category of behaviour. Leadership can be viewed from three standpoints:

- an **attribute** or a position, e.g. the managing director;
- a **characteristic** of a person – a natural leader;
- a **style** of behaviour.

Various writers on leadership suggest anywhere from three to twenty one dominant characteristics of a leader, but the main ones are that a leader:

- articulates a vision for the organisation that others find inspiring and motivating;
- manages by principle rather than by policy and serves as a role model for others;
- effectively coaches individuals and teams and helps them develop their potential;
- understands and communicates business information;

- eliminates barriers to team effectiveness and challenges the status quo;
- facilitates and develops team members bringing together the necessary tools, information and resources to get the job done;
- focuses on the customer's perspectives.

4.3 The characteristics of an entrepreneur

DEFINITION

An entrepreneur is a person with a strong need for achievement, who continually seeks opportunities to innovate and drive change, and who seeks the power and independence necessary for success.

We discussed entrepreneurship in Chapter 4 (see Section 2).

An entrepreneur can be defined as a person with a strong need for achievement, who continually seeks opportunities where they can innovate and drive change, and who seeks the power and independence necessary for success. Entrepreneurs are people who organise, operate, and assume the risks for starting up a business venture.

Carloff (1991) believes that an entrepreneur has a number of characteristics: he prefers to make decisions immediately; he is open to new approaches, is focused on achieving results (in his activities); he is open for constructive criticism and approval; he tries to be actively involved in doing business, and thus very often is happy in a small organisation. He loves fast development and innovations; in a business environment he is very comfortable during the business growing stage; he is very demanding to himself and to his partners' capabilities.

Very often they are outstanding strong-willed people, who do not fit in any corporate culture.

Other writers suggest that entrepreneurs share a number of common characteristics. They have found that, in general, the entrepreneur:

- likes to compete;
- is constantly searching for opportunities;
- is able to determine risk and has the courage to take risks but is not a gambler;
- is innovative, creative, and has dreams and goals;
- is independent and self-confident, yet knows when to get help;
- is able to do many things at once;
- likes a challenge and sees change as the norm and as healthy – is ready to adapt to new conditions;
- likes to work for him/herself and be in control;
- is hardworking and willing to stick with a project;
- is not easily discouraged;
- is in good health, has lots of energy and can handle stress;
- has a strong sense of self-worth;
- focuses his/her attention on the chances of success rather than the chances of failure.

Entrepreneurs do not function well in structured organisations and do not like someone having authority over them. They are self-confident and have a compelling need to do their own thing in their own way. Most believe they can do the job better than anyone else and will strive for maximum responsibility and accountability. They enjoy creating business strategies and thrive on the process of achieving their goals. Once they achieve a goal, they quickly replace it with a greater goal. They strive to exert whatever influence they can over future events.

Successful entrepreneurs can comprehend complex situations that may include planning, making strategic decisions, and working on multiple business ideas simultaneously. They are farsighted and aware of important details, and they will continuously review all possibilities to achieve their business objectives. At the same time, they devote their energy to completing the tasks immediately before them.

Entrepreneurs are natural leaders and are usually the first to identify a problem to be overcome. However, they are more concerned with people's accomplishments than with their feelings, and their lack of sensitivity to people's feelings can cause turmoil and turnover in their organisation. Entrepreneurs are impatient and drive themselves and everyone around them. They lack the tolerance or empathy necessary for team building and will delegate very few key decisions.

4.4 Manager or leader?

What distinguishes management from leadership? Management describes a position and set of responsibilities and roles, whereas leadership is the process by which a leader influences others to work willingly towards the organisation's goals and to the best of their abilities. A leader can be a manager, but a manager is not necessarily a leader. The leader of the work group may emerge informally as the choice of the group. If a manager is able to influence people to achieve the goals of the organisation, without using formal authority to do so, then the manager is demonstrating leadership.

Generally speaking, **leadership** deals with the **interpersonal** aspects of a manager's job, whereas planning, organising, and controlling deal with the administrative aspects. Leadership deals with change, inspiration, motivation, and influence. Management deals more with carrying out the organisation's goals and maintaining equilibrium. Successful leadership depends not only on the knowledge, skills and personality of the leader, but also on the task to be achieved, the skills and motivation of the team.

The key point in differentiating between leadership and management is the idea that employees willingly follow leaders because they want to, not because they have to. Leaders may not possess the formal power to reward or sanction performance because leadership does not necessarily take place within the hierarchical structure of the organisation. However, employees give the leader power by complying with what he or she requests. On the other hand, managers may have to rely on formal authority to get employees to accomplish goals

Activity 3

Fayol listed the functions of management as:

(a) commanding, co-ordinating, controlling, planning and monitoring

(b) planning, organising, commanding, co-ordinating and monitoring

(c) planning, organising, commanding, co-ordinating and controlling

(d) organising, commanding, co-ordinating, negotiating and controlling.

State which one is correct.

Feedback to this activity is at the end of the chapter.

5 Theories of management style

5.1 Behavioural theories

DEFINITION

Leadership is a dynamic process where one individual influences others to contribute voluntarily to the achievement of group tasks in a given situation.

Leadership is a dynamic process where one individual influences others to contribute voluntarily to the achievement of group tasks in a given situation.

Early theories of leadership focused on the character traits that appeared to be common to successful or 'great' leaders: leaders were born and not made. Trait theorists tried to seek out the common personality characteristics (or traits) so that they had a basis on which to recognise actual and potential leaders and find a way for others to acquire these traits through learning and experience. In the 1940s the ideas of unique leader traits were questioned and it was considered that the qualities of leaders could be analysed better by looking at their behaviour or their style that causes others to follow them.

In this section we will look at theories which concentrate on what a manager or leader does – their **behaviour** or **style**. The early approaches sought to identify one style that was 'best'.

KEY POINT

Most styles have been classified in terms of how authoritarian or democratic they are. The two extremes of leadership style could be described as task centred or group centred.

Since the 1950s several theories about leadership and management style have been put forward. Most have been expressed in terms of authoritarian versus democratic styles, or people-oriented versus task-oriented styles. The two extremes can be described as follows:

- **Task-centred leadership** – where the main concern of the leader is getting the job done, achieving objectives and seeing the group as simply a means to an end.
- **Group-centred leadership** – where the prime interest of the leader is to maintain the group, stressing factors such as mutual trust, friendship, support, respect and warmth of relationships.

Contributors to behavioural theory include Likert, White and Lippitt, Blake and Mouton, McGregor, and Tannenbaum and Schmidt.

5.2 Likert

KEY POINT

Likert distinguished between four key styles or 'systems' of leadership: exploitative authoritative, benevolent authoritative, participative and democratic.

Likert distinguished between four key styles or 'systems' of leadership.

- **System 1: Exploitative authoritative** – is the epitome of the authoritarian style.
- **System 2: Benevolent authoritative** – is basically a paternalistic style. There is a limited element of reward, but communication is restricted. Policy is made at the top but there is some restricted delegation within rigidly defined procedures. Criticism or dissent is not tolerated and is frequently suppressed.
- **System 3: Participative** – the leader has some (incomplete) confidence in subordinates, listens to them but controls decision-making, motivates by reward and a level of involvement and will use the ideas and suggestions of subordinates constructively.
- **System 4: Democratic** – management gives economic rewards, rather than mere 'pats on the head', utilises full group-participation and involves teams in goal setting, and improving work methods and communication flows up and down. There is a close psychological relationship between superiors and subordinates. Decision-making is permitted at all levels and is integrated into the formal structure with reference to the organisational chart. Each group overlaps and is linked to the rest of the organisation by link pins that are members of more than one group.

Likert recognised that each style is relevant in some situations; for example, in a crisis, a system 1 approach is usually required. Alternatively when introducing a new system of work, system 4 would be most effective. His research shows that effective managers are those who adopt either a System 3 or a System 4 leadership style. Both are seen as being based on trust and paying attention to the needs of both the organisation and employees.

5.3 White and Lippitt

KEY POINT

White and Lippitt researched the impact of authoritarian, democratic and laissez-faire leadership styles and found the democratic style to be the most successful.

White and Lippitt argued that to research the effectiveness of various styles, it is necessary to hold the situation constant. They set up an experiment, which concentrated on the impact of three leadership styles in task-oriented groups. The study involved directing groups of schoolchildren in four different clubs. They were carefully matched for IQ, popularity, energy and so on and all worked on the same project of making masks. They had three types of leader assigned to them:

- **Authoritarian** – this leader was to remain aloof and to use orders without consultation in directing the group activities.
- **Democratic** – this leader was to offer guidance, encourage the children and participate in the group.
- **Laissez-faire** – this leader gave the children knowledge, but did not become involved and generally participated little in the group's activities.

The results showed the democratic leadership style seemed to be the most successful:

- **Authoritarian** – groups became aggressive and/or apathetic, high dependence on leader, rebellious, attention-seeking, outbursts of horseplay but group got the work done.
- **Democratic** – friendly group, a lot of individual differences but strong group mindedness, steady work, better results.
- **Laissez-faire** – group lacked achievement; members asked lots of questions, unable to plan or reach a decision, played about, did not get a lot done.

5.4 Blake and Mouton

KEY POINT

The management grid of Blake and Mouton addresses two key dimensions of managerial behaviour: concern for production, and concern for people.

Robert Blake and Jane Mouton in their Ohio State Leadership Studies, observed two key dimensions of managerial behaviour, namely: concern for **production** (the task), and concern for **people**. Concern for production includes the manager's attitude towards procedures, processes, work efficiency, and volume of output. Concern for people includes personal commitment, sustaining the esteem and trust of the group, maintaining interpersonal relationships and ensuring good working conditions.

Blake and Mouton recognised that it was possible for concern for production to be independent of concern for people. It was therefore possible for a leader to be strong on one and weak on the other, strong on both, weak on both, or any variation in between. They devised a series of questions, the answers to which enabled them to plot these two basic leadership dimensions as the axes on a grid structure, now commonly referred to as Blake's Grid (see below).

Blake and Mouton's Managerial Grid (for assessing managerial behaviour)

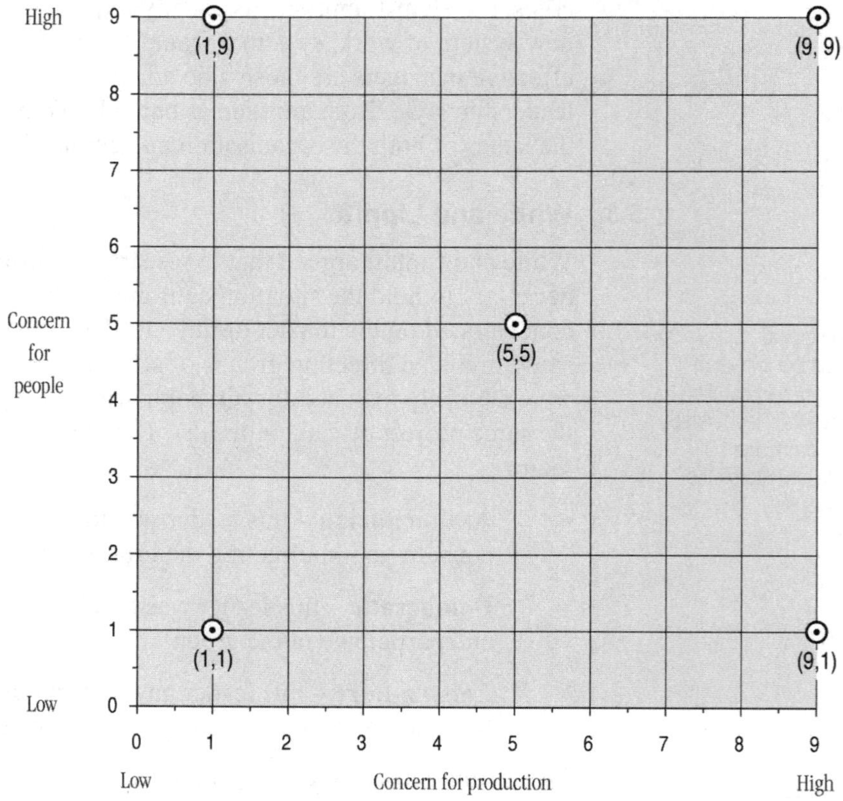

A high concern for production will score 9 and a high concern for people will also score 9, the two co-ordinates on the grid indicating the proportion of each concern present. Blake and Mouton picked out these two elements of a manager's job as characterising the leadership role.

In Blake's terminology, someone scoring 1 on the 'concern for production' scale and 9 on the 'concern for people' scale is described as a 'country club manager' because production or activity is incidental to good fellowship and camaraderie; the opposite, 9,1 style, is characteristic of the dictator. The unfortunate 1,1 executive is traditionally known as 'impoverished', having minimum concern for either production or people. A 5,5 score indicates an average, middle-of-the-road 'organisation manager' and is sometimes referred to as the 'dampened pendulum'. Blake and Mouton emphasised from the outset that managers switch from one style to another, or combine elements of several in running their operations. The successful ones adjust purposefully to achieve their ends, the less successful act involuntarily.

The implication is that managers should aim for the 9,9 combination; a goal-centred team approach that seeks to gain optimum results through participation, involvement, commitment and conflict solving, where everyone can contribute. According to Blake and Mouton, individuals can adapt their style to become more effective personally and, working in a team, can build the synergy needed to raise output above the level that could be achieved individually.

Activity 4

Blake and Mouton define 9,9, team-centred results based leadership, as the theoretical ultimate. Identify some situations where 9,9 may not be the best approach but 1,9 or 9,1 may provide a better basis.

Feedback to this activity is at the end of the chapter.

5.5 Douglas McGregor

The managerial grid is based on the assumption that concern for production and concern for people are not incompatible. In this respect they draw from the motivational ideas of **Douglas McGregor**, who examined basic assumptions about human behaviour, which underlie management actions. He defined two opposing images of human nature, which he called **Theory X** and **Theory Y** and suggested that the style of supervision or management adopted would depend on the view taken as to how subordinates behave.

KEY POINT

McGregor proposed that management style is based on managers' assumptions about workers, on a continuum between two extremes: Theory X and Theory Y.

Theory X: assumes that people dislike work and responsibility. Therefore they must be coerced or manipulated, with supervision likely to be task-driven, and managers having a high score on the 'concern for production' axis.

Theory Y: assumes that people value work. Because individuals are motivated by seeking self-achievement, supervision is more likely to be concerned with the individual and thus managers will have a high score on the 'concern for people' axis.

Theory X manager – the **authoritarian** – is tough and supports tight controls with punishment/reward systems. The contrasting style is that of the **Theory Y** manager – the **democrat** – who is benevolent, participative and a believer in self-control.

5.6 Tannenbaum and Schmidt's leadership continuum

The adaptation of leadership styles to varying contingencies was initially defined by **Tannenbaum and Schmidt** in 1958 with their idea of a **leadership continuum**, which is represented in the diagram below.

KEY POINT

Tannenbaum and Schmidt suggested that leadership style was best described as a continuum.
The appropriate style depends on the characteristics of the leader, subordinates and the situation.

Tannenbaum and Schmidt's leadership continuum

Dictatorship **Abdication**

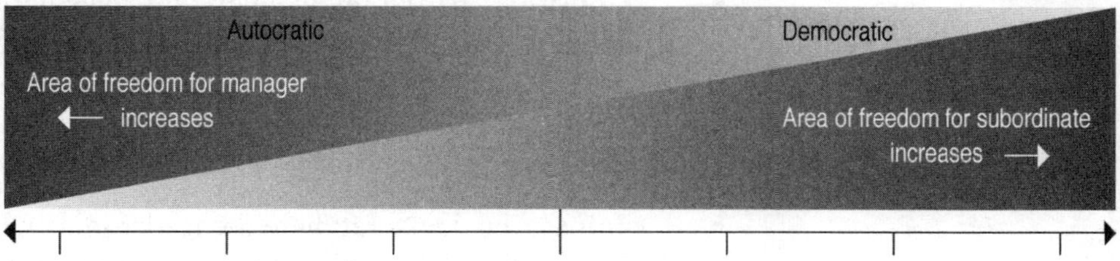

Manager...

able to make unchallenged decisions	persuades workers to accept	presents decision - invites questions	presents draft decision - invites questions	presents problem - decides after worker input	gives limits - all discuss - group decides	gives limits - group discuss & decide on own

Manager...

tells	tells and sells	tells and talks	consults	involves	delegates	abdicates

Tannenbaum and Schmidt suggested that leadership style was best described as a continuum. The appropriate style depends on the characteristics of the leader, subordinates and the situation.

They found that managers were often uncertain how to handle specific types of problem. In particular, distinguishing between the types of problem they should handle themselves and those that should be resolved with their subordinates. They concluded that in making an appropriate choice of how autocratic or democratic to be, a manager needed to consider three sets of issues:

- their personal concerns (personality, values, natural style, level of confidence etc.);
- the subordinates – managers had to consider their subordinate's needs for responsibility and independence, their knowledge, experience, attitude, etc.);
- the situation – includes concern for the nature of the problem, the competence of the group handling the problem, the organisation's culture, time pressures, levels of authority and responsibility, etc.

Re-appraising their theory in 1973, Tannenbaum and Schmidt added the influence of the environment on management style, for example, ecology pressures, education changes, union power base.

5.7 The Ashridge studies

KEY POINT

Ashridge Management College suggested four distinct management styles as a development of the continuum idea. These are: 'Tells', 'Sells', 'Consults' and 'Joins'.

A further development of the continuum was published by the **Ashridge Management College** in 1966. Basically, they suggest four distinct management styles:

- **Tells** – the autocratic dictator: the manager makes decisions, issues orders and expects obedience. Communication is downward with no feedback until after the event.
- **Sells** – the persuader: the manager makes the decisions and tries to persuade staff that it represents their best interests.
- **Consults** – partial involvement: the manager retains the decision-making authority but seeks to elicit other opinions before reaching a decision. Ashridge points out that this must be an honest approach, not an attempt to hoodwink staff where the manager has no intention of changing a predetermined decision.
- **Joins** – the democrat: here the leader joins with the staff and operates from within the team, seeking to reach a consensus decision. It is clearly most effective where all members within the group have knowledge and experience to contribute so that an evenly balanced informed discussion can lead to the best decision.

The findings from the study are that employees prefer to receive the 'consults' and 'joins' styles, but most managers were scored as being 'tells' and 'sells'. This was further reflected in the fact that staff satisfaction in work tended to be higher with staff who saw their manager's style as 'consults' and 'joins'.

A further important conclusion was the need for consistency in leadership style. The least favourable attitudes were found in staff who professed themselves unable to see a consistent style in their boss.

5.8 Advantages and disadvantages of different styles of management

Tannenbaum and Schmidt's continuum suggests a range of styles between autocratic and democratic without any suggestion that any one style is right or wrong. In fact, there are probably advantages and disadvantages associated with most management/leadership styles.

Advantages of autocratic style	**Disadvantages of autocratic style**
• It is very appropriate in times of crises or emergencies. • Decision-making is faster when only one person is involved in the process. • It is appropriate when a person is training others who don't know enough about the task to make decisions. • It is appropriate when there is rebellion and the situation is filled with disturbances, then one person needs to take over.	• It fails to develop leadership in followers. • It stifles creativity and discourages innovation. • Work may actually stop when the leader is not physically present, because no one else can make a decision. • Generally an autocratic leader will not develop an organisation that can continue after he/she leaves.
Advantages of democratic style	**Disadvantages of democratic style**
• It helps to train followers in leadership as they participate in planning and decision making, which gives them a stronger sense of ownership of goals and decisions. • Followers get to listen and learn from the free exchange of ideas and even the praise and criticism of ideas. • Wisdom is accumulated as one participates in the give and take of discussion of ideas. • It is appropriate when there is rebellion and the situation is filled with disturbances, then one person needs to take over.	• The democratic process will take more time than a more autocratic approach. • In time of crises this delay may be costly. • The followers must know enough to contribute good ideas and they must be motivated enough to want to be involved.
Advantages of laissez faire style	**Disadvantages of laissez faire style**
• It can be an excellent style to use with a trained and motivated group. • Professionally trained and experienced staff can be given the freedom to do their work.	• Some people need more direction and some may even feel that the leader does not care for them because there is so little contact (control). • Co-ordination is also a problem.

6 Contingency approaches to management

6.1 Contingency or situational models

KEY POINT

Contingency theories state that the appropriateness of the actions of a manager/leader depend on the actual situation in which actions are taken.

Contingency theories state that the appropriateness of the actions of a manager/leader depend on the situation in which actions are taken. They avoid the notion that there is a 'best style' or a 'best way' of managing. An autocratic style may be suitable for managers in a factory but not for managers of development and design staff. There is no one right way to lead that will fit all situations, rather it is necessary to lead in a manner that is appropriate to a particular situation.

The contingency models of leadership include:

- Adair's action centred leadership model;
- Fiedler's contingency model;
- Maturity of followers model – Hersey and Blanchard.

6.2 Adair's action-centred leadership model

Behavioural theories have emphasised the functions of the leader (what the leader does) and the style of the leader. However, leadership is seen as an active process, a process of goal attainment involving complex relations between leader and follower with actions performed both by and for the leader.

KEY POINT

Adair's model stresses that leadership focuses on the needs of the task, group and individuals.

Professor **Adair's action-centred leadership model** (which we discussed in Chapter 9) is used for leadership training. It is a functional approach, which identifies the functions of a leader in relation to the basic needs that are common in all leadership situations. Training is organised around eight elements: defining objectives, planning, controlling, evaluating, motivating, organising, briefing and setting an example. Individual needs are distinguished from group needs and the needs of the task to be done. There will never be a perfect match between the elements and the job of the leader is to be sufficiently sensitive to these aspects and manage each situation by giving suitable priority to the variables. The diagram below shows the overlap of the task, group and individual needs, and indicates some measure of interrelation between these factors.

Adair's action-centred leadership model

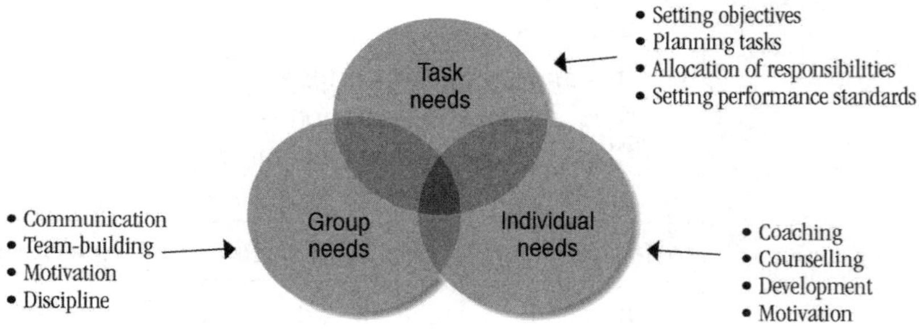

6.3 Fiedler's contingency theory

Contingency theory sees effective leadership as being dependent on a number of variable or contingent factors. There is no one right way to lead that will fit all situations; rather it is necessary to lead in a manner that is appropriate to a particular situation. The theory also provides a basis for developing people as leaders. By making people aware of the factors affecting the choice of leadership style and providing a basis for increased self-awareness the theory gives a useful starting point for leadership training.

The major difficulty for any leader seeking to apply contingency theory is to actually modify their behaviour as the situation changes.

Fiedler's contingency theory can be of practical advantage to managers, offering a systematic way of analysing situations and then prescribing the most effective leadership response to that situation. First of all Fiedler developed a new way of assessing leadership style based on the measurement of the leader's LPC (least preferred co-worker) score. This score is obtained by asking the leader to think of the person with whom they can work least well – their **least preferred co-worker**. Then they are required to rate that person on 16 dimensions, each with a positive and negative aspect. Examples of these dimensions are given below:

Some dimensions of the least preferred co–worker

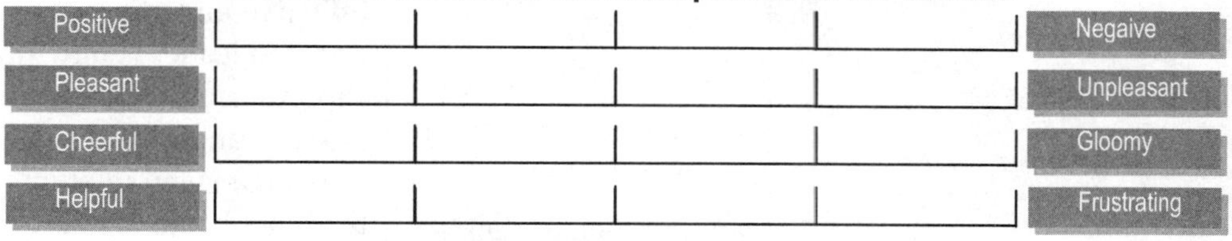

The leaders who rate their least preferred co-worker negatively get lower LPC scores and are said to be task orientated. Those who get high scores and see positive value even in those they find it difficult to get on with are said to be relationship oriented. These measures provide a new and original method of assessing a person's leadership orientation.

Fiedler goes on to show that there is no direct correlation between a leader's LPC score and his effectiveness as a leader. People with very different LPC scores can be equally successful and people with identical scores are seen to succeed or fail as leaders independent of whether they are task or relationship orientated. He argues that effective leadership is also dependent on a further set of variables namely:

- the extent to which the task in hand is structured;
- the leader's position power;
- the nature of the existing relationships between the leader and the group.

Since these factors are likely to vary from group to group there is no one way of leading; rather the approach to leading must be modified in the light of task structure, position power and whether existing relationships are good or bad. From his analysis Fiedler is able to identify three typical situations, which require a very different response from a leader.

Situation 1 • The task is highly structured. • The leader's position power is high. • Subordinates feel the relationships with the leader are good.	Under these conditions the task-oriented leader (low LPC) will get good results. Operating under these favourable conditions the low LPC leader will detect that events are potentially under control, set targets, monitor performance and get excellent results. The relationship-oriented leader (high LPC) does not perform well under these circumstances. This type of leader seeks to get work done by maintaining good inter-personal relations but here these relations are already good. The relationship orientation is irrelevant here and the group may well under-achieve under such leadership.

Situation 2 • The task is unstructured. • The leader's position power is low. • Subordinates feel that their relationships with the leader are moderately good.	Relationship-oriented leaders get the best results under these conditions. Maintenance of good relations is important here both to the ability of the leader to exert influence over subordinates and to the accomplishment of the task. The task oriented leader will not succeed in these circumstances because any deterioration in relationships will be ignored and, since the task lacks structure and position power is low, leadership/subordinate relations will be the key factor in producing good results.
Situation 3 • The task is unstructured. • The leader's position power is low. • Subordinates feel that their relationships with the leader are poor.	Fiedler says that task-oriented leaders are most effective under these conditions. A relationship-oriented leader is unwilling to exert pressure on subordinates, avoids confrontations that might upset or anger them, gets involved in attempts to repair damaged relations and ignores the task. On the other hand, the task-oriented leader will be impatient, attempt to structure the situation, ignore resistance from subordinates, reduce ambiguity and uncertainty surrounding the work and thus achieve a good performance.

From an analysis of these three situations it does appear that leadership depends on the particular requirements of a situation and there is no single style suitable for all occasions. For Fiedler, the effective leader is the person who can successfully identify the important features of the context (the contingent factors) and then adopt the style relevant to that context.

6.4 The Hersey-Blanchard situational leadership model

KEY POINT

The Hersey-Blanchard situational leadership model is based on the direction and socio-emotional support required by the maturity level of the followers.

The **Hersey-Blanchard** situational leadership model is based on the amount of **direction** (task behaviour) and amount of **socio-emotional support** (relationship behaviour) a leader must provide given the situation and the '**level of maturity**' of the followers.

- **Task behaviour** is the extent to which the leader engages in spelling out the duties and responsibilities to an individual or group. This behaviour includes telling people what to do, how to do it, when to do it, where to do it, and who's to do it. In task behaviour the leader engages in one-way communication.
- **Relationship behaviour** is the extent to which the leader engages in two-way or multi-way communications. This includes listening, facilitating, and supportive behaviours. In relationship behaviour the leader engages in two-way communication by providing socio-emotional support.
- **Maturity** is the willingness and ability of a person to take responsibility for directing their own behaviour. People tend to have varying degrees of maturity, depending on the specific task, function, or objective that a leader is attempting to accomplish through their efforts.

To determine the appropriate leadership style to use in a given situation, leaders must first determine the **maturity level** of their followers in relation to the specific task that they are attempting to accomplish through the effort of the followers. As the level of followers' maturity increases, leaders should begin to reduce their task behaviour and increase relationship behaviour until the followers reach a moderate level of maturity. As the followers begin to move into an above average level of maturity, leaders should decrease not only task behaviour but also relationship behaviour.

Once the maturity level is identified, the appropriate leadership style can be determined. The four leadership styles are:

- **delegating** to subordinates;
- **participating** with subordinates;
- **selling** ideas to subordinates;
- **telling** subordinates what to do.

High task/low relationship behaviour (S1) is referred to as '**telling**': the leader provides clear instructions and specific direction. Telling style is best matched with a low follower readiness level.

High task/high relationship behaviour (S2) is referred to as '**selling**': the leader encourages two-way communication and helps build confidence and motivation on the part of the employee, although the leader still has responsibility and controls decision-making. Selling style is best matched with a moderate follower readiness level.

High relationship/low task behaviour (S3) is referred to as '**participating**': with this style, the leader and followers share decision-making and no longer need or expect the relationship to be directive. Participating style is best matched with a moderate follower readiness level.

Low relationship/low task behaviour (S4) is labelled '**delegating**': this style is appropriate for leaders whose followers are ready to accomplish a particular task and are both competent and motivated to take full responsibility. Delegating style is best matched with a high follower readiness level.

7 Cross cultural management

7.1 Differences in culture

It is clear that national culture influences the way that people behave at work, and the expectations that they have of their colleagues, careers and organisation. Pümpin, for example, noticed that his four characteristics of dynamic cultures are quite close to Swedish culture. Perhaps the contrasts are most noticeable when Europeans and East Asian cultures are contrasted.

The economies of East Asia and South East Asia – Japan, China, Taiwan, South Korea, and Hong Kong – have recently been among the most dynamic in the world. Although this is partly attributable to their general political and economic policies, these countries have also benefited from the competitive activity of their business organisations. Japanese, Chinese and Korean management systems have all proved to be highly competitive in their different ways.

A common feature of these management approaches has been their tradition of holding together an organisation as a dynamic group. This suits the norms of Asian cultures.

The traditional model of management and competitiveness in the West has been based on Max Weber's study of the Protestant ethic in the rise of capitalism. Weber argued that a connection exists between the religious and cultural beliefs by which an individual is surrounded and the attitude to economic activity held by that individual. His analysis led to a view of strategic management activity based on individualism, mastery over the world, laissez faire economic principles, and the supremacy of market mechanisms.

Analysts studying comparative management have seized on Weber's ideas by trying to show how the different religious and cultural values held in Asian countries have been translated into different styles of management. These commentators have emphasised certain aspects of a 'Confucian' ethic that are believed to underlie much management theory and practice in Japan and other Eastern nations.

- While the Protestant ethic is highly conscious of rights, the Confucian ethic instead emphasises obligation. Individuals should be conscious of their group responsibilities.
- Western approaches to management emphasise adversarial relations, while Eastern approaches are based instead on a fiduciary community. This emphasis on trust implies that laissez faire principles are unwelcome; leadership and intervention by the government are the norm.

7.2 The Hofstede model

In the past, it has been assumed that there are significant differences in organisations across the world, which can be attributed to culture. However, one should be wary of overstating this view since some academic research now points to a somewhat different conclusion.

While research does not prove that national culture transcends organisational factors, it does suggest that management style in different countries may reflect personal values, attitudes and beliefs. On the basis of national differences in a large-scale research project into the impact of national culture on a single multinational business, Geert Hofstede (*Cultures and Organisations,* 1991) has identified four dimensions in which national culture seems to vary:

KEY POINT

Hofstede, identifies four dimensions in which national culture varies:

- Power distance
- Individualism versus collectivism
- Masculinity versus femininity
- Uncertainty avoidance.

Power distance – how much society accepts the unequal distribution of power, for instance the extent to which supervisors see themselves as being above their subordinates. In some cultures, particularly South American ones, disparities of power were tolerated more than in North European cultures.

Individualism versus collectivism – how much people prefer a tight-knit social framework based on 'loyalty' to an involvement based on individual cost and benefit. Some cultures are more cohesive than others, with Anglo Saxon cultures more individualistic than the collectivist cultures of South America.

Masculinity versus femininity – used as shorthand to indicate the degree to which 'masculine' values predominate: e.g. assertive, domineering, uncaring and competitive, as opposed to 'feminine' values such as sensitivity and concern for others. A masculine culture is one where gender roles are distinct, with the male focus on work, power and success. Such cultures include Japan, and Italy. Feminine cultures, such as Finland, have smaller differences in gender roles and success is likely to be regarded as a social, rather than personal activity.

Uncertainty avoidance – how much society dislikes ambiguity and risk, and the extent to which people feel threatened by unusual situations, paralleled by how far persons and ideas deviate from the accepted norm. Some cultures, such as France and Japan, dislike uncertainty and use planning and bureaucracy to reduce it. Other cultures, such as Jamaica and Denmark, tend to be less uncomfortable with uncertainty and ambiguity. High uncertainty avoidance traits means risk taking is discouraged.

Hofstede's four dimensions of culture

Individualistic Australia United States United Kingdom	Individualism/Collectivism ←————→	**Collectivist** Colombia Pakistan Venezuela
Low power distance Austria Denmark Israel	Power distance ←————→	**High power distance** Mexico India Philippines
Low uncertainty avoidance Singapore Hong Kong Denmark	Uncertainty avoidance ←————→	**High uncertainty avoidance** Japan Portugal Greece
Masculine Japan Austria Venezuela	Masculinity/Femininity ←————→	**Feminine** Sweden Denmark Norway

It is important to see that Hofstede was attempting to model aspects of culture that might influence business behaviour, rather than produce national stereotypes or explain the differences he found in historical or socio geographic terms. He mapped each nationality as a mixture of traits. In general, these traits were positions on a continuum rather than absolute.

Hofstede also looked at cultural differences in work related attitudes. These include:

- **Leadership** – in some countries, such as those in Latin America, leaders are expected to take a strong personal interest in employees and appear at private social functions such as weddings, etc whereas in other countries such as Germany such social contact is discouraged. In other countries, notably in Asia and Africa, public criticism is intolerable as the loss of self-**respect brings dishonour to the employee and his family.**
- **Motivation** – the incentives for effective performance must match the culture. It is pointless offering individual bonuses to workers where there are strong group and company loyalties, as in Japan, or where loyalty to an individual's superior is paramount as in Turkey and the Near East.
- **Structure** – research showed that French firms are bureaucratic with orders and procedures set from above whereas German work organisation relies more on the professional expertise, which derives from the trained knowledge and skill of the more junior employees.

Summary

- Authority is the right to use power, and delegation is the act by which a person transfers part of their authority to a subordinate person.
- Reasons for delegation include: training subordinates; management succession; performance evaluation; relief of stress; job satisfaction.
- McGivering distinguishes five types of power: reward power; coercive power; legitimate power; expert power; referent power.

- Fayol identified five functions of managers: planning; organising; commanding; co-ordinating; controlling.
- Mintzberg's analysis of managers' functions distinguishes between interpersonal roles, informational roles and decisional roles.
- Many authorities have described a spectrum of managerial styles and have tried to analyse which style is most effective. Relevant authorities include: Likert; White and Lippitt; Blake and Mouton; Douglas McGregor; Tannenbaum and Schmidt.
- Contingency models of leadership include Adair's action centered leadership model, Fiedler's contingency model, and Hersey and Blanchard's situational theory.
- Hofstede identifies four dimensions in which national culture varies: power distance; individualism versus collectivism; masculinity versus femininity; and uncertainty avoidance.

Having completed your study of this chapter you should have achieved the following learning outcomes.

- Explain the concepts of power, bureaucracy, authority, responsibility, leadership and delegation.
- Analyse the relationship between managers and their subordinates.
- Discuss the importance of national cultures to management style.

Self-test questions

1 How did Fayol define authority? (1.2)

2 Describe Weber's model of bureaucracy. (1.4)

3 Outline the process of delegation. (2.3)

4 What are the five types of power according to McGivering? (3.2)

5 Describe Fayol's functions of management. (4.1)

6 List the main characteristics of a leader. (4.2)

7 What do the axes on Blake and Mouton's managerial grid represent? (5.4)

8 What are the three major goals in Adair's action-centred leadership? (6.2)

9 According to Fiedler, under which conditions are task-oriented leaders most effective? (6.3)

10 Briefly describe Hofstede's four dimensions of national culture. (7.2)

Multiple-choice questions

Question 1

What kind of power is a management accountant most likely to have over a line manager in another department?

A Reward power

B Legitimate power

C Expert power

D Referent power

Question 2

The assumption that people dislike work and responsibility and must be coerced or manipulated to perform adequately is called:

A System 1

B 9, 1

C Theory X

D Theory Y

For the answer to these questions, see the 'Answers' section at the end of the book.

Exam-type questions

Question 1: Super Auto Machines plc (SAMs)

During the 1980s Super Auto Machines plc (SAMs) enjoyed a reputation as one of the world's leading makers of high-quality luxury cars. During the early 1990s, however, under the leadership of a new chief executive, Hu Song, SAMs embarked on a new strategy. Hu Song transformed SAMs from a company focused on producing luxury cars and trucks under the SAMs label into one of the country's largest conglomerates. Hu Song achieved this by acquiring a number of major companies, including electronics and consumer goods manufacturers, an aerospace company, a mini steel mill and an aluminium plant.

The logic underlying Hu Song's diversification strategy was based on a number of factors. First, he believed that the intensity of rivalry in the world automobile industry would increase. Pacific Rim manufacturers were beginning to move up-market into SAMs' territory, making it difficult for SAMs to hold on to its differential advantage. Secondly, Hu Song believed that in the new competitive environment, the companies that would succeed would be those that were able to incorporate leading-edge technology into their cars before competitors did. Thirdly, Hu Song reasoned that by acquiring electronics and aerospace businesses, SAMs could gain access to just such technology. Fourthly, Hu Song hoped that by purchasing steel and aluminium processing facilities, the organisation could ensure that the quality and type of materials required in its end products could be controlled. In brief, Hu Song believed that technological developments were creating significant opportunities for sharing know-how across the aerospace, automobile and electronics businesses.

To date, however, Hu Song's plans have yet to bear fruit. Since the early 1990s the company's profits have fallen. A major reason had been the poor performance of SAMs' new businesses. As a result, by the mid-1990s SAMs' car business, even though it made up only 50% of SAMs' total revenues, accounted for 85% of profits. But the future prospects look even worse. In 1997, for the first time ever, SAMs' main competitor sold more cars than SAMs. In fact it sold almost 10% more.

Hu Song has played down this worrying turn of events and argued that these problems are short-run ones and that, in the long run, the diversification strategy will pay off. Some of Hu Song's fellow executives, however, are not convinced by his arguments. A number of them have always thought that Hu Song's view of the potential for sharing technology among aerospace, cars and electronics businesses was too optimistic. These doubters also found it difficult to understand why a diversified conglomerate had to be constructed to share such technological know-how when some of their competitors were sharing know-how through strategic alliances. Similarly, the wisdom of acquiring steel and aluminium processing facilities has been questioned.

The current state of the company has given rise to serious morale problems. Managers of SAMs' auto business are unhappy at having to use most of their profits to finance the loss-making aerospace and electronics businesses. There is also is a widespread belief among the staff of SAMs' car business that Hu Song's diversification strategy has been responsible for the recent loss of leadership in the luxury car industry to its main rival.

Unfortunately, the problems of SAMs are not confined to Hu Song's strategic moves. SAMs' auto manufacturing costs are amongst the highest in the industry. A high proportion of this cost is accounted for by the labour force which enjoys pension, sick pay, holiday entitlement and other benefits unrivalled elsewhere. Many of SAMs' rivals went through a process of downsizing a few years ago, but a strong trade union presence in SAMs' main country of operation has so far limited the ability of SAMs to cut the labour force significantly or, for that matter, to restrain ever-rising costs of labour.

Required:

(a) Describe the sources of power and authority that would enable someone in Hu Song's position to make and implement major strategic decisions. **(12 marks)**

(b) Hu Song is accountable to various stakeholder groups. Identify these groups and explain why Hu Song is accountable to each. **(13 marks)**

(Total: 25 marks)

Question 2: Blake and Mouton's managerial grid

Six supervisors from accountancy departments are on a management development course. A, one of them, has reported his proposals about a case which they have been studying. The other five have rated A by placing crosses on Blake and Mouton's managerial grid. The results are as shown.

Explain what the consultant in charge of the exercise should tell the group about the significance of the result and make suggestions to improve A's management style.

(10 marks)

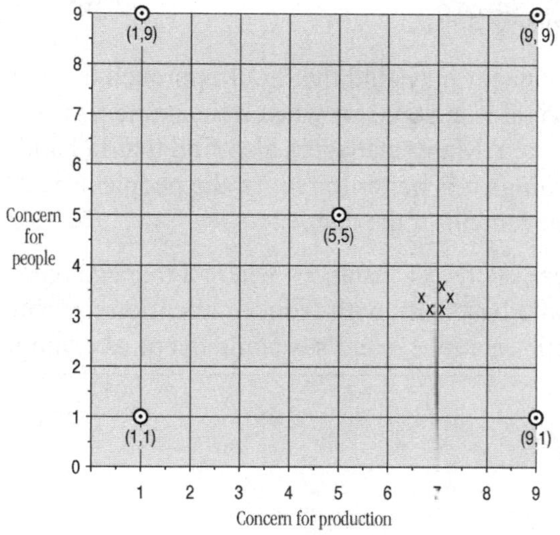

For the answer to these questions, see the 'Answers' section at the end of the book.

Feedback to activities

Activity 1

Example A, because the flow of authority is shown as passing down from the machine room manager to the assistant manager and then on to the operatives. In example B the machine room manager can delegate to the assistant manager and to the operatives, but the assistant manager is not shown as having any authority over the operators.

Activity 2

More reasons for delegation include:

- Managers can be relieved of less important or less immediate responsibilities.
- It enables decisions to be taken nearer to the point of impact and without the delays caused by reference upwards.
- It gives organisations a chance to meet changing conditions more flexibly.
- It makes a subordinate's job more interesting.
- It allows career development.
- It brings together skills and ideas.
- Team aspect is motivational.
- It allows performance appraisal.

Activity 3

Fayol listed the functions of management as:

(c) planning, organising, commanding, co-ordinating and controlling.

Activity 4

A manager may find that a 9,1 approach is better in situations of crisis where survival is at stake, or when a timetable has gone wrong and urgent action must be taken. Many managers also find that in handling dismissals or issuing final warnings it is better to reduce the people aspect and concentrate only on the achievement of the task.

There are fewer instances where a manager can move from 9,9 or 9,1 towards a people-based 1,9 with reduced attention to results. Staff welfare issues and some public relations exercises could occur as examples.

Chapter 12

CONTROL, COMMUNICATION AND NEGOTIATION

Syllabus content

- The use of systems of control within the organisation (e.g. employment contracts, performance appraisal, reporting structures).
- Theories of control within firms and types of organisational structure (e.g. matrix, divisional, network).
- Personal time management.
- Communication skills (i.e. type of communication tools and their use, as well as the utility and conduct of meetings) and ways of managing communication problems.
- Negotiation skills.
- Creativity and idea generation.
- Information gathering techniques (e.g. interviews, questionnaires).

Contents

1 Organisation control

2 Control systems

3 Personal time management

4 Conducting research and collecting data

5 Communication

6 Interpersonal skills

7 Creativity

1 Organisation control

1.1 Theories of organisation

There are many writers on organisation and management with as many different approaches to co-ordination and control within the organisation. The classical writers placed emphasis on structure and formal organisation, sets of principles to guide managerial actions, standard procedures and the exercise of rules and regulations to create consistency and predictability in behaviour.

Frederick Winslow Taylor believed that each worker should be controlled by having a large, clearly defined daily task with standard conditions to ensure the task is more easily accommodated. High payment was to be made for successful completion of the task and workers should suffer loss when they failed to meet the standards laid down. A distinctive feature of Taylor's writing was that workers should be controlled not only by the giving of orders and maintenance of discipline, but also by removing them from any decisions about the manner in which they carried out their work. Taylor's ideas are referred to as scientific management.

Henry Gantt introduced task setting (goals for the worker to achieve) and Gantt charts (to plan and control production).

Frank Gilbreth introduced micro-motion analysis based on defined elements of work. This formed the basis of time study.

Henri Fayol developed several principles of management as guides to managerial action:

- division of work leading to specialisation;
- authority – the right to give orders and the power to exact obedience;
- discipline – the military tag 'discipline constitutes the chief strength of armies' should be followed by 'discipline is what leaders make of it',
- scalar chain through which formal lines of authority should pass.

Max Weber stated that bureaucracies should have:

- clearly defined duties and responsibilities for all organisational members;
- hierarchically arranged staff with each member reporting to a superior and responsible for subordinates (except for those at the top or bottom of the structural pyramid);
- an elaborate system of rules governing the manner in which each official carries out his duties.

The human relations approach offered an alternative view of control. They emphasised the social needs of individuals in the workplace and saw a high level of control as self-defeating, producing a negative response and increasing internal conflict. They argued that control is more a feature of interpersonal influence and takes place within a network of interaction and communication.

Henry Mintzberg advances the view that:

- all labour in an organisation has to be divided into distinct tasks;
- co-ordination is needed between the people carrying out the different tasks.

Co-ordination is achieved in one or more of the following ways; the relative complexity of the work affects the method chosen:

- **Standardised work processes** – the work is specified, and everybody works in the same way.
- **Standardised outputs** – through such things as product or service specifications. Whilst the results are standardised, the means are not.
- **Standardised skills and knowledge** – even though each job is performed independently. This is an important co-ordinating mechanism in professional activities and specifies the kind of training needed to perform the work.
- **Direct supervision** – exists throughout the hierarchy where individuals issue instructions and monitor performance. One person has a specific co-ordinating role.
- **Mutual adjustment** – co-ordination results from internal communication and through informal contact between the people performing their organisational roles. This exists in simple structures where people work closely together. It also applies to some complex tasks e.g. in a research project if the outcome is uncertain, colleagues will adjust their activities in the light of new findings.

1.2 Control process

Control is concerned with regulating the activities within an organisation so that the causes of deviations from standards specified in policies, plans and targets are identified and corrected. The purposes and methods of organisational control are therefore to:

- **standardise performance** – e.g. by quality assurance and control systems, supervision, procedure manuals, production schedules;
- **prevent losses** through theft, fraud, wastage or misuse, e.g. by record keeping and audit procedures;
- **correct deviances**, e.g. by statistical quality control, supervisory management, disciplinary procedures;
- **define and limit authority** by job descriptions, policy statements, rules and procedures;
- **define and direct performance** by management, by objectives, budgets, sales and production targets. Control is an integral part of management. It is a general concept that is applied to both organisational performance and individual behaviour.

1.3 Internal control systems

DEFINITION

An internal control system is the whole system of controls and methods to: ensure adherence to management policies; safeguard the organisation's assets and secure, as far as possible, the completeness and accuracy of its records; and promote operational efficiency.

Internal control can be defined as: 'The whole system of controls and methods, both financial and otherwise, which are established by management to:

- safeguard its assets;
- secure, as far as possible, the completeness and accuracy of the records;
- promote operational efficiency;
- monitor adherence to policies and directives'.

At its simplest, companies need internal controls to stop things going missing and to make some sense of how the business is doing.

Activity 1

What are the main functions of control systems within organisations?

Feedback to this activity is at the end of the chapter.

1.4 Reporting and control structures

Managers should have a plan of their organisation, defining and allocating responsibilities and identifying lines of reporting for all aspects of the organisation's operations. The delegation of authority and responsibility should be clearly specified.

Organisational structure was discussed in Chapter 3. You may wish to review the basic organisational forms with a focus on their control issues.

- Classical **hierarchical organisations** (whether structured functionally or geographically) are able to exercise more or less centralised control via the scalar chain of authority. Bureaucracies also exercise control through a system of clearly defined roles and rules.

- **Divisional structures** give greater autonomy (or decentralised control) to specialised or geographically dispersed units.

- **Network structures** (such as virtual organisations, Chapter 4) exercise control via shared goals and, in the case of inter-organisational collaborations, contractual arrangements. Their formal structures are deliberately loose and flexible, giving responsiveness at the expense of direct managerial control.

- **Matrix structures** are a mechanism of dual control, giving a measure of management control to both functional (departmental) and project (or product/client) managers.

In Mintzberg's terms (as discussed earlier): hierarchical organisations co-ordinate by direct supervision; bureaucracies by standardisation of processes; divisionalised structures by standardisation of outputs; and network/matrix organisations by mutual adjustment.

Another key point to note is that control/supervision issues – or the extent of centralisation or decentralisation of control – effectively shapes the overall organisation structure.

DEFINITION

Span of control is the number of subordinates that can be supervised effectively by one manager.

The '**span of control**' or 'span of management' refers to the number of subordinates reporting directly to one person. The scalar chain refers to the number of different levels in the structure.

Narrow spans of control result in tall organisational structures, having many levels of supervisors. Tall structures have the advantages of close supervision and control and fast communication between subordinates and superiors. The disadvantages are high costs due to the numerous levels and undue delays because information has to be carried through several levels (upwards and downwards).

Wide spans of control result in flat structures, where supervisors have to delegate and ensure that clear policies are laid down. The disadvantages include the possible loss of control and the need for high quality of managers, as their workload tends to be so high that bottlenecks may occur.

Span of control

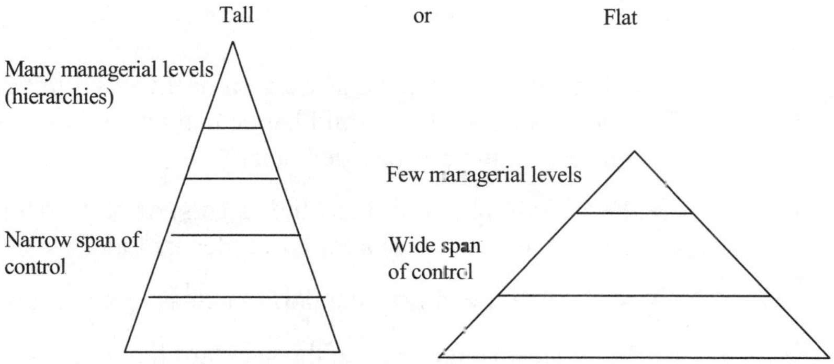

Although classical theorists, such as Fayol, claimed that ideally a manager should have between three and six subordinates, there is no ideal span, although an 'optimum span' may depend on:

KEY POINT

The span of control depends on the nature of work, type of personnel and the management methods/style.

- **nature of work** – the more repetitive the work, the greater the number that can be controlled;
- **type of personnel** – the ability, competence and skills of managers and subordinates depend to some extent on profession and training;
- **management methods/style** – depends on computerisation and automated management techniques and the staff/specialist assistance available.

Urwick favoured structures with wide spans of control and few hierarchical levels (flat structures) because this encouraged delegation and the exercise of meaningful responsibility.

Generally, classical theorists believed that flat organisation structures were more efficient in terms of cost, communications and motivation. Tall organisations tended to encourage bureaucracy and slow market response.

2 Control systems

2.1 Basic system

Whatever the nature of control, there are at least five elements to a control system, shown in the diagram below.

A basic control system

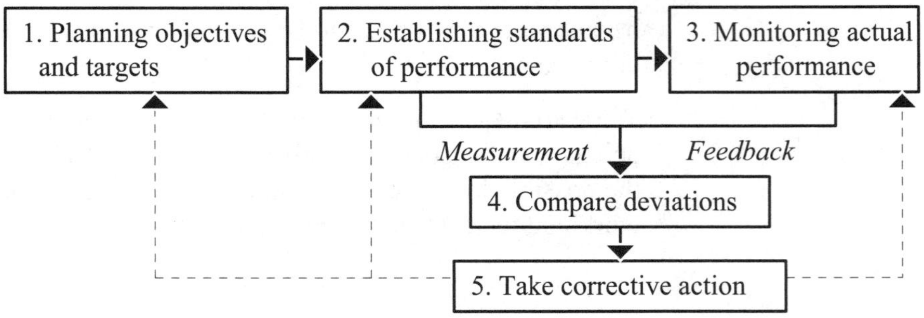

Planning – involves clarification of the goals to be achieved. People need to know exactly what should happen and what is required of them. Objectives and targets should be specified clearly.

Establishing standards (and targets) of performance against which the level of success can be measured. Examples include:

- manufacturing standards such as units of raw materials per unit produced;
- cost standards e.g. the standard labour cost of making product X might be three hours at £7 per hour = £21;
- the achievement of stated goals such as meeting a profit objective;
- revenue targets such as turnover per square metre of floor space in a warehouse;
- intangible standards such as motivation, corporate image, goodwill and quality of service which might be measured using attitude surveys, market research, etc.

Monitoring actual performance – requires feedback and a system of reporting information that is accurate, relevant and timely and in a form that enables management to highlight deviations from the planned standard of performance. Feedback also provides the basis for decisions to adjust the control system e.g. to revise the original plan.

Comparing actual performance against planned targets – requires a means of interpreting and evaluating information to give details of progress, reveal deviations and identify possible problems.

Taking corrective action – requires consideration of what can be done to improve performance. It requires authority to take appropriate action to correct the situation, to review the operation of the control system and to make any adjustments to objectives, targets or standards of performance.

2.2 Budgetary control systems

Budgets can be stated in financial terms (capital and revenue expenditure budgets) or in non-financial terms (units of production). In a budgetary control system the performance of a department is compared with the budget. Action is then taken to improve the department's performance if possible.

Budgetary control system

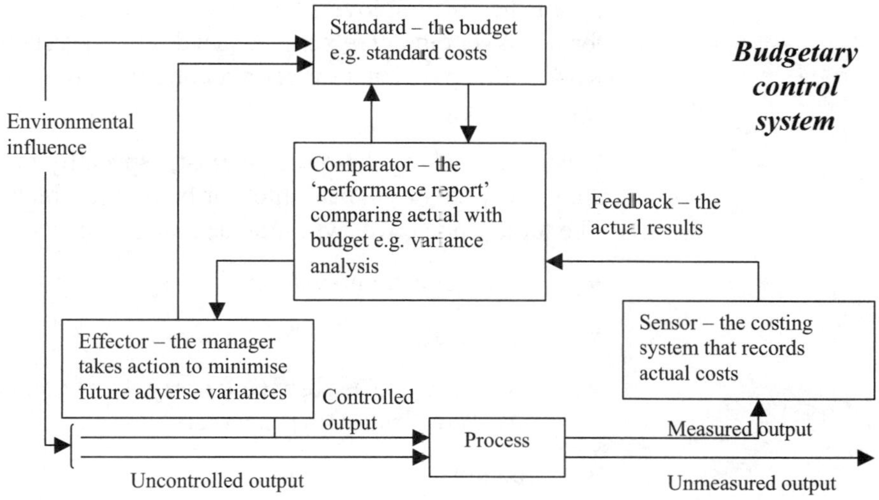

Budgetary control system

The opportunity may also be taken to adjust the standard (i.e. the budget) if it is seen to be too easy or too difficult to achieve.

A number of complications have been included in the budgetary control system illustrated:

- the impact of the environment on the system e.g. prices of raw materials may rise uncontrollably or interest rates may increase;
- differences between actual and budgeted results may not be controllable directly by the departmental manager (e.g. rises in certain input costs may be caused by another department);
- the accounting system cannot measure all the output of the department, hence feedback may be incomplete e.g. an investment for longer-term profits may have been made at the expense of short-term cost control.

Control is maintained through a network of information flow, which is the means of control. When such information is not fed back it is of no value to the system. This process of routing back into parts of the system is known as 'feedback'. It is a fundamental aspect of any control system.

KEY POINT

Feedback control is the measurement of differences between planned outputs and outputs achieved, and the modification of subsequent action and/or plans to achieve future required results.

Feedback control is the measurement of differences between planned outputs and outputs achieved, and the modification of subsequent action and/or plans to achieve future required results. The control system responds to the information received from the comparator and initiates corrective action. In order to take any action, the comparator e.g. a manager, must consider:

- the accuracy of the information fed back (the feedback);
- the significance of the variation from standard or norm;
- what inputs are required to restore the system to an acceptable standard or a reasonable degree of stability.

2.3 Contracts of employment and other rules

Contracts of employment (discussed in more detail in Chapter 14) form the most basic control tool for the relationship between employer and employee. They contain, often in great detail, standards of behaviour and expected performance required of the employee, and the duties and responsibilities of the organisation. In the case of disciplinary proceedings, the contract (and any accompanying code of conduct) is used as a basis for corrective action.

In addition to contract terms, there are working rules, which have been established by employers and unions, and these are normally issued in booklet form and set out agreements reached on issues such as public holidays, night work shifts, payments for certain conditions (e.g. for dirty work), bonuses and tea breaks, etc.

Organisational regulations also exist, especially in very large firms, and these are usually set out in pamphlets or booklets, which are available to employees. The topics they cover will include matters such as:

- the suggestions system;
- punctuality;
- special leave of absence for, say, local councillors who are employees, or for Territorial Army members;
- complaints procedure;
- medical examinations; and
- parking.

Finally, there are always informal rules and regulations, which have arisen as conventional, acceptable standards of behaviour in the organisation. These have a very wide range, from the unofficial inferences drawn concerning some official (formal) rules, which have arisen over the years, to understood ways of going about things. A new recruit has to learn of these from colleagues, usually by experience.

2.4 Performance measurement systems

KEY POINT

Performance measurement aims to establish how well something or somebody is doing in relation to the planned activity and desired results.

Performance measurement aims to establish how well something or somebody is doing in relation to the planned activity and desired results. The 'something' may be a machine, a factory, a subsidiary company or an organisation as a whole. The 'somebody' may be an individual employee, a manager, or a group of people.

Performance measurement is a vital part of control: it generates the results which are fed back for comparison with objectives.

A typical organisation requires performance measurement:

- in terms of its relations with external parties (its customers or market, suppliers and competitors);
- across the organisation as a whole (divisional performance measurement);
- within each of the main sub-divisions of the organisation;
- at the level of individual activities.

Three possible points of reference for measurement are profitability, activity and productivity.

The types of performance measures include:

- **Quality and service** – The *quality of output* can be measured by the number of production items rejected on inspection, or the number of items returned by customers as faulty. The *quality of a service* could be measured by the level of complaints or by favourable reaction e.g. the quality of a training course could be monitored by asking trainees to complete an assessment form when the course has finished. The training manager's performance could be assessed on the basis of the responses.

- **Ratios and percentages** – Ratios relate one item to another, and so help to put performance into context. For example the profit/sales ratio sets profit in the context of how much has been earned per £1 of sales, and so shows how wide or narrow profit margins are. A percentage expresses one number as a proportion of another and gives meaning to absolute numbers. For example, a company may aim to achieve a 25% share of the total market for its product, and measure both its marketing department and the quality of the product against this.
- **Sales performance** – is traditionally measured in terms of price and volume variances, and also perhaps a sales mix variance. Other possible measures include revenue targets and target market share.
- **Materials measurement** – traditional measures are standard costs for materials, and price and particularly usage variances. Stock turnover is a particularly relevant measure in a just-in-time production environment, where the aim is to minimise all stocks.
- **Performance measures for people** – labour costs are traditionally reported by rate and efficiency variances against standards. Qualitative measures of labour performance concentrate on matters such as ability to communicate, interpersonal relationships with colleagues, customers' impressions and levels of skills attained.
- **Reward systems** – there are many examples of reward systems being used as an incentive to give credit to good performance. Salary may be linked to clear performance criteria, or a bonus may be paid for exceptional work. For project-based work, project team members may be paid a bonus on completion that is linked to cost, time or quality criteria.

2.5 Performance appraisal

KEY POINT

Performance appraisal may be defined as 'the regular and systematic review of performance and the assessment of potential with the aim of producing action programmes to develop both work and individuals.'

The general purpose of any assessment or appraisal is to improve the efficiency of the organisation by ensuring that the individual employees are performing to the best of their ability and developing their potential for improvement. Performance appraisal may be defined as 'the regular and systematic review of performance and the assessment of potential with the aim of producing action programmes to develop both work and individuals.' It is a procedure where the managers or supervisors in an organisation discuss the work of their subordinates. They see each person individually and consider the progress they have been making in their job, their strengths and weaknesses and their future needs as regards training and development and the employee's potential for promotion. In some circumstances it may be used to assess the level of reward payable for an individual's efforts, e.g. in merit payment systems.

The organisation's appraisal scheme is inextricably linked to its control structure. It clarifies specific jobs, it assesses competencies, it uses feedback and reward to improve performance, it links performance to organisational goals and it aims to make the behaviour of employees predictable and, hence, controllable.

The diagram below shows the process of performance appraisal.

Performance appraisal

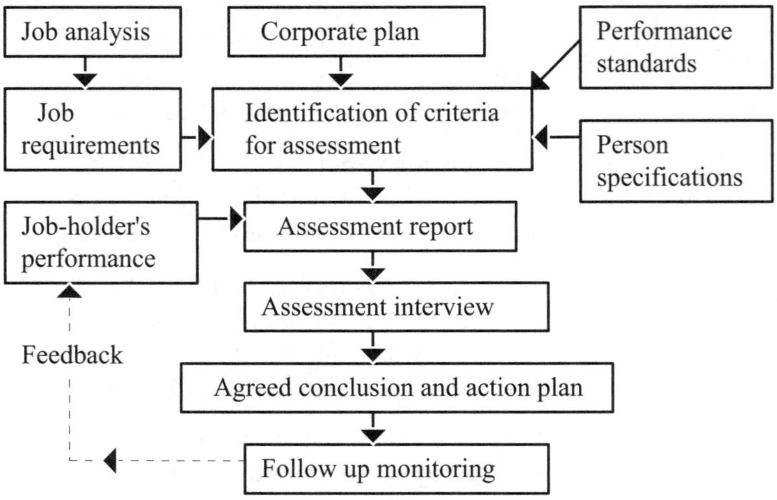

The **benefits of appraisal** include:

- Effective appraisal is grounded in the belief that feedback on past performance influences future performance, and that the process of isolating and rewarding good performance is likely to repeat it.
- Agreement on challenging but achievable targets for performance motivates employees by clarifying goals and setting the value of incentives offered.
- Effective appraisal can allow employees to solve any workplace problems and apply creative thinking to their jobs.
- Performance appraisal data can be used as predictors in the planning, recruitment and selection processes and can determine employee rewards.

3 Personal time management

3.1 Use of time

A major aspect of efficiency is the effective management of time. Time is a unique resource – you cannot hire, rent or buy more time. The supply is totally irreplaceable and everything requires time. One of the learning outcomes for this chapter is that you should demonstrate personal time management skills. For most of us, this will mean more than just reading this section.

DEFINITION

Time management implies planning the best use of time, including cutting down on time wasting, devoting more time to the really important issues and completing more in the time available.

Time management implies planning the best use of time, including cutting down on time wasting, devoting more time to the really important issues and completing more in the time available. It is fundamental to job performance and effective delegation.

The absence of time management is characterised by last minute rushes to meet dead-lines, meetings which are either double booked or achieve nothing, days which seem somehow to slip by unproductively, crises which loom unexpected from nowhere. This sort of environment leads to inordinate stress and degradation of performance.

3.2 Demonstrate your time management skills

An essential objective of looking at time management is to enable you to save at least some of the time you presently waste in one way or another at work, and to use this time better in tackling jobs which really require your undivided attention and effort. It is of course unlikely you will never waste time in the future, but even a 10% saving in the first year could give you up to four hours a week extra productive time.

What follows is a list of practical suggestions and hints to help you improve and demonstrate your time management skills. You will need to:

- cost your time;
- define your work priorities;
- keep an activity log;
- draw up an action plan;
- set priorities on a 'to do' list;
- schedule the tasks.

(i) Cost your time

The first part of your focus on results should be to work out how much your time costs. This helps you to see if you are spending your time profitably.

Activity 2

If you work for an organisation, calculate how much you cost it each year. Estimate the number of working days per annum by deducting holidays, including public holidays, days spent training and sick days. Add together the direct and indirect cost of your employment. Include your salary, taxes, pension, the cost of office space you occupy (rental per square metre), equipment and facilities you use, expenses, administrative support, etc. If you are self-employed, work out the annual running costs of your business.

There is no feedback to this activity.

(ii) Define your work priorities

This stage concentrates on three areas – clarifying what you enjoy, understanding what your strengths and weaknesses are, and working out both what your job is and what constitutes excellent performance.

- If you know broadly what you like and dislike, you will be more able to move your job towards doing things that you enjoy. This is important as you are much more likely to do your job effectively if you love it.
- It is also important to know what your talents and weaknesses are. A good way of doing this is to carry out a SWOT analysis. This provides a formal approach to evaluating your strengths and weaknesses, and the opportunities and threats that you face. This helps you to play to your strengths, minimise weaknesses, and move in the right direction.
- Understanding how to be excellent at your job – clarify your job with your employer, and concentrate on doing well in the areas he or she considers to be the most important.

Activity 3

Draw up your own SWOT chart like the one below and start by writing down the answers to these questions. Be realistic. If you are having any difficulty with this, try writing down a list of your characteristics. Some of these will hopefully be strengths!

There is no feedback to this activity.

Strengths	**Weaknesses**
What advantages do you have? What do you do well? What resources do you have access to? What do other people see as your strengths?	What could you improve? What do you do badly? What should you avoid?
Opportunities	**Threats**
Where are the good opportunities facing you? What are the interesting trends you are aware of?	What obstacles do you face? Are the required specifications for your job or products changing? Is changing technology threatening your position? Could any of your weaknesses seriously threaten your job/business?

Activity 4

You should ask the following questions:

- What is the purpose of the job?
- What are the measures of success?
- What is exceptional performance?
- What are the priorities and deadlines?

There is no feedback to this activity.

If you have answers to these questions, you will know how to do your job in precisely the right way. If you know what exceptional performance is, you can plan to achieve it using all the resources you have available.

(iii) Keep an activity log

What counts is not the number of hours you put in but what you put into the hours! Keeping an activity log for several days helps you to understand how you spend your time, and when you perform at your best.

Activity 5

Draw up an activity log or print out a blank from the following web site www.deskdemon.com/advice/timemanagementtimelog.pdf

Without modifying your behaviour any further than you have to, note down the things you do as you do them and their degree of importance and urgency. Every time you change activities, whether answering the phone, working, in a meeting, making coffee, gossiping with colleagues or whatever, note down the time of the change. As well as keeping track of activities, you could also write down how you feel – are you wide awake, concentrating, tired, full of energy? Do this at various points throughout the day.

There is no feedback to this activity.

Your effectiveness may vary depending on the amount of sugar in your blood, the length of time since you last took a break, routine distractions, stress, discomfort, or a range of other factors. There is also some good evidence that you have daily rhythms of alertness and energy.

Once you have logged your time for a few days, analyse the log. Evaluate your results by asking yourself, 'Did I accomplish what I was supposed to accomplish? Was I often pressed for time? At what time of the day was I most productive? Least productive? Using your insights make changes in three areas:

1 **Compare** – look at each activity and decide objectively how much time each was worth to you, and compare that with the time you actually spent. You may need to limit time spent on lower priority activities and increase the time available for more important matters.

2 **Correlate** – schedule your activities so that they correlate with your energy levels. Note the times of day at which you are most effective and alert, so that you can carry out your most important tasks during these times. When you are alert, you can process information more quickly and save time as a result.

3 **Combine** – try to combine activities. While you are waiting for that report to print make a phone call. Also combining similar tasks together will prove more efficient. Errands, phone calls, filing, and other tasks will be more efficient when done only once or twice during the day.

With these simple changes, you will find yourself more productive and make the most of your minutes.

(iv) Draw up an action plan

An action plan is a list of tasks that you have to carry out to achieve an objective/goal. Set goals that are specific, measurable, realistic and achievable. They give your life, and the way you spend your time, direction. Your optimum goals should cause you to 'stretch' but not 'break' as you strive for achievement. In work terms you could probably set specific goals by reference to your job description.

Activity 6

Make a list of everything you plan to do, dividing the list into fixed commitments and flexible commitments. List the tasks, the deadlines, the people to see or write to etc. This allows you to concentrate on the stages of that achievement, and monitor your progress towards it.

There is no feedback to this activity.

Fixed commitments are those tasks that you absolutely must complete by a specific deadline. Flexible commitments are obligations you can meet on a time available basis. Assign priorities to your list and set aside enough time to do the designated tasks.

Learn how to schedule. We all have best times to work and play, so plan your work schedule around your peak energy times. Also, there are additional steps that you can take that will help you accomplish your goals:

- Compile a 'to do' list each week of tasks that must be completed.
- Prioritise the tasks on your list in order of importance and according to deadlines.
- Try to complete tasks with a minimum of interruptions.

- Delegate responsibility, when appropriate.
- Allow time for breaks, personal time, and social activities.

(v) Set priorities on a 'to do' list

A 'to do' list is a list of all the tasks that you need to carry out. It consolidates all the jobs that you have to do into one place. You can then prioritise these tasks into order of importance. This allows you to tackle the most important ones first.

Activity 7

Write down the tasks that face you and, if they are complex, break them down into smaller manageable pieces, and focus on one at a time. If these still seem large, break them down again. Do this until you have listed everything that you have to do. Review your list and decide on the priority of each task. Give the highest priority to the tasks that get you closer to your goals. A proven simple technique is an ABC rating of your priorities, an A being those that are directly related to your goals which should be done that day.

There is no feedback to this activity.

KEY POINT

Prioritisation involves identifying key results and key tasks (those things that must be done on time and to the required standard if the key results are to be achieved).

If you do decide to use a planning aid such as a daily work schedule, then at the start of any day you will be faced with a mixture of activities to sort out. Some will be long-term priorities, some short-term priorities, and yet more will have much lower priorities still. Additionally, some activities will be imposed upon you by others e.g. meetings and visitors. Prioritisation involves identifying key results (objectives which must be achieved if the section/department is to fulfil its aims) and key tasks (those things that must be done on time and to the required standard if the key results are to be achieved) i.e. considering tasks in the order of their importance for the objective concerned. A job will be critical or 'high-priority' compared to other tasks, if it has to be completed by a 'deadline' in order to fulfil its objective, if other tasks depend on its completion or if the potential consequences of failure are long-term, difficult to reverse, far reaching and costly.

Eliminate the urgent – urgent tasks have short-term consequences while important tasks are those with long-term, goal-related implications. Too often the urgent and unimportant jobs get done to the detriment of the important. One way of resolving the dilemma is to use the Urgent versus Important matrix, shown below. Tasks that are both important and urgent should get top priority (A). The ones that are urgent but not very important (B) need to be done soon, but spend as little time as possible on each. Important but not urgent tasks (C) should be started as soon as possible as they have disaster potential i.e. they could suddenly become both important and urgent. Tasks that are neither important nor urgent (D) go to the back of the queue.

		Important	
		High	Low
Urgent	High	A	B
	Low	C	D

(vi) Schedule the tasks

Scheduling is the process by which you look at the time available to you, and plan how you will use it to achieve the goals you have identified. When choosing your tasks and allocating time, remember the 80-20 rule: 80 percent of the reward comes from 20 percent of the effort. If you start from those most important 20 percent, you progress much faster.

By using a schedule properly, you can:

- understand what you can realistically achieve with your time;
- plan to make the best use of the time available;
- leave enough time for things you absolutely must do;
- preserve contingency time to handle 'the unexpected'; and
- minimise stress by avoiding over-commitment to yourself and others.

There are many good scheduling tools available, including diaries, calendars, paper-based organisers and integrated software packages like MS Outlook® or GoalPro 6®. The key things are to be able to enter data easily, and to be able to view an appropriate span of time in the correct level of detail.

Scheduling is best done on a regular basis, for example at the start of every week or month.

Activity 8

Scheduling is a five-step process:

1 Identify the time you have available.

2 Block in the essential tasks you must carry out to succeed in your job and your studies.

3 Review your To Do list and schedule in high priority urgent tasks as well as the essential maintenance tasks that cannot be delegated and cannot be avoided.

4 Block in appropriate contingency time to handle unpredictable interruptions.

5 In the time that remains, schedule the activities that address your priorities and personal goals.

There is no feedback to this activity.

4 Conducting research and collecting data

4.1 Measuring performance

Measuring performance requires a system for collecting, analysing and distributing management information. Performance indicators are an important component of this system. An indicator may link two separate pieces of data as a ratio (e.g. absenteeism rate = the number of staff absent divided by the number of staff employed). They can be constructed from a wide variety of different data sources and, properly developed and used, can enable managers to make comparisons between similar organisations and also measure changes over time for their organisation.

Careful analysis of the information provided and presented can help to reveal not only progress towards targets but background reasons why performance towards these objectives is good or poor and what lessons might be shared and applied elsewhere within the organisation. Using indicators as part of a continuous monitoring process helps managers to address questions such as 'How does our organisation compare with similar organisations?' 'What have we achieved over the past year?' and 'How can we do better?'

4.2 Basic steps in planning and conducting research

There are six steps to the information research process. These steps are basic to any type of research. They represent an organised and systematic method:

1. **Define the task** – what needs to be done? Define the problem, select topic, narrow down the topic, comprehend task and requirements, identify the information needed, and draft a personal time line for the project.
2. **Develop a search strategy** – what can I use to find what I need? Brainstorm; browse; use general sources for background information; write questions and keywords down; organise outline.
3. **Locate and access the information** – where can I find what I need? Specify the data collection procedures and select the data analysis methodology. Execute the research.
4. **Use the information** – what information can I use? Take detailed notes on interesting facts and ideas, categorise notes, identify need for any additional information and obtain it.
5. **Synthesise the information** – how can I put my information together? Organise notes, quote / paraphrase / summarise as appropriate, connect information taken from various sources, extend the information, write your draft paper and bibliography, edit and correct.
6. **Evaluate the product** – how will I know if I did my job well? Judge the result: How well does your finished product meet or exceed the requirements of the task? Identify what worked in the research process and what didn't.

4.3 Information gathering techniques

The overall goal in selecting business research methods is to get the most useful information to key decision makers in the most cost-effective and realistic fashion.

Note that, ideally, the researcher uses a combination of methods, for example, a questionnaire to quickly collect a great deal of information from a lot of people, and then interviews to get more in-depth information from certain respondents to the questionnaires. Perhaps case studies could then be used for more in-depth analysis of unique and notable cases, e.g., those who benefited or not from the program, those who quit the program, etc.

There are a wide variety of methods that are common in qualitative measurement. Here we discuss a few of the more common methods.

Participant observation – requires that the researcher become a participant in the culture or context being observed. It often requires months or years of intensive work because the researcher needs to become accepted as a natural part of the culture in order to assure that the observations are of the natural phenomenon.

Direct observation – the observer does not try to become a participant in the context but does strive to be as unobtrusive as possible so as not to bias the observations. Because the researcher is watching rather than taking part, technology can be a useful part of direct observation e.g. videotape or from behind one-way mirrors.

Unstructured interviewing – involves direct interaction between the researcher and a respondent or group. There is no formal structure – each interview tends to be unique with no predetermined set of questions asked of all respondents. The interviewer is free to move the conversation in any direction of interest that may come up.

Case study – is an intensive study of a specific individual or specific context. There is no single way to conduct a case study, and a combination of methods (e.g. unstructured interviewing, direct observation) can be used.

Questionnaires – when most people think of questionnaires, they think of the postal survey. Response rates from postal surveys are often very low and they are not the best vehicles for asking for detailed written responses.

A second type is the group-administered questionnaire. A sample of respondents is brought together and asked to respond to a structured sequence of questions. In the group interview or focus group, the interviewer facilitates the session. People work as a group – listening to each other's comments and answering the questions. Someone takes notes for the entire group –people do not complete an interview individually.

Interviews – are a far more personal form of research than questionnaires. A face-to-face interview is an excellent way to obtain detailed, in–depth information and to handle the problems or queries of individuals, allowing confidentiality and flexible response to personal factors where necessary. It is one of the major investigative methods and requires good communication skills from the manager.

Almost everyone is familiar with telephone interviews. They enable a researcher to gather information rapidly. Like personal interviews, the telephone interview allows for some personal contact between the interviewer and the respondent and allows the interviewer to ask follow-up questions. But they also have some major disadvantages. Many people do not have publicly-listed telephone numbers. Some only have mobile telephones. People often do not like the intrusion of a call to their homes. And, telephone interviews have to be relatively short or people will feel imposed upon.

5 Communication

5.1 The purpose of communication

In any organisation, the communication of information is necessary to achieve co-ordination and control. It is essential for internal functioning and also used to relate the organisation to the external environment. In an effective organisation communication flows in various directions. As well as flowing in and out of the organisation, it can flow downwards, upwards, horizontally and diagonally within the organisation hierarchy.

Management need communication to make the necessary decisions for planning, co-ordination and control; managers should be aware of what their departments are achieving, what they are not achieving and what they should be achieving. Communication is needed to:

- establish and disseminate the goals of the organisation;
- develop plans for their achievement;
- organise human and other resources in the most effective and efficient way;
- select, develop and appraise members of the organisation;
- lead, direct, motivate and create a climate in which people want to contribute;
- control performance.

Departments – all the interdependent systems for purchasing, production, marketing and administration can be synchronised to perform the right actions at the right times to co-operate in accomplishing the organisation's aims.

Individuals – employees should know what is expected from them. Effective communication gives an employee's job meaning, makes personal development possible, and acts as a motivator, as well as oiling the wheels of labour relations.

As well as facilitating the managerial function, communication allows the organisation to interact with its environment. It is through information exchange that managers become aware of the needs of customers, the availability of suppliers, the claims of shareholders, the regulations of government and the concerns of the community.

5.2 The process of communication

KEY POINT

The communication process involves six basic elements: sender (encoder), message, channel, receiver (decoder) and feedback.

Communication is the process of passing information and understanding from one person to another. The communication process involves six basic elements: sender (encoder), message, channel, receiver (decoder) and feedback. Managers can improve communication skills by becoming aware of these elements and how they contribute to successful communication. Communication can break down at any one of these elements, through various forms of interference, known technically as 'noise'. The process of communication can be modelled as shown in the following diagram:

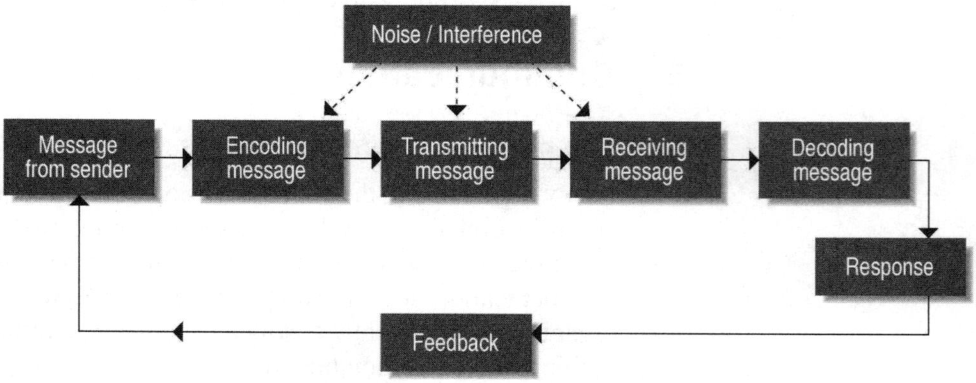

As a sender, the manager should define the purpose of the message, construct each message with the receiver in mind, select the best medium, time each transmission thoughtfully, and seek feedback. Whether written or spoken, words are used to create pictures and stories (scenarios), and are used to create involvement.

Within the communication process it is also important to note the problem of 'noise': anything in the environment that impedes the transmission of the message is significant. Noise can arise from many sources, e.g. factors as diverse as loud machinery, status differentials between sender and receiver, distractions of pressure at work or emotional upsets. The effective communicator must ensure that noise does not interfere with successful transmission of the message.

As illustrated in the above diagram, it is **feedback** that makes communication a two-way process rather than a series of send-receive events. Feedback is a vital and often neglected aspect of the process, which indicates to the sender whether or not his message has been successfully received, understood and interpreted. Failure to seek or offer feedback, or ignoring feedback offered, is one of the major problems in communication.

Feedback takes various forms. In a conversation it can be immediate (e.g. the changed expression on a person's face). In business it might be delayed.

5.3 Managing communication problems

There are many barriers and breakdowns that impede the effective communication of information. They can exist in the sender, in the transmission of the message, in the receiver or in the feedback. They include poorly expressed messages – awkward sentence structure, platitudes, omissions and unnecessary jargon that cause lack of clarity and precision, which can be avoided through greater care in encoding the message. The receiver can also wrongly interpret the message – this is often the case with cultural differences. A company's policies, plans, instructions and information need to be known and understood if the corporate plan is to be a success. This communication is only seen by some companies to be necessary from the top echelon downwards to lower ones. It is, however, equally essential for information, ideas and experiences to flow upwards from the lower levels. If communication is only one way, there is no feedback and this is a severe disadvantage. Apart from anything else, employees will not feel a real part of the company.

Some examples of managing communication problems are as follows:

- Individual bias and selectivity – we hear or see what we want to hear or see. By adopting feedback the 'two-way' nature of communication is ensured, so that the receiver seeks clarity and the sender seeks acknowledgement
- Lack of trust, fear and other emotional overtones can cloud the communication message. If a person has bad news to pass on, which is almost certain to upset the recipient, there will be a tendency to avoid the whole truth and be content to pass on part of the message only. Also with natural reserve and status differences subordinates may well read more than was intended into a manager's message.
- Verbal difficulties are a frequent source of confusion and misunderstanding. These may arise because of lack of fluency on the part of the sender, or because of the use of jargon (specific application of words in technical and professional contexts).
- Other important barriers to communication include 'noise' (the message is confused by extraneous matters) and information overload (where a person is overloaded with memos, reports, letters, telephone messages, etc.).

- The traditional line and staff approach to organisation can itself be an inhibiting factor in establishing and maintaining effective communications. The advent of new technologies has if anything created new problems here. For example, if a company has workers carrying out their duties from home, paid on a 'piece work' basis and communicating largely by electronic methods, the barriers imposed by the organisational structure itself can impede the processes necessary to transmit messages. Many companies have made changes to their organisation structures in order to address these problems, moving away from the line and staff model and towards more flexible structures.
- With a wide range of media to choose from, barriers to communications can arise from choosing an inappropriate method for the message. For example, routine messages between individuals can be conveyed in both directions by e-mail whilst more complex ones require alternative media such as hard copy, briefings or meetings. Company results can be prepared and published for all to read, but motivation towards achieving better results is usually better achieved in small face-to-face teams
- As business relationships become more remote, it is important to constantly address the question of how people feel in terms of what they can contribute to the team and how they personally would like to develop. Proper feedback systems are vital here in order to avoid alienating the worker and, more positively, utilise their skills and personal qualities to the optimum.

Activity 9

One definition of business communication is 'the transmission of information so that it is received, understood and leads to action'. Explain the key items included in this definition.

Feedback to this activity is at the end of the chapter.

6 Interpersonal skills

6.1 Interpersonal skills

Interpersonal skills can sometimes be called interactive, face-to-face or social skills. They involve inspiring, motivating, leading and controlling people to achieve goals, which are often poorly defined. Managers need interpersonal skills to:

- understand and 'manage' the roles, relationships, attitudes and perceptions operating in any situation in which two or more people are involved;
- communicate clearly and effectively;
- achieve their aims from an interpersonal encounter.

A manager or supervisor who develops skills in dealing with others gets action and is influential and effective. The type of skills needed to develop effective working relationships include:

- the ability to get co-operation, make contacts and work with others to solve problems;
- the ability to maintain the enthusiasm to persuade, negotiate and propose new possibilities/solutions;

- perseverance – the ability to keep going back to the same people to raise the same issues if they remain unresolved;
- Flexibility – the ability to adjust to fit in with other people's ideas or constraints.

Managers use many interpersonal skills (and related communication tools) but we will only be looking at a few, which include negotiating, mentoring, meetings and interviews, including grievance and disciplinary interviews (in Chapter 13).

6.2 Negotiation and the role of the manager

Negotiating is an activity that seeks to reach agreement between two or more starting positions.

The skills of a negotiator can be summarised under three main headings:

- **Interpersonal skills** – the use of good communicating techniques, the use of power and influence, and the ability to impress a personal style on the tactics of negotiation.
- **Analytical skills** – the ability to analyse information, diagnose problems, to plan and set objectives, and the exercise of good judgement in interpreting results.
- **Technical skills** – attention to detail and thorough case preparation.

A negotiation is a special kind of interpersonal interaction between two or more parties.

DEFINITION

Negotiation is an interaction in which people try to meet their needs or accomplish their goals by reaching an agreement with others who are trying to get their own needs met.

It can be defined as an interaction in which people try to meet their needs or accomplish their goals by reaching an agreement with others who are trying to get their own needs met. Whether we call it problem solving, bargaining, cooperative decision-making, or communicating, when two or more people reach a voluntary agreement about something, they are negotiating.

A manager's involvement in negotiation within the organisation covers three categories:

- on his/her own behalf when securing a pay rise, for instance, or an improvement in the terms and conditions of employment;
- on behalf of a department or functional area e.g. securing an acceptable departmental budget;
- with the external environment on behalf of the organisation e.g. obtaining planning permission for an extension to the warehouse.

For the managers involved, the aim in any negotiation is to achieve a settlement that is acceptable to the other parties but which also comes as close as possible to their desired outcome. To do this they need to address the ways in which they can maximise their negotiating effectiveness.

6.3 Types of negotiating situation

The negotiating techniques adopted will depend on the type of bargaining situation. Walton and McKersie in *A Behavioural Theory of Labour Negotiations* identify two main types of negotiation: distributive and integrative bargaining.

Distributive bargaining is that which is aimed at resolving pure conflicts of interest on, for example, hours of work and rates of pay, in other words the substantive issues.

In most bargaining situations it is usual to find that there are some topics that are best discussed on the basis of an integrative, or joint, approach aimed at finding a solution from which both sides will benefit substantially.

6.4 The negotiation process

The negotiation process can be divided into three distinct stages. The problem arises; this is followed by the interaction or the negotiation, and hopefully ends in agreement and conciliation.

Stage 1

The *pre-negotiation* stage involves:

- a situation where each of the parties involved is prepared to seek a mutually acceptable solution;
- determining an ideal outcome, an *expected* outcome and a minimum acceptable outcome;
- planning the meeting, including agreeing an agenda

Before entering into the negotiation process managers need to assess the situation in terms of the perceived conflict over the stakes and the perceived importance of the relationship in the future.

Perceived conflict over stakes

Perceived importance of future relationship		High	Low
	High	Balanced concerns	Relationships
	Low	Transactions	Tacit co-operation

The stakes/relationship priority matrix

Balanced concerns – the future relationship and the immediate stakes are in *balanced tension*. You want to do well but not at the cost of the future relationship. Examples include many employment disputes, partnerships, mergers, long-term supplier relationships, family business issues, and relationships between different units of the same organisation. The best strategies will be problem solving or compromise.

Relationships – here, the relationship matters a lot and the particular matter being negotiated is secondary. We strive to treat the other party well and play by the rules. Examples include friendships and well functioning work teams. The best strategies will be accommodation, problem solving or compromise.

Transactions – the stakes matter more than a continuing relationship. Leverage counts. Examples include buying goods and many market-mediated deals. The best strategies will be competition, problem solving or compromise.

Tacit co-operation – these situations do not require formal negotiation so much as the tactful avoidance of conflict. Examples include cars meeting at a cross roads or choosing seats in an unassigned bus or train. Best strategies are avoidance, accommodation or compromise.

Stage 2

The negotiation stage itself involves argument and persuasion, strengthening one's own case, undermining the opposition's, helping the other side to move, conceding trivial points and searching for common ground.

Stage 3

Agreement and conciliation – a final compromise is agreed at this stage.

- After the negotiation has been concluded, the agreement will be publicised and implemented.
- A programme for implementation should be included in the agreement, covering such matters as date of commencement and who is to undertake the work.

6.5 Negotiation strategies and tactics

The strategies will vary depending on issues and circumstances under negotiation. An awareness of the history of the conflict and the implications for the future is essential.

Negotiation attempts to resolve and accommodate differing interests by moving towards an end point, which is acceptable to both sides – a 'win-win' situation. A 'win-lose' situation culminates where one group has achieved its objectives at the clear expense of the other. This solution tends to cause dissatisfaction and the situation could deteriorate into a 'lose-lose' position where the benefits originally gained by the winner are continuously eroded by resistance and a lack of commitment.

The types of strategy could be classified as follows:

(a) **Power strategy** – where the two sides are unequal, one possessing a kind of sanction over the other. This type of strategy is likely to cause resentment and dissatisfaction, at best resulting in compliance without a shift in attitudes. The worst scenario may result in sabotage, resistance or further dispute.

(b) **Consultation strategy** – involves encouraging the relevant parties to express their ideas, concerns and opinions on the subject under negotiation. However, this does not necessarily mean that these views are taken into consideration; the strategy may be no more than a PR exercise.

(c) **Resolve strategy** – where agreement and conciliation is achieved, even if it means that neither party has achieved the perfect result. One of the problems frequently encountered in negotiating is that sides take up positions that are incompatible. Skilled negotiators concentrate on the interests that lie behind the positions, as they are more likely to provide footholds for finding common ground.

6.6 Consultation

DEFINITION

Consultation is where one party seeks the views of another party before either party takes a decision.

True consultation is the process where, on a regular basis, management genuinely seeks the views, ideas and feelings of employees before a decision is taken.

Consultation is not the same as negotiation. Negotiation implies acceptance by both parties that agreement between them is required before a decision is taken. Consultation implies a willingness to listen to the views of another while reserving the right to take the final decision, with or without agreement on both sides.

For effective managers, using their interpersonal skills, a way of consulting subordinates is to discuss proposals with them. The: 'I have decided to give you X' approach is nowhere near as effective as the: 'I've been thinking – do you feel that you can tackle X?' approach.

KEY POINT

Consultation can help to improve the quality of decisions; lead to better co-operation; serve as a preliminary to negotiation; increase organisational efficiency; and help industrial relations.

The advantages associated with consultation include the following:

- improved quality of decisions – because the manager is using the collected knowledge and ingenuity of those who are most affected by the decisions;
- better co-operation between managers and employees – because people will accept even those decisions that they do not like, if their views have been taken into consideration, assuming they have been told why the decision has been taken;
- it serves as a valuable preliminary to negotiation – when representatives have been involved in the discussion of 'how', they will be better informed when it becomes a matter of 'how much';
- increased efficiency of the entire organisation by involving employees in achieving a better product or service;
- improved employee relations by allowing managers and their subordinates the opportunity to understand each other's views and objectives.

For a process of consultation to be genuine, it must not be used when managers have already reached a decision. Their minds will then be closed to alternatives; the meeting will sense that it is an insulting charade of 'guess what's in my mind'. Instead of gaining commitment to the decision, the pseudo-consultation will alienate. There will be resentment, which might result in non co-operation.

Consulting implies that decisions are only made after consultation. However, the final decision may not include any or all of the ideas put forward. Subordinates may feel cheated and not truly involved.

6.7 Meetings

Most managers seem to spend half of their life in meetings, so understanding how they work and how to make them more effective is very important. A meeting is a group of people coming together for the purpose of resolving problems or making decisions.

Meetings can be held for a wide range of purposes, but it is important that the purpose of the meeting is made clear to the participants in advance. If this is done, the meeting is more likely to be a success.

A well-organised, well-aimed and well-led meeting can be extremely effective in many different contexts:

- the relaying of decisions and instructions (e.g. briefings);
- the dissemination of information and the collection of feedback;
- participative problem solving;
- brainstorming: free exchanges with a view to generating new approaches and ideas;
- co-ordinating the efforts of a large number of people from different interest groups;
- a meeting may be responsible for taking a final decision on an issue of great importance.

There are two types of meetings at work:

- **informal meetings** – these may just be colleagues bumping into each other in the corridor or at the drinks machine;
- **formal meetings** – these are planned and structured and include board meetings, committees, working groups, public meetings, conferences, AGMs and EGMs, team meetings, appraisals, interviews and brainstorming.

6.8 Conducting effective meetings

Key points in the conduct of meetings include the following:

- A clear goal or expected outcome, understood and agreed by all participants. (This helps to ensure that there are no unnecessary meetings!)
- A clear **structure** or **agenda**: a list of matters for discussion or decision. The agenda should reflect the meeting's goal and priority, both in sequencing items of business (so that core time is given to the most important items) and in allocating target times for the discussion of each item (to keep the meeting on track). The agenda should be circulated in advance to enable participants to prepare.
- A **skilled facilitator/leader**, whose role is to: keep the meeting to the agenda; ensure fair opportunities for all participants to contribute; control the discussion according to agreed 'ground rules'; and facilitate decision-making (e.g. by vote, consensus or other means).
- A **secretary or scribe** whose role is to take notes or minutes of the meeting (i.e. decisions reached and follow-up responsibilities allocated) for circulation to participants afterwards.

6.9 Mentoring junior colleagues

DEFINITION

Mentoring is a process where one person offers help, guidance, advice and support to facilitate the learning or development of another.

Mentoring is a process where one person offers help, guidance, advice and support to facilitate the learning or development of another. It is used by some organisations to show junior employees how things are done. The mentor, who may be a more senior manager, agrees to guide the less experienced colleague through a development programme and 'socialise' them into the culture of the enterprise. In this way they gain access to a pool of experience that is larger, or at least different from theirs. Through their mentors, they also expand their network of contacts, thereby building their exposure and career options within the firm. The mentors get new takes on company processes and working practices, fresh ideas and the satisfaction of seeing their protégés progress.

For the system to work, these relationships cannot be based on authority, but rather a genuine wish by the mentors to share knowledge, advice and experience. The mentor plays a major role in establishing an environment conducive to effective communication, paying close attention to what is said, being an active listener, encouraging the junior colleague to ask questions when something is not clear and giving feedback with the intent of helping him or her improve.

The overall **purpose of coaching and mentoring** is to encourage and support people to manage their own learning in order that they may maximise their potential, develop their skills, improve their performance and become the person they want to be. This method of satisfying training and development needs is most suitable for managers where the benefits include:

- opportunity to learn from role model;
- integration of work activities with learning and development;
- quicker learning about the way the organisation works; and
- greater clarity of development goals.

The **mentoring process** consists of three core activities, which set it apart from other developmental activities:

- exchange of knowledge that is unique to a business, industry, profession or organisation;
- a sustained partnering relationship;
- measurable, beneficial outcomes for the individual parties involved and for the larger organisation

Mentoring should not be seen as an additional or supplementary management task. It is an approach to management that puts the learning and development of the person at the heart of the process, offering advice and guidance to facilitate development. It is a good way of breaking down internal barriers between departments or groups and promoting equal opportunities.

7 Creativity

7.1 Creativity and idea generation

DEFINITION

Creativity is the application of imaginative thought to problems.

Creativity is a vital means for the organisation to achieve viability. It involves the application of a person's mental ability or imaginative thought to a specific area, which results in the creation or discovery of something new. It can result in innovative solutions to many problems. Imaginative thought may lead to new ways of seeing things, which may be novel for the person or completely novel in time.

Actively creative people have a talent for getting to the heart of a problem. They are not confused by detail and by the need to invoke standard approaches.

There is a consensus in the literature that suggests that such individuals have a desire for originality, non-conformity and the opportunity to experiment and express new ideas. A difference can also be drawn between those people who are productive in terms of the number of ideas they can create and those individuals who have entrepreneurial capabilities and are able to bring the ideas to the market place.

The great creativity gurus – so far – are Alex Osborn, Edward de Bono, and George Prince, the founder of Synectics. The tools they have created include brainstorming, affinity diagrams, knowledge mapping and mind-mapping, and flowcharts.

- **Brainstorming** – this is simply listing all ideas put forth by a group in response to a given problem or question. Creativity is encouraged by not allowing ideas to be evaluated or discussed until everyone has run dry. Any and all ideas are considered legitimate and often the most far-fetched are the most fertile. Structured brainstorming produces numerous creative ideas and if it is done right, it taps the human brain's capacity for lateral thinking and free association. However, a brainstorm cannot help you positively identify causes of problems, rank ideas in a meaningful order, select important ideas, or check solutions.

- **Affinity diagrams** – focus on idea grouping, instead of idea generation, but it is still supposed to be a gut-level activity, not a rational, analytical one.

- **Knowledge mapping and mind-mapping** are tools used to try to see all the threads of knowledge about a given issue, breaking it down into fine points, and trying to arrange them spatially. The classic brainstorm does not worry about arranging ideas; it just lists them. The knowledge map tries to arrange those ideas so that gaps in knowledge become evident, or so that connections can be seen.

- **Flowcharts** – are maps or graphical representations of a process. Steps in a process are shown with symbolic shapes, and the flow of the process is indicated with arrows connecting the symbols. They can help you see whether the steps of a process are logical, uncover problems or miscommunications, define the boundaries of a process, and develop a common base of knowledge about a process. Flowcharting a process often brings to light redundancies, delays, dead ends, and indirect paths that would otherwise remain unnoticed or ignored.

7.2 Creative organisations

Many of the characteristics found in highly creative organisations seem to match those of highly creative individuals. The comparison by Steiner illustrates the similarity of characteristics

The creative individual	The creative organisation
Has conceptual fluency. Is able to produce a large number of ideas quickly.	Has idea people. Has open channels of communication. Has suggestion systems and idea units with no additional responsibilities. Encourages contact with outside sources.
Is original. Generates unusual ideas.	Hires a variety of personality types. Assigns non-specialists to problems. Allows eccentricity.
Considers ideas on the basis of their merit, not their source. Is motivated by interest in problem itself; follows wherever it leads.	Has objective, fact-founded approach. Evaluates ideas on their merits, not status of originator. Selects and promotes on merit only.
Suspends judgement; avoids early commitment. Spends considerable time in analysis, explanation.	Exhibits lack of financial material commitment to present products, policies. Invests in basic research. Has flexible long-range planning. Experiments with new ideas and does not prejudge them on rational grounds. Gives everything a change.
Is less authoritarian. Is flexible. Accepts own impulses. Undisciplined exploration	More decentralised. Provides time and resources to absorb errors. Tolerates and expects taking risks. Is not run as a 'tight ship'. Employees have fun, have freedom to choose and pursue problems. Free to discuss ideas.
Has independence of judgement. Is less conformist. Is often deviant from accepted ideas. Sees self as different	Has original and different objectives. Is not trying to follow the leader.
Has rich, bizarre fantasy life, and a clear view of reality	Has enough security of routines. Allows creators to roam. Has separate units or occasions for generating versus evaluating ideas. Separates creative from productive functions.

This comparison tends to contradict the general belief that group creativity is necessarily dependent on a very few highly creative individuals, and if an organisation is lacking then it has to recruit such individuals.

On the contrary, many organisations have creativity spread throughout their employees, and the characteristic culture of a creative organisation usually reflects the personalities of its members as creative characteristics can be found throughout the organisation.

Creative organisations tend to:

- recruit creative/innovative people;
- develop objectives which are original and different;
- be more decentralised in structure;
- use compensation strategies to select and promote on merit only;
- use less talented employees to provide a stable environment that allows creators to develop.

Summary

- Approaches to organisational control have included Taylor's scientific management (backed up by the work of Gilbreth and Gantt), Fayol's principles of management (e.g. scalar chain), and the human relations approach.
- The combination of span of control and scalar chain determines whether an organisation has a tall or a flat structure.
- Organisational structure reflects the control system. Possible structures include functional, divisional, hybrid and matrix.
- There are at least five elements to a control system: planning objectives; establishing standards; monitoring actual performance; compare deviations; take corrective action.
- Improving time management involves six steps: cost your time; define your work priorities; keep an activity log; draw up an action plan; set priorities; schedule the tasks.
- Basic steps in planning and conducting research: define the task; develop a search strategy; locate and access the information; use the information; synthesise the information; evaluate the product.
- The communication process involves six basic elements: sender; message; channel; receiver; noise; feedback.
- Mentoring is a process where one person offers help, guidance, advice and support to facilitate the learning or development of another.

Having completed your study of this chapter you should have achieved the following learning outcomes.

- Demonstrate personal time management skills.
- Identify methods of conducting research and gathering data as part of the managerial process.
- Discuss the roles of negotiation and communication in the management process, both within an organisation and with external bodies.
- Explain the process of mentoring junior colleagues.

Self-test questions

1 What is an internal control system? (1.3)

2 Give two examples of intangible standards of control. (2.1)

3 List the steps that you have used to demonstrate your personal time management skills. (3.2)

4 Describe two business research methods. (4.3)

5 Why is feedback vital to the communication process? (5.2)

6 Explain the differences between a power strategy and a resolve strategy of negotiation. (6.5)

7 Give three suggestions for enhancing the effectiveness of meetings. (6.8)

8 Outline the benefits of mentoring. (6.9)

9 List some techniques for creative thinking. (7.1)

Multiple-choice question

Question 1

A narrow span of control results in:

A tall organisation structures with many levels of supervision

B wide organisation structures with many levels of supervision

C tall organisation structures with few levels of supervision

D wide organisation structures with few levels of supervision.

For the answer to this question, see the 'Answers' section at the end of the book.

Exam-type questions

Question 1: Time management

It was getting to the end of Henry Owen's appraisal interview. He was pleased with it so far. His boss, Tania Bostock, had been complementary about his year's work.

'Now for what I see as a problem area,' said Tania. 'Time management – not yours. Henry – but Joy Kent's.' (Joy was one of the supervisors in the department of which Henry was manager.)

Tania continued, 'Over the past three months I've noticed that:

(a) Joy always seems to have a mound of paper in her in-tray;

(b) despite this she spends most of her time on the telephone or typing away at her electronic mail keyboard;

(c) she submitted a report to me the other day – 14 pages of well researched work, very well presented. It must have taken her days to produce the report – but it concerned only a minor part of the job and I'd emphasised to her when briefing her that I only wanted a half-page opinion;

(d) she's submitted annual appraisal reports on two of her staff which have been over a week late.

I've checked her holiday records – she's not taken a major holiday for 12 months, and did you notice that last week she struggled in every day despite being obviously ill?'

'I know,' said Henry, 'I've already spoken to her about this. I confirm everything you say. I told her to sort herself out but she's made no effort. She says she has no way of knowing how much work will hit her desk on any one day. Do you think I should reprimand her?'

'Henry, is it you or Joy who's at fault?' said Tania. 'You selected her; we both agreed she was the right person for the job. Have you identified what's wrong with her time management? Have you given her guidance or support or advice?'

'No,' said Henry.

Required:

(a) Explain what aspect of poor time management each of Joy's symptoms suggests. **(10 marks)**

(b) What suggestions could Henry make to Joy to help her overcome her time management difficulties? **(15 marks)**

(Total: 25 marks)

Question 2: Communication skills

Sam Browne is a sole trader. He runs a very profitable newsagents in a leafy town in the English midlands. His shop is very close to the railway station. His customers are the many people who commute daily into Birmingham and the executives who park their cars at the station before catching the early morning express trains to London. Sam is a good salesman, whatever the weather he has a cheery smile for his customers, and he has a shrewd notion of what to stock and the margins available. His weakness is that he can't keep records. His idea of record-keeping is sticking everything into a shoe box.

Not surprisingly, Sam's accounts are in a mess, his tax affairs are getting out of hand and he ignored the need to make a Return last year. There is a risk that the Revenue will start an investigation and Sam has come to you, as an Accountant in practice, for help. You feel the accounting problems are straight forward if only you can get the full background information from Sam.

You are meeting Sam next Saturday afternoon, when Mrs Browne can look after the shop. First you need to think about how you should approach the meeting.

Required:

Draft some notes for the meeting with Sam showing:

(a) the types of information you require; **(6 marks)**

(b) how you will manage the communication process; **(7 marks)**

(c) the skills you will contribute to the process. **(12 marks)**

(Total: 25 marks)

For the answer to these questions, see the 'Answers' section at the end of the book.

Feedback to activities

Activity 1

Control ensures that management knows how the organisation is progressing towards objectives and what corrections need to be made to 'stay on course'.

Controlling activities are concerned essentially with measuring progress and correcting deviations. The basic functions of control are:

(i) *To establish standards of performance*

Once plans have been made, standards of performance need to be clearly stated. Budgets are a useful means of setting quantifiable standards. Where standards are qualitative, they should be expressed in terms of end results rather than methods.

(ii) *To measure actual performance against standards*

This involves analysing actual information in a manner, which is consistent with the standards set. The management accounting department will be responsible for identifying and analysing variances to find out whether they can be avoided if adverse or encouraged if favourable.

(iii) *To take corrective actions where appropriate*

When comparing actual performance against standard, management will require action to be taken when the variances against standard are significant.

The control function must be responsive to the environment in which it operates. Changes in the environment may result in the standards set being inappropriate. For this reason, the managerial control process must be flexible.

Activity 9

The main items are:

1 **'Transmission'**, i.e. the onus is on the sender to send the information.

2 **'Information'**, not data. Data is dead, historic or irrelevant; information tells the recipient something they do not know.

3 **'Received and understood'**, i.e. in the sense intended by the sender.

4 **'Leads to action'**, i.e. if it does not lead to action was communication necessary?

Chapter 13

MANAGING GROUPS

Syllabus content

- Theories of group development, behaviour and roles (e.g. Tuckman, Belbin).
- Disciplinary procedures and their operation, including the form and process of formal disciplinary action and dismissal (e.g. industrial tribunals, arbitration and conciliation).
- The sources of conflict in organisations and the ways in which conflict can be managed to ensure that working relationships are productive and effective.

Contents

1 Theories of group development, behaviour and roles

2 Sources and dynamics of conflict

3 Managing conflict

4 Dealing with grievances and disciplinary matters

5 Dismissal

1 Theories of group development, behaviour and roles

1.1 Groups

DEFINITION

A group can be defined as two or more individuals engaged in some social interaction, for the purpose of achieving some goal or goals.

A group can be defined as two or more individuals engaged in some social interaction, for the purpose of achieving some goal or goals. In the work situation these goals are usually work related if the group is a formal working group. (We defined **teams** in Chapter 9.)

A random collection of people does not necessarily constitute a group and, for management purposes, a group should be a collection of people with the following characteristics:

- a common sense of identity;
- having a common aim or purpose;
- having expected and accepted standards of behaviour)i.e. group norms exist);
- having communication and interaction within the group.

Elton Mayo arrived at the following conclusions which are pertinent to group dynamics:

- individual members cannot be treated in isolation, but must be seen as members of a group;
- the need to belong to a group and have status within it is more important than monetary incentives or good physical working conditions;
- informal (or unofficial) groups at work exercise a strong influence over the behaviour of workers;
- supervisors and managers need to be aware of these social needs and cater for them if workers are to collaborate with the organisation, rather than work against it.

People come together in groups for a number of reasons that fall under two broad headings: 'personal' or 'situational'. Under the heading of 'personal' such reasons as achieving personal goals, developing common interests (e.g. a football team), achieving satisfaction of personal needs, or seeking protection from outside threats could be included. In the case of situational groupings however the reasons for coming together are a bit more precise – the need to perform a specific task, to pass information amongst themselves, or because people are in the same geographic location. In the case of situational groups it may also be that the reasons for the grouping will also persist, as in the case of a research group who have a specific task to carry out.

1.2 Group development and maturity

Groups are not static. They mature and develop. The degree of cohesiveness is affected also by the manner in which groups progress through the various stages of development.

We discussed Tuckman's model of group development in Chapter 9 (see Section 2.4).

Woodcock also developed a model, classifying the groups into four categories:

- **Undeveloped** – the leader makes most of the decisions because the group is not sure what the objectives are. Personal interaction is not open – feelings are hidden.
- **Experimenting** – the group turns in on itself and key issues are raised and addressed.
- **Consolidating** – the task and its objectives are clear and members begin to agree on procedures; they also begin to get along with each other on a personal level.
- **Mature** – working methods are methodical and members are open with their feelings.

1.3 Behaviour of groups

As they develop, groups exhibit certain characteristics and behaviours.

- **Structure** – they form a structure based on patterns of relationships, or who relates to who; these patterns can be determined on the basis of status, expertise, attraction.
- **Status hierarchy** – who is held in high esteem and respect and who isn't; this may have little to do with formal hierarchy. For example, a competent line worker may be held in higher esteem than an incompetent supervisor.
- **Roles** – behaviour that persons in each position are expected to display; people can have multiple roles because they are members of different groups. For example, a supervisor is both manager and member of line staff.
- **Norms** – agreed upon standards of behaviour that develop over time; are often unwritten or discussed. For example, be on time, always wear a coat and tie, feel free to steal company property.
- **Leadership** – leaders emerge to influence group activity.
- **Cohesiveness** – strength of group members' desire to be part of the group; a social force that binds people together.

The advantages associated with cohesive groups include:

- **atmosphere** – an effective, cohesive group will work in an informal, relaxed atmosphere;
- **participation** – the group will discuss the work and will participate in the decision-making;
- **commitment** – as a result of effective communication and acceptance of the objective, there will be a high degree of commitment and desire to complete the task(s);
- **communication** – there will be a good rapport between group members.
- **leadership** – informal leaders are more likely to have the total support of the group;
- **progress** – the group monitors its progress and quality, always trying to perform better.

Members who belong to cohesive groups appear better adjusted to the organisation. Such workers are likely to have higher rates of job satisfaction and lower rates of tension, absenteeism and labour turnover. This better adjustment is due to the satisfaction and psychological support that groups provide.

1.4 Group member roles

We covered Belbin's model of group member roles in detail in Chapter 9 (see Section 2.5).

1.5 Managing for group effectiveness

KEY POINT

Handy's contingency approach should be carefully examined since it provides an analytical method for improving group effectiveness.

Handy takes a contingency approach to determine what makes a group successful, in which, he proposes, three categories need to be considered:

- **the givens** – the group, the task, the environment;
- **the intervening factors** – motivation of group, processes and procedures, leadership style;
- **the outcomes** – the productivity of the group and the satisfaction of the group members.

Handy stated that in the short term group leaders cannot vary the 'givens' but they must understand each aspect since it presents a constraint within which they must operate. Within the givens, the characteristics of the group include the size of the group, member characters, group norms, individual members' objectives and roles, and stage of development of the group.

On the other hand 'intervening factors' are within the influence of the team leader and should be operated to maximise the 'outcomes'. It should be noted that two outcomes are specified as reflecting effectiveness:

- productivity or task performance;
- team member satisfaction.

Activity 1

Describe Tuckman's four stages of group development as applied to the production of a play by an amateur dramatics group.

Feedback to this activity is at the end of the chapter.

To develop effective work teams/groups the manager will be concerned with the factors that either contribute to group cohesiveness or cause frustration or disruption to the operation of the group. These factors can be developed under four broad headings:

(i) **Membership**

- **Size of the team** – as a team or group gets larger, communication and co-ordination problems arise. Large teams are more difficult to handle and require a higher level of supervision. Absenteeism also tends to be higher.
- **Permanence** – relationships and team spirit take time to develop. Cohesiveness is more likely when members are together for a reasonable length of time and changes occur slowly. A frequent turnover of members is likely to have an adverse affect on morale and on the cohesiveness of the team.
- **Compatibility of members** – the more homogeneous the team in terms of features such as shared backgrounds, interests, attitudes and values of its members, the easier it is to promote cohesiveness. Variations in other individual differences, such as personality and skills of members, may serve to complement each other and make for a cohesive group. Alternatively, such differences may be the cause of disruption and conflict.

(ii) **Organisational factors**

- **Management and leadership** – the form and style adopted will influence the relationship between the team and the organisation and will be a major determinant of group cohesiveness.
- **Personnel policies and procedures** – if they are well developed and seen to be equitable with fair treatment for all members, harmony and cohesiveness within the team are more likely to be achieved.
- **External threats** – such as changes in the methods of work or the appointment of a new manager will tend to enhance cohesiveness and co-operation within the team. Even when the threat is removed the team may still continue to have a greater degree of cohesiveness than before the threat arose.
- **Success** – is usually a strong motivational influence on the level of work performance. The more successful the group, the more cohesive it is likely to be.

(iii) **Work environment**

- **The nature of the task** – where workers are involved in similar work, share a common task, or face the same problems, this may assist cohesiveness. The nature of the task may serve to bring people together when it is necessary for them to communicate and interact regularly with each other in the performance of their duties e.g. members of a research and development team.
- **Physical setting** – where members of a group work in the same location or in close physical proximity to each other this will generally help cohesiveness.
- **Communications** – the more easily members can communicate freely with each other, the greater the likelihood of group cohesiveness. Communications are affected by the work environment, by the nature of the task, and by technology. There may be difficulties in communication where physical conditions limit effective communication. For example, the technological layout and high level of noise with some assembly line work can limit contact between workers. Restrictions on opportunities for social interaction can hamper internal group unity.
- **Technology** – the nature of technology and the manner in which work is carried out has an important effect on cohesiveness, and relates closely to the nature of the task, physical setting and communications. Where the work process involves a craft or skill-based technology there is a higher likelihood of group cohesiveness

(iv) **Group development**

The degree of cohesiveness is also affected by the way the group progresses through the various stages of development and maturity – as we saw from Tuckman's model in Chapter 9.

2 Sources and dynamics of conflict

2.1 The nature of conflict

DEFINITION

Conflict is any personal divergence of interests between groups or individuals.

Conflict is any personal divergence of interests between groups or individuals. It occurs when organisational units are interdependent, share resources, and perceive their goals as incompatible. It can be identified on three levels:

- **Perception** – realisation that conflict exists because goals of the two parties are incompatible and the opportunity for interference is present.
- **Feelings** – conflict may cause feelings such as anger or mistrust between the groups.
- **Behaviour** – conflict results in behaviour which is a reaction to the first two levels.

Conflict can be either 'organised' or 'unorganised'. The feelings of 'organised' conflict are often expressed through recognised procedures, e.g. grievance and disputes procedures between company and union, strikes and restriction or reduction of output, or activity, which jeopardises income. 'Unorganised' conflict tends to be personal and ad hoc, expressing itself through poor morale, grumbling, lack of trust, absenteeism, lack of discipline, sabotage and high labour turnover etc.

A certain amount of conflict in an organisation is not only inevitable, it is often beneficial, for conflict is both a cause and an effect of change. An organisation where there was no active debate, no contrary views about future plans, no difference of opinion would be a dull, unimaginative and boring place to work in.

Mary Parker Follett distinguished between the two types of extreme conflict – constructive and destructive.

Constructive conflict is beneficial to the organisation because it can:

- challenge accepted, 'old-fashioned' ideas;
- stimulate the development of a climate of change and innovation;
- define responsibility and authority limits more closely;
- provide an opportunity for anxieties or personality challenges to be brought out into the open;
- provide a fresh approach, often widening the range of options available for dealing with a problem.

KEY POINT

Conflict can be constructive (generating new ideas) or destructive (destroying morale and motivation).

The essence of constructive conflict is that it is not personality-based and therefore does not create a legacy of 'bad will'.

Destructive conflict, on the other hand, is usually damaging to personal working relationships. It is, therefore, detrimental to both the organisation and the individuals involved. Such conflict can cause alienation between individuals, between groups and between the individual group and the company.

The essence of destructive conflict is that it is often personality-influenced and creates 'bad will'. This will encourage negative, 'dog in the manger' attitudes and block achievement of company goals.

Activity 2

Identify the ways in which conflict may manifest itself

Feedback to this activity is at the end of the chapter.

2.2 Causes of conflict

While there are many different manifestations of conflict, the causes are often difficult to determine, as individuals may themselves be unsure of their motivation and behaviour. Some authorities suggest the following:

- misunderstandings;
- insensitive and non-supportive relationships;
- failure to communicate openly and honestly;
- a climate of distrust, unreasonable pressure, or competition.

KEY POINT

Causes of conflict generally arise from differences over territory and/or objectives and ideologies.

Handy explains that the causes of conflict can be many and various but they all start from two fundamental issues: differences over territory and/or objectives and ideologies.

Differences over territory can cause conflict in the following circumstances:

- where there is violation of territory, i.e. infringing another department's responsibilities;
- overcrowding where there are too many people for the amount of work or responsibility;
- territorial jealousy – the drive to obtain and enjoy the role and privileges of others; for example, to become a member of a particular committee or control a particular routine.

Differences in objectives and ideologies leading to conflict can be caused by:

- the overlapping of formal objectives;
- the overlapping of role definitions, e.g. possible conflict for an accountant between professional codes and organisation needs;
- the contractual relationship is unclear, where parties may view their priorities differently;
- the existence of concealed objectives.

The conflicts that arise from these causes will often cause individuals to distort the communication process. To win the conflict, an individual might be selective in the information that they are willing to release, or narrowly interpret rules and regulations to enhance their own influence.

Dessler classifies four major sources of conflict:

- **Interdependence and shared resources** – conflict is most likely to occur where groups are dependent on each other to achieve their goals and use shared resources in pursuit of these goals. An example of this might be a dispute between a production department and a research and development department where both claim priority over access to a particular piece of equipment.

- **Differences in goals, values and perceptions** – groups are distinctive social units and will have special interests, particular views of what is important and what is not and will tend to see the world in a way which supports the maintenance and success of the group.
- **Authority imbalance** – where a group's authority is inconsistent with its responsibilities or prestige conflict is likely to occur. If it has too little then it will aggressively seek more; if it has too much it will be the target of others who feel the need to enhance their own authority or prestige.
- **Ambiguity** – conflict is a familiar event where a group's responsibilities are unclear or ambiguous. Power vacuums arise and inter-group conflicts ensue as each department or group seeks to fill the vacuum.

2.3 Types of inter-group conflict

Types and sources of inter-group conflict include:

Vertical conflict:

- Institutionalised conflict – e.g. that between Trade Unions and management.
- Hierarchy based conflict – those based on inequalities of power built into the organisational hierarchy.

Horizontal conflict:

- Functional conflicts – interdepartmental conflicts of a lateral (rather than hierarchical) nature where departments conflict over goals and resources, e.g. a conflict between production and sales.
- Line/staff conflicts – professional staff employed in a staff capacity often regard line management as being unimaginative, dull and inflexible whilst line management sees the staff group as abstract, impractical, over-educated, inexperienced and too young.

Formal/informal conflict – the existence of two sorts of group, one determined by the formal structure and rules of the organisation and the one resulting from social interaction can often result in conflict; custom and practice may well be at variance with formal procedures and the two can easily come into conflict

Status conflict – where groups compete for status and prestige conflict often follows

Political conflicts – these can take many forms; political processes, such as the formation of cliques and conspiracies, are commonplace features of organisational life

2.4 The dynamics of inter-group conflict

When groups come into conflict the patterns of the group behaviour change, relationships between groups change, new strategic moves are adopted and at the final stage of the conflict the parties have to adjust to winning or losing. Changes within the group experiencing conflict include:

- Loyalty to the group becomes more important.
- Perceptions about one's own group and the other group are distorted. Out-group members are often stereotyped whilst, in one's own group, it is common only to perceive the strengths and deny any weaknesses.

- There is increased hostility to the rival group. People become part of the 'enemy' rather than colleagues.
- There is an increased concern for task accomplishment, i.e. more pressure for the group to perform at its best.
- Interaction and communication between groups decrease. Groups become more isolated, overlooking shared interests and exaggerating differences.
- Leadership in the group becomes more autocratic.

There is a move from a problem-solving orientation to other groups to a win/lose orientation. Ignoring long-term consequences of the conflict, groups become obsessed with winning in the particular situation.

2.5 Strategies groups use to gain power

- **Contracting** – this refers to the negotiation of a *quid pro quo* agreement between two groups. Each side makes some concessions to the other. This is often found in union/management bargaining.
- **Co-opting** – this takes place when a group gives some of its leadership position to members of other groups and thus blunts any criticism of its activities by the out-group.
- **Forming coalitions** – two or more groups can combine to increase their power over groups not in the coalition.
- **Influencing decision criteria** – this is sometimes referred to as 'moving the goal posts' and involves trying to win by changing the criteria by which success and failure are judged.
- **Controlling information** – by selectively giving or denying information a group can strengthen its position.
- **Forcing and pressure tactics** – this consists of the use or threat of direct action, e.g. the use of a strike or work to rule.

3 Managing conflict

3.1 Possible approaches to dealing with conflict

There are obviously a variety of different ways to handle conflict and you have probably heard some of the following said in your own organisation:

- 'Try to avoid things going too far; provide friendly counsel; avoid trouble at all costs.'
- 'Keep personalities out of this; let's concentrate on the facts.'
- 'Let's get this out in the open; come to the point; don't drive the conflict underground.'

KEY POINT

The conditions for avoiding conflict include a positive atmosphere with common recognised goals, a clear understanding of tasks and a steady environment.

One writer has suggested that at least three essential conditions are required to **avoid conflict**:

- a friendly **atmosphere** with clear **common goals** that are recognised and accepted by other group members;
- a clear idea of the various tasks to be accomplished;
- a reasonably **steady environment** such as the market in which a firm operates.

KEY POINT

The two main strategies for managing negative conflict are to convert the conflict into a positive one using a **team-building approach** or to respond to the conflict by trying to **avoid**, **defuse** or **confront** it.

There are many approaches to the management of conflict; the suitability of any approach is to be judged only in terms of its relevance in a particular situation. There is no universal right way – it depends on the goals and requirements of management in a specific setting. In some situations it is correct to compromise, in others nothing less than complete victory is required.

The two main strategies for managing negative conflict are:

- to convert the conflict into a positive one using a team-building approach;
- to respond to the conflict by trying to **ignore** it, **calm** it or **resolve** it – **avoid**, **defuse** or **confront**.

Obviously, the first strategy is the most beneficial. The second strategy has a set of possible approaches for dealing with the conflict:

- **Avoid the problem** – You might want to pretend to yourself that the situation does not exist or you might bottle up your feelings and turn the other cheek. This is the type of approach that is used when you cannot bring yourself to face the difficulties. Not only will you be left with the bad feelings because of your inaction but the conflict is still out there.
- **Defuse the conflict** – By trying to calm everyone down you may buy some time. However, the problem may suddenly reappear and be much more of a threat.
- **Confront the problem by bringing it out into the open** – Getting to the bottom of the problem is a difficult, high-risk strategy but you may be sure that this is the only certain and dependable way to resolve the conflict.

Confrontation can be by **negotiation** or by **power**. The **power** strategy will work if there is adequate real power behind the conflict manager, e.g. having enough money could resolve a confrontation between the union and management or having an army can solve a war conflict. Unfortunately, the power option means one party (the one with the power) wins and the other loses. A win–lose situation is not satisfactory because there is often resentment on the part of the losing side that may damage working relations.

The **negotiation** strategy is not an easy option, but it is one that has much more of a positive outcome than the other choices.

3.2 Strategies for managing conflict

These are the broad strategies for managing conflict in organisations as explained by Mainwaring in *Management and Strategy* (1991):

Conflict stimulation and orchestration. This approach actively encourages conflict as a means of generating new ideas and new approaches or of stimulating change. It is a characteristic of matrix structures which deliberately build role conflicts into organisational relationships. There are obvious dangers in generating conflict, not least that they will escalate and perpetuate in a destructive way. However some conflict is necessary to prevent organisational stagnation. This approach involves the maintenance and management of constructive conflict as a means of continuous renewal.

Conflict suppression. This involves the use or threatened use of authority or force, or the avoidance of recognition that a conflict situation exists, or smoothing over the conflict by de-emphasising the seriousness of the situation. Such strategies are essentially short-term, and are likely to be perceived as such by those involved.

Conflict reduction. This involves building on areas of agreement and on common objectives, and changing attitudes and perceptions of the parties involved. Techniques that can be used include compromises and concessions. These can be facilitated by independent third party interventions, such as conciliation and arbitration.

Conflict resolution. This seeks to eliminate the root causes of conflict by establishing a consensus. Attitude change is a key element, particularly regarding the possibility of 'win/win' situations where the parties involved are aware of the mutual gains to be derived from co-operation and collaboration.

The mix of strategies used will depend not only on the situation, but also on the assumptions that managers make about conflict.

3.3 The Handy way

KEY POINT

Handy suggested two sets of strategies for tackling conflict: 'control by ecology', which creates the environment for constructive relationships, and 'short-term regulation'.

Handy suggests that in tackling conflict a manager should seek to turn the conflict into a possible argument or engender fruitful competition. Only if this is not possible should the conflict be controlled. Handy nominates two types of strategy for tackling conflict.

The first set of strategies he terms 'control by ecology', because they create the environment for constructive relationships. Such strategies include:

- agreement and knowledge of common objectives;
- providing meaningful information to the participants;
- building communication and trust between the individuals/groups;
- ensuring that individuals' roles do not counteract the organisation's goals;
- developing suitable co-ordination mechanisms for the departments involved.

The second set include 'short-term regulation' strategies such as:

- the use of an arbitration authority;
- the development of detailed rules of conduct;
- creating a position to manage the area of conflict, e.g. a budget liaison officer;
- using confrontation or inter-group meetings to analyse the conflict openly;
- separating the conflicting parties;
- ignoring the conflict problem in the belief that it is a temporary situation that will 'blow over'.

3.4 Pluralist approach to conflict

In contrast to the human relations' approach, the underlying assumptions of the pluralist approach to conflict are:

- Conflict is often desirable, but it should be managed in such a way as to prevent it getting out of hand.
- Conflict is the sign of a healthy organisation.
- Conflict is inevitable and results from:
  - a struggle to achieve the needs of (for example) food, power, status and responsibility;
  - innate instincts in man of aggression and competitiveness.

- Genetic and physiological determinations of aggressive behaviour are more important than the environmental influence.
- Man is driven by the instincts of selfishness, competitiveness and aggression.

The views of this school of thought are supported by Follett and Tannenbaum. Experimental studies of creativity and innovation suggest that groups are more productive when a dissenter is present than when dissenters are absent, although, given the opportunity, the dissenter is the first person the group gets rid of. The weaknesses of this approach are:

- conflict of interest can be dysfunctional;
- dissension among union members can reduce the effectiveness of the union; and
- differences can be magnified out of all proportion; and, for example in collective bargaining, the resolution of even moderate differences may be difficult to achieve.

Whereas the human relations' supporters try to obviate conflict, the pluralists try to make constructive use of it by exploiting conflict to effect changes and enhance organisational performance. According to Follett, there are three methods of dealing with conflict:

- **Domination**. A strong management can win against a weak union, or a strong union can completely destroy a company; this type of behaviour only results in grievances being perpetuated.
- **Compromise**. In a compromise situation, both sides give ground in the interests of a short-term solution to the dispute; it is often not a real solution to the underlying problems.
- **Integration**. This is Follett's suggestion as the best approach; from the conflict of ideas and attitudes, the opposing forces move towards common objectives. She believed that this would happen if there were frank and open discussion of the real problems. This led to her view of power with, rather than over people, and of joint responsibility.

More recent research suggests that the pluralist approach to conflict management is most effective when:

- neither party dominates the other;
- both parties see some advantage in their continued association, even though their relationship may change as a result of the conflict;
- neither party is able, or wishes, to annihilate the other;
- cross loyalties or affiliations exist which prevent complete separation of conflicting parties into distinct camps.

3.5 Blake and Mouton's model of conflict management

Blake and Mouton plotted various conflict styles according to a manager's position on their managerial grid (see Chapter 11).

The diagram below illustrates five key orientations or conflict styles.

Blake & Mouton's conflict styles grid

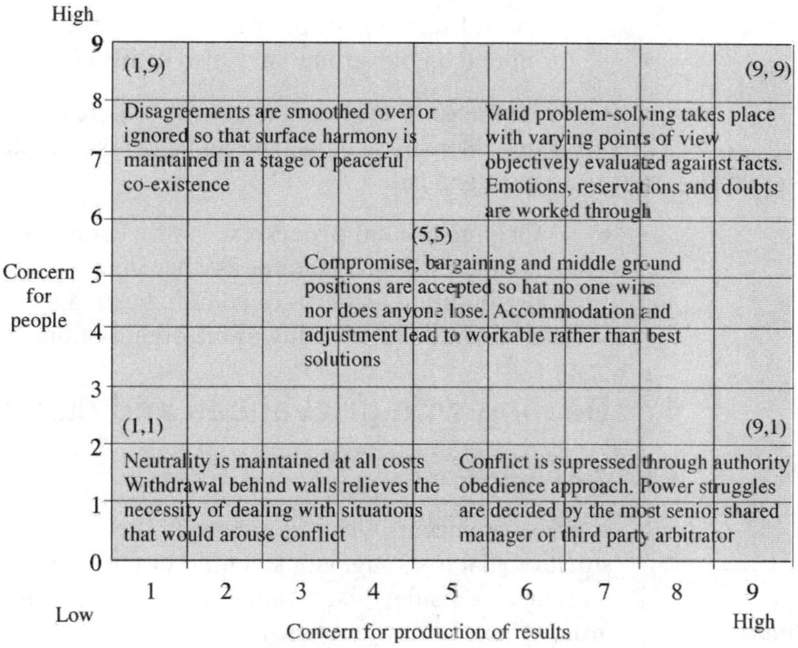

Blake and Mouton believe that on the whole people do conform to the expectations of others; this readiness tc conform reduces conflict and is what permits regularity, order and predictability

3.6 Tools for managing individuals, teams and networks, and for managing group conflict

Throughout this text we have outlined management tools and tactics to deal with many situations. Although conflict resolution techniques, including mediation and negotiation, are valuable tools, conflict management procedures that prevent the escalation of conflict are preferable. These include:

- **Clarification of goals and objectives**. Focusing attention on super-ordinate goals that are shared by the parties in conflict may help to defuse hostility and lead to more co-operative behaviour.
- **Resource distribution**. Although it may not always be possible for managers to increase their allocated share of resources, they may be able to use imagination and initiative to help overcome conflict situations – for example, making a special case to higher management; greater flexibility to transfer funds between budget headings; delaying staff appointments in one area to provide more money for another area.
- **Personnel policies and procedures**. Careful and detailed attention to just and equitable personnel policies and procedures may help to reduce areas of conflict.
- **Non-monetary rewards**. Where financial resources are limited, it may be possible to pay greater attention to non-monetary rewards.
- **Development of interpersonal/group process skills**. This may help to encourage a better understanding of one's own behaviour, the other person's point of view, communication processes and problem-solving. It may also encourage people to wcrk through conflict situations in a constructive manner.

- **Group activities**. Attention to the composition of groups and to factors that affect group cohesiveness may reduce dysfunctional conflict. Overlapping group membership with a 'linking-pin' process, and the careful selection of project teams or task forces for problems affecting more than one group, may also be beneficial.
- **Leadership and management**. A more participative and supportive style of leadership and managerial behaviour is likely to assist in conflict management.
- **Organisational processes**. Conflict situations may be reduced by attention to such features as: the nature of the authority structure; work organisation; patterns of communication and sharing of information; democratic functioning of the organisation.

4 Dealing with grievances and disciplinary matters

4.1 Grievances

DEFINITION

Employees have a grievance when there is something in the work situation that they feel is unfair, wrong, unjust or unreasonable.

A grievance occurs when an employee feels that there is something in the work situation that is wrong, unjust, unfair or unreasonable. Some grievances are individual – dislike of something that is said or a manager's approach. Others are group grievances, where one person volunteers to represent others. Many grievances are about pay but in times of economic uncertainty, grievances may be about job security and employees will express this in 'territory defending' behaviour.

A grievance may become a complaint to express the employee dissatisfaction or it may become a dispute, which is a formal expression of dissatisfaction at organisational level.

When an individual or group has a grievance, there should be a procedure to enable the problem to be resolved. Some grievances are resolved informally by the appropriate manager but, if an informal solution is not possible, there should be a formal grievance procedure.

4.2 Discipline

The word discipline tends to be associated with authority, force, warnings, threats and/or punishment. However, discipline can also be used to maintain sensible conduct and orderliness. Most mature people accept the idea that following instructions and fair rules of conduct are normal responsibilities that are part of any job. They believe in performing their work properly, in following instructions, in coming to work on time and in refraining from fighting, drinking, stealing or taking drugs at work.

The types of disciplinary situations that require attention by the manager include:

- excessive absenteeism;
- defective or inadequate work performance;
- breaking safety rules and other violations of rules, regulations and procedures;
- improper personal appearance.

The purpose of discipline is not punishment or retribution. The goal of disciplinary action is to improve the future behaviour of the employee and other members of the organisation. The purpose is avoidance of similar occurrences in the future.

Many organisations adopt a progressive discipline approach following a list of suggested steps:

- **The informal talk** – where the infraction is of a relatively minor nature and the employee's record has no previous marks of disciplinary action. The manager discusses with the employee his or her behaviour in relation to standards that prevail in the organisation.
- **Oral warning or reprimand** – emphasises the dissatisfaction with the subordinate's repeated violation, which could lead to serious disciplinary action.
- **Written or official warning** – become a permanent part of the employee's record and may be used as evidence in the case of grievance procedures.
- **Disciplinary layoff or suspension without pay** – used when previous steps were of no avail.
- **Demotion** – a form of constant punishment due to losing pay and status over an extended period of time.
- **Discharge/dismissal** – a drastic form of disciplinary action reserved for the most serious offences.

4.3 Role of procedures in handling conflict

An important part of any employee relations policy is to set out the broad standards of conduct that the organisation intends to follow in respect of unacceptable behaviour on the part of the employee (disciplinary matters) and grievances raised by the employee.

The role of procedures in handling conflict is to:

- create a means of solving problems and grievances while allowing work to go on;
- provide a means by which justice can be seen to be done;
- allow time for issues to be judged more calmly;
- remove problems from immediate source of dispute for examination at objective levels;
- give protection to the individual against personal animosity;
- redress the balance of power towards the individual;
- specify time scales and appeals procedures.

4.4 Grievance procedures

Grievance procedures should provide a speedy means by which employees can seek redress for any grievances they may have at work. A good procedure aims to achieve a solution to a grievance as near as possible to the point of origin or to process the grievance without delay to a higher level in the management chain. In a grievance situation, the manager concerned should aim to establish the facts relating to the grievance and eventually reach a mutually acceptable solution.

Formal grievance procedures should be set out in writing and do the following:

- clarify the categories of employees to which they apply and ensure they are aware of their rights;
- specify who employees can take their grievance to in first instance (usually their immediate boss) and subsequent steps;
- allow friend or representative involvement;
- define time limits between processes;
- define distinctions between collective and individual grievances.

A typical grievance procedure usually follows the stages set out below:

- The employee should first raise the matter with the immediate supervisor or manager and may be accompanied by a fellow employee. The supervisor or manager will endeavour to resolve the problem without delay.
- If the employee is not satisfied with the response of the superior, he or she may refer the grievance to the department manager or other senior manager, who will hear the grievance within five working days. A fellow employee may accompany the employee and the company HR manager will be present.
- If the employee is still dissatisfied after the second stage, he or she may appeal to a director who will arrange to hear the appeal within five working days. The results of the appeal will be recorded and distributed to all the parties concerned.

4.5 Disciplinary procedures

The aim of this type of procedure is to correct unsatisfactory behaviour, rather than punish it. A good disciplinary procedure should be clearly stated, in writing and should enable employees to feel assured of fairness and consistency of treatment if ever they should become subject to the procedure. It should specify as fully as possible what constitutes 'misconduct' and 'gross misconduct' and state what the most likely penalty is for each of these categories and how long an offence is kept on the records. In cases of proven gross misconduct, this is most likely to be immediate dismissal, or suspension followed by dismissal.

There should be a definition of who has the authority for dismissal. In cases of less serious misconduct, the most likely consequence is that a formal warning will be given. For repeated acts of misconduct, it is likely that the employee concerned will be dismissed.

The Advisory, Conciliation and Arbitration Service (ACAS) has issued a Code of Practice which recommends that disciplinary procedures:

- should be in written form;
- must identify to whom they apply (all, or some of the employees);
- should be able to deal speedily with disciplinary matters,
- should indicate the forms of disciplinary action which may be taken (e.g. dismissal, suspension or warning);
- should specify the appropriate levels of authority for the exercise of disciplinary actions;

- should provide for employees to be informed of the nature of their alleged misconduct;
- should allow employees to state their case, and to be accompanied by a fellow employee and/or union representative;
- make sure that every case is properly investigated before any disciplinary action is taken;
- must inform employees of the reasons for any penalty they receive;
- should state that no employee will be dismissed for a first offence, except in cases of gross misconduct;
- should provide for a right of appeal against any disciplinary action;
- should specify the appeals procedure.

4.6 External means of dealing with grievance and disciplinary matters

ACAS was established under the Employment Protection Act 1975, and operates services of conciliation, both on an individual and group basis, arbitration, mediation and enquiry. In addition ACAS offers advice to organisations, particularly in its preparation of Codes of Practice, e.g. in the area of disciplinary procedures.

Where employees feel that they have been unfairly dismissed they have the right to take their case to an Employment Tribunal. The tribunal will normally refer the case to ACAS in the hope of gaining an amicable settlement. Most cases are settled by some form of conciliation and arbitration.

Employment tribunals always compare the company procedures with ACAS recommendations when making judgements. If an organisation follows the ACAS procedures, an employee will be less successful in suing for unfair dismissal.

4.7 The role of management

Because of the serious implications of disciplinary action, only senior managers are normally permitted to carry out suspensions, demotions or dismissals. Other managers and supervisors are restricted to giving the various types of warnings.

When it comes to handling grievances, all supervisors and managers will have a role to play because one of the key features of an effective grievance procedure is that it should aim to settle the dispute as near as possible to the point of origin. Another important role of the manager when conducting the grievance interview is to aim for a mutually beneficial outcome. The employee concerned should be able to go away feeling reassured that, either there is no problem or, if there is, it has been tackled constructively by the immediate superior. The manager should feel that the grievance has been handled correctly and that both parties had 'won'.

4.8 Disciplinary interview

These are very formal affairs where managers control the proceedings and can plan in advance how they will deal with the guilty party and future consequences. This type of interview seeks to establish the facts and, assuming the complaint is valid, confirms that a company rule has been broken to the offending employee.

The employee is warned that a penalty is, or will be, enforced either now or in the event of further misconduct. The seriousness of the offence, such as gross misconduct, is identified, and at this stage the consequences of further offences must be discussed. It is hoped by this means to prevent further misconduct and so ensure the future efficiency and appropriate conduct of the employee.

An employee has the right to bring a friend or colleague as a witness to the details of the interview.

Activity 3

Can the manager plan a grievance interview in advance?

Feedback to this activity is at the end of the chapter.

5 Dismissal

5.1 Introduction

Dismissal is usually seen as the last step, the ultimate sanction in any disciplinary procedure. However, dismissals occur most frequently in the form of redundancy. Statistics published by the Department of Employment list the major reasons for dismissal as redundancy, sickness, unsuitability and misconduct in that order.

5.2 Fair dismissal

There is a statutory obligation for an employer to show that a dismissal is fair. In this case a dismissal is fair if it is related to:

- **Redundancy** (provided that selection for redundancy can be shown to be fair).
- **A lack of capability or qualifications**

  This involves cases where the employee lacks the qualifications, skill, aptitude or health to do the job properly. However, in all cases the employee must be given the opportunity to improve the position or in the case of health be considered for alternative employment.
- **Misconduct**

  This includes the refusal to obey lawful and reasonable instructions, absenteeism, insubordination over a period of time and some criminal actions. In the last case, the criminal action should relate directly to the job; it can only be grounds for dismissal if the result of the criminal action will affect the work in some way.
- **A statutory bar**

  This occurs when employees cannot pursue their normal duties without breaking the law. The most common occurrence of this is the case of drivers who have been banned.
- **Some other substantial reason**

  This is a separate reason and will include good work-related reasons for dismissal (e.g. a need for the business to change and the employees refusing to adapt to the change required).

5.3 Unfair dismissal

In all cases of unfair dismissal there are two stages of proof. Firstly, the circumstances which represent fair grounds for dismissal must be established, and secondly, the tribunal must decide whether dismissal is fair in the circumstances of the case in question.

For dismissal to be automatically unfair, it must be for one of the following reasons:

- trade union membership or non-membership;
- pregnancy, maternity or exercising rights to parental leave;
- discrimination (on any grounds covered by law);
- assertion of a statutory right (e.g. under Equal Pay Provisions);
- participation in official industrial action (for the first 8 weeks);
- disclosure of illegal practices by the employer ('whistle blowing').

5.4 Provisions for unfair dismissal

Where employees feel that they have been unfairly dismissed they have the right to take their case to the Employment Tribunal. The tribunal will normally refer the case to ACAS (Advisory Conciliation and Arbitration Service) in the hope of gaining an amicable settlement. Most cases are settled by some form of conciliation and arbitration. The possible solutions or remedies for unfair dismissal are set out below.

- **Withdrawal of notice** – by the employer. This is the preferred remedy as stated in the Employment Protection Act.
- **Reinstatement (order of Employment Tribunal)** – this treats the employee as though he had never been dismissed. The employee is taken back to his old job with no loss of earnings and privileges.
- **Re-engagement (order of Employment Tribunal)** – in this case, the employee is offered a different job in the organisation and loses continuity of service.
- **Compensation (order of Employment Tribunal)** – if an employer refuses to re-employ then the employee receives compensation made up of a penalty award of 13 – 26 weeks' pay (more in the case of discrimination), a payment equivalent to the redundancy entitlement and an award to compensate for loss of earnings, pension rights and so on. Some form of compensation may also be appropriate in cases of reinstatement and re-engagement.

Summary

- To foster effective work teams managers will be concerned with four main factors: membership of the team; organisational factors; work environment; group development.
- Handy argued that group leaders cannot alter the 'givens' of group, task and environment, but should work on the 'intervening factors' (motivation; processes and procedures; leadership style).
- While constructive conflict may benefit the organisation, destructive conflict may destroy morale and motivation.

- Dessler classifies four main sources of conflict: interdependence and shared resources; differences in goals, values and perceptions; authority imbalance; ambiguity.
- Mainwaring identifies strategies for managing conflict: conflict stimulation and orchestration; conflict suppression; conflict reduction; conflict resolution.
- ACAS proposes that disciplinary procedures should follow defined guidelines.

Having completed your study of this chapter you should have achieved the following learning outcomes.

- Explain how groups form within organisations and how this affects performance.
- Construct a set of tools for managing individuals, teams and networks, and for managing group conflict.
- Recommend ways to deal effectively with discipline problems.

Self-test questions

1 Describe any of the group development models. (1.2)

2 Outline the advantages associated with cohesive groups. (1.3)

3 What are 'process roles', according to Belbin? (1.4)

4 What does Handy mean by 'givens' and 'intervening factors'? (1.5)

5 In what circumstances can differences over territory cause conflict? (2.2)

6 According to Dessler what are the four major sources of conflict? (2.2)

7 Describe one of Mainwaring's strategies for managing conflict. (3.2)

8 What is the difference between grievance and discipline? (4.1, 4.2)

9 What does ACAS stand for? (4.5)

10 What are considered unfair reasons for dismissal in UK law? (5.3)

Multiple-choice questions

Question 1

Integrative bargaining requires:

A an adversarial approach

B a problem-solving orientation

C an ability to 'bluff' effectively

D an ability to ignore the other side's interests and priorities.

Question 2

Which of the following suggests a settling period when standards and roles are accepted?

A Storming

B Performing

C Norming

D Forming

Question 3

A thoughtful and thought-provoking person in a group is described by Belbin as the:

A plant

B team worker

C co-ordinator

D finisher.

For the answer to these questions, see the 'Answers' section at the end of the book.

Exam-type question

Managing conflict

Because of its failure to serve a sufficient number of clients and/or to provide a service of the required quality, a state-owned business (SOB) has had its funding cut for three consecutive years. This is putting pressure on people throughout the organisation. Departments and individuals have been set more demanding targets and large-scale redundancies have recently been announced. This has resulted in considerable conflict. The service professionals are convinced that the marketing and sales department is responsible for the troubles of the organisation. This view is not shared by the marketing and sales people. They believe that the poor quality of service offered is the real reason for the decline in demand for services and for the resulting cuts in government funding. The effect of these differences between departments is one of declining co-operation between the direct service providers and the personnel in marketing and sales.

Of more immediate concern to senior management, however, is the threat of industrial action by the trades unions determined to protect their members' jobs. Even individuals such as the management accountant are finding themselves in conflict with departmental managers with whom they have previously enjoyed good relations. Requests for information on costs of providing services are being met with hostility and the management accountant's job becomes more difficult day by day.

Required:

(a) Discuss the potential consequences arising from the conflicts between various departments and groups within SOB. **(12 marks)**

(b) Describe how senior management can best manage the conflicts between various parties. **(13 marks)**

(Total: 25 marks)

For the answer to this question, see the 'Answers' section at the end of the book.

Feedback to activities

Activity 1

Forming – the members meet and perhaps decide what production they are going to stage.

Storming – here members compete for roles and challenge how the play is to be performed and who is in charge.

Norming – plans are made, the script modified, and early rehearsals occur to test the chosen roles.

Performing – the play is now in full swing, lines are learnt and the group is getting ready to put on the play.

Activity 2

Conflict may manifest itself in many different ways:

- official or unofficial strikes
- restriction or reduction of output, or activity which jeopardises income
- demarcation disputes
- lock-outs
- absenteeism
- sabotage
- high labour turnover
- poor time-keeping
- refusal to obey instructions
- working to rule
- unwillingness to accept more efficient methods of production
- racial prejudice
- unhealthy rivalry between groups and between individuals
- refusal to work with colleagues, or the ostracism of individuals.

Activity 3

It is very difficult to plan in advance, because the subordinate will want to determine the content of the interview. Prior to the interview the manager should have some idea of the grievance and its possible source, and should have done some investigations in preparation.

Chapter 14

LEGAL AND ETHICAL ISSUES

Syllabus content

- The nature and effect of legal issues affecting work and employment, including the application of relevant employment law (i.e. relating to health, safety, discrimination, fair treatment, childcare, contracts of employment and working time).
- Introduction to corporate governance, including business ethics and the role, obligations and expectations of a manager.

Contents

1 Employment law

2 Equal opportunities and discrimination

3 Corporate governance and business ethics

1 Employment law

1.1 Background

Because of concern by successive governments to avoid exploitation and discrimination, human resource management is perhaps more subject to legislation than any other aspect of corporate management.

When we consider employment law, we are dealing almost exclusively with civil law, where a plaintiff takes action against a person who committed a wrongful act. This means that the outcome of any successful case will normally be an award of compensation and/or damages, as opposed to prosecution and possible imprisonment under criminal law. Employers can be imprisoned under certain specific conditions e.g. where negligence is proved under the health and safety legislation, but there are very few cases.

In the UK, Acts of Parliament mainly determine the conduct of employment relations. Codes of Practice are also important; these are recommended procedures that describe good practice in such areas as recruitment, discipline, equal opportunities and redundancy, even though there are laws surrounding these areas. Bodies such as ACAS (Advisory, Conciliation and Arbitration Service), the EOC (Equal Opportunities Commission) and the CRE (Commission for Racial Equality) are among the main providers of such recommendations.

1.2 Contract of employment

When a person is newly employed, a contract of employment has to be issued. This is of considerable significance in the determination of the legal rights and obligations of both parties. In some parts of the world, this individual contract is not so significant since the obligations, rights and remedies of the parties involved in it are determined by collective agreement. However, in the UK these collective agreements themselves create legalities if and when they are specifically incorporated into the contract.

Note that there are two kinds of terms to a contract of employment: express and implied.

KEY POINT

The implied terms and conditions of the contract of employment are established by custom or general usage in the industry or in the organisation.

Implied terms – the contract does not have to be in writing. There are implied terms and conditions, which are established by custom or general usage in the industry or in the organisation. What is *implied* is that the employer should pay the agreed wages/salaries, and adopt reasonably safe procedures in the workplace. But, as a rule, the employer is not *obliged* to provide work. Also, on the part of the employee, he or she must co-operate with the employer, use skill and care in obeying lawful instructions, and give a faithful service.

Express terms – the present trend is for contracts of employment to be in writing.

In the UK an employer must give employees, within 13 weeks of the beginning of the period of employment, a written statement which:

- Identifies the parties.
- Gives the date when the period of continuous employment began, and where employment with a previous employer counts as part of the employee's period of continuous employment, the date when the previous employment began. If the contract is for a fixed term the statement has to give the date of expiry.

- Gives particulars of the following terms of employment:
  - the scale or rate of pay and payment intervals;
  - hours of work;
  - holidays, holiday pay and entitlement to accrued holiday pay;
  - sick pay/leave provisions;
  - pensions and pension schemes;
  - notice required for termination by employer and employee;
  - job title (not job description).

There are, in addition, certain statutory conditions laid down in respect of particular industries (e.g. for road haulage, hotel and catering, etc.) and these cannot be in any way limited by any employer-employee agreement. Additionally, the written statement must have a note stating what disciplinary rules are applicable, to whom the employee can appeal against a disciplinary decision or to whom the grievance can be taken. Any appeals procedure must also be stated.

1.3 Health and safety at work

In the UK, the Health & Safety at Work Act 1974 is the most significant piece of legislation in relation to health and safety issues. Employers have to take reasonable steps to ensure the health, safety and welfare of their employees at work. The employer's responsibility to the employee might include a duty to provide safe plant and machinery and safe premises, a safe system of work and competent trained and supervised staff. Certain groups of employees may require more care and supervision than others, for example disabled workers, pregnant workers, illiterate workers, etc.

Usually the employer's responsibility is only to his or her own employees and premises; however, the responsibility can be extended in some circumstances. For example:

- Where employees from different firms are employed on one job, the main contractor will then be responsible for coordinating the work in a safe manner and must inform all workers of possible hazards whether they are his actual employees or not.
- Where the employee is sent to work for someone else (but remains employed by the same employer), and an accident happens at the place where he has been sent to work, the responsibility may fall on the original employer.
- The employer may also have responsibility to customers or visitors who use the workplace.

It is always advisable for employers to have a written code of conduct, rules regarding training and supervision, and rules on safety procedures. This should include information on basic health and safety requirements.

In any event an employer must establish a health and safety policy if they employ five or more workers. Where there is a recognised trade union in the workplace, which has appointed a safety representative, that person must be consulted when drawing up the safety policy.

Additionally, the employer must provide a safe system of work. This may involve the selection of competent staff and proper supervision, the provision of safe premises, plant and materials, and the merger of all these factors into a system that ensures that the work may, with reasonable care, be executed in safety.

The standard is one of reasonable care. In assessing the reasonableness, the following factors may be relevant:

- foreseeability of risk of injury;
- the nature of the risk and the probable consequences of a breach of this duty by the employer;
- the known characteristics of the employee;
- the cost of prevention – this must be weighed according to what is practicable in the circumstances.

Where the work is simple and straightforward, the employer need not promulgate a system – he may rely on the employee's skill and discretion in approaching the job. The employer's duty to provide safe working conditions extends to employees working on premises belonging to a third party.

1.4 Working Time Regulations

The Working Time Regulations (1998) give full-time, part-time, agency and casual workers certain basic rights as follows:

- Limit of an average of 48 hours per week which a worker may be required to work. However, they can opt-out of this limit and work more if they want to.
- Limit of an average 8 hours work every 24 hours for night workers.
- Free health assessments for night workers.
- 11 hours rest in every 24 hours.
- A minimum of one day off per week.
- Rest break during working hours if the working day is longer than 6 hours.
- A minimum of 4 weeks paid leave per year.

2 Equal opportunities and discrimination

2.1 Legislation

In the UK, there are some key statutes relating to equal opportunities and discrimination:

1 **The Equal Pay Act 1970** (and subsequent regulations) is intended to prevent discrimination between men and women with regard to the terms and conditions of employment. It makes it clear that the provisions apply equally to men and women (i.e. a man can also claim if he has a less favourable term than a woman has). The Act covers all conditions and terms of employment and not just pay. Where men and women are employed in like work or work of an equivalent **value** (as determined by job evaluation), they should receive the same terms and conditions of employment.

KEY POINT

The Sex Discrimination Act renders it unlawful to make any form of discrimination in employment affairs because of marital status or sex.

2 **The Sex Discrimination Act 1986** renders it unlawful to make any form of discrimination in employment affairs because of marital status, sex or sex change. This applies especially to the selection process as it offers protection to both sexes against unfair treatment on appointment.

3 **The Disability Discrimination Act 1995** makes it unlawful for an employer (of more than 20 employees) to discriminate against a disabled person in terms of selection, promotion, benefits or dismissal.

4 **The Race Relations Act 1996** makes it unlawful to discriminate on grounds of race, colour, nationality and ethnic or national origin. The Race Relations (Amendments) Act 2000 adds the requirement for large public organisations to draw up detailed plans for achieving racial equality.

5 **The Employment Equality Regulations 2003** outlawed discrimination and harassment on the grounds of sexual orientation and religious beliefs; employers may be held responsible for conduct deemed offensive in regard to either issue, as well as discrimination (e.g. in regard to staff benefits).

Keep an eye on the professional and quality press. There are due to be changes to the law on sexual discrimination (including a first statutory definition of **sexual harassment**) and new legislation on **age diversity** in employment (currently the subject of voluntary self-regulation in the UK) in 2006.

2.2 Equal opportunity

'Equal opportunities' is a generic term describing the belief that there should be an equal chance for all workers to apply and be selected for jobs, to be trained and promoted in employment and to have that employment terminated fairly. Employers should only discriminate according to ability, experience and potential. All employment decisions should be based solely on a person's ability to do the job in question; no consideration should be taken of a person's sex, age, racial origin, disability or marital status.

A number of employers label themselves as *equal opportunity employers*, establishing their own particular kind of equal opportunity policy. However, while some protection is afforded by employment legislation, the majority of everyday cases must rely on good practice to prevail.

Developing and applying good working practice should cover all of the aspects of human resource management including the following:

- recruitment;
- terms and conditions of employment;
- promotion, transfer and training;
- benefits, facilities and services; and
- dismissal.

From the employer's point of view, an organisation's workforce is representative when it reflects or exceeds the demographic composition of the external workforce. A representative workforce reflects or exceeds the current proportions of women, visible minorities and persons with disabilities in each occupation as are known to be available in the external workforce and from which the employer may reasonably be expected to draw from.

This is a good indication that an employer is not limiting access to the skills and talents of workers by discriminating on the basis of sex, race, colour or disability. A non-representative workforce signals the need for evaluation and action, so that whatever is blocking or discouraging certain groups from employment and advancement may be corrected.

Some organisations set themselves goals on the representation of certain groups e.g. women in management positions To address this type of problem, a diversity assessment will show how an organisation's systems and culture may provide supports or may act as barriers to diversity.

Activity 1

What is a representative workforce?

Feedback to this activity is at the end of the chapter.

2.3 Managing diversity

Diversity can be defined as 'all the ways in which we are different and similar along an infinite number of lines'.

Diversity is a wider concept than 'equal opportunity' (as defined by law) because it recognises that individuals differ on a wider range of dimensions than the rather crude categories of sex, race, age and so on.

People have individual differences in personality, working and learning styles, personal needs and goals. In addition, society (and therefore the representative workforce) is increasingly diverse in terms of its:

- Educational patterns and qualifications: with non-standard educational pathways such as adult learning, re-skilling and e-learning; and issues of harmonising international qualifications in an increasingly global workforce.
- Family structures and responsibilities; with single households, dual income households, blended families and so on.
- Career aspirations and patterns, and ways of organising working life; with increasing part-time, temporary and freelance working.
- Cultural norms and values, with the rise in cross-cultural working.

A 'managing diversity' orientation implies a pro-active response to the needs of a diverse and changing workforce, to produce an open, flexible and supportive environment that values the uniqueness of employees. The award-winning diversity strategy of US multi-national Pitney-Bowes, for example, sets out five key goals for communication, education and training, career development, recruitment and work/life balance, in order to promote an understanding of individual differences ('including, but not limited to, age, gender, race, religion, ethnicity, disability, sexual orientation and family circumstances') and to create a culture and work environment supportive to all employees.

A **diversity assessment** is a structured process to gather information about the experience of current employees and perhaps former employees. Typically, a group of 10 to 12 individuals are asked a series of structured questions designed to identify policies and practices, both formal and informal, that either promote diversity or act as barriers. The practices, policies and systems include:

- job classification and descriptions;
- recruitment, training and development processes;

- performance evaluation systems;
- promotions and upward mobility;
- levels of compensation and access to benefits;
- facilities (building design) and access to assistance.

2.4 Family friendly policies and work-life balance

Child care support

One of the main barriers to work and equal opportunities for parents is the lack of good quality, affordable childcare. There are a number of ways in which employers, both large and small can support working parents in their search for quality childcare. The options include:

- providing information and advice for employees;
- opening nurseries and holiday playschemes;
- buying places in existing local nurseries or playschemes/ out of school clubs;
- setting up a childminding support network;
- supporting and fostering relationships with local providers of childcare;
- providing childcare allowances or vouchers.

These options are not necessarily exclusive. Employers may find that a combination of different forms of support is effective for their employees.

Flexible working

In addition to direct childcare support there are many options available to employers to help employees balance work and home life. Many employers have found that policies designed to support employees with care responsibilities benefit all employees by enhancing the quality of their working life. The options listed below fall into two basic types:

- arranging the pattern of working hours to accommodate the competing demands on the employee;
- changing the way in which a job is carried out.

KEY POINT

Flexible working options:

- Flexi-time
- Term-time working
- Annual hours
- Job sharing
- Part-time working
- Working from home
- Sabbaticals
- Special leave arrangements.

These options include:

Flexi-time – flexi-time schemes allow employees to choose, within limits, the hours that they start and finish work. They usually also allow any extra hours worked to be counted and taken as flexi-leave. Flexi-time is a popular option and is very suitable for employees who have childcare or other domestic responsibilities. Often, the 'core' time that must be worked falls within school hours permitting parents to care for their children before and after school. By working extra hours parents can accrue leave which can be taken during school holidays, or can help offset time needed for special activities such as school events, open evenings, nursery outings, etc.

Term-time working – this gives permanent employees the opportunity to take unpaid leave of absence during the school holidays. Each year there are about 13 weeks of school holidays and so for, an employee who is entitled to five weeks paid leave, there will be a chance to take a further eight weeks of unpaid leave.

Term-time working arrangements can particularly help to attract women with school age children into employment, as they will not have to arrange childcare cover during the school holidays.

Annual hours – in an annual hours scheme the period of time which employees must work is defined over a whole year. For example an average of a 37.5 hours per week becomes 1702.5 hours allowing for five weeks of holiday entitlement and 1.6 weeks of bank holidays. Annual hours schemes can be particularly suitable in industries where the workload is seasonal or spasmodic so that staffing levels can be high during periods of intense activity but reduced when demand drops. Often such schemes are administered by drawing up rotas, which cover the whole year.

Job sharing – this is an arrangement between two (or more) permanent employees to share the responsibilities, pay, holidays and benefits of a job according to the number of hours worked. It has become an accepted way of introducing part-time working into jobs, which have only been available on a full-time basis in the past. Many benefits arise from this arrangement. For example, employers find that the sharers bring two sets of skills to a job and during periods of illness or holidays part of the work continues to be done. Employees benefit from working at a more senior or skilled level on a part-time basis. Job sharers with children sometimes choose to share childcare arrangements with one carer, although this obviously depends on circumstances, needs and availability.

Part-time working – a part-time worker is defined as someone who works for less than 30 hours per week. Part-time staff can provide the employer with flexibility, e.g. having some staff work only during peak hours. For the employee, working part-time can reduce the need for childcare or give time to pursue other interests.

Part-time working has been associated with low pay, poor benefits and poor contractual rights, but this position is changing and more part-time options are becoming available at more senior and managerial levels.

Working from home – in some sectors employers can arrange for employees to work from home for all or part of their working day. Obviously the feasibility of this option depends upon the nature of the work being undertaken. With the rapid development of communications technology many tasks can now be performed remotely. Employees can communicate with their workplace and clients via fax, e-mail and videoconference. Working from home can also give employees greater flexibility to organise the pattern of their working day.

Sabbaticals – are periods of time off work in addition to annual leave. Generally a sabbatical is given as a reward for long service and the employee can choose to spend it as they wish. Increasingly this arrangement is being considered as a way to deal with employee stress as the consequences of over-stressed employees can be very expensive for employers.

Carer or special leave arrangements – many employers recognise that special leave arrangements assist employees when unexpected circumstances require them to take time off work. Some employers also allow time off by arrangement for particular responsibilities such as hospital visits/health checks for dependents or school/nursery events. Cover/special leave systems usually involve entitlement to a specific amount of days per year. For carers, special leave arrangements are crucial if dependents become ill, childcare arrangements break down, or school/nursery closures occur. Carer/special leave arrangements offer reassurance to employees and can be monitored effectively by employers.

3 Corporate governance and business ethics

3.1 Why is good corporate governance so important?

We introduced the key issues of corporate governance in Chapter 5. Corporate governance enables organisations to achieve their goals by providing appropriate:

- management structures – to ensure the proper functioning of executive groups and committees (e.g. Boards);
- management environment – including effective strategic planning and decision making mechanisms, clear accountability channels and meaningful monitoring of management performance;
- risk management procedures – integrated with the strategic planning and conformance and compliance processes;
- conformance and compliance processes – including control systems such as internal audit and quality assurance, organisational values and ethics, and integrated with risk management;
- performance monitoring – through timely, relevant and accurate indicators of performance that are used internally and by key stakeholders; and
- accountability to stakeholders – such as parliament, shareholders and community groups, through all of the above elements.

Pressure for good corporate governance is increasing because:

- recent failures of major organisations have shown up weaknesses;
- overwhelming legislative and information requirements demand robust corporate governance responses and safeguards;
- responsibilities of CEOs have never been greater;
- greater scrutiny is undertaken by many parties;
- complexity and pace of change in organisations demand it; and
- more rapid turnover of management and staff demand corporate responses to knowledge and skill retention and transfer.

3.2 Business ethics

Ethics refers to a code of conduct or behaviour that a society, a group or professional body, or an individual considers correct.

Donaldson, in *Key issues in Business Ethics*, describes business ethics as 'the systematic study of moral matters pertaining to business, industry or related activities, institutions or practices and beliefs'.

DEFINITION

Business ethics can be described as 'the systematic study of moral matters pertaining to business, industry or related activities, institutions or practices and beliefs'.

As discussed in Chapter 4, business ethics is concerned with the expectations of society, fair competition, advertising, social responsibilities and corporate behaviour (at home, as well as abroad), and with how organisations ought to relate to their external stakeholders and the community as a whole (corporate social responsibility).

Activity 2

To recap, see if you can recall the three **levels** at which ethical issues may affect business activity (see Chapter 4).

Feedback to this activity is at the end of the chapter.

Managers face ethical issues all the time. Examples are:

- dealing with direct and indirect demands for (or offers of) bribes, often in cultural contexts where these are ambiguous;
- compliance with legislative standards in relation to safety, wages, product description, etc;
- marketing policies – should they avoid manufacturing products detrimental to health, e.g. cigarettes, weapons?
- policies that imply social costs, e.g. pollution of rivers;
- whether or not to export to particular countries.

The **source** of management's ethical obligations include:

KEY POINT

Sources of ethical obligations:

- the law
- government regulations
- ethical codes
- social pressures.

- **The law** – this defines the minimum ethical standards in a given area of practice. For example, deceptive advertising is illegal and violators of this law are liable to large fines, court action and/or loss of goodwill. Some unethical behaviour is often not considered very illegal, such as head hunting employees from other companies, padding expense accounts etc.
- **Government regulations** – these are also fairly clear-cut outlining what is acceptable and what is not. These regulations set standards on issues such as unfair competition, unsafe products, etc. Failure to comply with these regulations could lead to criminal charges, or fines etc. Unfortunately, there are times when these regulations do not force ethical behaviour. In the U.S. cyclamates (artificial sweeteners) were banned because there was evidence that they were carcinogenic. Following the ban a major food manufacturer sold 300,000 cases of cyclamate sweetened food overseas. Similarly many banned food additives and pesticides etc are being sold overseas, mainly to third world countries.
- **Industry and company ethical codes** – are codes that clearly state the ethical standard a manager should follow within his or her organisation. These standard practices are usually followed if they are written down and the rules enforced. However many companies have 'unwritten' codes of practice or if written down, have no method of enforcing these rules. Generally, written codes clarify the ethical issues but leave the resolution to the individual's conscience.
- **Social pressures** for corporate social responsibility.

3.3 Managing ethics

Paine *(Managing for Organizational Integrity)* suggests that organisations should adopt one of two approaches to managing ethics.

- A **compliance-based approach** is designed to ensure that the organisation acts with regard for and compliance with the relevant law. Any violations are prevented, detected and punished.
- An **integrity-based approach** emphasises managerial responsibility for ethical behaviour, as well as a concern for the law. Ethics is an issue of organisational culture and systems. The task of ethics management is to:
  - create an environment that supports ethically sound behaviour;
  - define and give life to an organisation's values; and
  - instil a sense of shared accountability amongst members of the organisation.

Many successful organisations proactively use an ethical and socially responsible stance as a means of strategically differentiating from competitors to achieve competitive advantage.

A committed top management may:

- *establish corporate ethical codes* which, amongst other things, involve identifying required conduct in specific circumstances; training key personnel in ethical decision making; establishing channels of communication for reviewing ethical dilemmas; and appointing independent non-executive directors to bring independence to matters of conduct;
- *establish environmental strategies* which can highlight waste, inefficiency, recycling opportunities and the minimisation of potential environment-related liabilities;
- *analyse and assess current activities* in terms of product portfolio; packaging and distribution of raw materials and waste; process technology; energy efficiency; recycling; and potential threats of accidents;
- *identify impacts of activities on the environment* and establish policies to address issues raised after reviewing legislation, industry guidelines and competitor practice;
- *integrate into the corporate management system* the setting and implementation of ethical and social responsibility policies.

Key areas covered by an ethics programme or **ethical code** include:

- **The purpose and values of the organisation** – the service that is being provided, financial objectives and the business's role in society.
- **Employees** – how the organisation values employees and its policies on: use of company assets, working conditions, recruitment, development and training, rewards, health, safety and security, equal opportunities, retirement, redundancy, discrimination and harassment.
- **Customer relations** – the importance of customer satisfaction and good faith in all agreements, quality, fair pricing and after-sales service.
- **Shareholders or other providers of money** – the protection of investment made in the organisation and proper 'return' on money lent. Also a commitment to accurate and timely communication on achievements and prospects.
- **Suppliers** – prompt settling of bills, co-operation to achieve quality and efficiency and no bribery or excess hospitality accepted or given.
- **Society or the wider community** – compliance with the spirit of laws as well as the letter, the company's obligations to protect and preserve the environment, the involvement of the company and its staff in local affairs and the corporate policy on giving to education and charities.
- **Implementation** – the process by which the code is issued and used, the means to obtain advice, code review procedures and training programme.

3.4 Benefits of managing ethics in the workplace

Many people are used to reading or hearing of the moral benefits of attention to business ethics. However, there are other types of benefits, as well. The following list describes various types of benefits from managing ethics in the workplace.

Consideration of business ethics has substantially improved society. A matter of decades ago, children in the UK worked 16-hour days. Workers' limbs were torn off and disabled workers were condemned to poverty and often to starvation. Trusts controlled some markets to the extent that prices were fixed and small businesses choked out. Price fixing crippled normal market forces. Employees were sacked based on personalities. Influence was applied through intimidation and harassment. Then society reacted and demanded that businesses place high value on fairness and equal rights. Government agencies were established. Unions were organised. Laws and regulations were established.

Ethics programmes cultivate strong teamwork and productivity. They align employee behaviour with top priority ethical values preferred by leaders of the organisation. Usually, an organisation finds surprising disparity between its preferred values and the values actually reflected by behaviour in the workplace.

Ongoing attention and dialogue regarding values in the workplace builds openness, integrity and community – critical ingredients of strong teams in the workplace. Employees feel strong alignment between their values and those of the organisation. They react with strong motivation and performance.

Ethics programmes help ensure that policies are legal. It is far better to incur the cost of mechanisms to ensure ethical practices now than to incur costs of litigation later. A major intent of well-designed personnel policies is to ensure ethical treatment of employees, e.g., in matters of hiring, evaluating, disciplining, firing, etc.

Ethics programmes promote a strong public image. Attention to ethics is also good for public relations – admittedly, managing ethics should not be done primarily for reasons of public relations. But the fact that an organisation regularly gives attention to its ethics can portray a strong positive impression to the public. People see those organisations as valuing people more than profit, as striving to operate with the utmost of integrity. Aligning behaviour with values is critical to effective marketing and public relations programmes.

3.5 Ethical questions

There is often a tension between personal standards and the goals of the organisation – we can refer back to the example involving the sale of banned substances overseas. It is not illegal, but it may be against your personal values to sell these products to unsuspecting overseas clients. What would you do if this action were a direct order from a superior? Does this take away your responsibility? As with many ethical problems there are no easy answers.

According to Kenneth Blanchard and Norman Vincent Peale *(The Power of Ethical Management)*, there are three questions you should ask yourself whenever you are faced with an ethical dilemma.

- Is it legal? In other words, will you be violating any criminal laws, civil laws or company policies by engaging in this activity?
- Is it balanced? Is it fair to all parties concerned both in the short-term as well as the long-term? Is this a win-win situation for those directly as well as indirectly involved?
- Is it right? Most of us know the difference between right and wrong, but when push comes to shove, how does this decision make you feel about yourself? Are you proud of yourself for making this decision? Would you like others to know you made the decision you did?

Summary

- An employment contract contains both express and implied terms regulating the relationship between employer and employee.
- An employer has a duty to maintain a safe and healthy workplace.
- UK legislation aims to promote equal opportunities and eliminate unfair discrimination.
- Many employers attempt to enhance their employees' quality of life by offering a range of options on flexible working.
- The importance of good corporate governance has become apparent from recent corporate failures.
- An organisation's ethical obligations are increasingly seen as important. Individual organisations may adopt a compliance-based approach or an integrity-based approach.

Having completed your study of this chapter you should have achieved the following learning outcome.

- Explain the importance of business ethics and corporate governance to the organisation and its stakeholders.

Self-test questions

1 What terms are implied in the contract of employment? (1.2)

2 When can the employer's responsibility be extended beyond its own employees? (1.3)

3 Does the Equal Pay Act just cover pay? (2.1)

4 When employing staff, in what areas can employers discriminate? (2.2)

5 How would you describe flexi-time? (2.4)

6 What are business ethics concerned with? (3.2)

7 What does an integrity-based approach to ethics emphasise? (3.3)

Multiple-choice question

Question 1

Which of the following does not relate to equal opportunities and discrimination?

A The Sex Discrimination Act

B The Health and Safety at Work Act

C The Disabled Persons (Employment) Acts

D The Rehabilitation of Offenders Act

For the answer to this question, see the 'Answers' section at the end of the book.

Exam-type questions

Question 1: Legal framework

You are the newly appointed Chief Accountant of the subsidiary of a publicly quoted company. You have just had a meeting with John Harrison, the senior Management Accountant, about a problem in his department. Your notes from that meeting are set out below.

Notes

Eileen Skinner joined the Accounts Department 4 years ago from Watt and Armitage, a local firm of accountants. She had already passed the final examinations of the Association of Accounting Technicians and came with excellent references. Her performance until recently has been good. She has scored well in every annual review, never getting an overall performance rating of less than 7 out of 10, and has been viewed as a strong candidate for promotion to a higher grade.

In recent weeks the quality of her work has deteriorated and she has taken to arriving late and leaving early. She has also begun to take days off, sometimes without offering a proper explanation. Her immediate superior has tolerated the situation because of Eileen's past record. However, other members of staff are beginning to complain that Eileen is not pulling her weight and, as one colleague put it, 'if she can get away with it, why can't we?'

John doesn't want Eileen Skinner to be dismissed but he can see no other way out if morale in the department is to be maintained. The parent company has a policy of being a ' good' employer and of meeting its legal obligations in full. Prepare a Memorandum for John Harrison setting out your proposals for dealing with the problem.

Required:

(a) Set out the legal framework covering the situation. **(15 marks)**

(b) What procedure would you follow if Eileen were to be disciplined or dismissed? **(10 marks)**

(Total: 25 marks)

Question 2: Food is Us

The supermarket chain 'Food is Us' has decided to tackle prejudice and discrimination in all its stores by establishing a policy applicable to all its stores. As part of this, it is challenging all employees, especially managers, to examine their attitudes towards people of a different race, sex and ability.

The reasons for introducing the policy are threefold. Plainly there is legislation on discrimination which must be complied with if the company is to avoid the risk of legal action against it. Also, from a marketing point of view, 'Food is Us' wish to be identified with its customer base by reflecting the racial diversity of the environments in which it operates. Most positively, the company wants to develop a workforce which can reflect sufficient diversity not only to avoid risk and to maintain its current market position, but also produce the initiatives which will develop the company in a successful and sustained manner.

During the course of the coming year, all store employees will be expected to attend an awareness-raising training programme. This programme is intended to help employees explore their own attitudes and highlight any prejudices that these employees might have.

The personnel director, Anne Healey, told shop operatives 'we want to make all our front line employees who deal closely with the members of the public aware of any subconscious prejudices that they might have.'

'It is very difficult to quantify the benefits of such specialist training, but it is one of our corporate principles that all people are treated fairly by employees, whether they are customers or work colleagues,' she added.

Initially small groups of employees will attend sessions to raise awareness. These sessions, to be held in-store, will take place during time already set aside for staff training and development.

The new policy is to be an extension of 'Food is Us' current equal opportunities scheme for managers. So far more than 1,500 managers have attended one day awareness-raising courses over the past 18 months.

The same course is to be revised and updated following feedback from previous participants and will also be extended to include senior executives for the first time.

Required:

With reference to the above scenario:

(a) Equal opportunities encompass many features. For 'Food is Us'. What would be the main features of a sex discrimination policy? **(10 marks)**

(b) Why should an organisation like 'Food is Us' have an equal pay policy? **(5 marks)**

(c) What is the difference between an equal opportunities policy and a managing diversity initiative within an organisation? **(10 marks)**

(Total: 25 marks)

For the answer to these questions, see the 'Answers' section at the end of the book.

Feedback to activities

Activity 1

From the employer's point of view, an organisation's workforce is representative when it reflects or exceeds the demographic composition of the external workforce. A representative workforce reflects or exceeds the current proportions of women, visible minorities and persons with disabilities in each occupation as are known to be available in the external workforce and from which the employer may reasonably be expected to draw from.

A representative workforce is a good indication that an employer is not limiting access to the skills and talents of workers by discriminating on the basis of sex, race, colour or disability. A non-representative workforce signals the need for evaluation and action, so that whatever is blocking or discouraging certain groups from employment and advancement may be corrected.

Activity 2

Ethical issues may apply:

1. At the **macro** level: the role of business in the national and international organisation of society.
2. At the **corporate** level: the ethical issues facing individual corporate entities. (This is often identified with Corporate Social Responsibility.)
3. At the **individual** level: the ethical issues facing individuals within organisations.

Chapter 15

ANSWERS TO MULTIPLE-CHOICE AND EXAM-TYPE QUESTIONS

Chapter 1

Multiple-choice questions

Question 1

The element most unlikely to be included is: B Profits – return on investment.

Question 2

C Employees are not connected stakeholders.

Exam-type questions

Question 1: Stakeholder groups

It is important that relationships are developed and maintained with each of these following main stakeholder groups:

- **Internal stakeholders** – the employees and managers of the hotel are the main link with the guests. The service they provide is vital to the hotel's value chain. The quality of the guest's experience at the hotel will be determined by their attitude and approach. They must perform with competence and efficiency without disturbing the enjoyment of the customers.

  The managers concerned should ensure that employees achieve the highest levels of service, are well trained and committed. This means that they must be prepared to support the staff and create an environment in which they feel valued.

- **Connected stakeholders** (shareholders, guests and suppliers) – the shareholders of the hotel will be concerned with a steady flow of income (e.g. dividends), possible capital growth and continuation of the business. It is important that relationships are developed and maintained, especially with those operating on behalf of institutions, to ensure their continued commitment and loyalty. The management must try to achieve improvements in the return on their investment by ensuring that customers are satisfied and willing to return.

  The hotel must also maintain good relationships with its guests because they provide the income to the hotel. Each guest will seek good service and satisfaction, although there will be differences in the services required e.g. some looking for relaxation and others wanting business services and conference facilities. Management must analyse the customer database regularly to make sure that all customer needs are being met.

Suppliers must be selected very carefully as they are an essential element in the hotel's value chain – providing goods and services such as food and laundry, which play an essential part in ensuring the satisfaction of the guests. They are generally concerned with being paid promptly for goods and services delivered and maintaining good relationships will ensure their continued support of the hotel.

- **External stakeholders** (the government and local regulatory authority) – the management of the hotel must maintain close relationships with this group and ensure that they comply with legislation and regulations relating to the health and safety of guests, staff and other members of the public. Failure to do so may give the local regulatory authority the power to close the hotel down.

Question 2: Synfib and Thetfib

The mission statement should set out the organisation's reasons for existence and provide a general sense of purpose to management and staff. It may also contain core corporate values that can act as a filtering mechanism in the setting of objectives and the design, evaluation and selection of strategy.

As well as indicating the sector focus of the organisation, the mission statement should outline the positioning of the business with regard to quality, service, price etc., and reflect the specific role it will fulfil within society over the long term.

C's mission statement should convey its purpose, social policy, spread of operations and position in the market. Unfortunately, its only features are 'highest quality' and 'reasonable price'. These relative adjectives should be placed in a context where the method of assessment is incontrovertible. They are both vague and stakeholders would find them confusing, especially as price and quality are conflicting ways of competing and often mutually exclusive. If it came to a choice of strategies, which of the two - the price or the quality - would be a critical factor?

The objectives should interpret the mission statement into measures of performance to be achieved and time frames to achieve them. For C this means that their stated objectives need to be augmented:

- The demands of the shareholders – could be defined in terms of achieving at least a certain percentage annual compounded increase in per share earnings, along with continuing attention to margin improvement and increase or maintenance of market share.
- Specific targets for pollution control should be set for both Home and Foreign.
- Methods to maintain secure employment should be defined, although this may be difficult with the current threat of transferring production to Foreign.
- Quality that satisfies customer requirements should be specified in terms of tolerances or pre-set standards.
- Wealth maximisation needs to be clearly defined in terms of cash returns from the present value of future cash flows being manifested in dividend payments and capital growth.

- Keeping shareholders' exposure to financial risk to a minimum – limits to risk should be defined and imposed. There should also be some reconciliation between risk and wealth maximisation.

Failure to establish a coherent framework of objectives for all parts of the organisation, and at all management levels, can lead to a lack of goal congruence and the taking of damaging, sub-optimal decisions.

Chapter 2

Multiple-choice questions

Question 1

The following comment is not a criticism of the rational model:

B The approach does not try to identify and review all the potential strategies available to the organisation

Question 2

One of the characteristics of a rational model is:

B Managers make present risk-taking decisions with the greatest knowledge of their futurity.

Question 3

D A system that does not communicate with its environment is not an open system

Question 4

The type of strategy that calls for being the low cost producer in an industry for a given level of quality is: A – cost leadership.

Exam-type questions

Question 1: Tub plc

(a) Johnson and Scholes in their influential text *Exploring Corporate Strategy* distinguish between three levels of strategy formulation: corporate strategy, business strategy and functional strategy. The relationship between them, as described by Johnson and Scholes, is as follows.

- *Corporate strategy* is concerned with what business or businesses the organisation is involved in or should be involved in, and the extent to which these businesses should be integrated with each other. Different businesses may well be conducted through separate *strategic business units* or SBUs, perhaps divisions or subsidiaries of the parent organisation. This appears to be the case with Tub plc.

- *Business strategy* determines how each business should attempt to achieve its mission within its chosen area of activity. Where the organisation operates through strategic business units there will be a separate business strategy for each SBU, framed within the context of the overall corporate strategy.

- *Functional strategy* determines how an individual function, such as marketing, finance or purchasing, can best support the corporate and business strategies.

As an example of the relationship, imagine that Tub plc's overall corporate strategy includes a commitment to quality. A manufacturing division of the organisation might incorporate this objective into its *business strategy* by focusing on a concept of no defects. The purchasing function might decide that this objective can only be attained by means of close 'partnership' relations with a small number of carefully selected suppliers. Thus the *functional strategy* adopted by purchasing might depend on a move away from adversarial management of supplier relations.

The strategic process is often depicted as a hierarchy of objectives. At the top of the hierarchy is the mission statement of the organisation. A statement of corporate mission is inextricably linked with the organisation's goals and objectives. Before setting about the preparation of a strategic plan the management of Tub plc should consider the mission of the organisation. This will provide all managers involved in the decision making process within the organisation with a clear indication as to what constitutes the raison d'etre of the organisation.

The existence of a mission statement should assist those responsible for the formulation of strategic plans since it will focus upon critical issues which will help to ensure that strategic plans are prepared in accordance with desired norms within the organisation. It is also important that strategy formulation is preceded by full investigation of Tub's strengths, weaknesses, opportunities and threats, including the challenge of competitors (perhaps using Porter's five forces analysis).

(b) In a large company such as Tub plc it can happen that the sheer magnitude of the separate product-market involvements is such that the traditional central strategic planning system becomes unmanageable. It may be extremely difficult for strategic planners to conceptualise the total and to plan, co-ordinate and integrate the range of diversity into coherent strategies. Tub plc has addressed this problem by creating eight operating companies.

The typical characteristics of each operating company in Tub plc will be as follows:

- It operates in one market segment or a number of related market segments.
- It has a product portfolio related to that market segment or segments.
- It is semi-autonomous and managed by its own board, who are accountable for implementing agreed strategies developed to achieve targets.
- Its targets and strategies are set by the corporate board of directors with the full participation of the individual board.
- Its targets and strategies are sufficiently broad for the individual board to make independent decisions relating to product-market moves and changes.

The operating companies also serve as a means of meshing the corporate (macro) perspective with local (micro) priorities, thus achieving meaningful vertical management teamwork. The three levels of planning link together as follows:

- The strategic task at corporate level is to develop a balanced product-market portfolio, which will achieve the objectives of the company and satisfy the values and expectations of its stakeholders.
- The strategic task at the operating company level is to achieve total customer responsiveness, succeed against competitors and operate within the broad guidelines and goal parameters established by corporate strategy.
- The task at functional level is to implement the strategies decided on at the operating company level.

At the operating company level it is important that business strategy links in well with overall corporate strategy.

(c) In practice, the neat division between three levels of strategy is obscured by a good deal of overlapping. Additionally, it is not safe to assume, as this analysis implies, that corporate strategy is determined first, then business strategy, and finally functional strategy. This is because influences travel in the other direction as well. For example, a purchasing function might pioneer new approaches to supplier relations, which open up the possibility of total quality management at the corporate level; this is a case of functional strategy helping to determine corporate strategy rather than the reverse.

The discussion above covers general issues relating to the percolation of strategy down from corporate level, through the business level and eventually to functions. This might give the impression that strategy formulation is a 'top-down' process, and in some organisations this is certainly the case. However, it is also possible to see strategy as an iterative process in which initiatives developed at top level must be brought into line with strategies applying at functional levels and vice versa.

Question 2: Cuddles Limited

(a) Some of the general environmental forces that may impact on Cuddles Limited over the next few years can be considered under the headings of political, economic, social and technological factors (known as PEST analysis).

Political

The UK is becoming more closely integrated with the rest of Europe. European Community legislation has a strong influence on UK companies, for example, legislation and regulations relating to working conditions for employees and consumer rights for customers. These are constantly changing.

Economic

The UK presently enjoys a strong economy, with stable and low rates of interest, inflation and unemployment. This has made the pound sterling very strong in relation to other currencies.

Cuddles may find that its customers find it much cheaper to import its products rather than manufacture them. The strong pound will also make it very difficult to export its garments.

Social

The demographic trends are that generally UK's population is ageing and the birth rate is declining in spite of government efforts to encourage marriage, "the family" and having children.

Fashions are changing more rapidly and there is a growing need for fashionable clothes for children by their parents.

This will affect the demand for Cuddles' garments.

Technological

The technology of garment manufacture, particularly computer aided design and manufacture (CAD-CAM) as well as production methods are constantly changing.

Unless Cuddles keeps abreast of the changes and has a programme of updating the technologies it uses, it will fall behind its competitors.

These are just a few of the factors influencing Cuddles' strategic and operational position now and in the future that Richard has to take into account in achieving his ambitions.

(b) The competitive forces that are likely to impact on Cuddles Limited as a small player in the children's garment industry can be considered under the five forces categorised by Michael Porter.

Threats from potential entrants

There would be very few barriers to entry for another competitor entering the market to compete against Cuddles. The barriers to entry as a major player are significant as the established large manufacturers have established strong brands and major investments in modern technologies and distribution channels.

The major threat of entry is from overseas, particularly suppliers from the Far East on a low price approach.

Threats from substitutes

There are likely to be many alternative substitute fashions for Cuddles' garments. In the absence of developing a strong brand image, Cuddles will face severe competition and from alternative firms who have their own designs supported by strong brands. This will lower the price Cuddles can charge for its products.

Threats from the power of buyers

The retail outlets have many domestic and foreign suppliers they can buy from and with the large quantities they buy, Cuddles' margins will be squeezed.

Cuddles will be in a relatively weak position with buyers compared to rivals who have more fashionable garments supported by strong brand image.

Threats from the power of suppliers

Cuddles, as a small firm, is unlikely to be buying significant raw materials and services from suppliers relative to larger competitors. It is unlikely to be in a position of demanding lower prices, as it will not have the scale of operations to enjoy such economies.

Rivalry and competition

Although Cuddles has decided to concentrate on garments for babies and infants, the market it is operating in is large and is dominated by several large firms. Cuddles is a very small player in this market.

The manufacturing industry for children's clothing is extremely competitive and the competition is intensified by the global nature of the market. Cuddles will be facing intense competition from both local and overseas firms.

The larger firms are often vertically integrated having their own retail outlets and their own manufacturing base.

Cuddles will find it difficult to compete with its limited resources to, for example, fight price reductions, introduce matching or better technologies or to market its products and develop a brand.

Overall, taking into account all five forces, Cuddles' position is weak relative to its competitors and its ambitions to grow will increase the intensity of competition and reduce or eliminate profitability.

(c) Michael Porter provides a range of strategic options that Cuddles can choose from in deciding how to compete in its market in order to grow and sustain competitive advantage.

Cuddles can choose from three generic strategies categorised as:

- cost leadership;
- differentiation;
- focus.

Cost leadership can be pursued through improved efficiency, low unit cost production, increased automation and generally achieving economies of scale. This approach would not be advisable for a small firm with limited resources such as Cuddles. It is an approach more suitable for the dominant firms in the market.

Differentiation would involve Cuddles in developing unique fashions, a strong brand based on quality with value and generally providing a distinctive service relative to its competitors. This is probably a better approach for a firm like Cuddles that does not have the resources to achieve economies of scale. Developing a strong brand image based on quality will give Cuddles sustainable competitive advantage.

Focus relates to specialising in a segment of the market. The specialisation can be based on product features, customer type, quality or geographical location, etc. Cuddles may be suited to a strategy of differentiation based on quality to focus on supplying a dedicated large customer, say a leading high street clothing retail chain.

This would give it a strong base for further growth at the risk of having a limited customer base.

Chapter 3

Multiple-choice question

Question 1

The odd one out is: C The number of employees at each level.

The chart only shows positions within the organisation and not the names, salaries or numbers of employees at each level.

Exam-type questions

Question 1: Resources and transactions

(a) One of the choices that businesses face is whether to carry out a process itself or whether to buy in the results of that process. The view taken by some writers is that the choice between carrying out a process in house and buying lies in the balance of the costs of production and those associated with transactions. A major consideration concerns the specificity of the assets involved. If the assets needed are very specific then it is unlikely that any organisation will wish to supply so the process must be conducted in-house.

Transaction costs arise from the effort that must be put into specifying what is required and subsequently co-ordinating delivery and monitoring quality. If the product or service is a standard design, then specification will be straightforward and the transaction costs will be low. But unfortunately, with sophisticated products and services there needs to be a great deal of negotiation between the organisation and its supplier.

The cost of supplies is not the same as the supplier is paid - there can be many additional costs. These include supplier selection, communications, drafting legal contracts, invoicing, delays and monitoring supply and quality.

Resource-based views of competitive advantage take the view that assets that cannot be easily imitated by other firms can act as a defence. Tangible resources, such as machines and buildings, as well as intangible resources such as scientific knowledge and budgetary systems, interact with members of the organisation to produce what anthropologists call 'material culture'. It is an understanding of the value activities undertaken in designing, producing, marketing, delivering and supporting its products and the linkages between them, which is crucial when assessing strategic capability.

Asset specificity refers to the relative lack of transferability of assets intended for use in a given transaction to other uses.

1 **Site specificity** – assets that are built in the same geographical proximity to increase efficiency, facilitate exchange and/or reduce costs e.g. transportation costs.

2 **Physical asset specificity** – physical characteristics specifically tailored to the transaction e.g. specialised machinery customised for one particular customer or transaction.

3 **Human asset specificity** – specific human capital comprised of firm-specific knowledge, skills, training or technical expertise. This asset has more value within the existing employment relationship than it has on the open market.

4 **Dedicated asset specificity** – investment in plant and/or equipment as a direct result of the needs of a particular buyer. It is customised for one particular customer or transaction.

5 **Brand name capital specificity** – consumers infer product quality from brand names e.g. franchise relationships take advantage of umbrella branding

6 **Temporal specificity** arises when the timing of performance and its effect on product value is critical. For example, temporal specificities may arise because a producer of a perishable product has difficulties finding alternative processors at short notice.

(b) Transaction cost theory helps us to understand how markets and hierarchies are chosen. There are two basic mechanisms for co-ordinating the flow of materials and services through the value chain: markets and hierarchies. Williamson classifies transactions into those that support co-ordination between multiple buyers and sellers - market transactions, and those supporting co-ordination within the organisation - hierarchy transactions.

The price a product is sold for consists of three elements:

1 **Production costs** – the primary processes necessary to create and distribute the goods or services being produced.

2 **Co-ordination costs** – the transaction costs of all the information processing necessary to co-ordinate the work of people and machines that perform the primary processes.

3 **Profit margin**

Most organisations will choose transactions that economise on co-ordination costs. As IT continues its rapid cost performance improvement, organisations will continue to find incentives to co-ordinate their activities electronically. Electronic developments have led to a greater awareness of choice and outsourcing. Using interconnected networks and easily accessible databases, economic theory predicts that a proportional shift of economic activity from single-source sales channels to electronic markets is likely to occur. Infomediaries can focus on particular product/service supply issues and by doing so they attract buyers and sellers. This allows them to acquire more expertise, which generates customer loyalty and participation. Electronic single-source channels will evolve from separate databases within the firm, to linked databases between firms (Electronic Data Interchange), to shared databases between firms.

The analysis of transactions cost has influenced the increase in the number of network organisations because it encourages organisations to investigate their supply costs and look at how well they meet their shareholder requirements. This has led them to take note of market forces in delivering their product or service in a cheaper manner, which may be facilitated by networks of contracts, both internal and external.

Question 2: Gensup plc

(a) The types of structure that might be appropriate include:

- functional;
- product;
- matrix.

With a functional structure, activities are grouped according to function. Typically this type of firm will have departments reflecting these functions – production, HR, IT, marketing, etc.

Elements of functional structure are already evident both in Unisal (e.g. the sales function) and in A, B and C (e.g. maintenance, purchasing, quality control and R&D).

With a product structure activities are grouped around each product type or line. Typically this type of firm will set up divisions (or even subsidiaries) to manage each product grouping. For example, a vehicle manufacturer may have a small cars division, a 4×4 division, etc. A key aspect of product-based structures is to decide which functions operate within each product division and which are centralised at head office. For example, each division may have its own production department but there is only one IT department for the whole firm, based at head office.

A product-based structure may well be an option in the group context to reflect the different outputs of the three manufacturing companies. This would need to be supported by specialised departments, such as corporate planning and finance, which apparently exist already.

Matrix structures attempt to reflect more than one emphasis simultaneously. IBM used to have a global matrix structure with three aspects of responsibility:

- There were functional heads, reflecting a global functional emphasis.
- There were product heads.
- There were also geographical heads.

A laptop salesman in the UK would thus report to three different bosses – head of laptops, head of sales and head of UK operations.

(b) *Functional structure*

The advantages usually claimed include stable hierarchies and expert staff. Career progression is well defined, and this is an aid to recruiting top quality personnel. This type of structure appears to have existed in A, B and C prior to the acquisition by Unisal.

The disadvantage is the compartmentalisation of activities, with possible problems in taking advantage of a wider perspective. Disagreements between different functions can be counter-productive and may stall development. There is a suggestion of this in the scenario, where high quality output by A, B and C was insufficient to enable them to capitalise on export opportunities.

Product structure

As the number of products produced by an organisation increases, functional design at all levels of the organisation may not be appropriate. In a multi-product organisation, such as Gensup has become, a product orientation may be used as a modification of the functional structure. Each major product or product line could be managed by a senior manager, who in turn reports to the chief executive or board member.

Each product manager is held accountable for the division's performance. Usually the product manager has control over most of the major functions that are involved with the product's production and sale. His responsibilities would include, for example:

- liaising with production management regarding processing/ production schedules;
- discussing pricing levels, sales and marketing budgets with the accounts function;
- working with R&D on new products and product changes.

The main attraction of divisionalisation by product is that by concentrating activities that relate to a product under one person, increased attention can be given to all phases of the product's manufacture and sales. Moreover, functional specialists working in a product environment can be more 'product oriented' in their thinking, rather than simply concerned with efficient performance of their own speciality. Problems concerning the product are likely to be given more attention by the division as a whole, regardless of the origin of the problem.

Matrix structure

The matrix structure may be appropriate where there are at least two significant criteria for success. For example, Gensup plc will be selling at least three different product lines (A, B and C) in at least two different markets (home and abroad). The management of each product range is equally important, as is the responsiveness to the needs of the different geographical areas. The product managers and area managers have equal weight.

Chapter 4

Multiple-choice question

Question 1

C – centralisation of control and decision-making is not a feature of virtual organisation. Decentralisation and worker empowerment are features of these structures, despite the co-ordinating possibilities of ICT networks.

Exam-type questions

Question 1: Classes of strategy

(a) (i) A company pursuing a growth strategy is aiming to expand earnings, probably through an increase in turnover and increased investment in the company. Variables which may be used to measure growth include return on capital employed, profit, sales, earnings per share, manpower.

A corrective strategy aims at correcting the balance of the company's operations so as to reduce risk and 'correcting' the organisation structure of the company in order to produce the most efficient operation.

A contingency strategy is designed to ensure that action can be taken quickly if an unexpected event occurs. It consists of saying 'if event E happens we shall take action A'. For instance, a company might have a contingency strategy that it could put into effect in the event that its demand forecasts turn out to be 20% wrong.

Selecting a growth strategy primarily concerns decisions about the firm's product-market posture. A corrective strategy also involves decisions about organisation and resources.

(ii) Growth may be achieved by market penetration, product or market development, or diversification. The first of these involves improvements to existing products and/or intensified marketing in order to sell more in the same markets; the other options involve developing new products or new markets or both. The firm pursuing a growth strategy should not, however, forget the importance of dropping some of its least profitable lines as well as developing new ones, especially if resources are scarce. Turnover might fall as a result of such divestment but earnings or return on capital employed can rise.

The same appreciation of the importance of the growth in profits rather than in turnover must guide the use of pricing policy as a means of pursuing a growth strategy. Cutting prices to increase sales might not be the right method.

A growth strategy will probably necessitate an active research department to develop new products, new markets, and new applications for existing products. It is possible, however, to buy know-how or to manufacture under licence in order to achieve internal growth. As an alternative to internal growth an acquisition or merger might be sought - either to strengthen the company's position in its own industry or to achieve diversification.

Firms which decide to diversify can often achieve rapid growth by taking advantage of the most profitable opportunities, although the risks increase the further away the firm moves from its original business.

A growing company can often take advantage of economies of scale or synergy to achieve higher return on capital.

(b) It is of course easy to criticise with hindsight, but it does appear that C Ltd has not been operating to a strategy. If they have it has been an inappropriate one. Nevertheless, one must recognise that recent years have been difficult for the automotive industry, which is very competitive. It is likely that whatever strategy a company adopted it might have been in difficulties.

Recent development of C Ltd

The overall drop in the number of customers was probably inevitable due to mergers in the industry and may itself pose no serious threat. Nevertheless, the dependence on a single customer is worrying as it makes

C Ltd very vulnerable to a change in its fortunes. Is the return it is getting sufficient compensation for the loss in flexibility?

The large number of products seems to suggest that while new product innovation has been good, there has been little attention to divestment. It would be interesting to see a breakdown of the returns from various products. Even if all are profitable the company would be able to increase its overall return on invested capital if it dropped the less profitable lines. Its objectives should probably be 'profit' or 'ROI' rather than simply 'market share' or 'turnover' – we are not told what its objectives actually are.

Future of C Ltd

First of all it is useful to summarise the strengths and weaknesses, opportunities and threats of C Ltd, as far as they can be deduced from the information given.

Strengths	**Weaknesses**
Good, innovative research and development dept. Well established company – good reputation.	Over-dependence on one customer. Cumbersome product range (needs pruning).
Opportunities	**Threats**
	Declining overall market. Peaks and troughs in trade.

It looks as though C Ltd needs to consider either new markets for components of a similar type or a product-market diversification. It should build on its strength in having (apparently) a good R&D department. A company cannot long continue to grow in a declining market even when it is increasing its market share. Nevertheless, it should enlarge that share as far as possible, by competitive pricing, trade advertising etc. We are not told whether the declining market is national or international but C Ltd could attempt to increase exports.

The company must discover in more detail **why** its sales have held up despite the declining market, and try and build on those strengths. It must examine the causes of failure amongst its competitors and try and avoid the same pitfalls.

The company appears to have a very good chance of survival in the short to medium term because it is so well established (though it should try to overcome its dependence on one customer) but whether it can survive as a worthwhile concern in the long term depends on its ability to find a new 'mission' for itself.

Question 2: Pharmaceutical companies

> ***Tutor's note***
>
> This question requires consideration of how a pharmaceutical company can satisfy what appear to be conflicting interests. Notice that there are really two requirements – a discussion on the ethical implications and comments on how the Directors reconcile the conflict.

Large pharmaceutical companies seem to be facing a conflict of interests between the long-term maximisation of shareholder wealth and their social responsibility – a term used to describe the duties an individual or an institution has towards the wider community or society.

The ethical environment refers to justice, respect for the law and a moral code. The conduct of an organisation, its management and employees will be measured against ethical standards by customers, suppliers and others with whom they deal. However, it could be argued that the ethics of doing business are not those of the wider society – taking advantage of a rival's mistake is perfectly fair in business, but not acceptable in, say, family life. Hence, adoption of some ethical principles would weaken a firm's competitive performance.

In most enterprises, managers have a duty to aim for profit. At the same time, modern ethical standards impose a duty to guard, preserve and enhance the value of the enterprise for the good of all touched by it, including the general public.

Many views have been expressed on the extent to which the pursuit of wealth maximisation is ethically acceptable. Some writers believe that business organisations have no social mandate to assert a moral code, or behave contrarily to their owner's best interests where this would conflict with some notion of ethical behaviour. Friedman argued that the search for profit is what motivates firms to respond to market needs, which in turn reflect the needs of society. He would argue that the pharmaceutical companies are maximising value to society by allocating resources in the most effective way to achieve the highest level of returns for the shareholders. Stenberg stressed that business organisations are distinguished from others in society by their pursuit of shareholder wealth. If businesses become involved in social responsibility concepts they are changing their role and invading the domain of charities, Governments, etc. She would argue that the pharmaceutical companies are carrying out their legitimate responsibility to maximise shareholder wealth.

Exam tips

You could concentrate more on the make-up of the stakeholders here and discuss how employees and suppliers might be more anxious about future employment. Pressure groups and Governments should also be mentioned because they play an important part in the pharmaceutical industry.

Stakeholders – people who have an interest in the organisation – believe that business success is a result of the organisation being a member of society. They would argue that business enjoys rights (such as the right to carry on its business interrupted), but in return the business has duties expected of it – the primary duty being to behave responsibly towards society as a whole. Organisational objectives are influenced and shaped by the stakeholders and pressure groups and they may set goals, which include constraints on profits, ecological considerations and staff welfare. The view of most stakeholders would imply that the Directors of the pharmaceutical companies should promote the research, development, manufacture and sale of medicines, which lead to elimination of diseases, even though this will ultimately affect their source of income.

There is also a political dimension to the issue – many people feel that medical and drug research should not be the responsibility of pharmaceutical companies. But if the only source of finance was the public sector, then this may stifle development due to lack of funds. Governments seem to welcome the new products that come on-stream and controls ensure that before drugs become available to the market, they must go through a rigorous testing process. We all benefit from profitable companies through taxation, which enables more investment in public amenities and infrastructure.

> ***Exam tips***
>
> There are more areas that could be discussed here, such as veterinary drugs, medicines in the third world and research into eradicating diseases of specific areas of the world. The whole area of genetics leaves plenty of scope for answers to differ.

How might the Directors reconcile conflicts between satisfying the demands of shareholders and discharging their social responsibilities? Because we are all susceptible to diseases but expect to live longer and stay healthy, it must be in everyone's interest that pharmaceutical companies develop improved medicines and work towards disease eradication. In the past, this process has led to many very profitable drugs/medicines being marketed, which has translated into enhanced shareholder value through higher sales volumes, meaning that we all win.

The new research into genetic code breaking is different because it focuses on what causes diseases to break out in the first place, rather than finding a cure for a condition that already exists. This could deny the shareholders of an end product to yield a profit unless research could identify ways to use the new information to prevent disease. Directors will probably feel that scientific breakthroughs will not affect the demand for existing products for a long time and will recognise their obligations to society and continue to invest in the development of products/services that contribute to the improvement in quality of life. This will hopefully improve their image, which will further enhance their sales.

Chapter 5

Multiple-choice question

Question 1

B Rewards and incentives

Exam-type question

Jetstreem

The term 'culture' is relevant to the organisation in two ways:

(a) It can be applied to the various societies and classes from which the company draws its management, its employees and those to whom it supplies its goods and or services.

(b) It can also be used to refer to the company's organisational structure. A simple level of culture is the particular way things are done in an organisation. The writer states that the culture of Jetstreem is different from that of his previous employer.

There are both static and dynamic aspects to culture: at any particular moment, culture refers to the total of the values, attitudes, beliefs, and norms or customs which are relatively common throughout a group, society or organisation; over a period of time, the culture is passed on from one generation or group to the next through social conditioning or socialisation. The writer notices that he is altering his behaviour to fit in with the new management culture. He suggests that Jetstreem values profit and is prepared to cut corners to achieve it. He implies that there is a culture clash between the culture of the delivery workers and the managerial culture.

Culture broadly refers to the distinctive way things are done (especially socially) in an organisation. For instance, in an organisation that values tradition, we would probably find that the culture could be traced back to the company's founders. For example, in the UK a number of firms can trace their company's culture back to their Quaker religious origins. Even though the founder may die the established values continue. The structure is often stable and hierarchical with precedent providing a strong argument for resisting change.

There are several key characteristics of organisational culture:

- **Beliefs and values** – beliefs are what is felt to be the case, which may not necessarily be true. Values are beliefs, which are relatively enduring and general. They are generally accepted as a guide to what behaviour is appropriate in the organisation. This is a standard of what is desirable and undesirable.

- **Norms or customs** are modes of behaviour, which are acceptable in particular circumstances. The importance and seriousness with which these norms are treated varies. The violation of a norm may be seen as mildly impolite or inappropriate to being a serious beach of behaviour, which must incur a grave sanction.

Organisational culture is:

- **Learned:** the process of socialisation passes on the culture to each new member.
- **Shared**: to be an element of culture the custom or belief must be common to a significant group of people.
- **Purposeful**: it offers order, direction and guidance in human problem solving and activity.
- **Dynamic**: culture must adapt and evolve otherwise it will die out or be discarded.

We can see examples of this in the culture of the delivery workers. There is a degree of common culture throughout the group. The writer states that when he joined the company he had a lot to learn. That included learning the group culture, which gives the writer information and guidance about how he should behave. As the writer admits in the last sentence, the culture of his group is not changing.

Culture as a concept is widely used by management both as an explanatory or analytical tool and also as something which needs to managed or changed to be appropriate, and is therefore a central element in the success or failure of the organisation.

Chapter 6

Multiple-choice questions

Question 1

The McKinsey 7S model has three hard and four soft Ss. The four soft ones are: D Staff, Skills, Style, and Shared Values.

Question 2

A traditional Appreciative Inquiry is based on the following four steps (the AI 4-D Cycle): C Discover, Dream, Design and Deliver.

Exam-type question

Project management

Memo

To: Jill Jackson

From: Jack Robinson

Date: January 200X

(a) Re: Distinguishing features of project management and likely management problems

There are several distinguishing features of project management, which are listed below.

- Clear aims – projects should have a specified duration, a beginning and an end. It is important for planning and control that they should have clearly defined purposes against which to measure progress, even if those purposes have to be clarified and redefined as the project progresses. Whilst a project may have a long duration, it is not an on-going and open-ended activity like 'business as usual'.
- The end result should conform to the proper specification i.e. the result should achieve what the project was supposed to do. A project generally has a detailed and defined set of objectives, including time and performance targets, which are more precise than 'business as usual' management.
- A project has a specific budget. Because it has a defined duration and purpose, its costs should and can be more specifically controlled than 'business as usual'.
- A project is geared to the introduction of change, whereas 'business as usual' management is geared to controlling operations in a stable environment.
- A project will have a hierarchy of detailed plans, unlike 'business as usual', which is an open-ended activity.
- A project will have a project team made up of experts in the disciplines required to complete the project. They are therefore likely to be drawn from various functions and various levels of the hierarchy (since relative status in the organisation may not be relevant).

(b) Project management is directed at an end. It is not directed at maintaining or improving a continuous activity. Because of this it has a limited objective within a limited time span. Most projects involve the projection of ideas and activities into a new challenge. No project can ever be exactly the same as anything which has gone before. The steps and tasks leading to completion can never be described accurately in advance. Therefore, the job of project management is to foresee as many dangers as possible, and to plan, organise and control activities so that they are avoided. There are therefore some special management problems.

- The work is carried out by a team of people usually assembled for one project, who must be able to communicate effectively and immediately with each other.
- There can be many novel expected problems, each one of which should be resolved by careful design and planning prior to commencement of work.
- There can be particular problems with a project working at the limits of existing and new technologies. There should be mechanisms within the project to enable these problems to be resolved during the time span of the project without detriment to the objective, the cost or the time span.
- There is normally no benefit until the work is finished. The 'lead in' time to this can cause a strain on the eventual recipient who feels deprived until the benefit is achieved (even though in many cases it is a major improvement on existing activities) and who is also faced with increasing expenditure for no immediate benefit.
- Contributions made by specialists are of differing importance at each stage. Assembling a team working towards the one objective is made difficult owing to the tendency of specialists to regard their contribution as always being more important than other people's and not understanding the inter-relationship between their various specialities in the context of the project.
- If the project involves several parties with different interests in the outcome, there might be disputes between them.

Chapter 7

Multiple-choice question

Question 1

The EST is established by: C working forwards from the start event, adding activity durations.

LFTs – latest finishing times – are established by a backward pass through the network: option A. Options B and D were pure red herrings.

Exam-type questions

Question 1: Drawing networks

There are both logical errors and departures from convention.

Logical errors

- two start events – 1 and 6
- dangling activities – H
- there is a loop joined by activities K, L, M and N.

Conventions broken

- event 7 precedes event 5
- activity J is drawn from right to left.

Question 2: Finding the critical path

Activity	Immediately preceding activity	Start event	End event	Duration (mins)
A	-	1	2	4
B	A	2	3	2
C	B	3	5	10
D	A	2	4	2
E	D	4	6	5
F	A	2	7	2
G	F	7	8	4
H	G	8	9	3
J	C	5	10	6
K	C, E	6	10	6
L	H	9	10	3
Dummy		5	6	

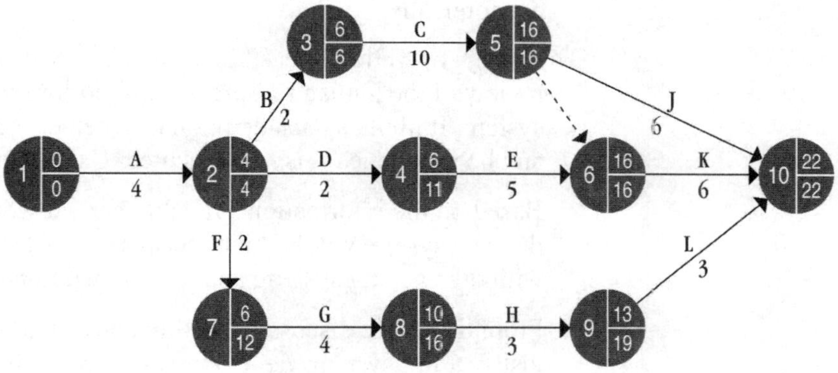

There are two critical paths – ABCJ and ABCK. The total duration is 22 hours.

Chapter 8

Multiple-choice questions

Question 1

The risk management planning process is: D Identify and classify risk, analyse risk, respond to risk and monitor risk.

Question 2

Configuration management is: A a means of monitoring and controlling emerging project scope against the scope baseline.

Exam-type question

Feasibility study

(a) Feasibility of a project is assessed in three main ways; operationally, technically and economically. A feasibility study is not a full-blown study; it gathers just sufficient information to enable management to make informed judgements on whether to proceed.

Technical feasibility relates to the adequacy of the existing technical resources, from the viewpoints of both equipment and technical expertise, to cope with the proposed system, or the ease with which those resources can be upgraded.

Technically, this project is feasible; the people in the system have the expertise, and the computer system can be updated to meet the new requirements.

Economic feasibility is the second aspect to be considered. Consideration is required here of the various costs that will be incurred in the development and operation of this system, and the monetary benefits that the system will bring to the organisation.

In this context, there is no pressing need for the new system, nor is there likely to be an immediate reduction in operating costs or efficiency. Depending on the final design, it is possible that some long-term benefits may be forthcoming, but they are intangible, and unlikely to justify the costs of systems development. The proposed system is therefore not economically feasible.

Finally, operational feasibility must be reviewed. This is dependent upon a review of the human resources required for the project and the new system. It implies consideration of whether the system will both operate and be used, once it is implemented. User attitudes are crucial here.

Based on the information available here, it would seem that resistance to the new system will be high, because users have expressed satisfaction with the existing system, and it is known to be operating satisfactorily.

From the above discussion, it is apparent that the new project does not justify a full systems development exercise. It is technically feasible but lacks economic and operational feasibility. That is not to say that a senior manager with 'a bee in his bonnet' might not succeed in pushing the proposal through regardless!

(b) The feasibility report should contain the following:

- introduction;
- terms of reference i.e. how the systems were selected for the study, and details about the scope of the study;
- existing system – i.e. a description of the system currently operating;
- system requirements i.e. derived from the existing system, and, for new requirements, from management, users and operators;
- proposed systems i.e. an outline logical system, including input and output definitions; highlighting the differences between old and new systems; identifying hardware, software and staff requirements;

- development plan – i.e. a suggested project plan, and how it will be implemented;
- costs and benefits i.e. detailed analysis of the costs that will be incurred in developing, installing and operating the system; and the monetary value of the various types of benefits that the new system will bring;
- alternatives considered i.e., identification of the various alternatives that have been considered, together with explanations of why they have been rejected in favour of the recommended approach;
- conclusions and recommendations;
- appendices.

(c) Given the decision to proceed, despite the adverse feasibility study report, then there are a number of techniques which the project team might utilise in order to gather detailed information. It is usual practice for staff involved in the earlier feasibility study to be members of the project team, as they will bring with them a nucleus of knowledge about the systems.

Analysts have to make a decision on two key issues:

(i) which of the many items of documentation associated with the system should be concentrated upon?

(ii) which people should analysts seek information from?

Information from documents

Analysts need to examine the 'hard data' contained in both quantitative and qualitative documents, i.e. reports, documents, financial statements, procedure manuals and memos. These provide information unavailable from any other fact-finding techniques. However, the analyst must always bear in mind such problems as accuracy, how up to date a document is, completeness, etc.

Interviewing

A major source of information about both existing and proposed system. The analyst listens for goals, feelings, opinions, and informal procedures, and attempts to sell the system and widen the knowledge of the interviewee.

Questions can be of two types: open, which leave all responses open to the interviewee; and closed, which limit the range of valid responses.

Interviews should be recorded, and reports written immediately afterwards to confirm what was said.

Questionnaires

These are useful if the people from whom the analyst needs to gather information are numerous and/or widely dispersed. They are most valuable when the information can be elicited by the use of simple, possibly multiple choice, questions.

The validity and reliability of the questionnaire is a problem of which analysts must be aware. Great care must be taken in their design, and they should be subjected to pilot test runs before being sent out.

Managers should have been consulted, agreed their use and made public their support for the technique in the particular context.

Observation

This technique provides analysts with an insight into what is actually done; they see at first-hand the relationships between the various types of users; they perceive the day-to-day activities which together make up the system, and may differ markedly from what documents or interviewees may reveal. It is essential that the analyst understand the nature of what he/she is observing.

The analyst can make use of event or time sampling, observe decision-making activities, and body language. There are various methods of recording observations, e.g. category systems, checklists, etc.

Prototyping

A useful information gathering approach, which may replace several stages in the traditional systems development life-cycle. It enables user reactions, suggestions, innovations and revision suggestions to be obtained, to improve the prototype, and system plans to be modified with minimum disruption and expense. It will require the use of a Fourth Generation Language with which to build this prototype.

A disadvantage of this approach is that managing the process is difficult because of the many iterations and the speed of the process. The user may pursue requests when the systems already fulfil the specified requirements. Sometimes an incomplete prototype may be pressed into service, and become regarded as the complete system.

Prototyping enables systems to be changed more easily during development; enables development to cease at an early stage if it becomes apparent that it is not progressing as required and will result in a system that more closely addresses the requirements of the user.

Chapter 9

Multiple-choice question

Question 1

The answer: B Executive assurance co-ordinator does not fit.

Exam-type questions

Question 1: Project management

Projects are special in that they have well-defined conclusions. A goal is to be achieved, and then the project will be over. The special management problems consequent on this, and possible solutions, are as follows.

Planning problems

If a project is to achieve a definite goal within a reasonable time and at a reasonable cost, the objective cannot be allowed to emerge over the course of the project: it must be clearly defined from the start. Thorough discussions are necessary to ensure that the objective is understood by the project manager. The manager must then communicate the objective to the team, so that everyone understands that they must not get diverted into work which will not help to achieve the objective.

Once the objective has been defined, the route to achieving it must be carefully planned. Techniques such as bar charts and networks can be helpful, but with a large project it may not be possible to foresee all the ways in which tasks will depend on each other. Unforeseen tasks may also arise, particularly if novel technology is being used. For example, a component may turn out not to perform as anticipated, so that time must be spent improving it, delaying the project as a whole. Reasonable margins of safety should be built into the planned duration and the budget, but there is then the problem of preventing team members from allowing planned work to fall behind schedule or run over budget because they know that slack has been allowed for.

Interface problems

A project team will normally work outside the client's management structure, and the client's managers may resent this. Tact in dealing with such managers is clearly necessary, and it is also helpful if the most senior management of the client issues a clear statement of the project team's role, their accountability to the client's management and their powers. Because of the position of the team outside the management structure, it is often better if the project manager is an outsider rather than one of the client's employees.

Team management problems

It is important to maintain the commitment of all members of the team to the project, even in the face of setbacks. In many projects, there are no real benefits before completion, but employees like to see the results of their work quickly. It may be worth creating interim goals which can be presented as achievements, simply to satisfy this desire.

Tensions may also develop within the team, particularly if some team members feel that others are not pulling their weight. In most projects, each member of the team relies on the work of others to facilitate their own work. Close monitoring by the project manager to ensure that everyone maintains the right level of effort is therefore important.

Control problems

A project should achieve its objective within the planned time and budget. It is not like the continuous provision of a service, where a temporary reduction in the level of service might be acceptable. Once deadlines start being missed, the problem can rapidly escalate because of the interdependence of tasks. The remedy is to take decisive remedial action as soon as problems start to develop, bringing in extra staff for a short period if necessary.

Question 2: Project processes

The conditions that are necessary to manage a successful information system project include:

Well-defined objectives – The overall aims of the project are well-defined, have been agreed by all who have an interest in them and have been tested throughout the relevant parts of the organisation.

Proper resourcing – There has been a proper analysis of the resources required to make the project a success. Resources include money, personnel, equipment, software, office space and other support resources. The resources have been fully discussed and full agreement to allocate the resources has been gained from those who control them.

Senior management support – Senior management have given their support to the project, do so very publicly, and their reasons for giving their support are sustainable such that the support will continue throughout the life of the system.

Application of project management techniques – All those involved with the project should be familiar with project management techniques and these should be appropriately applied to the project.

Capable project manager – There needs to be a single person who is in operational control of the project. This person should be experienced in the management of projects of the nature of the one to be carried out.

Correct balance of project team members – The project team should consist of individuals who have the necessary range of technical skills and organisational knowledge. In addition enough of the team members should have experience of projects of this nature to ensure the success of the project. Finally there needs to be a balance of personalities within the team to ensure that the team functions well as a group.

Communication strategy – There is an explicit strategy to communicate the project's:

- objectives;
- current state of progress;
- revisions from the original plan;
- methods of integrating the various needs of different groups.

This implies that there will be clear lines of communication between all concerned parties and there will be a general communications system to the wider organisation. Existing communications channels may be utilised or it may be necessary to set up communications systems specifically for the project.

Feedback channels – There should be properly established methods of gaining feedback from those that are affected by the project and whose commitment is needed to make the project a success.

Client focus – The project team need to ensure that they remain focused upon meeting the needs of the people that the project is intended to serve. This may well mean revising aspects of the project part way through.

Chapter 10

Multiple-choice questions

Question 1

A periodic document (e.g. biweekly, monthly) detailing time, cost, and resource performance is called: B a status report.

Question 2

The final steps in the close-out phase generally lead up to: C customer acceptance.

Exam-type questions

Question 1: Jim Ryan

(a) **Memorandum**

To: Jim Ryan – CityGo Bus Company

From: Management consultant

Date: October 200X

The responsibilities of a project manager include the following:

- *Agree the terms of reference of the project* – every project should start with Terms of Reference describing the objectives, scope, constraints, resources and project sponsor or client. It is the responsibility of the project manager to compile and agree these Terms of Reference. In particular he or she must be confident that the project can meet its objectives within the time agreed (a constraint) with the resources available. The Terms of Reference may be expanded into a Project Quality Plan, which will describe such issues as quality procedures, standards and a risk assessment. Producing the Project Quality Plan will also be the project manager's responsibility.

- *Plan the project* – the agreed project will have to be broken down into lower level tasks and activities, each of which will be given a time estimate. Precedents (which tasks must be completed before others can start) will also be agreed. The project task breakdown, the precedents of tasks, and task estimates will form the basis of the project plan. This will allow the project manager to determine the critical path and hence the elapsed time of the project. The project manager will also be able to see more clearly the resource requirements of the project. The project manager usually has the responsibility to produce and interpret the project plan, often using a computerised tool.

- *Monitor the project* – during the project the project manager must ensure that the overall project remains on target. Hence he or she will monitor the progress of tasks and record their completion on the project plan. Some of these tasks will over-run their original estimates and the consequences of this have to be carefully monitored and managed. The project will also be affected by new user requirements, staff illness and holidays and other external factors that cannot be predicted at the start of the project. The project manager has to reflect all these in the project plan and produce revised versions showing the effect of these changes.

- *Take corrective action* – if deficiencies are not corrected, the project manager can take corrective action. Falling behind schedule, because of some unforeseen circumstance at the planning stage might require the rescheduling of the project or a change in resource configuration. If the project is over budget, cost savings can be found, or alternatively more funds might be available from the client.

- *Report on project progress* – it is usually the responsibility of the project manager to report project progress both upwards (to the project sponsor or client) and downwards (to the rest of the project team). Progress reports usually specify what tasks have been completed in the last period, what tasks have been started but not completed (with perhaps an estimate to completion) and what tasks are scheduled to start in the next period. Reports should also highlight problems and changes, showing the effect of these on the project plan and suggesting a course of action. The project sponsor can then decide whether such changes are implemented in the project or left until a later phase of the development. Project reports may also contain important cost and time information showing the overall cost of the project to date.

- *Undertake post-project reviews* – a post-project review usually takes place at the end of the project and it will be the responsibility of the project manager to organise and chair this review and report on its conclusions and recommendations. The post-project reviews will consider both the products of the project (such as the robustness of the software, the satisfaction of users etc.) and the organisation of the project itself. It may review the estimates of project cost and duration and compare these with actual costs and duration. Large variances will be discussed and analysed and any lessons learnt recorded and fed back into the project management method.

- *Motivate the project team* – a multi-disciplinary team brought together for the purpose of undertaking the project undertakes most projects. Once the project is complete the team will probably be disbanded. During the project it is the responsibility of the project manager to motivate team members so that the tasks they are assigned are completed on time and to the required quality. Project managers have direct influence over the work that is assigned to the team members, the amount of responsibility individual team members are given and the recognition they are accorded on completion of their work. How the project manager goes about these management tasks will critically affect the morale and motivation of the team members.

Only five responsibilities were required.

(b) Risk management consists of the following steps:

(i) Identification of the risks involves an overview of the project to establish what could go wrong, and the consequences.

- What are the sources of risk?
- What is the likelihood of the risk presenting itself?
- To what extent can the risk be controlled?
- What are the consequences of that risk presenting itself?
- To what extent can those consequences be controlled?

(ii) Estimation of their downside effects i.e. the implications of what could go wrong.

(iii) Estimation of the probabilities of the events occurring - it will be difficult to establish precise probabilities, but it will be necessary to establish some type of prioritisation: some risks will be much more likely than others. Attention must first be paid to the more important threats.

(iv) Determine how the risks can be lessened, deflected or avoided.

(v) Decision on how the risks will be handled - set a risk management plan, including contingency plans where appropriate.

Most projects carry a degree of risk. There are two categories of risk involved:

- business risk – where the result might be a profit or loss
- an insurable risk – where the risk produces a loss only.

In a project like constructing a housing estate, items like the weather represent business risks: good weather will assist early completion, whereas bad weather may delay it. Insurable risks – which are not necessarily insurable – occur as a result of external unpredictable factors, many of which are legally based.

Risks can be handled as follows:

(i) Do nothing – this is appropriate where the effect is small or the chance of occurrence very remote.

(ii) Insure against the risk.

(iii) Off-load the risk e.g. by arranging for third parties to complete part of the project.

(iv) Investigate the risk further and try to protect against it e.g. arrange to have additional staff available in case of project overrun.

(c) **Threat identification and reduction**

The following can threaten the success of a project. Suggestions are included as to how the threats could be reduced.

Poor management – many project leaders will be from technical backgrounds and they may not have the proper management skills for controlling large projects.

Project leaders should be properly trained so that they have managerial skills as well as technical skills. They should not be given large critically important projects until they have proved themselves on smaller exercises.

Poor planning – managers have not made use of the various planning methods available: network analysis, PERT, Gantt charts. They have not broken the project down into its various activities and estimated a time and cost for each. Project tools and work breakdown structure techniques are used extensively to aid planning and reduce the threat.

Lack of control mechanisms – it is essential to be able to monitor the progress of projects otherwise it is impossible to decide whether they will meet cost and time budgets. Moving targets, where the project specification keeps changing as the project progresses, will certainly add costs and delay to the project. Reporting mechanisms and review dates should be set out in advance and communicated to the appropriate people.

Unrealistic deadlines – there is often pressure from users for projects to be completed quickly. Project teams, particularly if they have had to win the job competitively, may have suggested times that are unrealistic. Project managers must look critically at the deadlines. They should identify the critical activities of the project and ensure that these do not slip.

Insufficient budget – too few people are employed on the project, inadequate materials are bought and the cheapest (not the best) solutions are always sought. Of course, organisations cannot ignore costs and should try to get good value for money. However, it is important to be objective about what a given cost budget can produce by way of project outcomes. If money is tight, it might be better to do a smaller project thoroughly than a larger one poorly.

Make sure that for each threat that you identify, you have suggested a way of reducing the threat.

Question 2: Managing project objectives

Tutor's note

This question follows a 'define and apply' approach, combining rote learning of the attributes of project management with the application of their planning and management in practical situations.

The question has simplified the answer by outlining the areas to be discussed.

Although the diagram is not required, it helps to define the structure of the answer and highlight the relationship between the cost, time and quality objectives.

A project has boundaries and it is one of the activities of the project management team to set and keep the project within those boundaries. The set of attributes that are needed to achieve the project's objectives are shown in the diagram below:

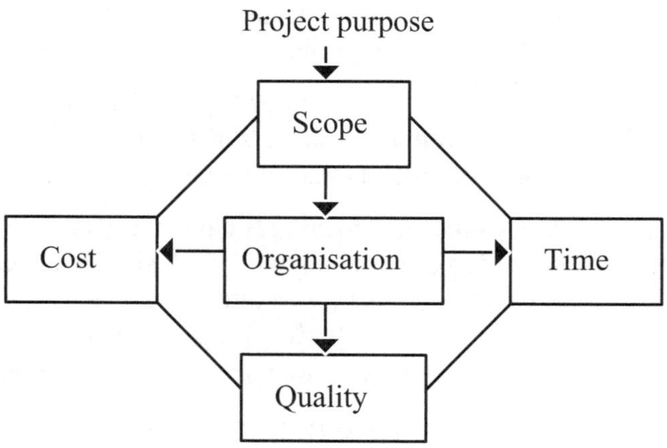

Scope

The scope of the project is to ensure that the project's purpose is achieved by specifying the work that must be done and excluding superfluous or otherwise unnecessary work. There are four stages in scope management; stages 1 and 2 are part of the planning stage.

1 The project definition is expressed in terms of the major objectives in a way that satisfies overall business objectives as well as the specific project purpose, scope and project objectives. The project objectives must be expressed in quantitative and qualitative measures by which the proper completion of the project can be judged.

2 Work breakdown techniques are used to define the scope in detail for management and control purposes.

3 Managers authorise, purchase or perform the work and monitor and control its completion.

4 The project is commissioned or released in order to realise the benefits.

Organisation

The aim of the project organisation is to assemble the appropriate resources (human, material, technical and financial) required to undertake the project. Management will be responsible for:

- approving plans;
- monitoring progress;
- allocating resources;
- assessing results; and
- recommending continuance or termination.

Relationships with other parties involved in projects will have to be managed.

These include:

- the client (or owner) – the person or group that will benefit from the project. Their objective is to achieve the best solution possible at the lowest price;
- the contractor, who may be internal to the organisation, delivers the project and has the objective of satisfying the client and maximising its own profit (performing within budget in an internal situation);
- the sponsor – who provides the funds and has a common interest with the client;
- the project manager – the contractor's representative responsible for planning, organising, controlling and delivering the project;
- the co-ordinators – who are responsible for integrating the work of the various teams working on the project;
- the supporters – the people that supply goods or services to the project.

To plan the organisation, it needs to be broken down in a manner, which runs parallel with and matches the work breakdown structure. The management process starts with contracts made between the contractor and the client, between the contracting groups for the project and between members of the project team.

In defining roles and responsibilities in detail, managers have to follow the same type of detailed scheduling used in work breakdown. This includes planning for the level and competence of resource to be applied.

Cost

The project cost is based on the budget, which includes an estimate of the resources (people, equipment and money) that will be used in the project. The costs may be internal or external and include suppliers, contractors, partners, statutory bodies, governments, banks, loans, grants, expert opinion (lawyers, accountants, consultants), etc.

There are two aspects to managing project costs. There is a budget available for project completion, which the project manager should not exceed without authorisation and there is the need, in most projects, to prove that the benefits of the project exceed the costs. An accountant is usually involved in planning project costing. A list of all the tasks, broken down into their constituent parts can be completed and analysed into direct and indirect costs (the cost breakdown structure) with columns for all the identifiable expenditure, including labour, materials and the project overhead costs. This structure can then be used for estimating or tendering for the project.

Time

Tasks need to be scheduled and planned in order to make the most effective use of the resources available. A variety of time-focused planning tools are available. In general they aim to break the project down into elements with the time required to complete each element. Project managers may also use simulations to assess possible outcomes for alternative assumptions, seeking the optimum combination with the existing time and cost constraints.

Quality

Developing the scope of the project means planning for quality. Good quality is managed through a total quality approach. It is about satisfying the client, which means both dealing with the client's perception of the outcome and performing to expectation.

A common problem in quality perception arises where the client has a change of mind, resulting in an altered specification.

The relationship between the cost, time and quality objectives means that, in the practical context of project management, there is often a trade-off. Each element is constrained at the outset but should change occur to one aspect during the project, there is generally an impact on one or both of the remaining aspects. For example, a change to the specification that increases its scope will logically require that either the timescale is extended or that resources are added to cater for the new parts of the specification in the same timescale. Conversely, a reduction in timescale will logically require that either the specification is reduced in scope or that resources are added to complete the same amount of work in less time.

Chapter 11

Multiple-choice questions

Question 1

A management accountant is most likely to have: C Expert power (depending on the extent to which he or she is perceived, by the line manager, to have expertise that the line manager needs).

Question 2

The assumption that workers must be coerced to perform adequately is:
C Theory X.

Theory Y is the opposite end of the continuum. You should have recognised System 1 as a reference to Likert, and 9.1 as a reference to Blake and Mouton: while they both reflect authoritarian leadership approaches, they do not refer (as Theory X and Y do) to managerial assumptions.

Exam-type questions

Question 1: Super Auto Machines plc (SAM)

(a) McGivering defines authority as 'the right to exercise power' and power as 'the ability to exert a positive influence over objects, persons or situations'. Authority stems from the power invested in an individual. It is the power to make and implement decisions, especially in a group environment. There are a number of different types of power associated with authority. The sources of Hu Song's power and authority may be outlined as follows:

Reward power – A person has power over another because he can secure rewards for him, such as promotion, recommendations, or answers to questions. Hu Song will have the power to adjust employees' pay and conditions.

Coercive power – This enables a person to punish others: for example, to dismiss, suspend, reprimand or embarrass them, or make them carry out unpleasant tasks. Hu Song will have this power and authority but will not use it as much as a manager at a lower level in the hierarchy.

Legitimate power – as holder of the post of chief executive, Hu Song enjoys the power vested in it. This form of power is based on agreement and commonly held values that allow one person to have power over another person e.g. the recognition given to the boss.

Expert power – this is based upon one person's perception that another person has expert knowledge of a given subject and is a recognised authority in a given situation. Hu Song's qualifications, reputation and background will lead many to defer to his perceived superior technical knowledge and judgement even if they do not concede his authority on other grounds.

Referent power – this is based upon identification with a person who has resources; or the desire to be like that person. It could be regarded as 'imitative' power, which is often seen in the way children imitate their parent. A strong personality can enjoy 'referent' power as people defer to the person they admire or wish to emulate. Hu Song's personal stature and credibility and his relationship with owners, employees, customers will bring strong support from these quarters and enhance his power as a chief executive.

Authority can arise from any of three main sources:

- **Formal** – where the organisation bestows the authority upon the individual by means of his job title and the reporting relationships specified. This is recognised in the organisation chart.

- **Technical** – where the authority arises due to personal skills or special knowledge or training. Here the authority exists only within the scope of that special knowledge or skill.
- **Personal, informal** – this authority is not recognised in any organisation chart. It exists because, without regard to the position he or she holds, the person is accepted as being particularly respected, or an elder citizen or is simply popular and recognised by colleagues as being efficient.

Because he has official power, high standing as a chief executive with a clear vision, and the backing of numerous stakeholders, Hu Song has been able to take decisions for change and see them through.

(b) Assessing the expectations of stakeholders enables an organisation to gauge whether its objectives will provide the means to satisfy their demands. A stakeholder is someone who has a stake in the well being of the organisation. The various stakeholder groups that Hu Song would be accountable to include the following.

Shareholders and other providers of capital – investors are concerned with the return on investment and capital appreciation. They can require information and participation in decision-making additional to that the company is required to give by law. In a large public company, this group includes institutions, markets and banks. Hu Song is accountable to this group because SAMs is using their money.

Fellow directors/managers – Hu Song is the leader and, as such, he needs loyal followers and a team of professional managers who can act to accelerate, slow or divert his plans for change. It is their commitment and control that he depends upon and it is their career development and rewards package that he is responsible for.

Customers and suppliers – Customers and final consumers are interested in value of money, ethical advertising and consumer protection. Suppliers want a fair price, regular business and payment on time. SAMs' management is accountable to those with whom it has trading relationships as these parties have a right to expect fair dealing and responsible management practices from the organisation.

Employees – are normally concerned with improving pay and conditions and, particularly in the current economic situation, job security. SAMs' management need to consider the well-being of those who work in the business, and those others who depend upon its success or who interact with it. The livelihood of these people may be at stake and they can be a strong block against Hu Song if mismanaged.

Government regulatory bodies, international agencies etc – are normally seeking finance through taxation and political support for its legislated activities. Officialdom has established several claims over the management decisions of large companies and Hu Song must comply with legislation and attempt to court influence and favour amongst those who control such bodies.

Society at large – normally want an improvement in the 'quality of life' through the reduction of pollution, the maintenance of an ecological balance by ceasing to rely on non-renewable resources, the minimisation of poverty, assistance with local community projects, help with the young and elderly. There is an obligation to humanity in issues such as the environment to the citizens of countries where SAMs has factories.

Management normally undertakes the responsibility of maintaining an equitable and working balance among the claims of the various directly interested groups, but usually the most powerful group of stakeholders, termed the dominant coalition, will determine the organisation's prime objectives.

Question 2: Blake and Mouton's managerial grid

The positions of the ratings on the managerial grid show a remarkable degree of unanimity on the part of the other participants. They are close enough to the central co-ordinates (5,5) to identify A as an example of Blake and Mouton's 'middle of the road' type of manager, and the exact position (around 7,3) shows more concern for production and less for people. Blake and Mouton believe that the compromise position of 5,5 results in inadequate attention being given to output and the needs of the employees. Given the close agreement of all the ratings the imbalance that this shows is probably significant enough to justify concern.

A's management style needs to show more concern for people if it is to improve and move towards Blake and Mouton's ideal of 9,9, where concern for both people and production reach a maximum. Possible ways of achieving this include the following means of improving his communications with his subordinates:

(i) showing greater confidence in them in the way he allocates and supervises work;

(ii) being prepared to accept their suggestions for improvements in work practices;

(iii) restructuring his decision making so as to involve them in it as fully as possible;

(iv) attempting to empathise more with their work problems and helping them to find solutions;

(v) being prepared to help them discover answers to problems rather than simply delivering a managerial decree;

(vi) providing them with proper feedback to motivate improvements in performance; and

(vii) showing a general interest in their current work and future career prospects.

Chapter 12

Multiple-choice question

Question 1

A narrow span of control results in: A Tall organisation structures with many levels of supervision.

Exam-type questions

Question 1: Time management

(a) Joy's poor time management

(i) Mound of paper in the in-tray. This indicates that Julia is bad at setting priorities. There is obviously a lot of work that she has not even looked at. Some of this perhaps could be delegated. She could also sort the work out into urgent and non-urgent tasks.

(ii) *Telephone and e-mail use*

We do not know the reasons for phone calls and the use of e-mail. Personal phone calls can obviously be reduced, but if most calls are related to her work it might suggest:

(i) she is searching for information and/or advice herself;

(ii) people demand to speak to her;

(iii) she constantly allows herself to be interrupted by the telephone or email;

(iv) she does not know how to refuse or delay unreasonable or unimportant requests.

Interruptions inevitably mean that other work takes a long longer to do, as it cannot be tackled in a long stretch. She probably deals with telephone enquiries, as they appear urgent. This shows a lack of assertiveness, and a poor setting of priorities.

(iii) *The over-long report*

A report of 14 pages, rather than a half page memo, would indicate that Joy is not really capable of controlling her work. The issue obviously interested her to take enough care, and she probably wanted to impress the supervisor with her diligence and knowledge. It shows a failure to assess priorities. To summarise, this indicates poor self-control, or even a lack of self-confidence.

(iv) *Late appraisal reports*

A staff appraisal is not an ad hoc request that must be dealt with. Staff appraisals take place regularly, and Joy must have had advance knowledge as to when they would be needed. The reports are often in a standard format.

This indicates poor forward planning.

(v) *Overwork*

Overwork can be a sign that there is genuinely too much work for a person to do. In Joy's case however, she has two assistants to help her, who do not appear to be suffering from the same problem. It is not her section which is overworking but Joy. This can be caused by:

(1) poor delegation, so that she does too much;

(2) inefficient working;

(3) bad planning;

(4) poor control and prioritisation;

(5) lack of self-assertiveness, as Joy might be incapable to saying no to colleague's work demands, even though the request is unimportant.

A final issue is that Joy appears to have been recruited relatively recently, as Tania and Henry both agreed that she was the right person for the job. It may be the case that Joy is still climbing a learning curve, and has yet to find her feet. Henry perhaps has been too relaxed in his approach to her.

(b) **What Henry can suggest**

First of all, Henry should take a more active, guiding role, in helping Joy with her work. She may not know what her priorities should be. Other specific suggestions could include the following.

(i) Identify *objectives* and the *key tasks* that are most relevant to achieving them. Joy must sort out what she must do from what he could do, and from what he would like to do. 'Urgent' is not always the same as 'important'. This is particularly relevant to phone interruptions.

(ii) *Prioritising and scheduling*. Assess key tasks for relative importance, amount of time required, and any deadlines or time-spans. Routine non-essential tasks should be delegated – or done away with if possible. Routine key tasks should be organised as standard procedures and systems. Non-routine key tasks will have to be carefully scheduled as they arise, according to their urgency and importance. An up-to-date diary with a 'carry forward' system (to check on consequences of decisions, follow-up action, etc) will be helpful to her.

(iii) *Planning and control*. She should avoid where possible, disruption by the unexpected. Schedules should be drawn up and regularly checked for 'slippage': priorities will indicate which areas may have to be set aside for more important or urgent interventions. Information and control systems in the organisation should be utilised so that problems can (as far as possible) be anticipated, and sudden decisions can be made on the basis of readily available information.

(iv) She should do a personal plan, in conjunction with detailed goal-planning or target setting for each day.

(v) She should delegate tasks to staff who are competent to perform them.

(vi) If assertiveness is a problem she could go on an assertiveness training course.

(vii) She should cut down on time-wasting activities, e.g. unnecessary or lengthy meetings and paperwork, and interruptions.

(viii) She should ensure that resources are available for forthcoming work, in sufficient supply and good condition.

(ix) She should ensure that files are to hand (not buried under irrelevant files, items or litter on a desk, nor 'somewhere else'). Tidiness is important for efficiency in the office as well as for the organisation's image: files and pieces of work should be easily locatable at all times (and should in any case never be left lying around, as a breach of security, fire hazard, etc).

(x) She should organising work in batches, while relevant files are to hand, machines switched on etc to save time spent in turning from one job to another.

(xi) She should work to plans, schedules, checklists, etc.

(1) She should not rely on memory alone for appointments, events and duties.

(2) She should work on one thing at a time, and finishing each task you start.

(3) She should not put off large, difficult or unpleasant tasks simply because they are large, difficult or unpleasant.

(4) She should learn to anticipate and allow for work coming up; recognise and set reasonable deadlines.

(xii) *Take advantage of work patterns*. Self-discipline is aided by developing regular hours or days for certain tasks: getting into the habit of dealing with correspondence first thing, filing at the end of the day.

(xiii) She should follow up tasks, and see them through. Uncompleted work, necessary future action, expected results or feedback etc should be scheduled for the appropriate time and entered in a 'follow-up' file or diary so that you will be reminded to check that the result/action has occurred when it was supposed to, or to give someone a decision as promised etc. Checklists are also useful for making sure an operation is completed, marking the stage reached in case it has to be handed over to someone else (because of illness, holiday, etc.) or temporarily laid aside (because of higher priority interruptions).

Question 2: Communication skills

(a) **Types of information**

There is a substantial amount of information that can be gathered before the meeting. Sam Browne's business is hardly unique; a firm of accountants which deals with sole traders could provide services to a number of newsagents. The accountant visiting Sam should already be aware of the nature of Sam's business, the types of supplier, the likely turnover and the expected profit margins on newspapers and journals, sweets and cigarettes.

The types of information which must be solicited at the meeting could be divided into:

- hard information, dealing with facts and documents, which will all be necessary to put Sam's chaotic affairs to rights, especially in relation to tax;
- soft information, such as feelings, point of view and morale. This information could include finding out about Sam's attitudes to the record keeping process, as this will affect the reliability of any additional information which he gives. If Sam is merely incompetent at keeping records, simpler procedures might help him overcome his problems. He might regard an accountant's presence there as an unnecessary waste of time, and this might attract some of the force of his resentment, which would be more appropriately directed at the tax authorities.

(b) **The communication process**

Communication is a way by which information is exchanged, which is the purpose of the meeting with Sam Browne. It can also involve instruction, encouragement or persuasion. Because his co-operation is required the purpose of the meeting will also be to establish a relationship with Sam, building trust and understanding, so that he responds with useful information. The communication model shown below demonstrates the elements in the process, emphasising that it is a two-way exchange in which the recipient is as important as the transmitter.

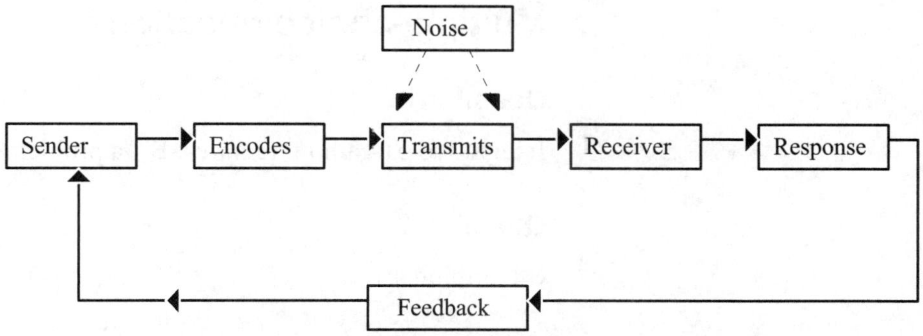

The hurdles to communication (in this case it may be Sam's attitude) may be overcome if:

- the communication is planned effectively. Prior knowledge of similar businesses will be of assistance here;
- direct, simple language is used;
- maximum feedback is obtained. This includes the acknowledgement that both the message and the response is understood, the proposal and clarification of ideas, checking up on any misunderstanding and further questioning and response to avoid confusion.

(c) **The skills contributed to the process**

While giving the appearance of a friendly chat, rather than an inquisition, interviewing skills must be used to put Sam at ease so that the two-way process of communication can go as planned.

Information given by Sam should be written down. A pre-planned sheet of questions and the types of response required would make this task easier and ensure that nothing is missed. Unless a tape recorder is used as a method of recording the information, skills in note taking and summarising will be used in the recording process and include the following:

(i) noting key facts, perhaps using a mind map;

(ii) questioning areas of uncertainty;

(iii) noting any follow-up questions;

If the summary is to be communicated to someone else then an assessment of Sam's approach to the record keeping problem should also be made.

The main skills required will be in effective listening to elicit the maximum information from the meeting. These include:

(i) being prepared to listen, not just simulating attention;

(ii) keeping an open mind and not assuming the expected;

(iii) providing Sam with feedback;

(iii) trying to grasp the gist of the matter rather than getting bogged down with Sam's problems.

Effective listening can be impeded by a low level of interest and other worries about the situation. Even worse, fixed ideas of what Sam is expected to say may prevent appreciation of the full situation. Effective listening will also help to reveal any gaps in Sam's logic.

Chapter 13

Multiple-choice questions

Question 1

Integrative bargaining requires: B a problem-solving orientation.

Question 2

C Norming.

Question 3

A Plant.

Exam-type question

Managing conflict

(a) The state-owned business (SOB) is suffering from many internal and external conflict situations. If the situation continues, it could lead to dire consequences.

The company is already failing to serve a sufficient number of clients and the service is of a poor quality. Customers will detect worsening levels of service as employees stop co-operating to meet customer needs. This will lead to further funding cuts, targets that are more demanding, redundancies and more conflict between groups and departments.

While SOB is experiencing difficulties, competitors who are pulling together internally could gain market share and suffer fewer setbacks. This could exacerbate the situation for SOB and make it very difficult for them to recover their clients even if the problems are resolved quickly.

The problems could lead to hostile and destructive behaviour by some employees. Hostility can lead to:

- poor communication – the withholding or distortion of information;
- interpersonal or inter group friction;
- denigration of others;
- low morale and commitment;
- annoying or disruptive behaviour.

Another consequence of conflict is that employees that are involved will be distracted from their work and suffer from stress. This could lead to under-performance and possible personal problems. Employees may decide to absent themselves from work, putting further strain on those that are left. As morale within the organisation sinks, key staff will consider leaving. This will lead to further morale problems, give rise to lost opportunities and lead to huge expenditure in recruitment and training.

Action by the trades union will worsen the company's capacity to compete. On top of the departmental rivalries, internal corporate cohesion will suffer further damage as the workforce clashes with the management. The management of the company could lose focus and direction as it becomes preoccupied with internal conflict and struggles to make optimal decisions as information stops flowing freely around the company.

(b) Because the threat of industrial action by the trades unions is of immediate concern, senior managers need to organise a meeting with the union representatives to stop the situation worsening. They should try to negotiate a package of measures broadly in line with reasonable expectations. This should form the basis for a forward-looking settlement.

When handling conflict, the management team might decide to deal first with the symptoms, by reducing the conflict behaviour, and then with the causes of the conflict by encouraging co-operative attitudes. Limiting the communication between the marketing and sales department and the service professionals could reduce the conflict behaviour. This is a short-term solution and senior managers need to examine and understand the various causes and effects of internal conflict in SOB, and find the pressure points they need to work on.

To control aggression between the management accountant and some heads of department, management needs to obtain consensus between individuals. This can be done by arbitration, the negotiation of rules and procedures, confrontation and role negotiation. Purely inter-personal clashes may be handled by removing the offending element or separating the people concerned.

Management can encourage co-operative behaviour using either integration devices such as joint problem-solving teams or confrontation and negotiation techniques. These require members in conflict to hammer out a solution. Consultants can be brought in as 'objective' arbitrators or catalysts for improving communications. Once a solution is found, senior management needs to be central in turning the agreed ideas for progress into an action that they will monitor and drive through. They need to reinforce the new settlement by improving internal communications (to reduce the build-up of friction in future) and police the settlement by rooting out obstinate non co-operators.

Different departmental goals might not be properly integrated into the organisation's goals as a whole. Senior managers need to raise the profile of common organisational goals, probably reinforcing this by having bonus incentives for all staff based in part on how they work together across the company.

The senior management at SOB must have the ideas and strength to tackle this serious internal threat to corporate survival. Without a clear policy, many will see the management as weak and the spiral of decline will accelerate further.

Chapter 14

Multiple-choice question

Question 1

A The Health and Safety at Work Act does not relate to equal opportunities and discrimination.

Exam-type questions

Question 1: Legal framework

MEMORANDUM

To: John Harrison

From: Chief Accountant

Date: 15th April 200X

Subject: Eileen Skinner

(a) Legal framework

There are a number of points to raise on the legal situation.

From the notes it is not clear whether Eileen is employed by the company i.e. has a contract of employment or is self employed and has a contract for services. Assuming she is an employee, working full time under a degree of supervision for a salary, Eileen has a contract of employment.

The Employment Protection (Consolidation) Act 1978 requires that all employees receive a statement of their terms and conditions of employment. As well as details of pay, this statement should outline the normal working hours, holiday entitlement, sickness procedures and periods of notice to be given by both the employee and employer. Where disciplinary and grievance procedures exist, these should be detailed in the statement. As a new recruit Eileen should have been informed of the following:

- disciplinary procedures, including the number of warnings, oral or written, which will be given before suspension or dismissal;
- grievance procedures, outlining who is responsible for dealing with complaints about any aspect of employment which the employee is not satisfied with;
- what constitutes a disciplinary offence;
- how many stages there are to the disciplinary procedure;
- what the rights of appeal and representation are.

A contract of employment places duties on both employer and employee. The employer's duties include provision of remuneration and work, holidays, sick pay and maternity provision. The employee's duties under the contract include fidelity, skill and care and obedience in carrying out lawful and reasonable instruction.

A contract of employment can end by either mutual agreement, by giving notice, by passage of time in the case of a fixed term contract, by dismissal or by redundancy.

Dismissal will be unfair if:

(i) it relates to trade union membership or activities;

(ii) the employer fails to prove the reason for dismissal relates to:

- the capability of the employee to perform the work;
- the conduct of the employee;
- redundancy;
- the employee contravening a restriction imposed by law by continuing employment;
- a female employee is dismissed because of pregnancy.

Acts of gross misconduct include the refusal to obey lawful and reasonable instructions, absenteeism, insolence and rudeness, committing a criminal act such as stealing or causing injury through practical jokes.

Other legal issues to take into consideration are:

- the *Equal Pay Act 1970*;
- the *Sex Discrimination Act 1986*, making it unlawful to discriminate, either directly or indirectly, because of sex or marital status;
- the *Disability Discrimination Act 1995*;
- the *Race Relations Act 1996*, making it unlawful to discriminate because of race, colour, nationality or ethnic origin.

(b) Recommendations

Eileen seems to have problems, which she is not sharing with either her colleagues or her superiors. She has not committed any gross misconduct, which would justify immediate dismissal and her behaviour is only recently changed.

The company's disciplinary code follows the guidelines laid down by ACAS and I suggest that we initiate this procedure. The steps, which should be agreed with Eileen and formally written down are as follows:

- Investigate and record the frequency of Eileen's late arrivals, early departures and days off work. Have an informal talk with Eileen to establish the cause of her recent change in behaviour. There may be problems at home or she may be unwell. She may be experiencing some difficulties in the office, such as sexual harassment or discrimination, which is making her behaviour different. Explain the feelings of the rest of the department and express your concern about the situation, using the results from the investigation.
- Eileen may have decided that she would like to work fewer hours or in a different department and the company may be able to help her, if this is the problem.
- If the poor conduct continues the disciplinary procedure will continue.
- An oral warning given to Eileen reminding her that her conduct is not acceptable. The quality of work and conduct we expect should be brought to her attention.
- A written warning, outlining the consequences of her continuing misconduct.
- A second written warning.

- Dismissal or other disciplinary action (which will be agreed with the personnel department after her oral warning).

Question 2: Food is Us

Overview

Organisations and businesses are made up of many individuals all working together. These individuals have different attitudes, perceptions and learning experiences, which together with gender and personality differences can be either a good source for developing creativity within an organisation or the root of an organisation's problems.

Managers need to be aware of the many factors that affect individual differences and their own attitudes and assumptions. They should recognise individual potential and harness talent to achieve the organisational goals.

(a) Equal opportunities is a generic term which describes the belief that there should be an equal chance for all workers in an organisation to apply and be selected for jobs, to be trained and promoted in employment and to have that employment terminated fairly. Employers should only discriminate according to ability, experience and potential. All employment decisions should be based solely on a person's ability to do the job in question; no consideration should be taken of a person's sex, age, racial origin, disability or marital status.

A sex discrimination policy would look at equality in all areas of employment. Such areas would include the selection process, opportunities for training, promotion, the provision of benefits and facilities and dismissal.

This policy would deem it wrong to make any form of discrimination within employment matters because of marital status or sex.

The policy should cover the three main categories of sex discrimination: direct discrimination, indirect discrimination and victimisation.

Direct discrimination incorporates the treating of a person on sexual or marital grounds less favourably than others would be treated. One act of discrimination is sufficient and must be directed against an individual. Such as a clause in the employment contract which states that it would be terminated on marriage.

Indirect discrimination consists in applying a term or condition applicable to both sexes but which one sex has considerably smaller ability to comply with it than the other. Such as all applicants for a post must be six feet tall. Victimisation is the discrimination against an individual who has brought proceedings or given evidence in another case. Such persons should not be treated less favourably than any other individual in the same circumstances.

(b) An equal pay policy means that a woman is entitled to identical pay with men and *vice versa* in respect of 'like work' or 'work that is rated as equivalent' or 'equal value' to that of a man in the same employment. 'Like work' means work of a broadly similar nature where differences are not of a practical nature. Work rated as equivalent requires equal pay. This is when work has been evaluated and graded to be equivalent as other work in relation to effort, skill and decision-making. Work of equal value is that of a woman's to that of a man's in the same organisation.

This should apply equally to men and women.

(c) **Equal opportunities and managing diversity**

There is a new generation of managers within organisations who regard the quality of their people as the distinguishing feature of a successful organisation.

People are the single sustainable source of competitive advantage. Nurturing high performance through the development of people is essential if organisations are to remain viable and competitive.

The promotion of equal opportunities has made good business sense. Equal opportunities has been promoted as a key component of good management as well as being legally required, socially desirable and morally right.

Managing diversity expands the horizons beyond equality issues and builds on recognised approaches to equal opportunities. It adds new impetus to the development of equal opportunities and the creation of an environment in which enhanced contributions from all employees will work to the advantage of business, people themselves and society more generally.

It offers an opportunity for organisations to develop a workforce to meet their business goals and to improve approaches to customer care.

Managing diversity is about having the right person for the job regardless of sex, colour or religion. Essentially the management of diversity is a quality assurance approach. It helps identify hidden organisational barriers, which make it more difficult for people who are perceived as being different from the majority of their colleagues to succeed and develop careers.

It also helps to effect cultural change and to create an environment in which people from all backgrounds can work together harmoniously. The management of diversity combats prejudice, stereotyping, harassment and undignified behaviour.

Index

A

Accountability, 225
Action-centred leadership model, 238
Actual cost of work performed (ACWP), 204
Adair, 238
Adaptive approach to strategy formulation, 36
Adaptors and Innovators, 191
Adhocracy, 70
Advisory, Conciliation and Arbitration Service (ACAS), 297
Agents of change, 136
Annual hours, 310
Ansoff, 32
Appreciative Inquiry (AI), 129
Approaches to strategy, 27
Ashridge studies, 236
Authority, 218
Authority and responsibility, 218
Authority relationships, 220

B

Bargaining power of buyers, 46
Bargaining power of suppliers, 46
Barriers to entry, 46, 47
Bartlett and Ghoshal, 40
Behavioural theories, 232
Belbin, 191
Blake and Mouton, 233, 292
Bounded rationality, 31
Buchanan and Huczynski, 87
Budgeted cost of work performed (BCWP), 204
Budgeted cost of work scheduled (BCWS), 203
Buffering, 178
Bureaucracy, 219
Burns and Stalker, 73
Business ethics, 98, 311
Business strategy, 4

C

Cadbury Report, 116
Chain of command, 144
Change decision meeting, 172
Change management, 172
Checkpoint meetings, 194
Child care support, 309
Classifying organisation structure, 61
Coase, 75
Coercive power, 226
Communication, 194
Competencies, 52
Competitive advantage, 39
Competitive environment – Five Forces Model, 45
Competitive rivalry, 47
Completion report, 210
Compliance-based approach, 312
Conflict, 286
Conflicting objectives, 17
Conformance management, 207
Connected stakeholders, 15
Constructive conflict, 286
Contingency approach to group effectiveness, 284
Contingency plans, 174
Contingency theory, 238
Continuous process improvement (CPI), 208
Contract of employment, 304
Control of time, cost and quality, 201
Core competencies, 52
Core-periphery models, 74
Corporate governance, 107, 116, 311
Corporate social responsibility, 98
Corporate strategy, 4
Corrective strategy, 86
Cost breakdown structure (CBS), 147Cost deviations, 205
Cost index, 206
Cost leadership, 39
Critical path, 154
Critical path analysis (CPA), 143, 150
Culture and structure, 110

D

Data Quality Objectives (DQO), 207
Decision-making, 7
Delegation, 222
Delphi model, 43
Demergers, 97
Demergers and divestment, 96
Determinants of culture, 109
Differences in culture, 241
Differentiation strategy, 40
Direct observation, 265
Disability Discrimination Act 1995, 307
Disciplinary interview, 297
Discipline, 294
Discrimination, 306
Dismissal, 298
Distinguishing competencies, 52
Distributive bargaining, 270
Diversity, 308
Divestment, 97
Divisional structure, 64, 252
Divisionalised form, 70
Drucker, 12, 17

E

Earliest start time (EST), 154
Earned value analysis (EVA), 203
Earned value management, 203
Ecological feasibility, 180
Ecological perspective on the firm, 78
Economic feasibility, 179
Emergent strategy – Mintzberg, 34
Employment law, 304
Employment Tribunal, 297, 299
Entrepreneur, 230
Entrepreneurial structure, 62
Entrepreneurial strategies, 35
Entrepreneurship, 87
Environmental analysis, 42
Equal opportunities, 306
Equal Pay Act 1970, 306
Ethics, 311
Evolutionary perspective, 37
Evolutionary theory, 37

Excellence concept, 114
Expert power, 226
Express terms, 304
External stakeholders, 15

F

Fact finding, 177
Fair dismissal, 298
Fayol, 227, 250
Feasibility stage, 179
Feedback, 267
Fiedler, 238
Financial objectives, 11
Five forces, 39
Five Ps, 3
Flexibility, 72
Flexi-time, 309
Flowcharts, 275
Focus strategy, 40
Follett, 286
Forecasting, 43
Forming, 189
Functional relationship, 220
Functional strategy, 4, 63
Fundamental strategies, 86

G

Gantt charts, 143, 148, 250
Gates and milestones, 143, 149
Generic strategies, 39
Geographic divisionalisation, 64
Gilbreth, 250
Global product companies, 68
Goals, 11
Grievance, 294
Group development, 282
Group-centred leadership, 232
Groups, 282
Growth strategy, 86

H

Handy, 74
Health and safety at work, 305
Hersey-Blanchard situational theory, 240
Hierarchy of objectives, 9
Hofer and Schendel, 30
Hofstede, 242
Holding company (group) structure, 65
Human relations approach, 250
Human resource management, 195

I

Idea generation, 275
Implied terms, 304
Information gathering, 264
Inspection, 207
Integrity-based approach, 312
Internal control, 252
Internal stakeholders, 15
International divisions, 68
International subsidiaries, 68
Internationalisation strategies, 41
Interpersonal skills, 268
Interviews, 265

J

JISC infoNet method, 162, 164
Job sharing, 310
Johnson and Scholes, 4, 7
Joint development, 93

K

Kaizen, 208
Kirton, 191
Knowledge mapping, 275

L

Latest finishing time (LFT), 154
Lawrence and Lorsch, 61
Leadership, 229
Leadership and management, 231
Leadership continuum, 235
Least preferred co-worker, 239
Legal and ethical issues, 303
Legitimate authority, 219
Legitimate power, 226
Likert, 232
Line authority, 220
Line management, 127
Logical incrementalism, 35

M

Machine bureaucracy, 70
Management, 227
Management buyout, 97
Management grid, 233
Management of change, 172
Management of configuration, 171
Management of risk, 173
Management style, 232
Managing diversity, 308
Matrix structure, 65, 252
Mayo, 282
McGivering, 225
McGregor, 235
McKinsey's 7S model, 127
Mechanistic structures, 73
Meetings, 272, 273
Mentoring, 274
Merger or acquisition, 92
Middle line management, 69
Miles and Snow, 111
Mind-mapping, 275
Mintzberg, 3, 69, 228, 250, 252
Mission, 10
Mission statement, 10
Missionary organisations, 70
Multinational companies, 67

N

National culture, 242
Negotiation, 269
Negotiation process, 270
Network analysis, 143, 150
Network diagram, 151
Network structures, 252
Neutral strategy, 86
New entrants into a market, 46
Non-growth strategy, 86, 96
Norming, 190

O

Objectives, 9, 11
Operating core, 69
Options evaluation, 178
Options generation, 177
Organic and mechanistic structures, 73
Organisation control, 250
Organisational configurations, 69
Organisational culture, 108
Organisational iceberg, 112
Organisational structure, 60, 61, 218
Outcome and process stakeholders, 133
Outsource, 74

P

Participant observation, 264
Performance appraisal, 257
Performance measurement, 202, 256

Performance-based management, 200
Performing, 190
Person culture, 111
Personal time management, 258
Planning, 8
Planning and decision-making, 8
Planning stage, 175
Population ecology, 78
Porter's value chain, 50
Position analysis, 177
Post Implementation Review (PIR), 211
Post-completion audit, 210
Power, 225
Power and channel relationships, 226
Power and leadership, 225
Power culture, 110
Power strategy, 271
Power/dynamism matrix, 19
Power/interest matrix, 19
Primary and secondary objectives, 13
PRINCE structure, 184
PRINCE 2, 162, 175
Processualists, 37
Product and geographical structure, 63
Professional bureaucracy, 70
Programme evaluation and review techniques (PERT), 150
Project champions, 136
Project change procedure, 172
Project completion, 208
Project control, 198
Project customer/user, 134
Project definition, 165
Project Initiation Document (PID), 143, 165
Project leader, 193
Project lifecycle, 125
Project manager, 135
Project management, 124
Project Management Body of Knowledge (PMBOK), 130, 162
Project management methodologies, 162
Project management tools, 142
Project organisation, 185
Project owner, 134
Project sponsor, 133
Project stakeholders, 133
Project structure, 184
Project team, 187
Project time management, 169

Q

Quality Assurance Project Plans (QAPP), 207
Quality assurance, 207
Quality control, 207
Quality management, 206
Questionnaires, 265
Quinn, 35

R

Random transformation, 78
Rational adaptation, 78
Rational model, 28
Recovery strategy, 86
Referent power, 226
Relationship marketing, 213
Reporting structures, 252
Research, 263
Resolve strategy, 271
Resource histogram, 143, 148
Resource-based view, 49
Responsibility, 221
Reward power, 226
Risk management, 173
Risk reducing contingency strategy, 86
Role culture, 110

S

Sabbaticals, 310
Scenario building, 43
Scenario planning, 178
Schedule deviations, 204
Scheduling, 198
Scientific management, 250
Scope definition, 168
Scope management, 167
Scope statement, 143
Sex Discrimination Act 1975, 307
Simple structure, 70
SLEPT analysis, 43
Small business structure, 62
SMART objectives, 171
Social and ethical objectives, 11, 101
Social or operational feasibility, 180
Social responsibility, 99
Sources of power, 21, 225
Staff relationship, 220
Stakeholders, 15, 118
Stakeholder analysis, 15, 136
Stakeholder expectations, 17
Stakeholder hierarchy, 184
Stakeholder marketing, 137, 213
Stakeholder planning, 137
Stakeholder power, 20
Steering committee, 134
Storming, 189
Strategic alliances, 93
Strategic analysis, 29
Strategic apex, 69
Strategic business unit (SBU), 4
Strategic choice, 29, 30
Strategic decision-making, 7
Strategic implementation, 29, 31
Strategic management, 5, 85
Strategic planning, 6
Strategies, 35
Strategy and scope for a project, 166
Strategy and structure, 59
Strategy formulation, 2, 28, 34, 42
Strategy identification and selection, 86
Substitute products, 47
Support staff, 69
SWOT analysis, 42, 143, 144, 177
Systematic planning process, 32, 33
Systemic perspective, 38
Systems model, 38

T

Tannenbaum and Schmidt, 235
Task culture, 110
Task-centred leadership, 232
Taylor, 250
Team building, 192
Team development, 189
Team roles, 191
Team selection, 188
Technical feasibility, 179
Technostructure, 69
Term-time working, 309
Theories of organisation, 250
Theory X and Theory Y, 235
Threshold competencies, 52
Time management, 258
Total quality management (TQM), 208

Trade-off between objectives, 14
Transaction costs, 75
Transnational corporations, 68
Tuckman, 189

U

Unfair dismissal, 299
Unstructured interviewing, 265

V

Value chain, 50

W

Weber, 219, 250
White and Lippitt, 233
Williamson's 'transaction cost theory', 76
Work Breakdown Structure (WBS), 143, 145, 168
Work environment, 285
Work priorities, 259
Working from home, 310
Working Time Regulations, 306

KAPLAN PUBLISHING
FOULKS LYNCH

STUDY TEXT REVIEW FORM
Paper P5

Thank you for choosing a Kaplan Publishing Foulks Lynch CIMA Study Text. As we are constantly striving to improve our products, we would be grateful if you could provide us with feedback about how useful you found this Study Text.

Name: ....

Address: ....

....

Email: ....

Why did you decide to purchase this Study Text?

Have used them in the past ☐
Recommended by lecturer ☐
Recommended by friend ☐
Saw advertising ☐
Other (please specify) ☐

Which other Kaplan Publishing Foulks Lynch products have you used?

Exam Kit ☐
Distance Learning Course ☐
Pocket Notes ☐

How do you study?

At a college ☐
On a distance learning course ☐
Home study ☐
Other ☐

Please specify...

Overall opinion of this Study Text

	Excellent	*Adequate*	*Poor*
Introductory pages	☐	☐	☐
Syllabus coverage	☐	☐	☐
Clarity of explanations	☐	☐	☐
Clarity of definitions and key points	☐	☐	☐
Diagrams	☐	☐	☐
Practice/exam-type questions	☐	☐	☐
Self-test questions	☐	☐	☐
Layout	☐	☐	☐
Index	☐	☐	☐

If you have further comments/suggestions or have spotted any errors, please write them on the next page.

Please return this form to: Mirjana Jeremic, Editor, Freepost RRAT-HLYC-5KXA, FTC Foulks Lynch, Unit 2 The Business Centre, Molly Millars Lane, Wokingham, RG41 2QZ

Other comments/suggestions and errors

KAPLAN
PUBLISHING
FOULKS LYNCH

CIMA Publications
Student Order Form

Please send your completed order form by post to:
Leeds NDL, West Gate, 6 Grace Street, Leeds LS1 2RP
Tel (UK): 0845 678 0022
Tel (International): + 44 (0) 113 200 6360
Fax: +44 (0) 113 243 0133
Order online: www.kaplanfoulkslynch.com
Email: cimaflexiblelearning@ftckaplan.com

Examination date: Nov 06 ☐		**Study Text £28.00 each**	**Exam Kits £15.00 each**	**Pocket Notes £10.00 each**	**Practice 4 Success CDs 100Qs £10.00 300Qs £25.00**		**Course in a Box** (Text, Kit, P/Notes, Tests, CD, Folder) **£150.00 each**	**Total Value**
		Quantity	Quantity	Quantity	100Q	300Q	Quantity	
Professional level								
Paper P1	Management Accounting Performance Evaluation	☐	☐	☐	☐	☐	☐	
Paper P2	Management Accounting Decision Making	☐	☐	☐	☐	☐	☐	
Paper P3	Management Accounting Risk and Control Strategy	☐	☐	☐	-	-	☐	
Paper P4	Organisational Management & Information Systems	☐	☐	☐	☐	☐	☐	
Paper P5	Integrated Management	☐	☐	☐	☐	☐	☐	
Paper P6	Management Accounting Business Strategy	☐	☐	☐	-	-	☐	
Paper P7	Financial Accounting and Tax Principles	☐	☐	☐	☐	☐	☐	
Paper P8	Financial Analysis	☐	☐	☐	☐	☐	☐	
Paper P9	Management Accounting Financial Strategy	☐	☐	☐	-	-	☐	
TOPCIMA								
Test of Professional Competence in Management Accounting Study Text		£28.00 ☐		The Knowledge			£28.00 ☐	

SUB TOTAL	£
PLUS DELIVERY CHARGE (see chart below)	£
TOTAL	£

Cardholder Details

Name on card: ....

Address:

....

....

....

Telephone:

....

Delivery address (if different from above – a signature will be required)

Name:

....

Address:

....

....

....

Telephone: ....

Payment

1 I enclose Cheque/Postal Order/Bankers Draft for £.....................................

Please make cheques payable to '**Kaplan Publishing Foulks Lynch**'.

2 Charge MasterCard/Visa/Switch/Delta no:

Valid from:

Expiry date:

Issue no: (Switch only)

Security Code:

Signature: .... Date: ....

POSTAGE	**Text Books**	**Pocket Notes**	**Course in a Box**
UK	£5 for one book + £2 for each extra	£2 for one book + £1 for each extra	£6 for one package + £4 for each extra
Europe	£7 for one book + £4 for each extra	£3 for one book + £2 for each extra	£12 for one package + £8 for each extra
Rest of World	£22 for one book + £8 for each extra	£8 for one book + £5 for each extra	£30 for one package + £20 for each extra

Please note that all prices on this form are subject to change.

KAPLAN PUBLISHING
FOULKS LYNCH

CIMA Publications
College & Bookshop Order Form

Please send your completed order form by post to:
Kaplan Publishing Foulks Lynch,
Unit 2 The Business Centre,
Molly Millars Lane, Wokingham RG41 2QZ
or by fax to 0118 979 7455

For all queries relating to this order please call 0118 912 3000 or e-mail info@kaplanfoulkslynch.com

ACCOUNT:

Examination Date: Nov 06 ☐

		Study Text £28.00 each	Exam Kits £15.00 each	Pocket Notes £10.00 each	Practice & Success CDs 100Qs £10.00	300Qs £25.00	Course in a Box (Text, Kit, P/Notes, Study Notes, Tests, CD, Folder) £150.00 each	Total Value
Certificate (Current syllabus only)		Quantity	Quantity	Quantity	100Q	300Q	Quantity	
Paper C1	Management Accounting Fundamentals	☐	☐	☐	☐	☐	☐	
Paper C2	Financial Accounting Fundamentals	☐	☐	☐	☐	☐	☐	
Paper C3	Business Mathematics	☐	☐	☐	☐	☐	☐	
Paper C4	Economics for Business	☐	☐	☐	☐	☐	☐	
Paper C5	Business Law	☐	☐	☐	☐	☐	☐	
Professional								
Paper P1	Management Accounting Performance Evaluation	☐	☐	☐	☐	☐	☐	
Paper P2	Management Accounting Decision Making	☐	☐	☐	☐	☐	☐	
Paper P3	Management Accounting Risk and Control Strategy	☐	☐	☐	-	-	☐	
Paper P4	Organisational Management & Information Systems	☐	☐	☐	☐	☐	☐	
Paper P5	Integrated Management	☐	☐	☐	☐	☐	☐	
Paper P6	Management Accounting Business Strategy	☐	☐	☐	-	-	☐	
Paper P7	Financial Accounting and Tax Principles	☐	☐	☐	☐	☐	☐	
Paper P8	Financial Analysis	☐	☐	☐	☐	☐	☐	
Paper P9	Management Accounting Financial Strategy	☐	☐	☐	-	-	☐	

TOPCIMA

Test of Professional Competence in Management Accounting Study Text	£28.00 ☐	The Knowledge	£28.00 ☐	

SUB TOTAL	£
LESS ________% DISCOUNT	£
TOTAL	£

Account details

Contact name: ....

Address: ....

....

....

Telephone: ....

Delivery address (if different to above)

Name: ....

Address: ....

....

....

....

Telephone: ....

Payment

1 Please invoice account ....

under Purchase Order Reference ....

2 I enclose Cheque/Postal Order/Bankers Draft for £..

(Please make cheques payable to '**Kaplan Publishing Foulks Lynch**')

3 Charge MasterCard/Visa/Switch/Delta no:

Valid from: Expiry date:

Issue no: (Switch only) Security Code:

Signature: .... Date: ....

Please note that all prices on this order form are subject to change